COGAT®
TEST PREP
GRADE 1 AND 2

- 2 MANUSCRIPTS
- COGAT® TEST PREP GRADE 1
- COGAT® GRADE 2 TEST PREP
- LEVEL 7 AND 8 FORM 7
- 290 PRACTICE QUESTIONS
- ANSWER KEY
- 108 BONUS QUESTIONS ONLINE

Nicole Howard

PLEASE LEAVE US A REVIEW!

Thank you for selecting this book.

We'd love to get your feedback on the website where you purchased this book.

By leaving a review, you give us the opportunity to improve our work.

Nicole Howard and the SkilledChildren.com Team

www.skilledchildren.com

Co-authors: Albert Floyd and Steven Beck

Copyright © 2021 Nicole Howard All rights reserved. No part of this publication may be reproduced, stored or transmitted in any form or by any means, electronic, mechanical, photocopying, recording, scanning, or otherwise without written permission from the publisher. It is illegal to copy this book, post it to a website, or distribute it by any other means without permission.

By reading this document, the reader agrees that under no circumstances is the author responsible for any losses, direct or indirect, that are incurred as a result of the use of the information contained within this document, including, but not limited to, errors, omissions, or inaccuracies.

First edition.

Cognitive Abilities Test™ (CogAT®) is a registered trademark of Riverside Assessments, LLC and its affiliates ("Riverside"), which is not affiliated with Nicole Howard and SkilledChildren.com.
Trademarks referring to specific test providers are used by Nicole Howard and SkilledChildren.com for nominative purposes only and are the exclusive property of their respective owners.

TABLE OF CONTENTS

INTRODUCTION 7
- Which Students Are Eligible to Take the Levels 7 and 8?. 7
- When in the School Year Does the CogAT® Take Place? ... 8
- An Overview of the CogAT® Levels 7 and 8 8
- The Length and the Complete Format of the Test 8
- The Test Breakdown 10
- How to Use the Content in These Books 11
- Tips and Strategies for Test Preparation 12
- Before You Start Test Preparation 12

COGAT®TEST PREP GRADE 1 15

VERBAL BATTERY GRADE 1 17
- Picture Analogies 18
- Tips for Solving Picture Analogies 19
- Picture Classification 28
- Tips for Solving Picture Classification Questions 28
- Sentence Completion 38
- Tips for Sentence Completion 38

PRACTICE TEST NON VERBAL BATTERY 57
- Figure Matrices 58
- Tips for Figure Matrices 59
- Figure Classification 68
- Tips for Figure Classification 69
- Paper Folding 78
- Tips for Paper Folding 78

PRACTICE TEST QUANTITATIVE BATTERY 85
- Number Puzzle 86
- Tips for Number Puzzle 86
- Number Analogies 93
- Tips for Number Analogies 94
- Number Series 103
- Tips for Number Series 104

ANSWER KEY GRADE 1 113
- Picture Analogies Practice Test 114
- Picture Classification Practice Test 116

    Sentence Completion Practice Test 118
    Figure Matrices Practice Test 120
    Figure Classification Practice Test 122
    Paper Folding Practice Test 124
    Number Puzzle Practice Test 127
    Number Analogies Practice Test 129
    Number Series Practice Test 131

HOW TO DOWNLOAD 54 BONUS QUESTIONS 134

COGAT®GRADE 2 TEST PREP 135

PRACTICE TEST VERBAL BATTERY 137
    Picture Analogies 138
    Tips for Solving Picture Analogies 139
    Picture Classification 149
    Tips for Solving Picture Classification Questions 150
    Sentence Completion 160
    Tips for Sentence Completion 160

PRACTICE TEST NON VERBAL BATTERY 181
    Figure Matrices 182
    Tips for Figure Matrices 183
    Figure Classification 193
    Tips for Figure Classification 194
    Paper Folding 204
    Tips for Paper Folding 204

PRACTICE TEST QUANTITATIVE BATTERY 213
    Number Puzzle 214
    Tips for Number Puzzle 214
    Number Analogies 220
    Tips for Number Analogies 221
    Number Series 231
    Tips for Number Series 232

HOW TO DOWNLOAD 54 BONUS QUESTIONS 242

ANSWER KEY FOR GRADE 2 243
    Picture Analogies Practice Test 244
    Picture Classification Practice Test 247
    Sentence Completion Practice Test 250

Figure Matrices Practice Test 253
Figure Classification Practice Test 256
Paper Folding Practice Test 259
Number Puzzle Practice Test 263
Number Analogies Practice Test 265
Number Series Practice Test 268

INTRODUCTION

INTRODUCTION

The Cognitive Abilities Test (CogAT®) is an assessment of a student's verbal, quantitative, and nonverbal reasoning ability. Administered to grades K-12, the CogAT® is designed to identify gifted students.

These books will increase the student's chances of success by providing an overview of the different types of questions for Grade 1 and 2, Level 7 and 8, Form 7 of the CogAT® test.

Two practice tests and their answer key, with clear explanations, are all included in each book to allow students to understand the testing structure and the different types of questions within it.

Additionally, by reading these books, you will gain free online access to 108 bonus practice questions. You will find the link and password on the page 134 and 242 of each book.

It is highly recommended to read this introductory section to understand how the CogAT® works.

Which Students Are Eligible to Take the Levels 7 and 8?

These books are dedicated to gifted seven and eight-year-old children and therefore focus on level 7 and level 8, form 7 of CogAT®.

Most Grade 1/2 teachers implement CogAT® Level 7/8 to identify which of their students will benefit from faster curriculum training modules. Used as a starting evaluation, these tests deliver reasonably accurate results.

INTRODUCTION

When in the School Year Does the CogAT® Take Place?

Several school districts choose to implement these tests at the end of the school year for more reliable and accurate results. If you are the parent or teacher of a student who could potentially qualify for this test, you will probably need to consult your school to determine how to enroll a child for this test.

An Overview of the CogAT® Levels 7 and 8

The CogAT® is administered to a group of students at a single time.

There are three autonomous sections of the test, specifically:

1. Verbal testing

2. Nonverbal testing

3. Quantitative testing

These autonomous sections can be used individually, and some students may only be asked to take one or two parts of the test based on the evaluations of their tutors.

Although there are resources that support students prepare for these tests, the content of the CogAT® isn't generally the same content that is seen in the conventional school curriculum, and students will be asked to think creatively to solve certain questions.

The Length and the Complete Format of the Test

The total time given for the three sections of the test is 112 minutes for grade 1 and 122 minutes for grade 2.

INTRODUCTION

Tests will vary, depending on the grades that are being assessed, but the Level 7 of CogAT® is divided into 136 multiple-choice questions. The Level 8 of CogAT® is divided into 154 multiple-choice questions. The questions are categorized as follows:

Verbal Section

- "Sentence completion" has 16 questions for grade 1 and 18 questions for grade 2.

- "Verbal classification" has 16 questions or grade 1 and 18 questions for grade 2.

- "Verbal analogies" has 16 questions for grade 1 and 18 questions for grade 2.

Nonverbal Section

- "Figure matrices" has 16 questions for grade 1 and 18 questions for grade 2.

- "Paper folding skills" has 12 questions for grade 1 and 14 questions for grade 2.

- "Figure classifications" has 16 questions for grade 1 and 18 questions for grade 2.

Quantitative Section

- "Understanding number analogies" has 16 questions for grade 1 and 18 questions for grade 2.

- "The number series" has 16 questions for grade 1 and 18 questions for grade 2.

- "Solving number puzzles" has 12 questions for grade 1 and 14 questions for grade 2.

The total number of questions for these three sections equals 136 for grade 1 and 154 for grade 3.

INTRODUCTION

The Test Breakdown

The verbal section of the test is designed to assess a student's vocabulary, ability to solve problems associated with vocabulary, ability to determine word relationships, and their overall memory retention. The verbal section of the Levels 7 and 8 of CogAT® has three subtypes of questions that need to be answered:

1. Sentence Completion: The teacher reads aloud a question. Children must choose the picture that best answers the question in a complete, logical way.

2. Verbal Classification: Students are required to classify pictures into like groups in this section. They will be given three pictures that have something in common and will be asked to identify a fourth picture that completes the set.

3. Verbal Analogies: Students are required to identify analogies. They will be given two pictures that go together, as well as a third, unrelated picture. They must pick the most fitting pair for the third picture from the answer choices given, based on the logic used for the original pair of pictures.

4. **The nonverbal section** of the test is designed to assess a student's ability to reason and think beyond what they've already been taught. This section includes geometric shapes and figures that aren't normally seen in the classroom. This will force the students to use different methods to try and solve problems. There are also three subtypes of questions that need to be answered in the nonverbal section of the CogAT®:

1. Figure Classification: Students are required to analyze three similar figures and apply the next appropriate figure to complete the sequence in this section.

2. Figure Matrices: Students are introduced to basic matrices (2x2 grids) to solve for the missing shapes within them. Three of the four squares will already be filled out, and they must choose which image fills the last square from the options provided. This is similar to the verbal analogies section, except it is now done using shapes instead of words.

3. Paper Folding Skills: Students are introduced to paper folding and will need to ascertain where punched holes in a folded piece of paper would be after the paper is unfolded.

INTRODUCTION

The quantitative section introduces abstract reasoning and problem-solving skills to learners and is one of the most challenging sections in the test. This section is also structured into three different parts:

1. Interpreting a Series of Numbers: Children are required to determine which string of beads is needed to complete a sequence that follows a specific pattern, by observing an abacus.

2. Solving Number Puzzles: In grade 1 test, Children see two trains. They must choose the answer picture that makes the second train carrying an equal number of things as the first one. In grade 2 test, students will need to solve number puzzles and simple equations. They will be provided with equations that are missing a number.

3. Understanding Number Analogies: Children will be provided with 2x2 basic matrices. Each box of the matrices contains a certain number of objects. In the lower row, the child must identify the same relationship as in the upper row and select the answer option that best fits the box with the question mark.

How to Use the Content in These Books

Since the CogAT® is an important test in all students' schooling careers, the correct amount of preparation must be performed. Students that take the time to adequately prepare will inevitably do better than students that don't.

These books will help you prepare your student(s) before test day and will expose them to the format of the test so they'll know what to expect. These books include:

- One full-length CogAT® Level 7 practice questionnaire.
- One full-length CogAT® Level 8 practice questionnaire.
- Question examples for teachers/parents to help their students approach all of the questions on the test with confidence and determination.
- Answer key for each book with clear explanations.

INTRODUCTION

Take the time to adequately go through all of the sections to fully understand how to teach this information to younger students. Many of the abstract versions of these questions will be difficult for some students to understand, so including some visual aids during preparation times will be greatly beneficial.

Tips and Strategies for Test Preparation

The most important factor regarding the CogAT® is to apply the time and effort to the learning process for the test and make the preparation periods as stress-free as possible. Although everyone will experience stress in today's world, being able to cope with that stress will be a useful tool. All students will experience varying amounts of anxiety and stress before these types of tests, but one of the ways to adequately combat this is by taking the time to prepare for them.

The CogAT® has difficult questions from the very beginning. Some of the questions will range from difficult to very abstract, regardless of the age group or level.

It's necessary to encourage your students to use different types of strategies to answer questions that they find challenging.

Students will get questions incorrect in some of the sections, so it's vital to help younger students understand what errors they made so they can learn from their mistakes.

Before You Start Test Preparation

There are multiple factors that may stress students out, regardless of their age and maturity levels. It's imperative for you as an educator to help your students cope with the anxiety and stress of upcoming tests. The tests themselves are going to be stressful, but there are other, external factors that can increase the amounts of stress that children experience.

The first aspect that needs to be focused on is teaching the learners how to deal with stress. Breathing techniques are important, and having a quiet place to use

INTRODUCTION

when studying is imperative to decreasing the amount of stress that students experience.

There are other aspects that can help alleviate stress, like teaching your students what pens and pencils they need to bring on the test day and how to successfully erase filled out multiple-choice questions on the test questionnaire.

PRACTICE TEST GRADE 1

COGAT®TEST PREP GRADE 1

PRACTICE TEST GRADE 1

VERBAL BATTERY GRADE 1

This section of the CogAT® test assesses the child's use of language, particularly the skill in identifying the correlation between words. These questions often involve the use of analogy.

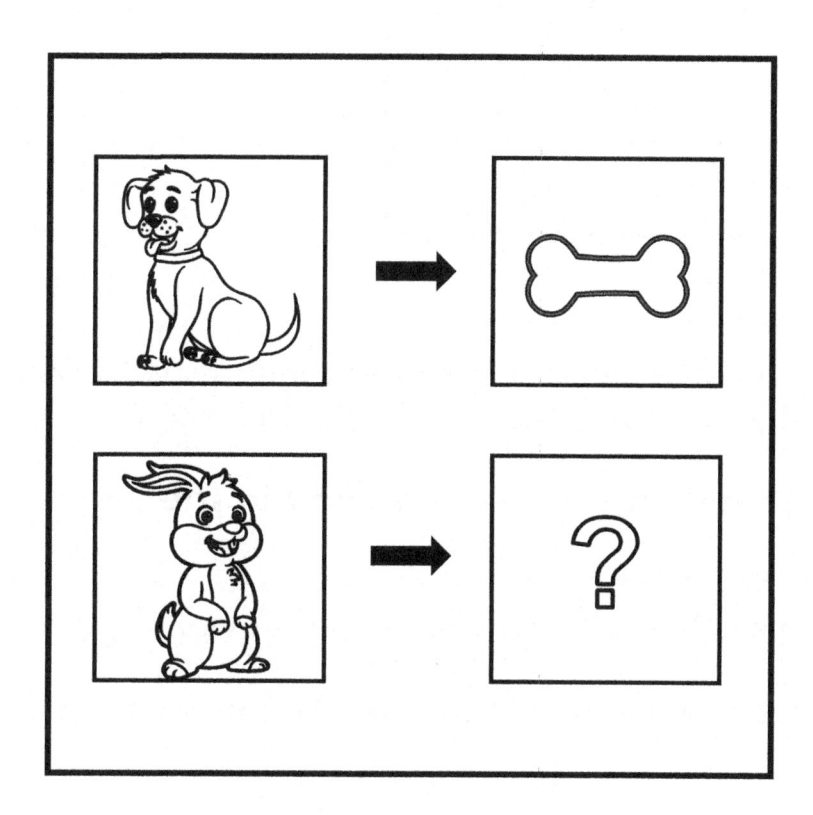

17

PRACTICE TEST GRADE 1

Picture Analogies

A picture analogy traces a similarity between a pair of objects and another pair of objects.

Example

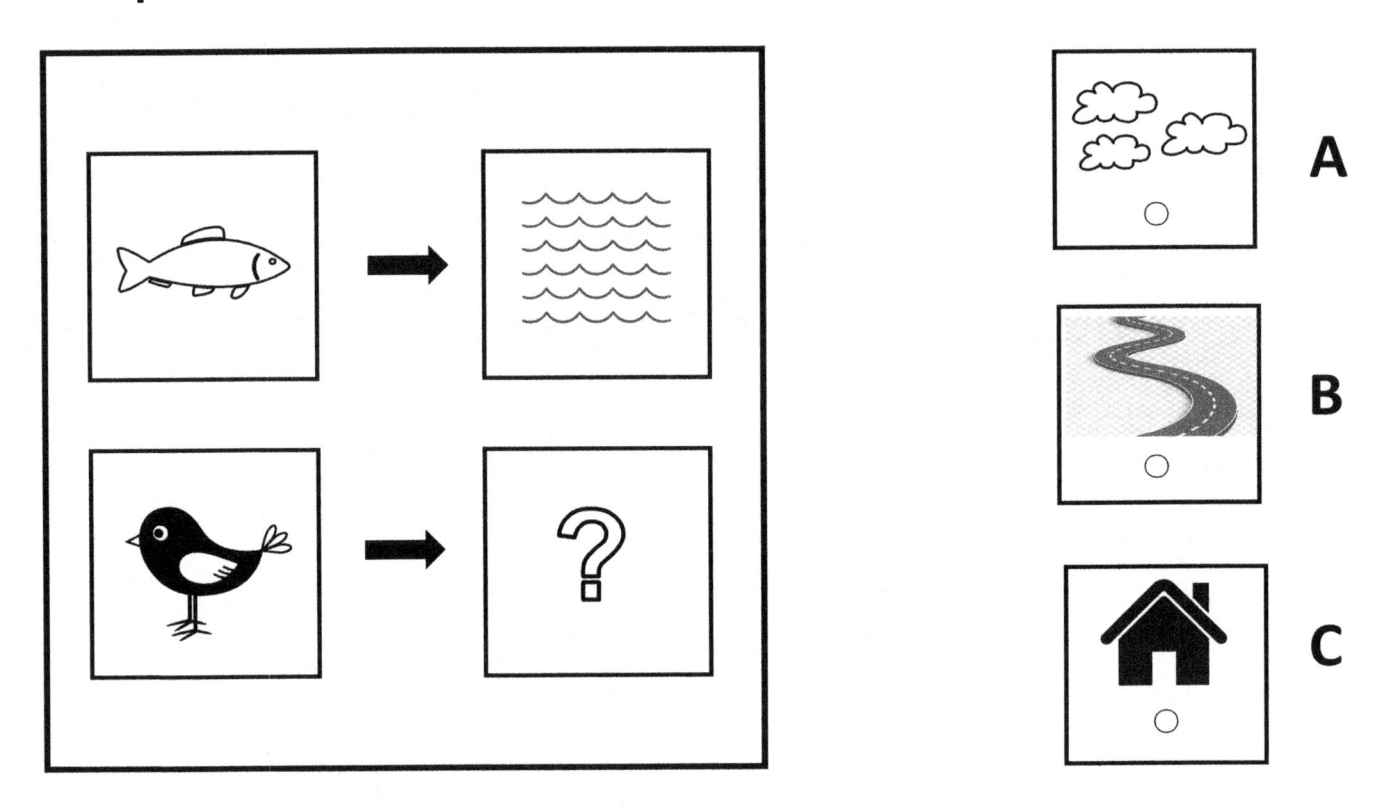

- First, identify the relationship between the first pair of objects.
- How do the objects "fish" and "sea" go together?

Fishes move by swimming in the sea.

- Now, look at the object "bird".
- Which of the possible choices follows the previous rule?

Birds move by flying in the sky, so the correct answer is A.

Tips for Solving Picture Analogies

- Try to identify the correlation between the first two pictures.

- Review all answers before you make a choice.

- The best approach to answering questions that might seem difficult is to proceed by elimination. Only one of the given answers will be correct. In case of doubt, find out which choice is less likely to be the correct one and eliminate it. This way of proceeding will leave fewer options and make it easier to find the right one.

- Evaluate the possible alternative uses of the objects.

- Try to transform analogies into sentences that have a logical meaning.

- Finally, the best way to improve the resolution of verbal analogies is through practice.

PRACTICE TEST GRADE 1

1.

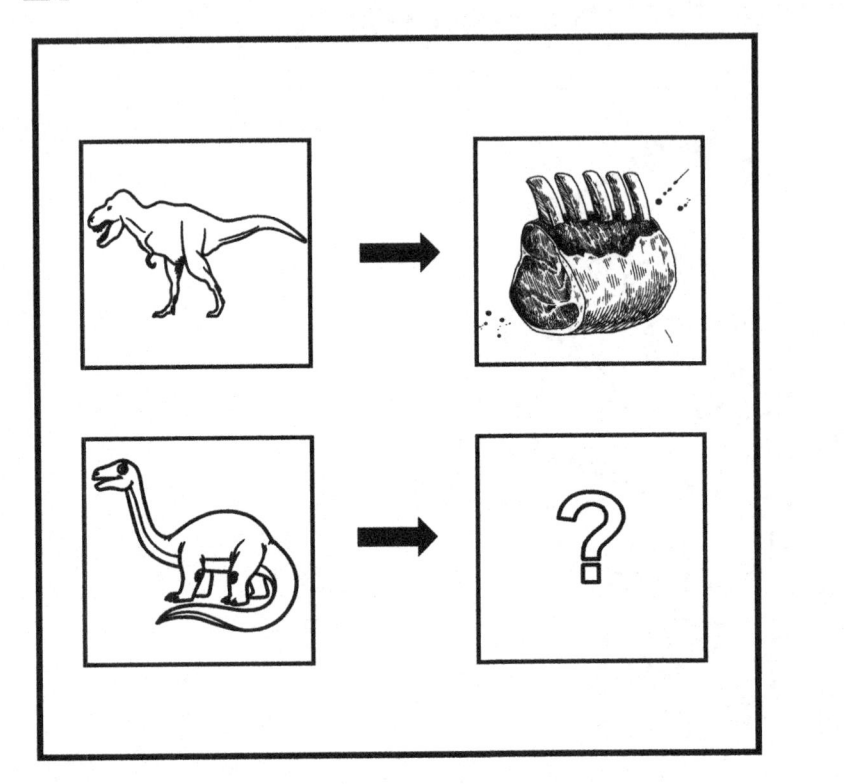

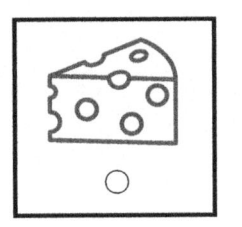

2.

20

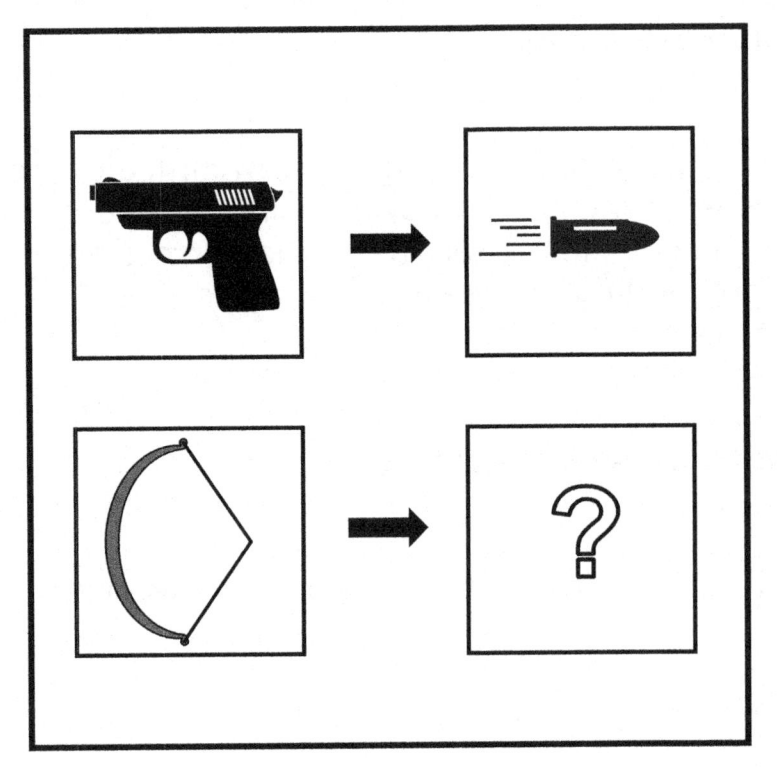

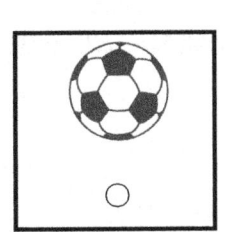

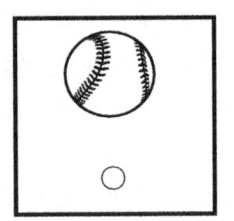

PRACTICE TEST GRADE 1

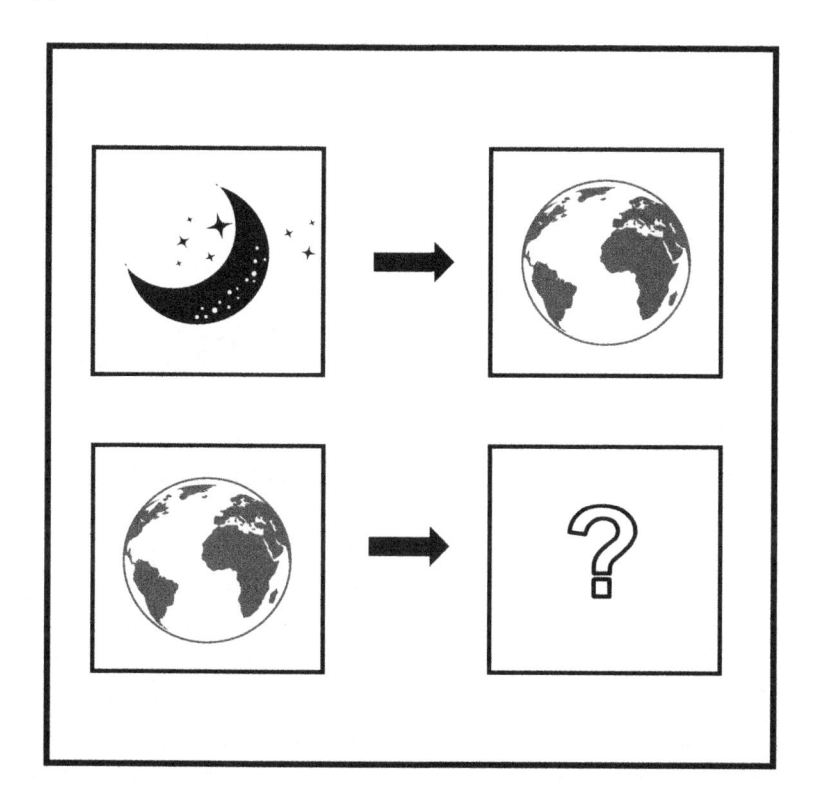

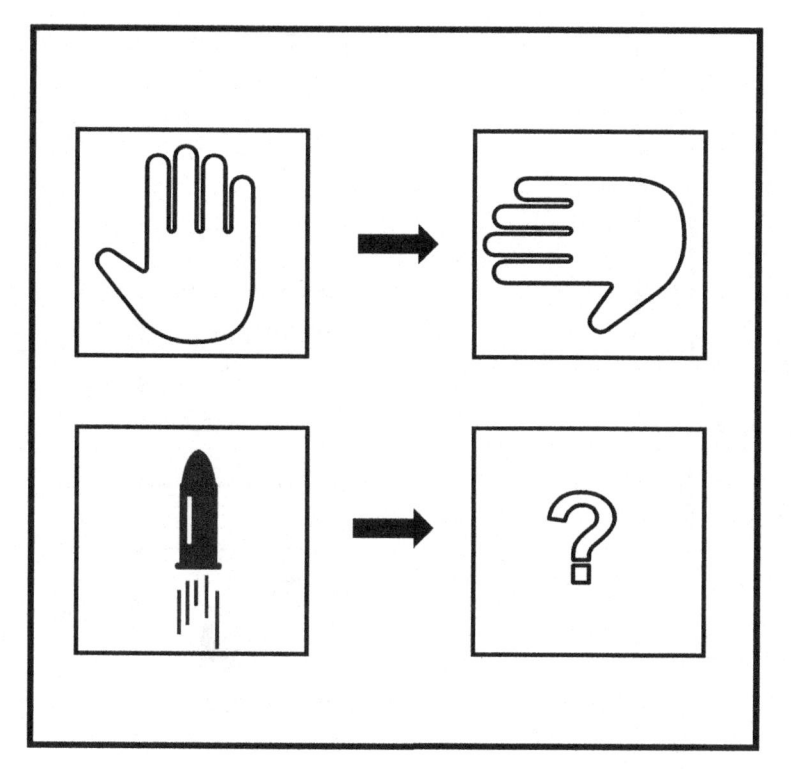

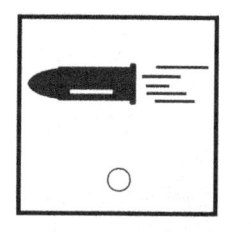

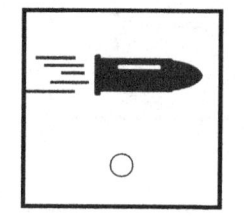

3

4.

PRACTICE TEST GRADE 1

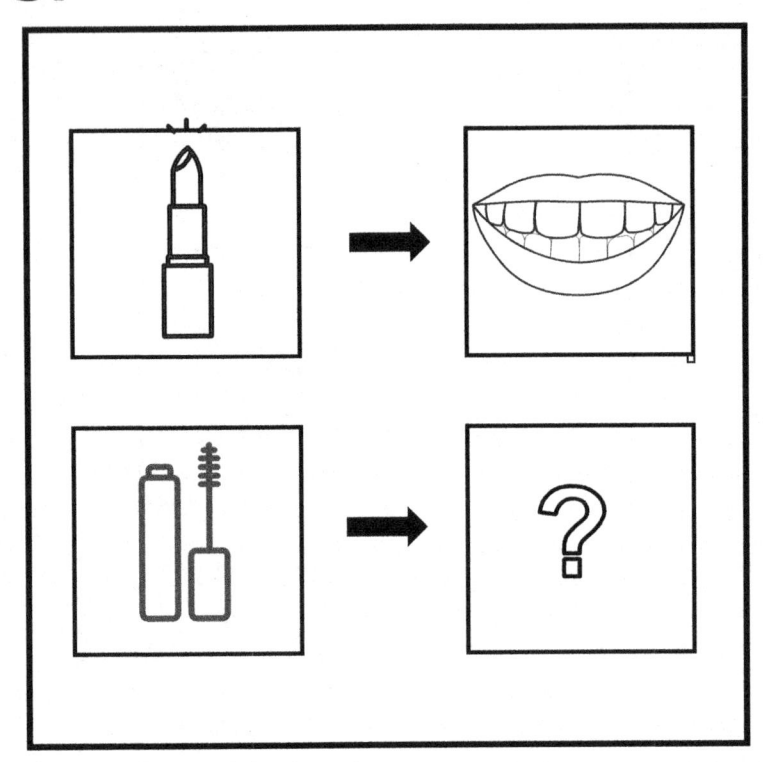

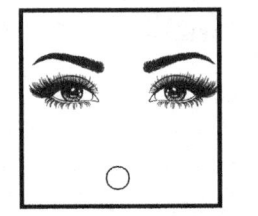

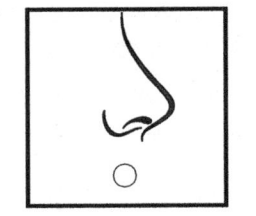

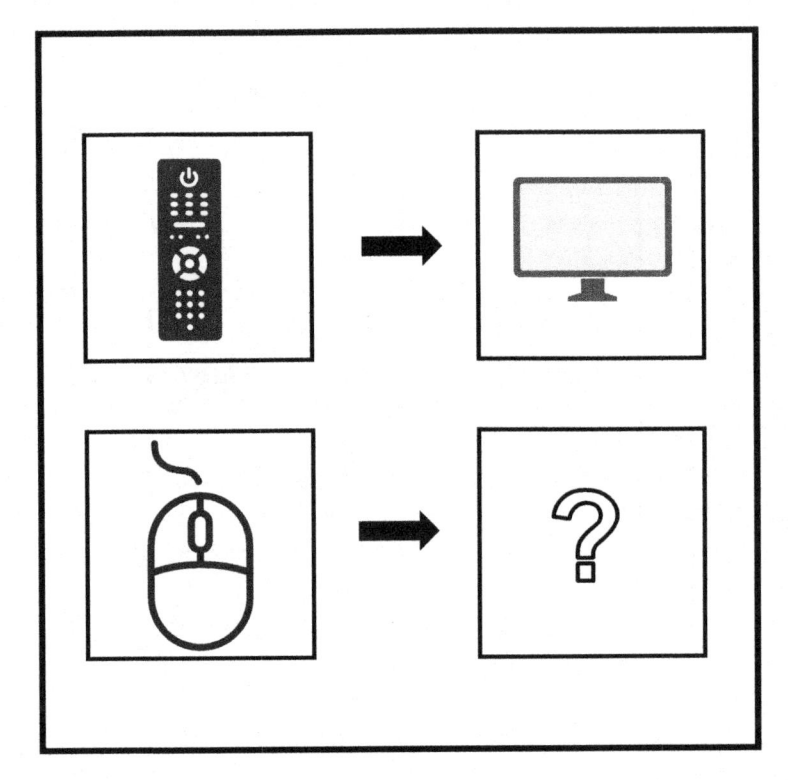

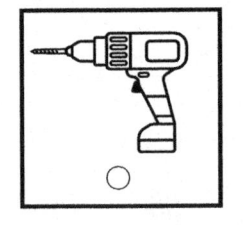

5.

6.

PRACTICE TEST GRADE 1

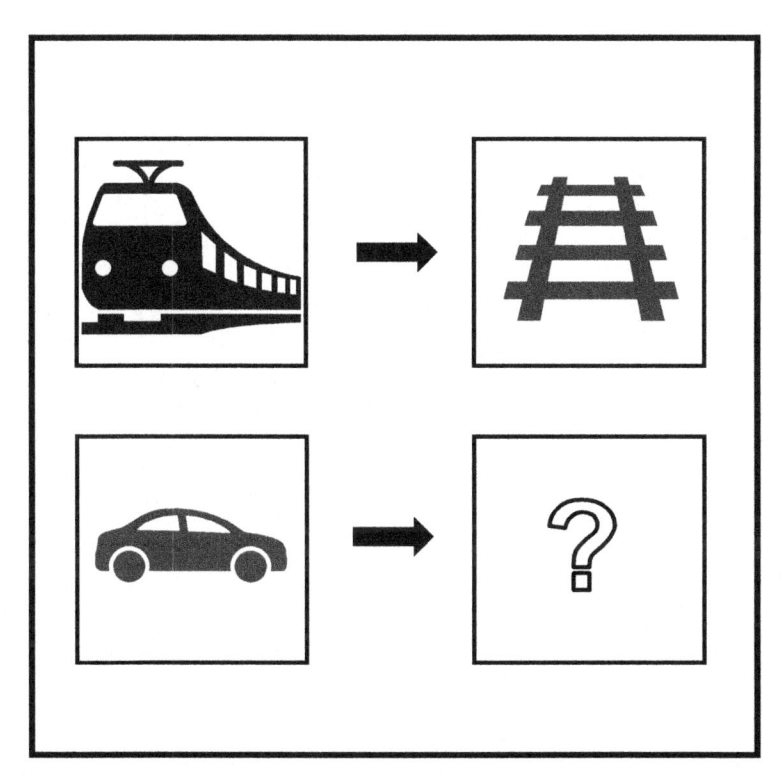

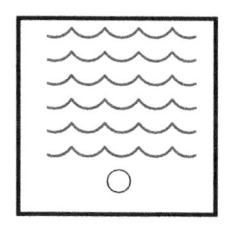

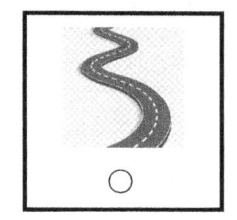

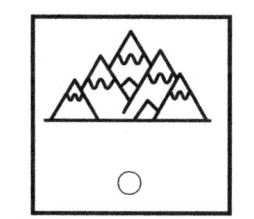

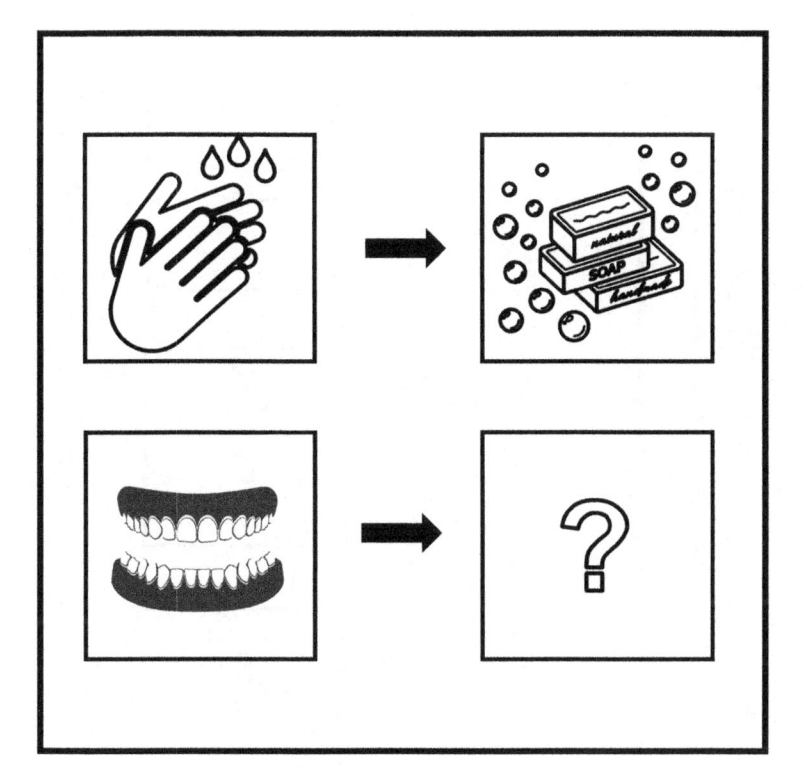

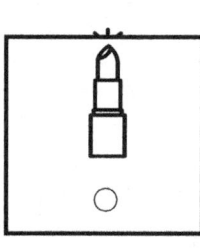

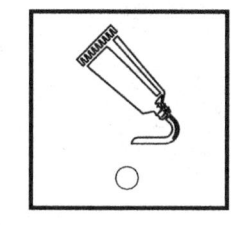

7.

PRACTICE TEST GRADE 1

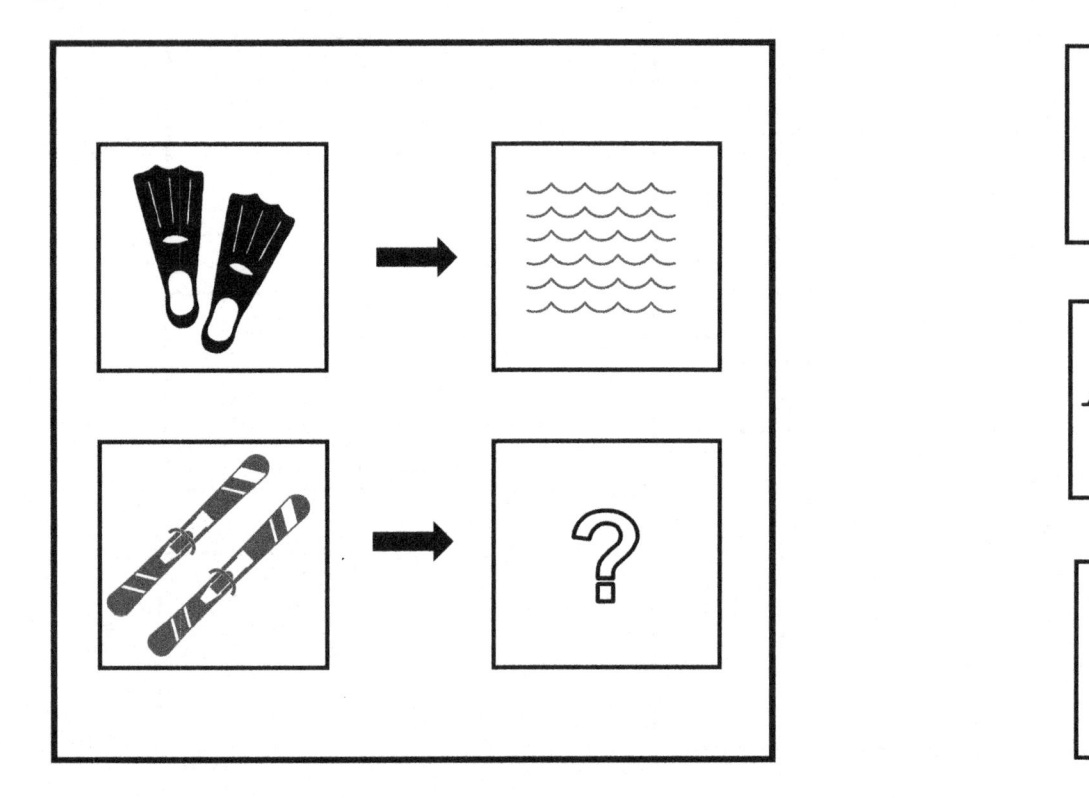

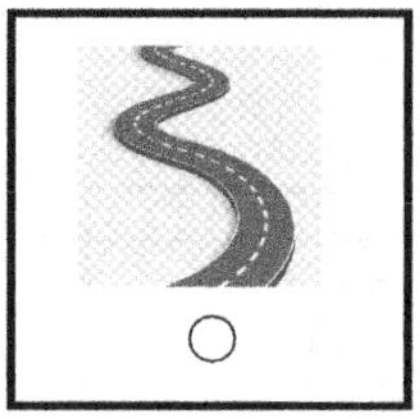

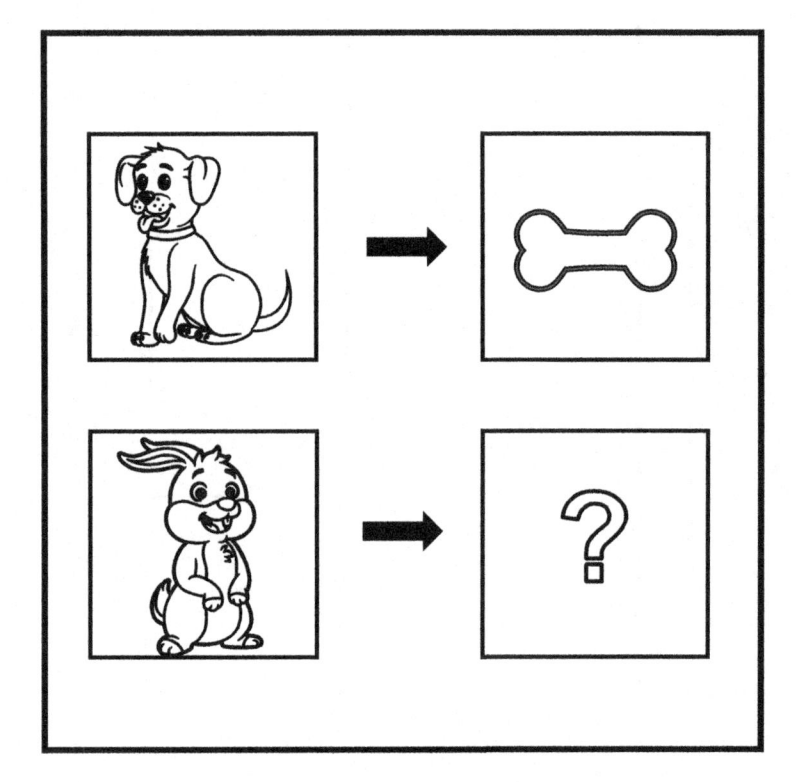

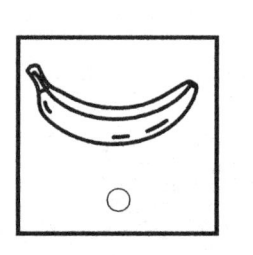

9.

10.

24

PRACTICE TEST GRADE 1

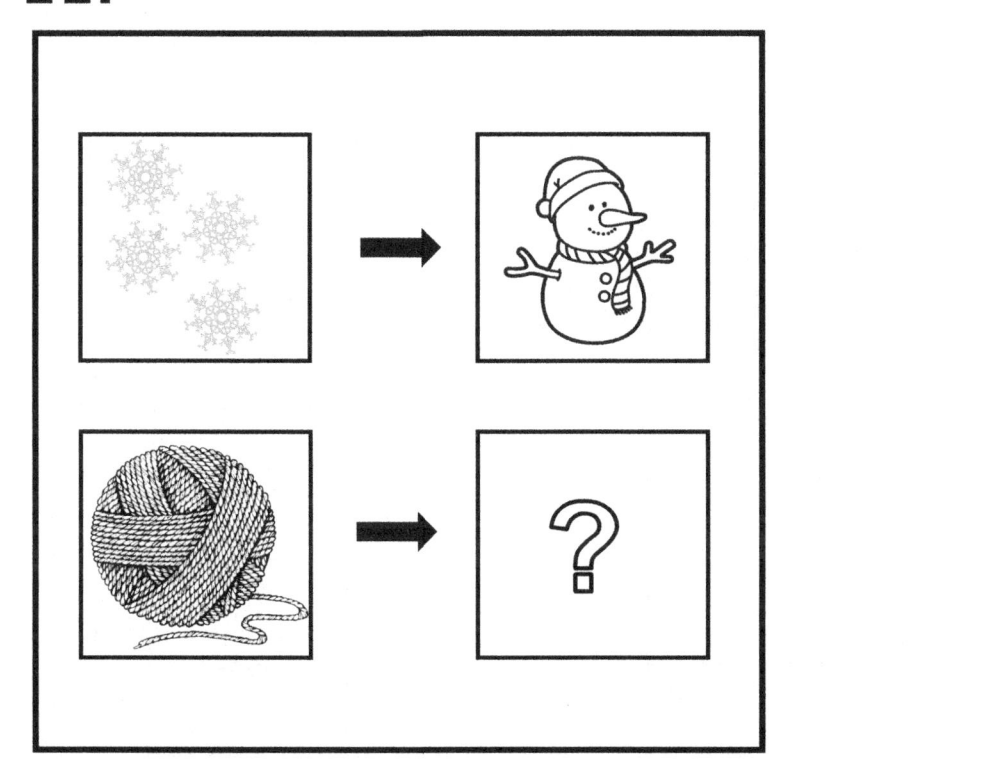

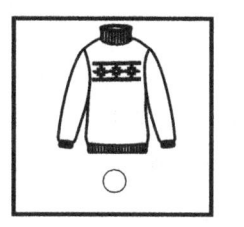

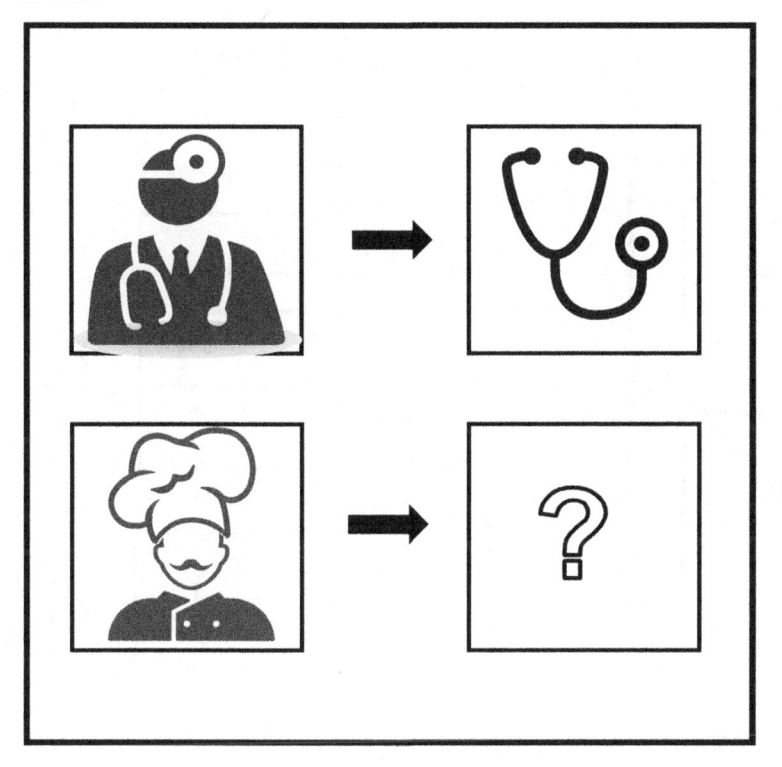

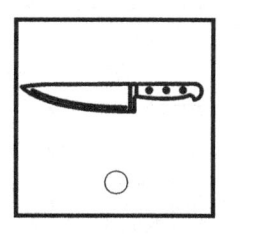

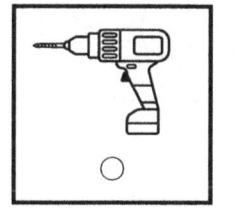

11.

12.

25

PRACTICE TEST GRADE 1

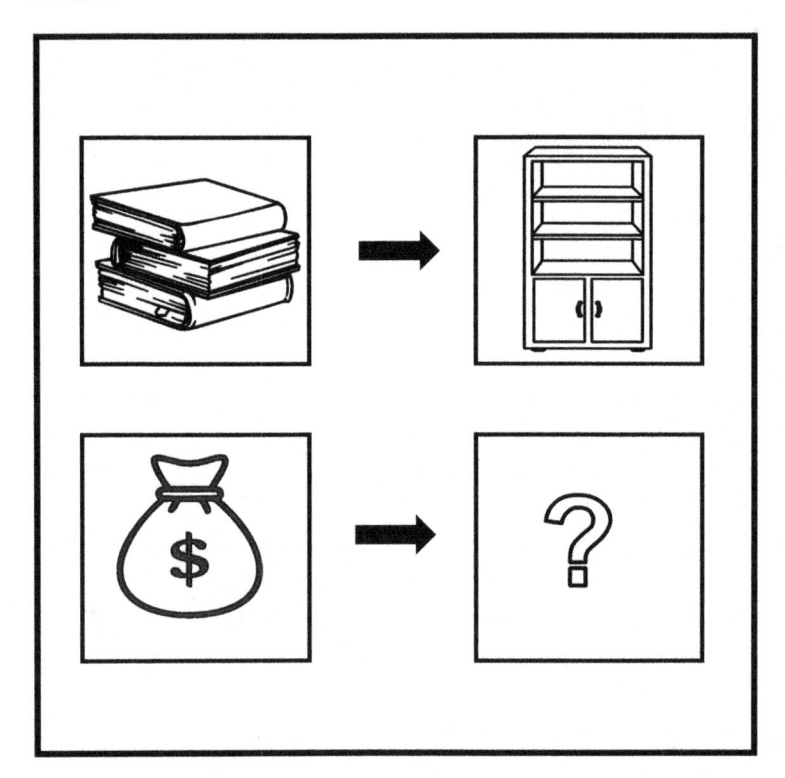

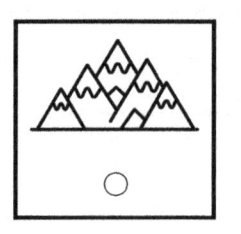

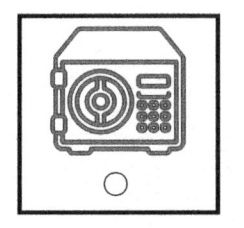

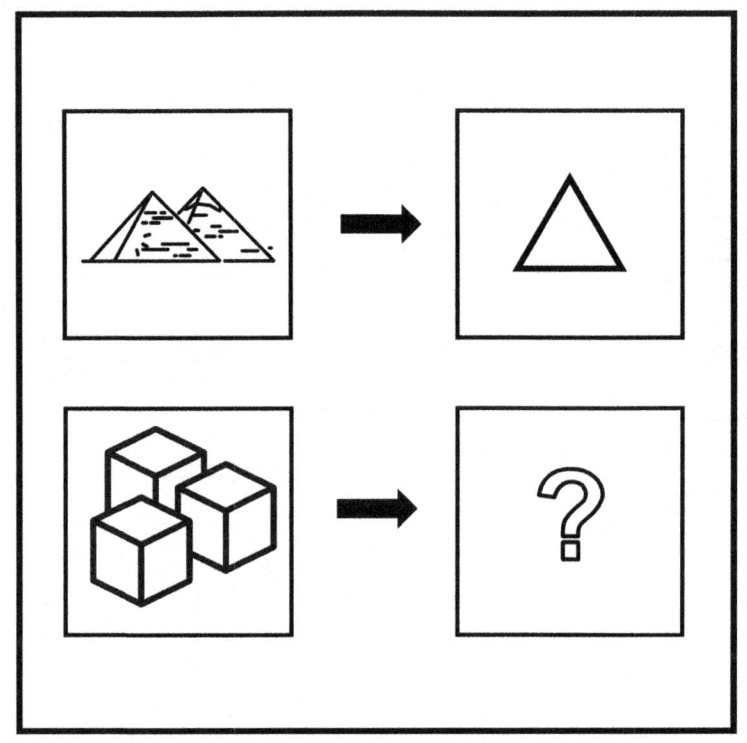

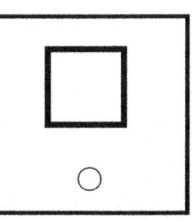

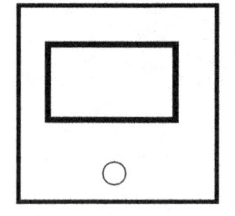

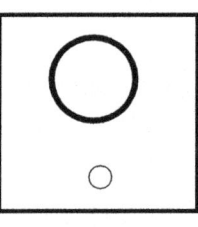

13.

14.

26

PRACTICE TEST GRADE 1

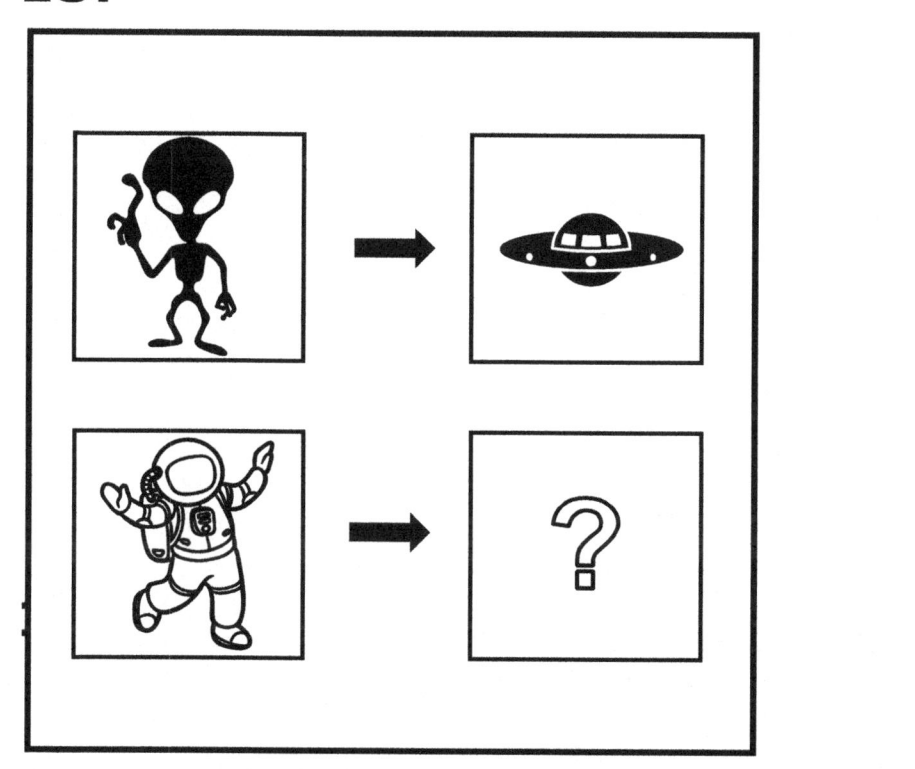

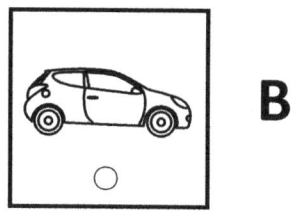

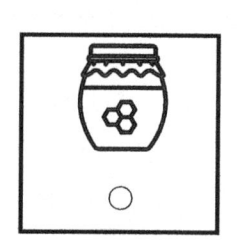

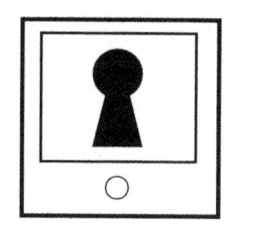

15.

16.

27

PRACTICE TEST GRADE 1

Picture Classification

Picture classification questions ask the student to choose the picture that belongs to a group of three images.

Example

A   **B**   **C**

- First, identify the relationship between the three pictures in the first row.
- What do the objects "rhinoceros", "sheep", and "tiger" have in common?

Rhinoceros, sheep, and tiger are all animals.

- Now, look at the three pictures in the lower row: cat, banana, and tree. Which picture goes best with the three images in the top row?

Cat is also an animal, so the correct answer is A.

Tips for Solving Picture Classification Questions

PRACTICE TEST GRADE 1

- Try to identify the correlation between the three pictures in the top row.

- Review all answers before you make a choice.

- Remove the pictures in the answers that don't have any kind of relationship with the three pictures in the top row.

- When you work on questions, always dedicate some time to review the incorrect answers. You will learn more from them than from the correct answers.

- Encourage your child to learn how to classify and sort toys, leaves, fruits or other objects into "similar" groups.

PRACTICE TEST GRADE 1

1.

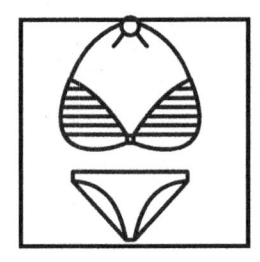

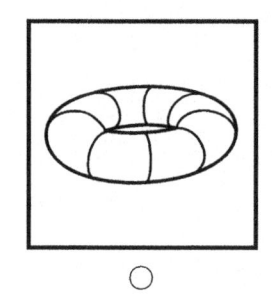

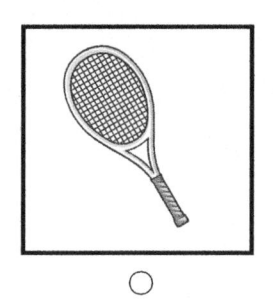

○ A   ○ B   ○ C

2.

○ A   ○ B   ○ C

PRACTICE TEST GRADE 1

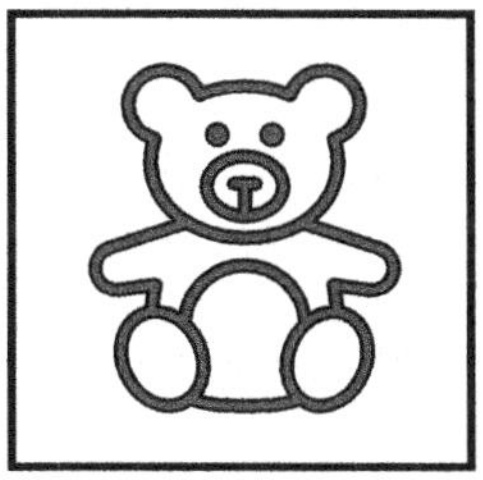

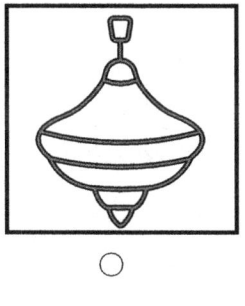

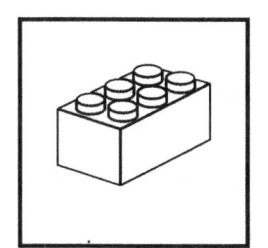

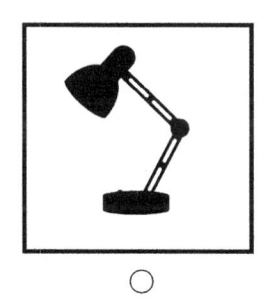

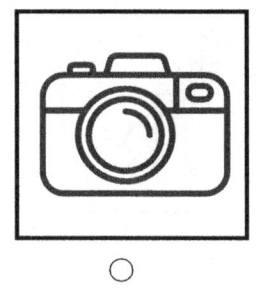

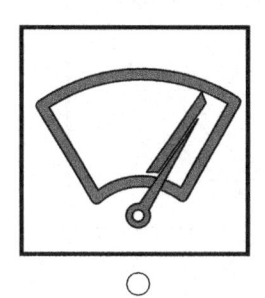

3.

4.

31

PRACTICE TEST GRADE 1

5.

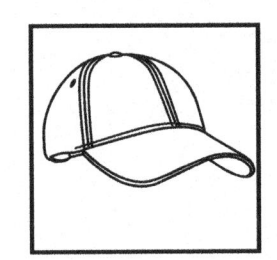

A	B	C

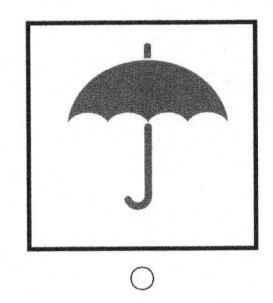

6.

A	B	C

32

PRACTICE TEST GRADE 1

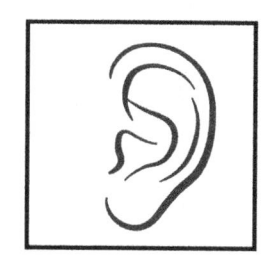

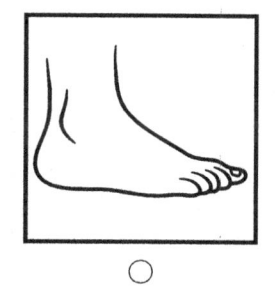

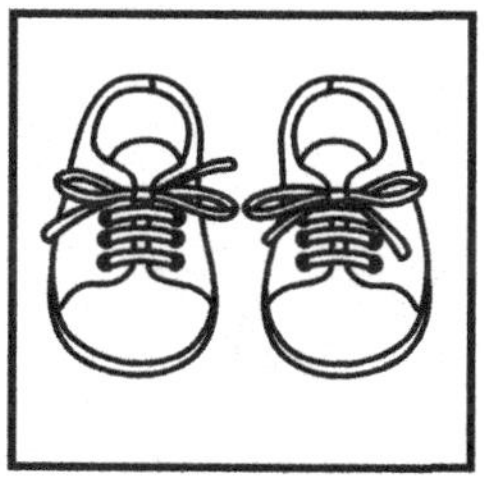

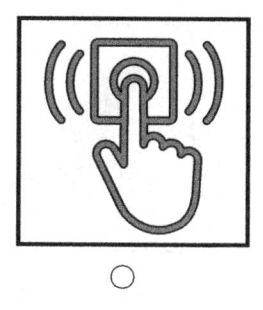

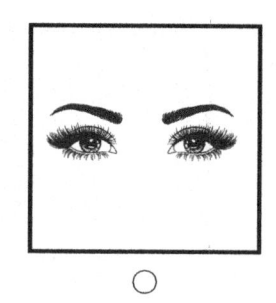

7.

8.

33

PRACTICE TEST GRADE 1

9.

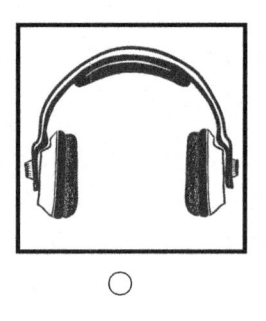

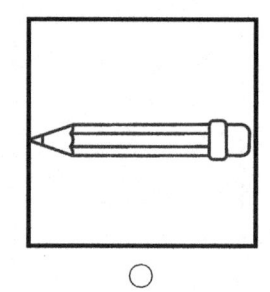

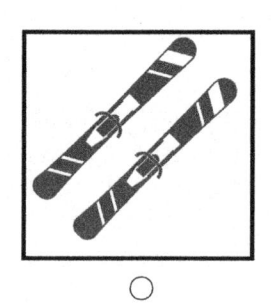

○ ○ ○
A B C

10.

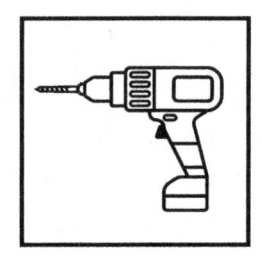

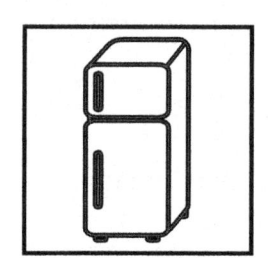

○ ○ ○
A B C

34

PRACTICE TEST GRADE 1

11.

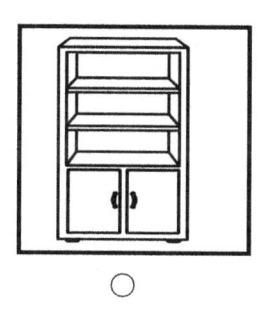

○ A   ○ B   ○ C

12.

○ A   ○ B   ○ C

PRACTICE TEST GRADE 1

13.

A

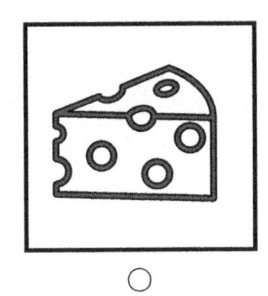

B

C

14.

A

B

C

36

PRACTICE TEST GRADE 1

15.

A   B   C

16.

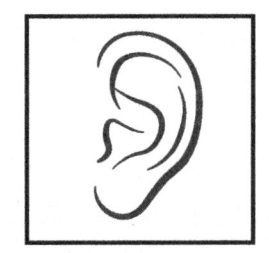

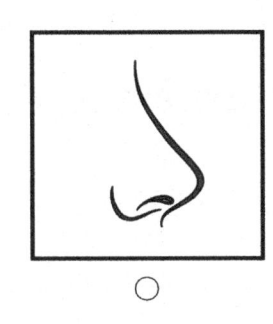

A   B   C

37

PRACTICE TEST GRADE 1

Sentence Completion

The teacher reads aloud a question and does not repeat it a second time. Children must choose the picture that best answers the question in a complete, logical way.
To answer correctly, the child must be very focused on the meaning of the sentence as a whole.

Example

Which tool is needed to make a hole in the wall?

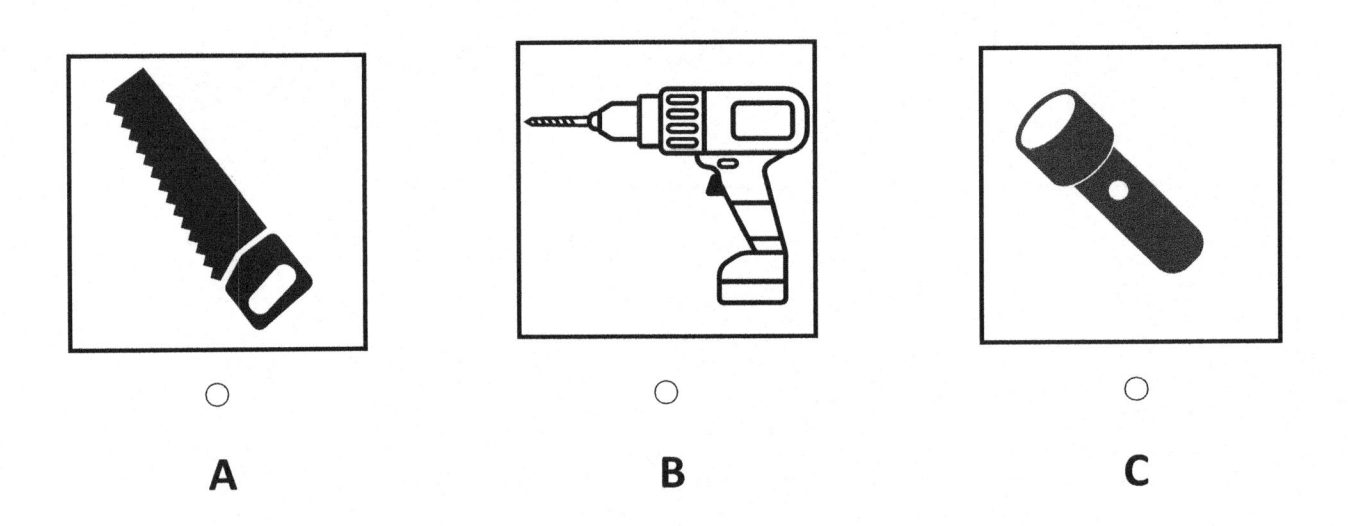

  A   B   C

- First, think about the meaning of the sentence as a whole.
- Look at the answer choices.
- Try to see these tools in your mind as they are used in everyday life.

The only tool you can use to make a hole in the wall is the drill. Therefore, the right choice is "B".

Tips for Sentence Completion

- First, listen carefully to the sentence.
- Look at the three pictures in the answer row.
- Remove the pictures that don't have any kind of relationship with the main sentence.
- Try to see objects with your mind, placing them in the real world.

PRACTICE TEST GRADE 1

Directions for Sentence Completion

- On each page, you will find two questions.

- Read aloud the first question to your child.

- Turn the page and show him the possible choices.

- Proceed with the next question.

PRACTICE TEST GRADE 1

1.

Which tool can be used to cut a log?

2.

Which object could you sit on?

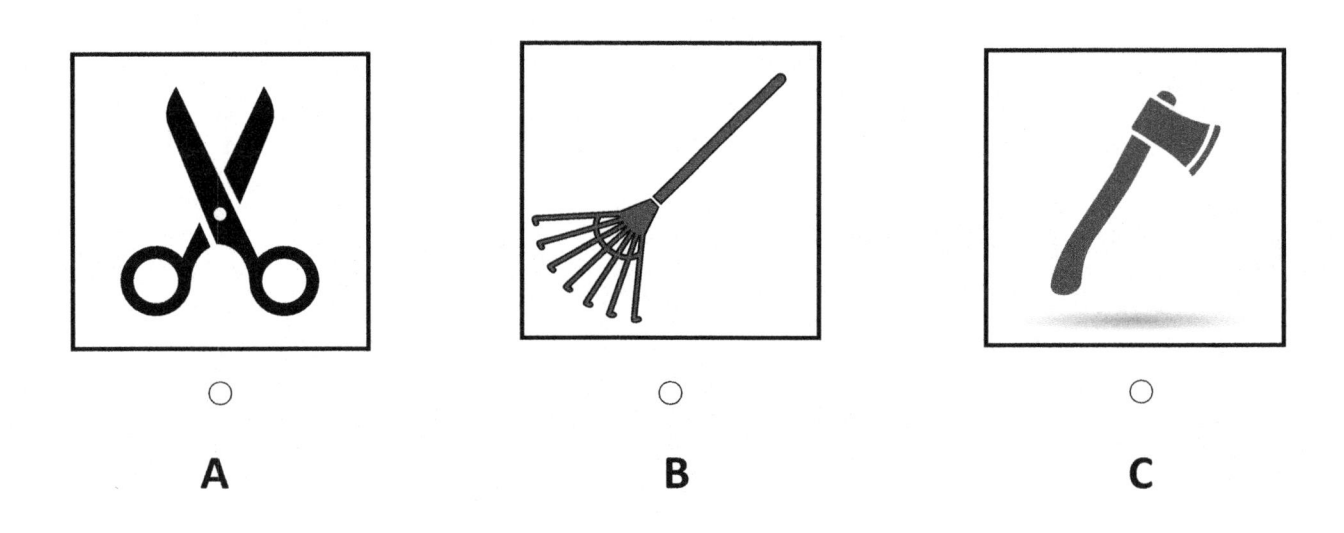

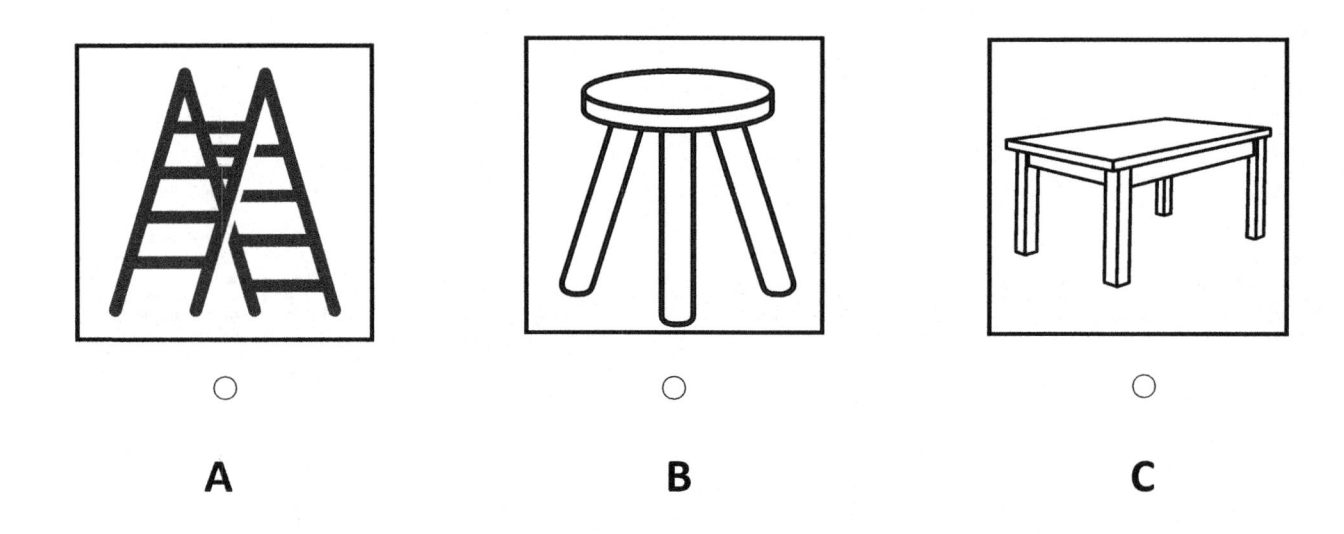

PRACTICE TEST GRADE 1

1.

A	B	C
○	○	○

2.

A	B	C
○	○	○

42

PRACTICE TEST GRADE 1

3.

Which one of these objects will not be found in a kitchen?

4.

Which image shows a reptile?

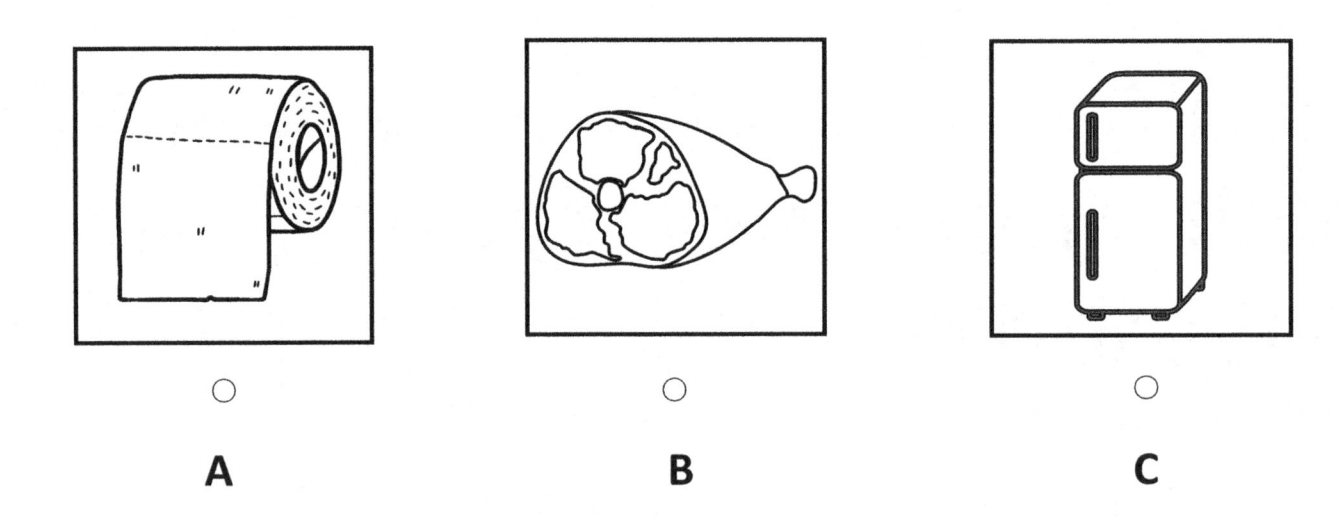

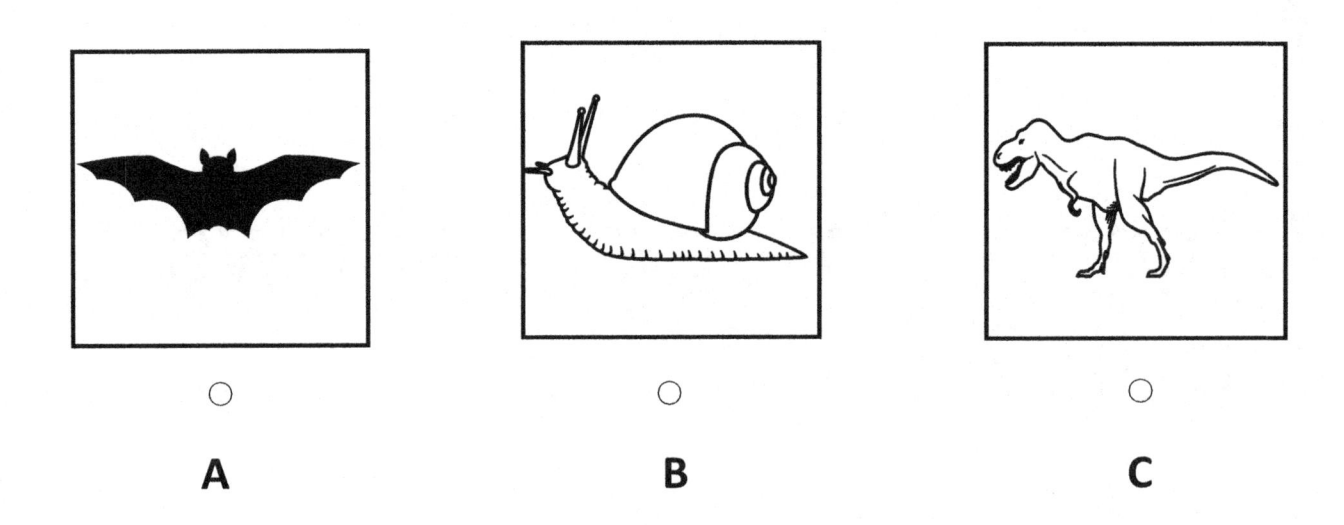

PRACTICE TEST GRADE 1

3.

| A | B | C |

4

| A | B | C |

44

PRACTICE TEST GRADE 1

5.

Mary wants to take his dog for a walk. Which one of these objects will she use?

6.

Which one of these pictures does not show a wild animal?

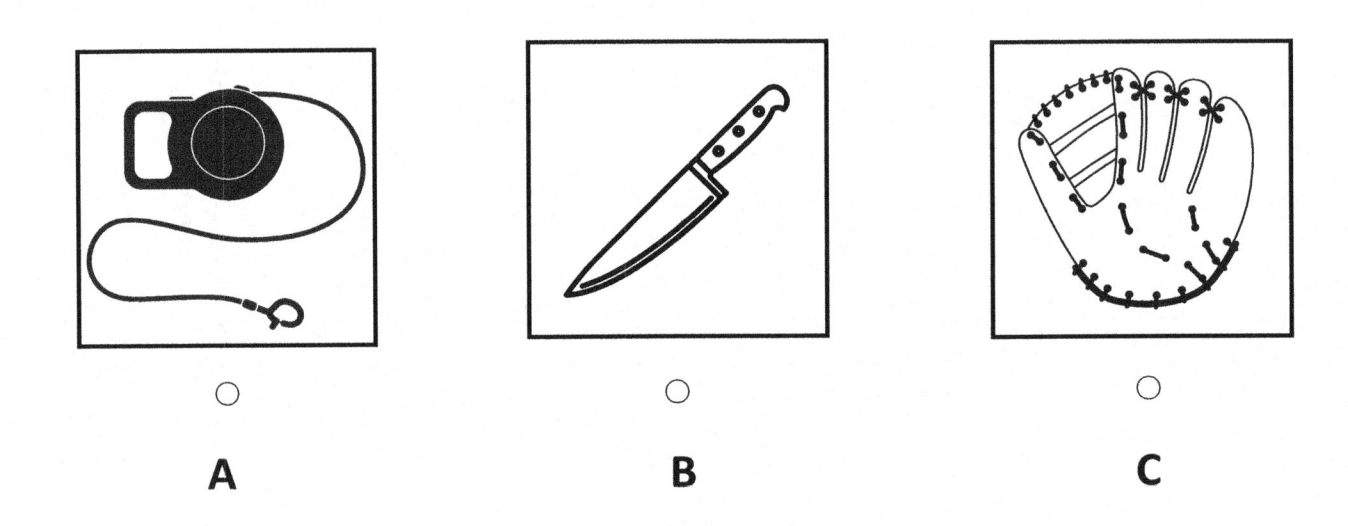

PRACTICE TEST GRADE 1

5.

A   B   C

6.

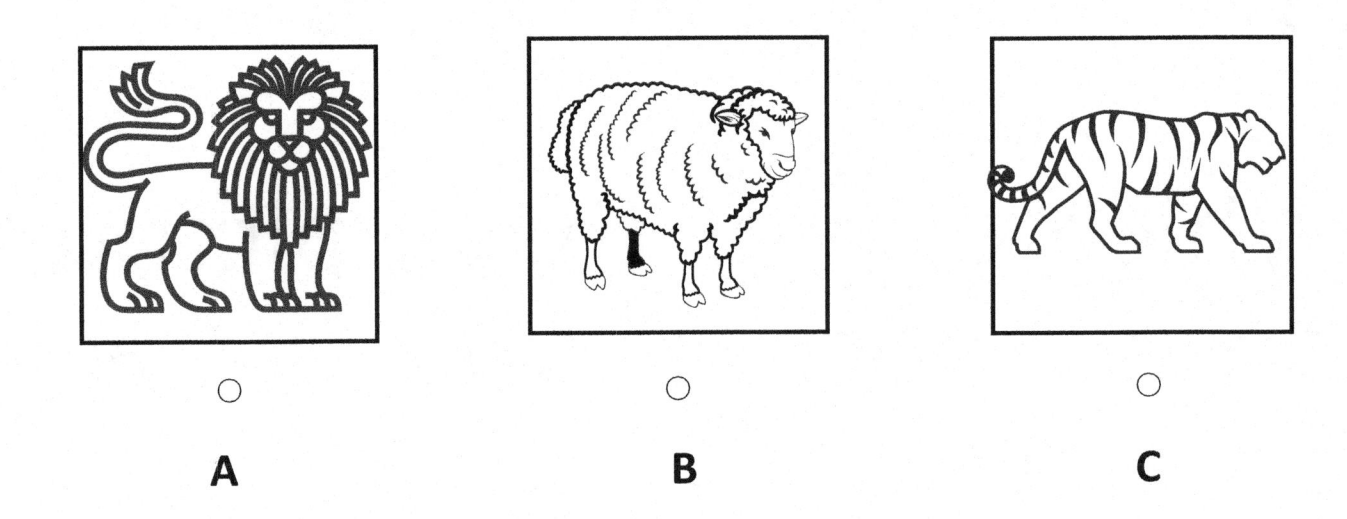

A   B   C

46

7.

Mary's dad is a chef. Which one of these images shows Mary's dad at work?

8.

Which one of these images shows less than four fruits?

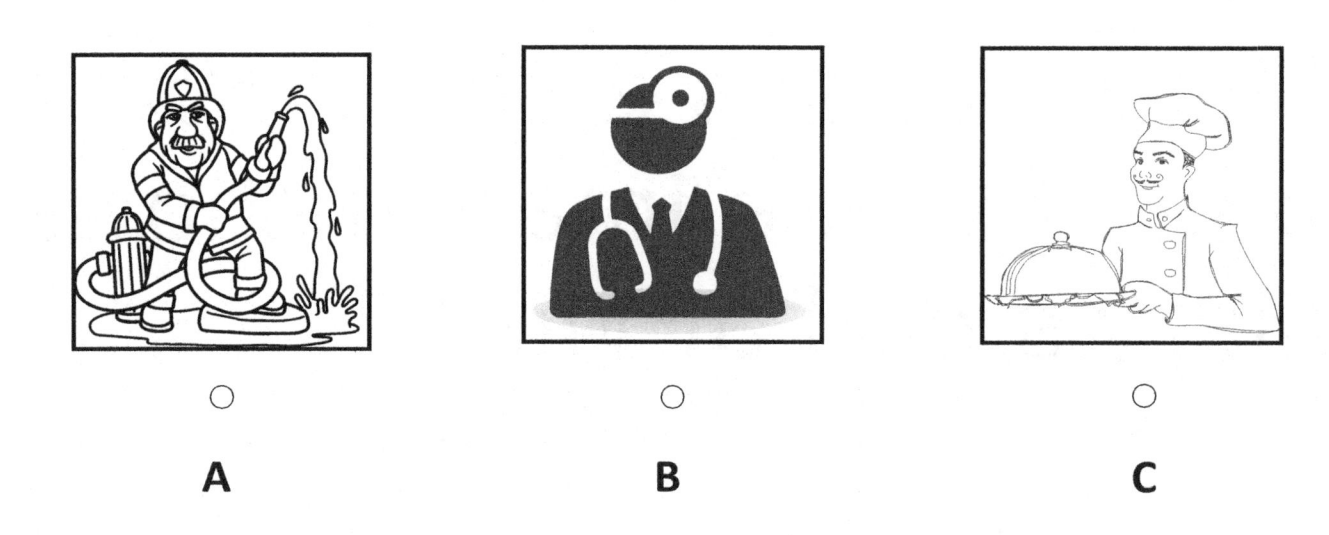

PRACTICE TEST GRADE 1

7.

A   B   C

8.

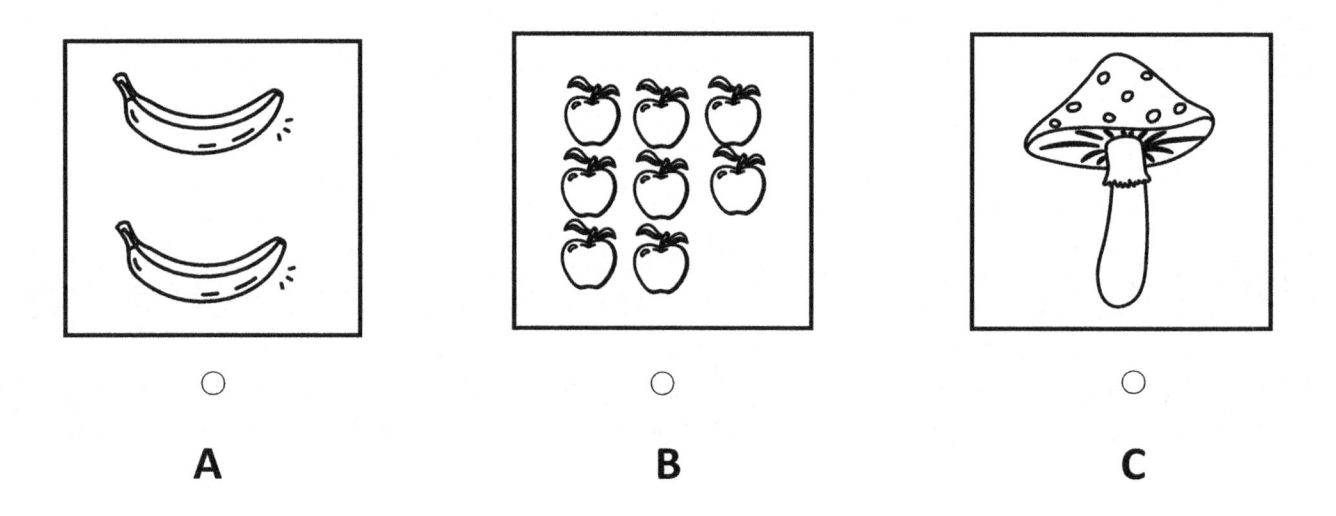

A   B   C

48

PRACTICE TEST GRADE 1

9.

Mom is making a birthday cake. Which ingredient will she not need?

10.

Which one of these images shows an apple on a table?

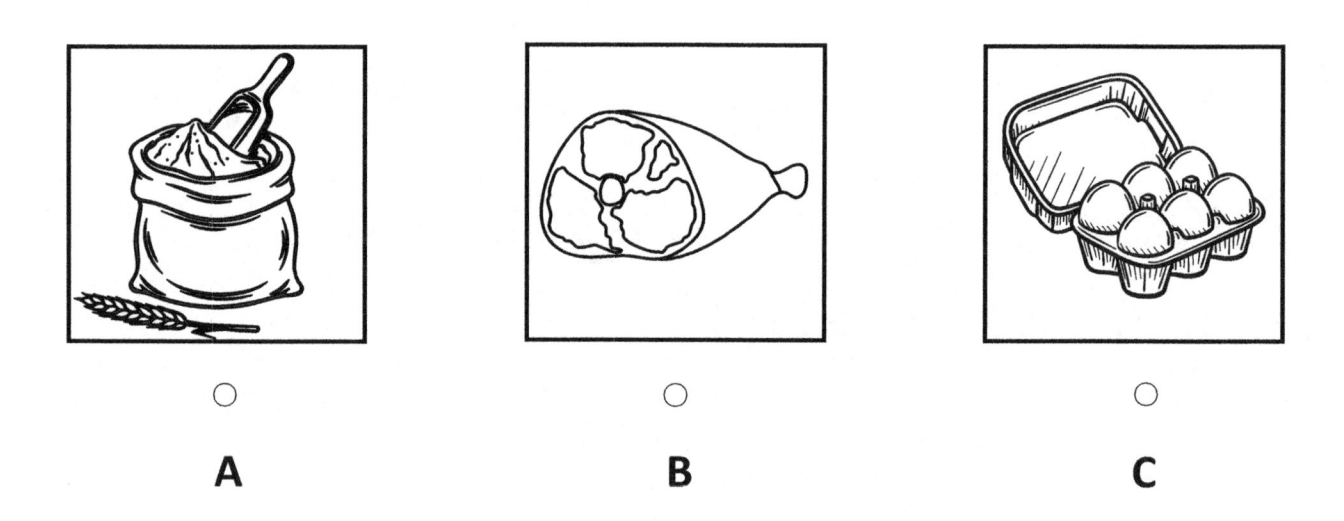

PRACTICE TEST GRADE 1

9.

○ A   ○ B   ○ C

10.

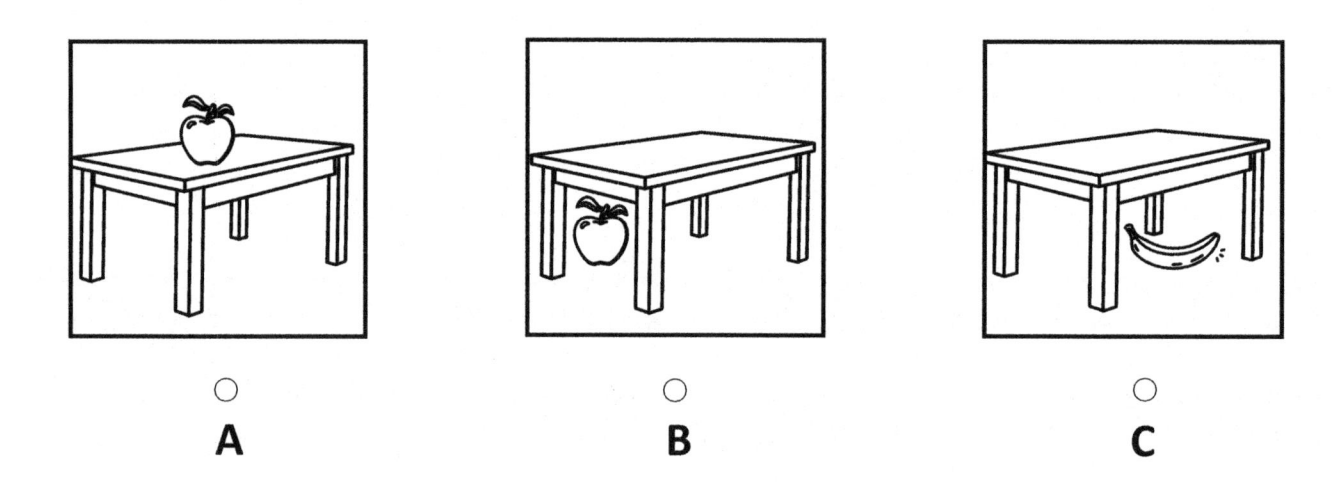

○ A   ○ B   ○ C

11.

It's raining. Mike wants to go out for a walk. Which of the following items will he not need?

12.

Which of these pictures does not show a part of a house?

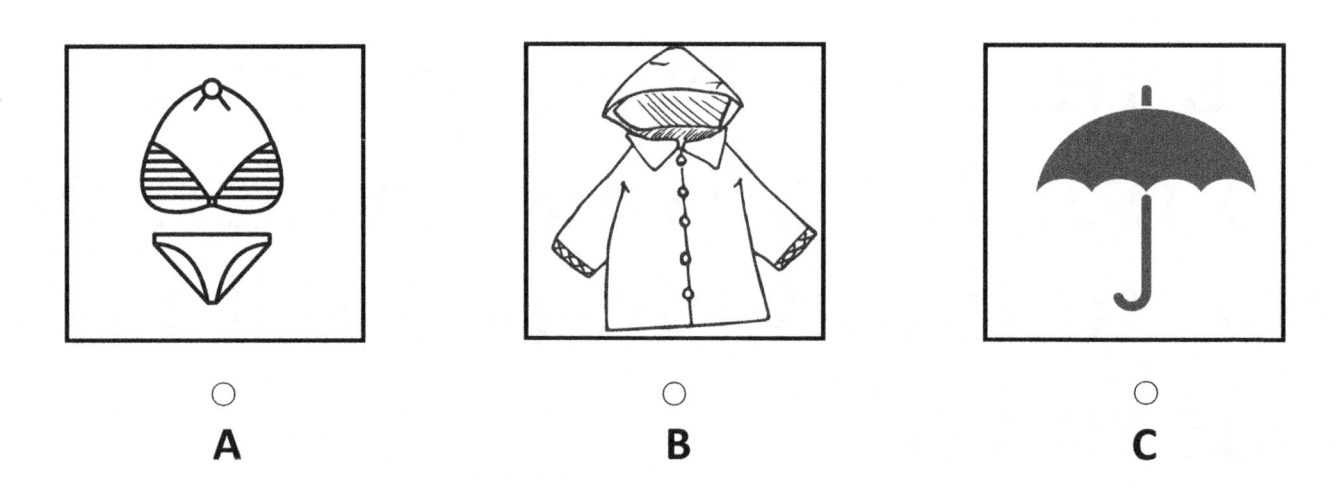

PRACTICE TEST GRADE 1

11.

○ A

○ B

○ C

12.

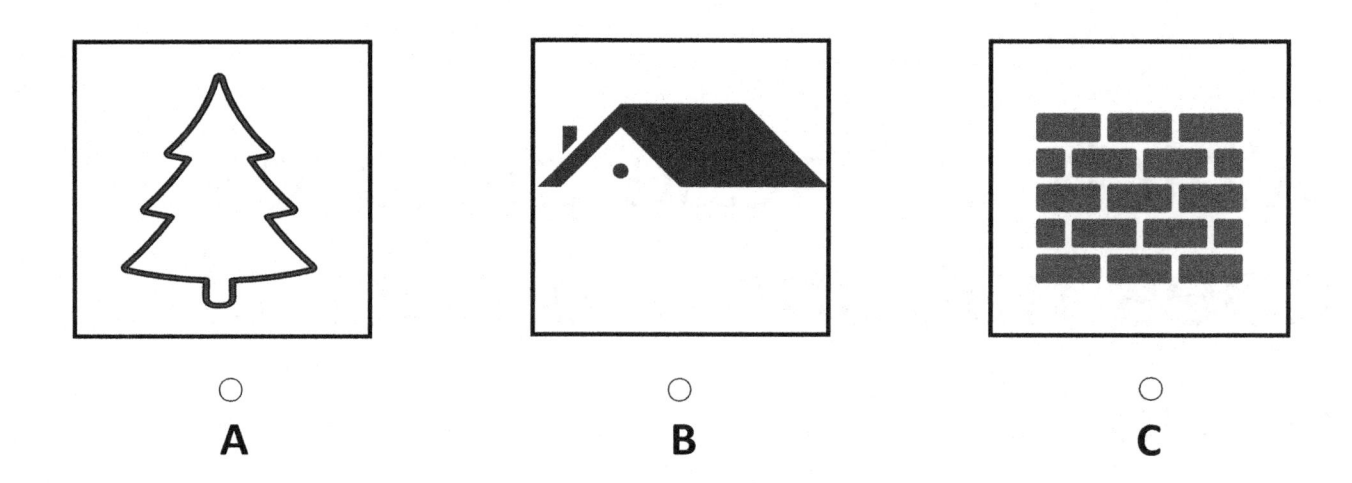

○ A

○ B

○ C

13.

Oscar wants to go camping with friends. Which object will he not need?

14.

Which of these images does not show a jumping animal?

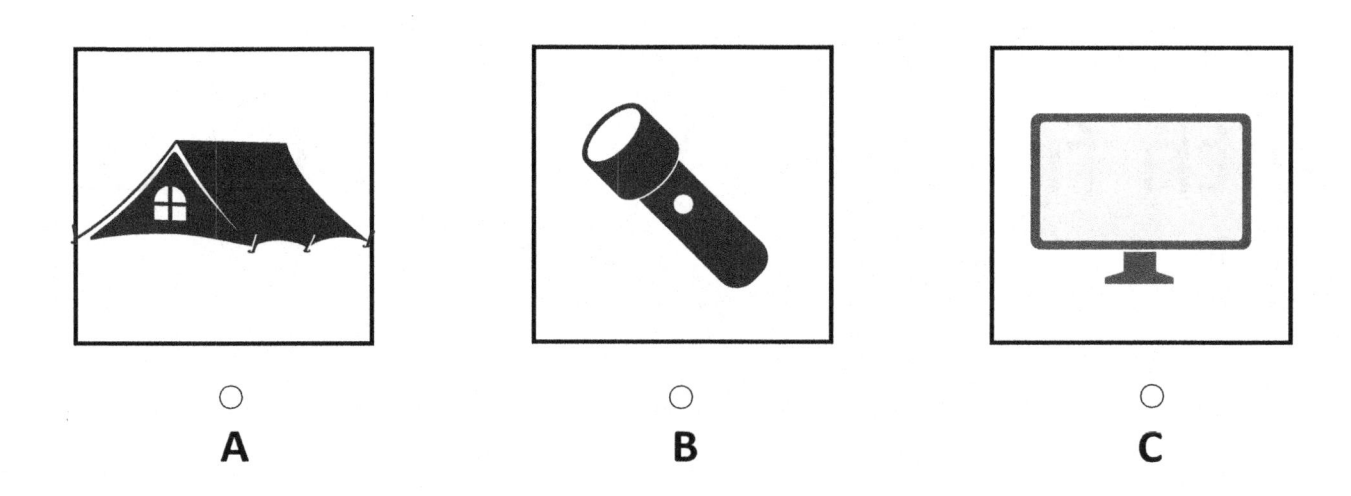

PRACTICE TEST GRADE 1

13.

○
A

○
B

○
C

14.

○
A

○
B

○
C

54

15.

Which fruit is needed for making wine?

16.

Mary is going to Africa. Which animal will she not meet?

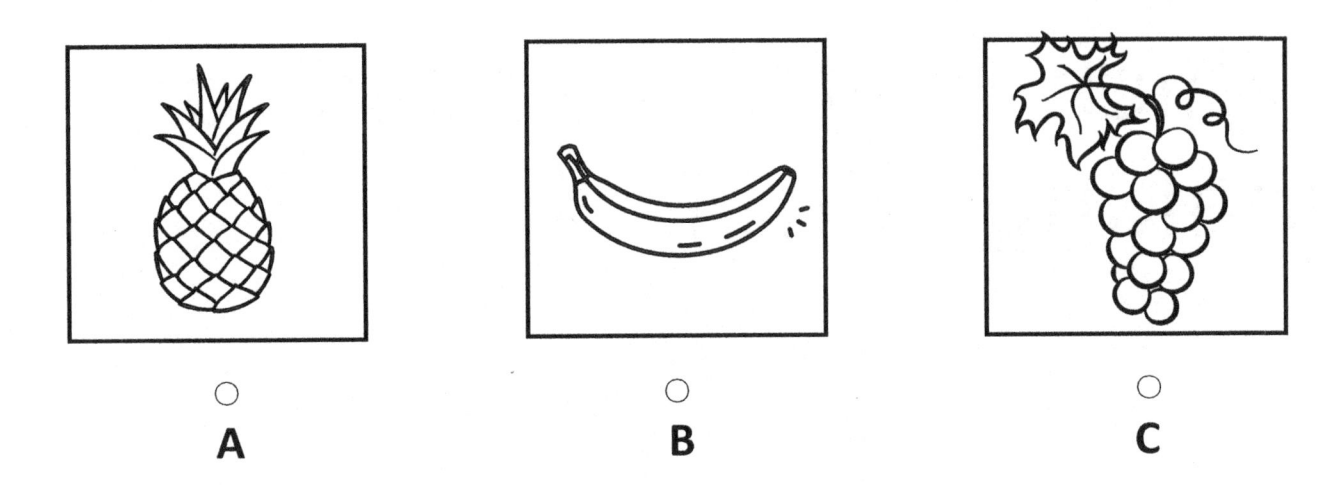

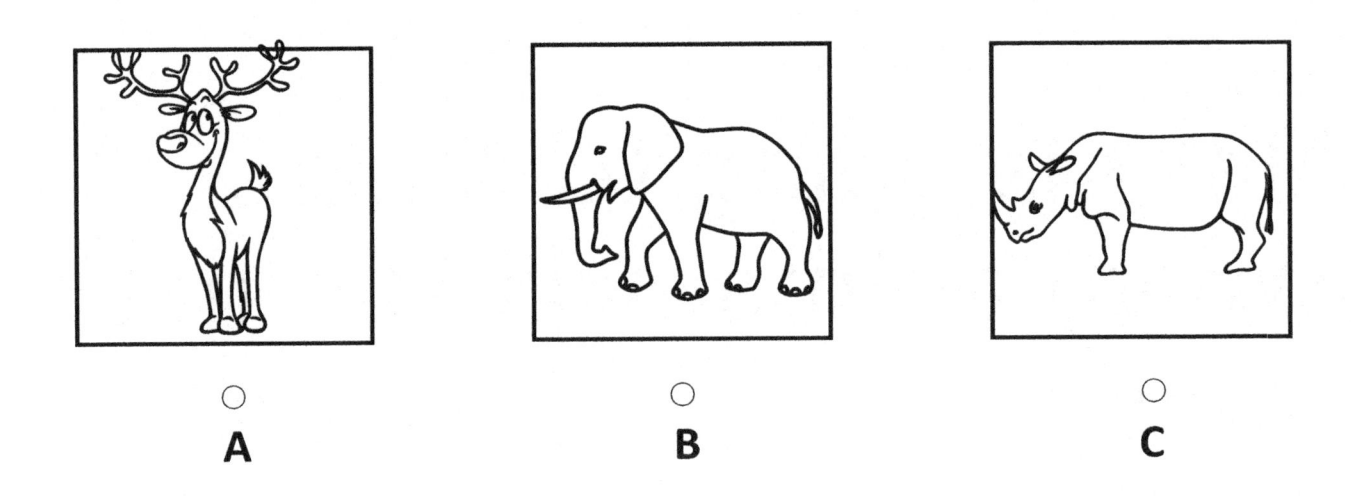

PRACTICE TEST GRADE 1

15.

○ A

○ B

○ C

16.

○ A

○ B

○ C

PRACTICE TEST GRADE 1

PRACTICE TEST NON VERBAL BATTERY

This section is designed to assess a student's ability to reason and think beyond what they've already been taught. This section includes geometric shapes and figures that aren't normally seen in the classroom.

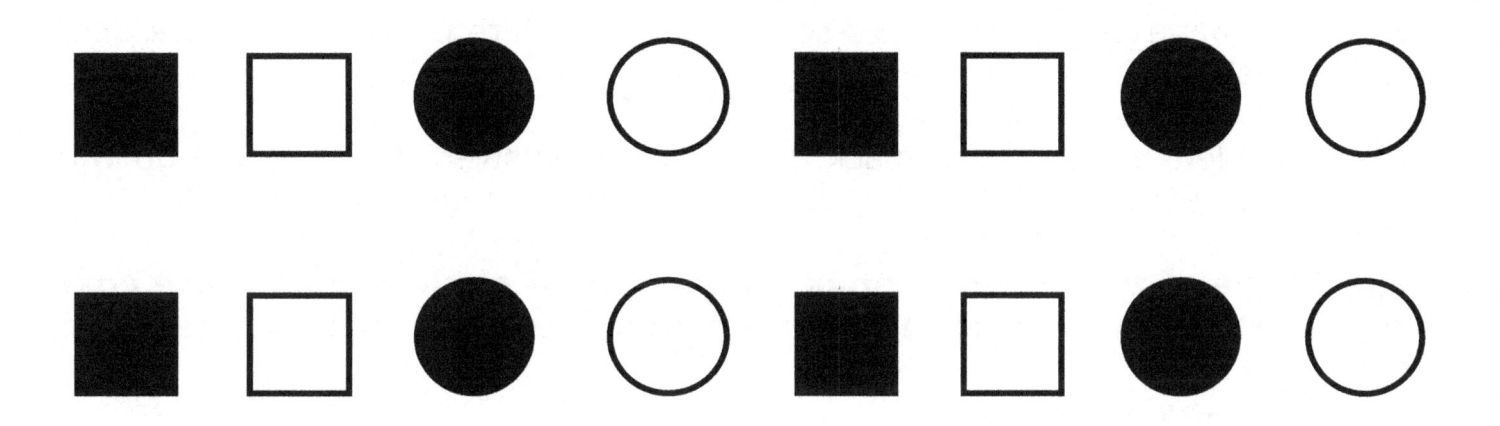

PRACTICE TEST GRADE 1

Figure Matrices

Children are provided with a 2X2 matrix with the image missing in one cell. They have to identify the relationship between the two spatial shapes in the upper line and find a fourth image that has the same correlation with the left shape in the lower line.

Example

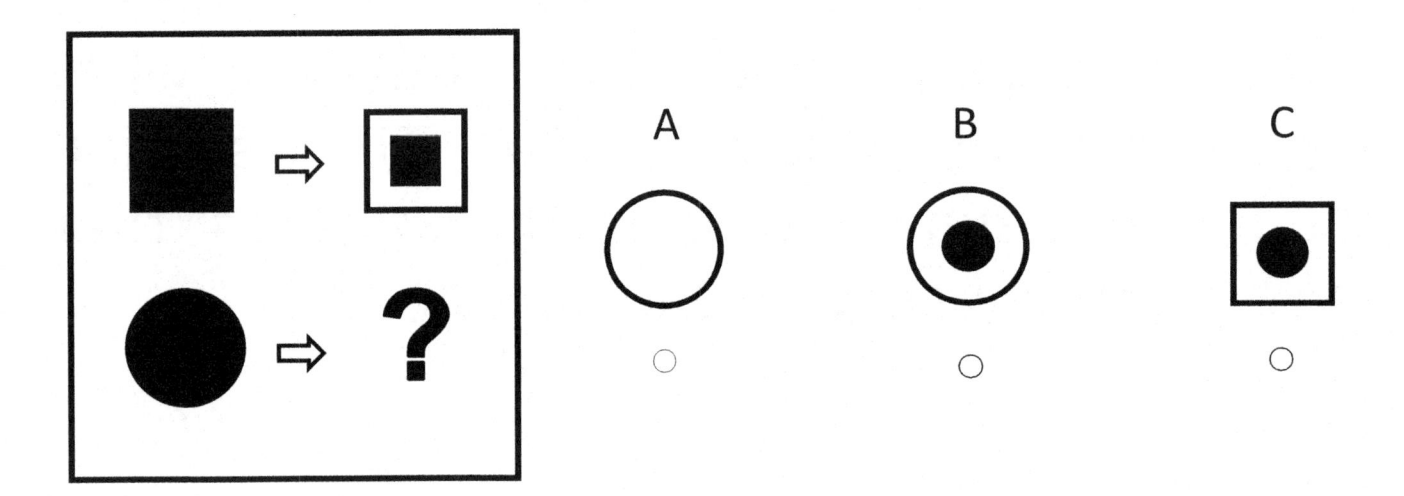

In the upper left box, the image shows a black square. In the upper right box, the image shows the same square, but in white color with a little black square inside.

The lower left box shows a black circle. Which answer choice would go with this image in the same way as the upper images go together?

**The image of the answer choice must show a circle but in white color with a little black circle inside, following the same logic of the upper shapes.
The right answer is "B".**

Tips for Figure Matrices

- Consider all the answer choices before selecting one.

- Try to use logic and sequential reasoning.

- Eliminate the logically wrong answers to restrict the options.

- Train yourself to decipher the relationship between different figures and shapes.

- Try using real shapes to better understand their relationships and similarities.

PRACTICE TEST GRADE 1

1.

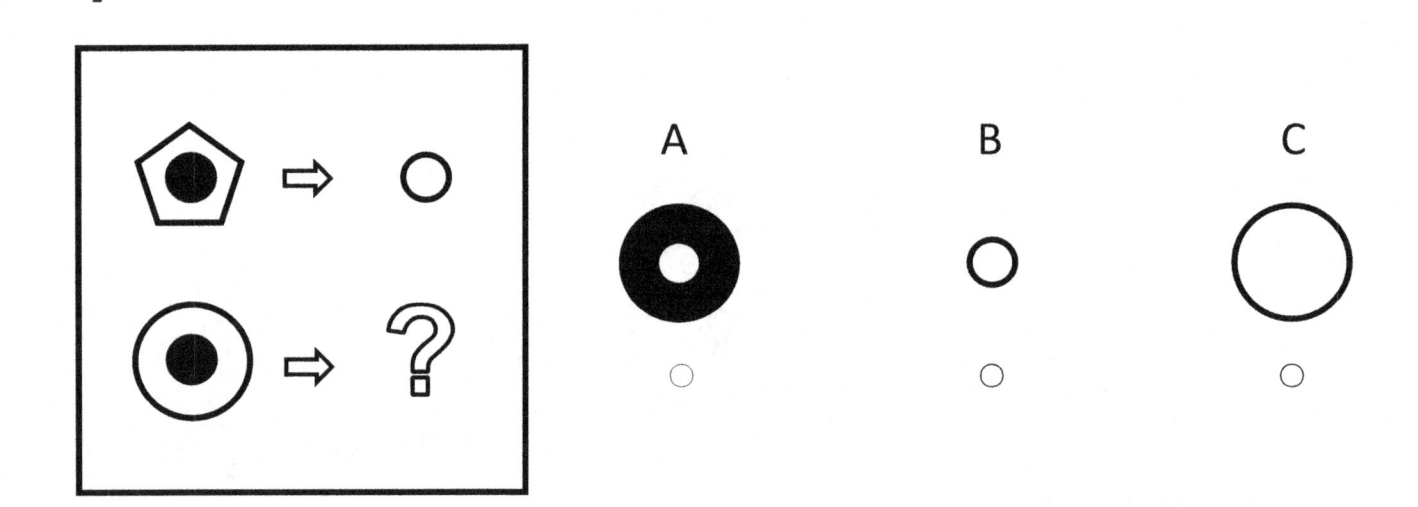

2.

60

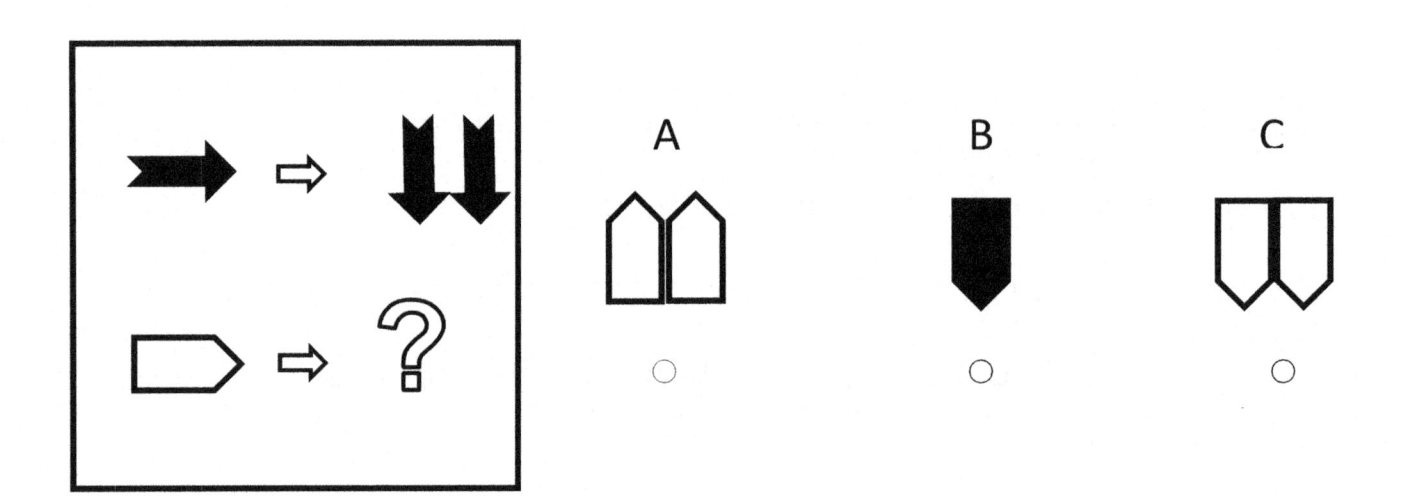

PRACTICE TEST GRADE 1

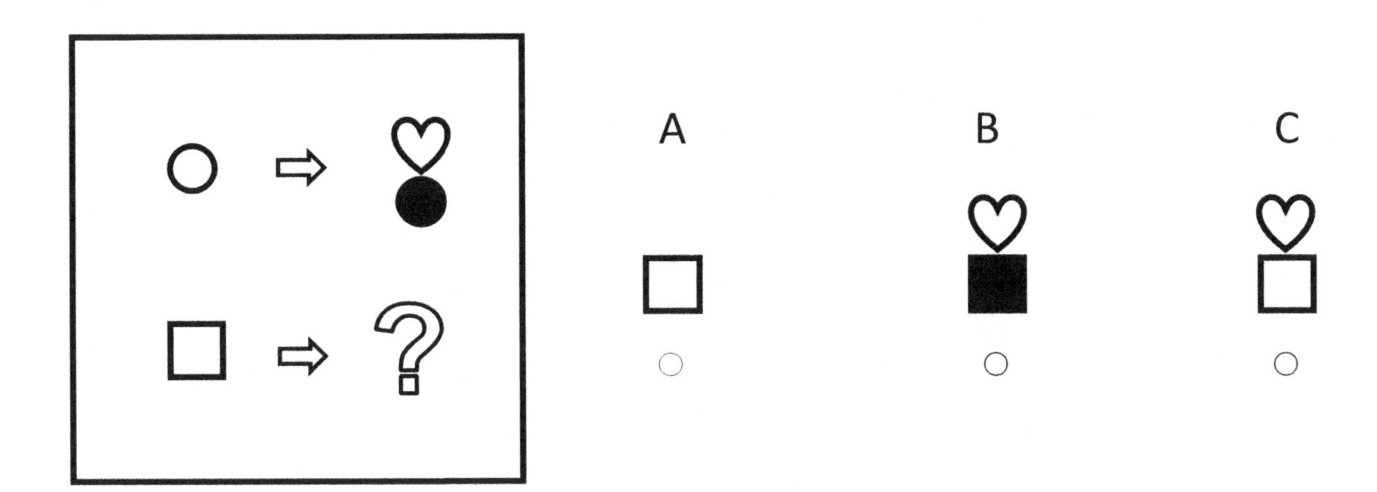

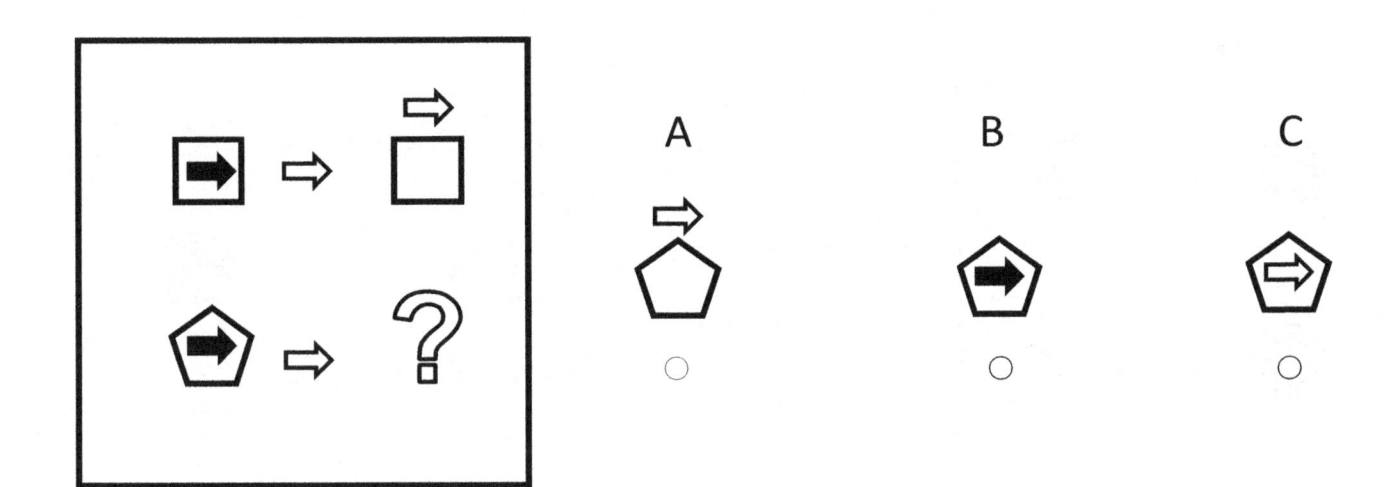

3.

4.

61

PRACTICE TEST GRADE 1

5.

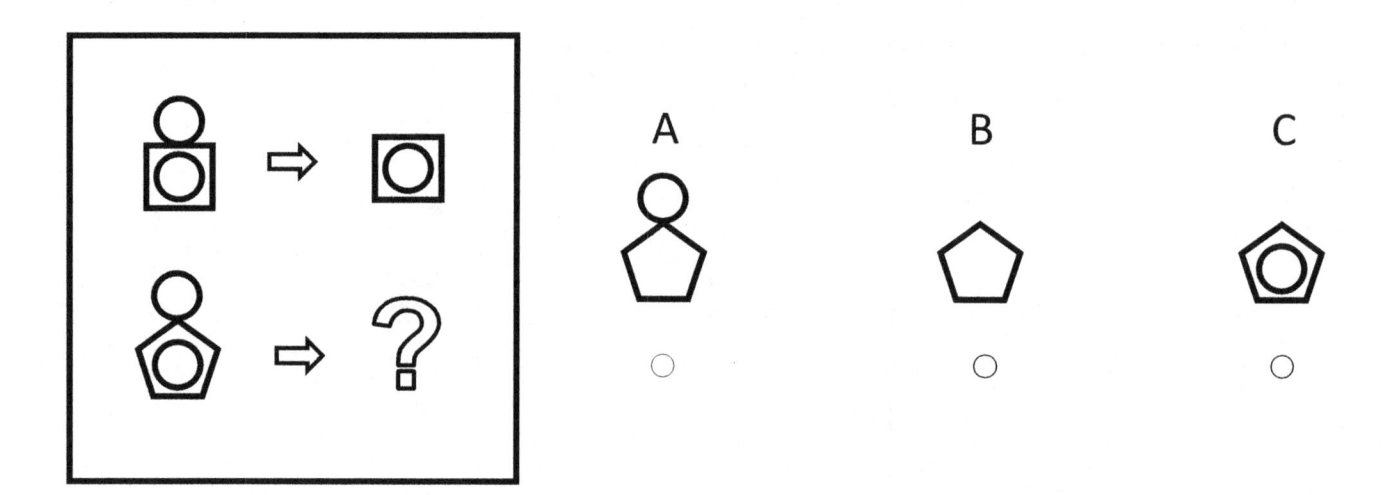

6.

62

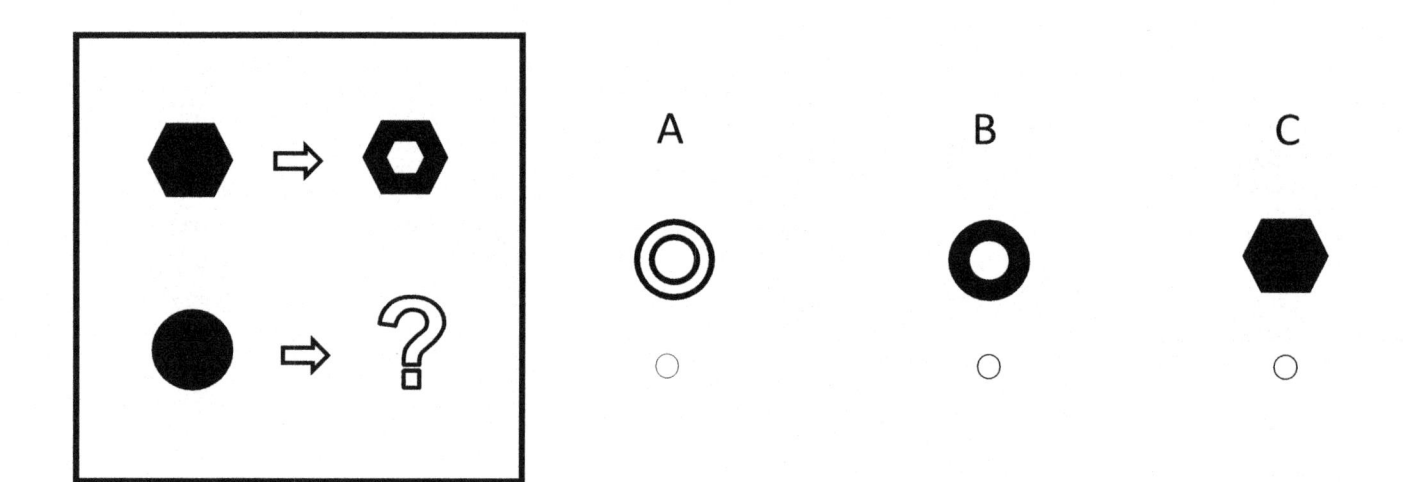

PRACTICE TEST GRADE 1

7.

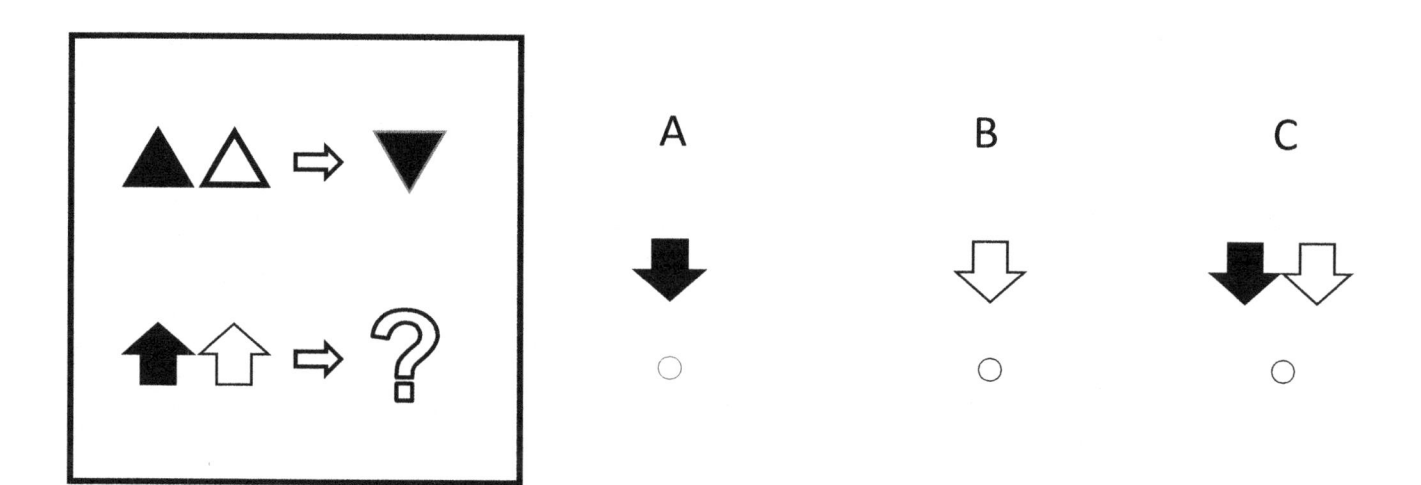

8.

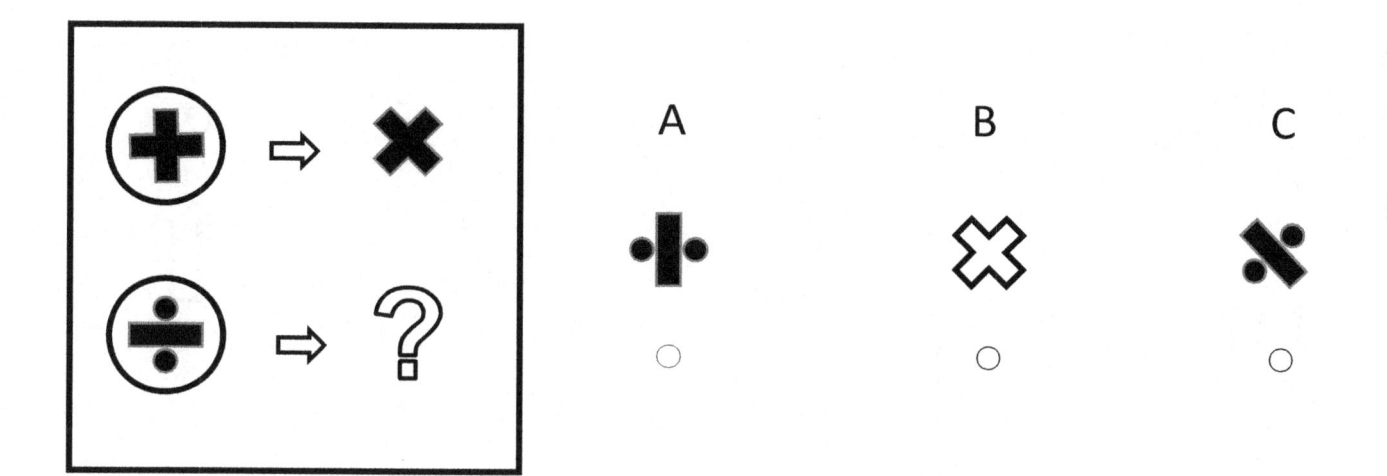

PRACTICE TEST GRADE 1

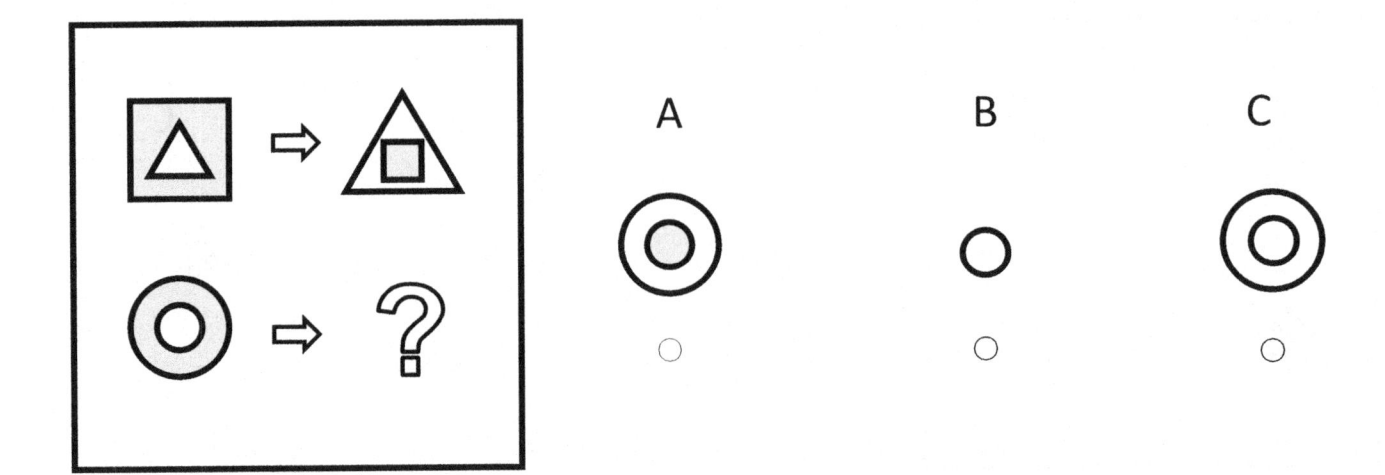

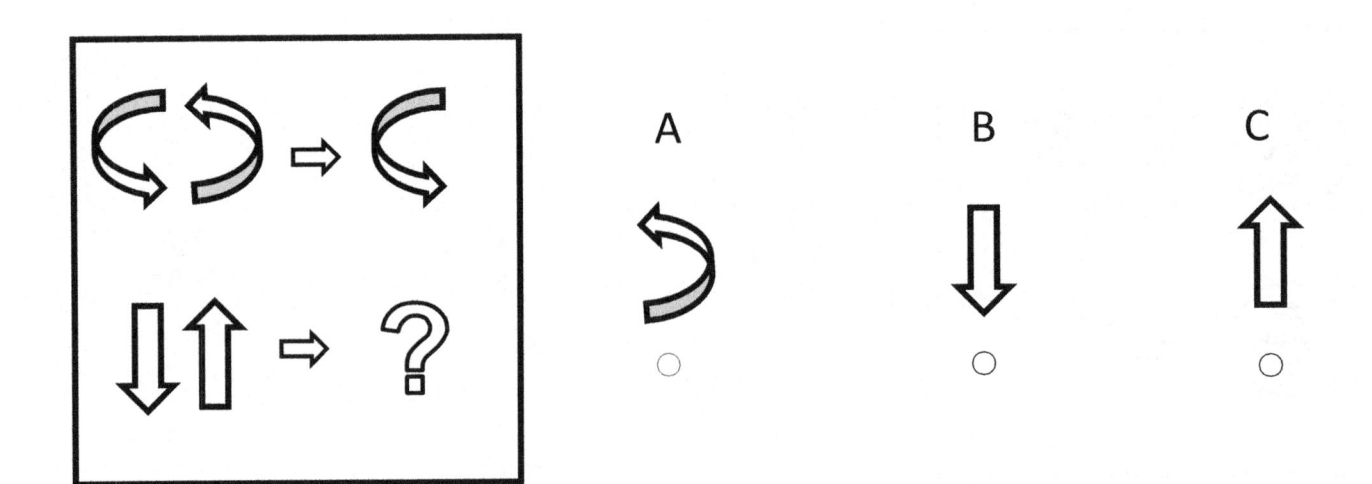

9.

10.

64

PRACTICE TEST GRADE 1

11.

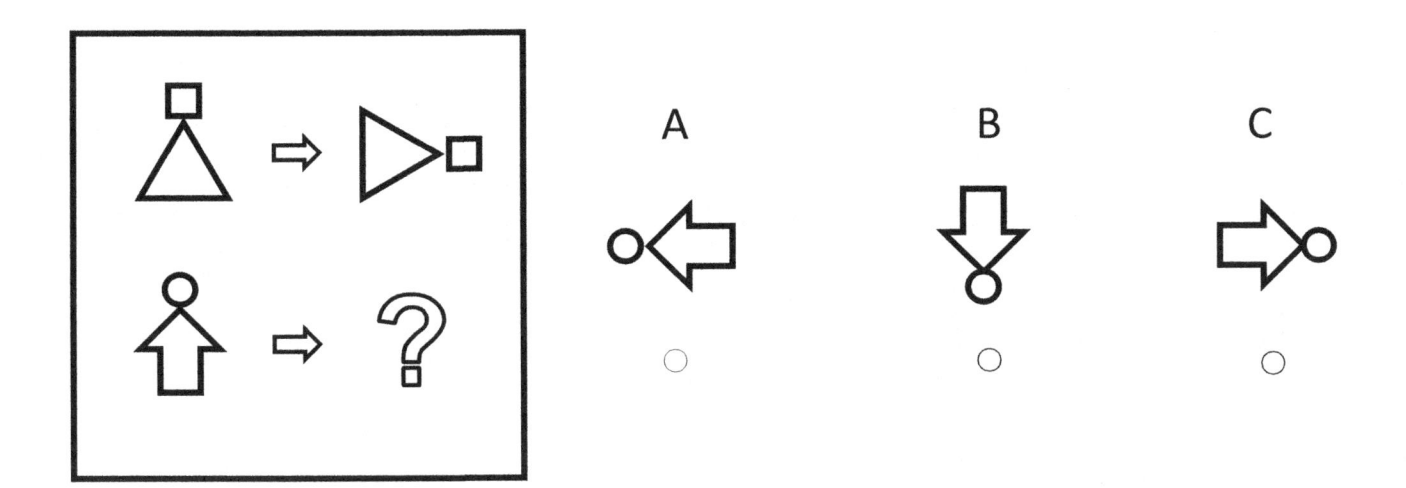

12.

65

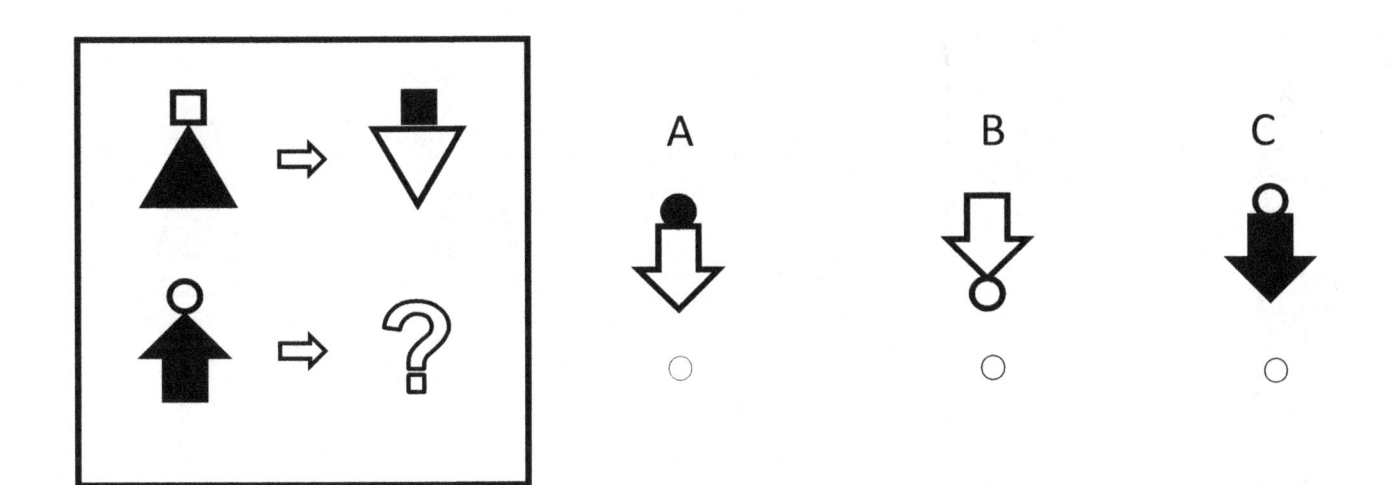

PRACTICE TEST GRADE 1

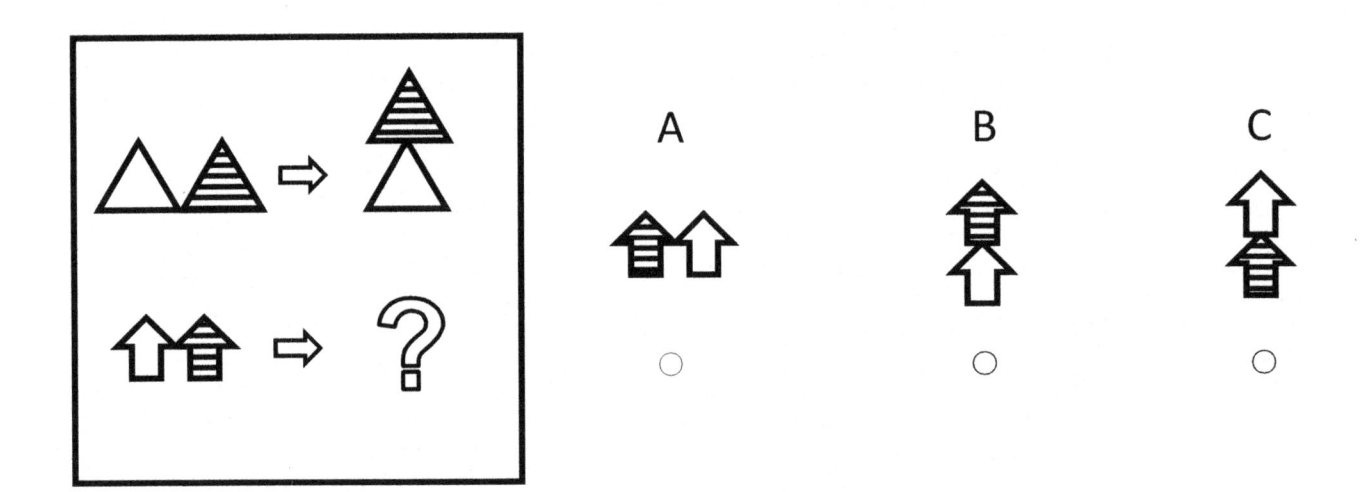

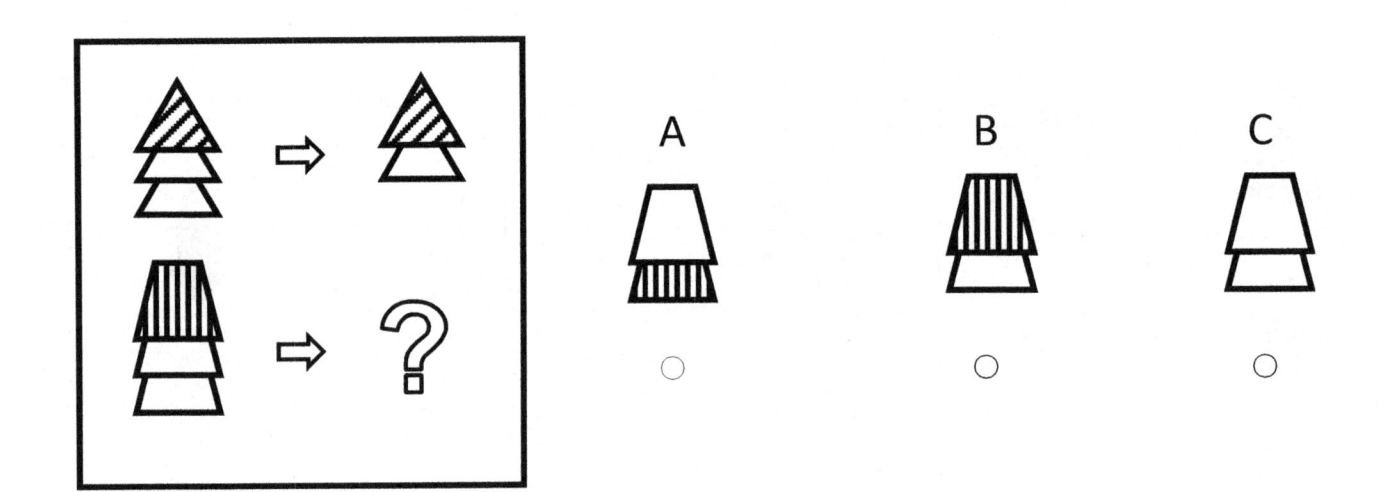

13.

14.

66

PRACTICE TEST GRADE 1

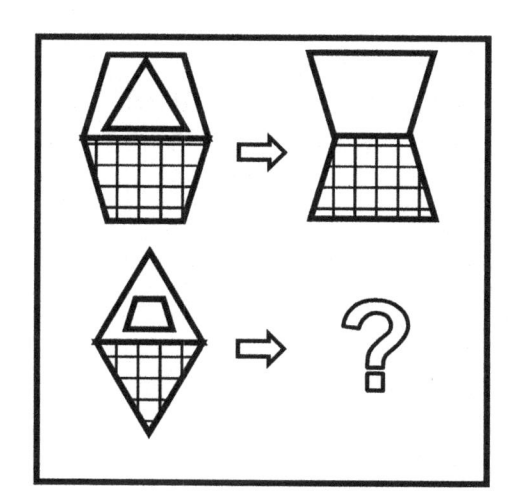

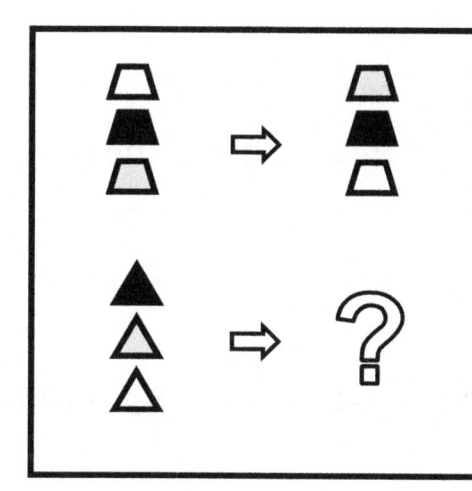

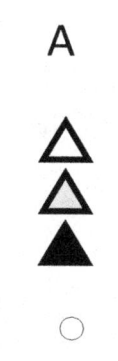

15.

16.

67

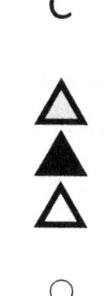

PRACTICE TEST GRADE 1

Figure Classification

Students are provided with three shapes and they have to select the answer choice that should be the fourth figure in the set, based on the similarity with the other three figures. The intention is to test the student's ability to recognize similar patterns and to make a rational choice.

Example

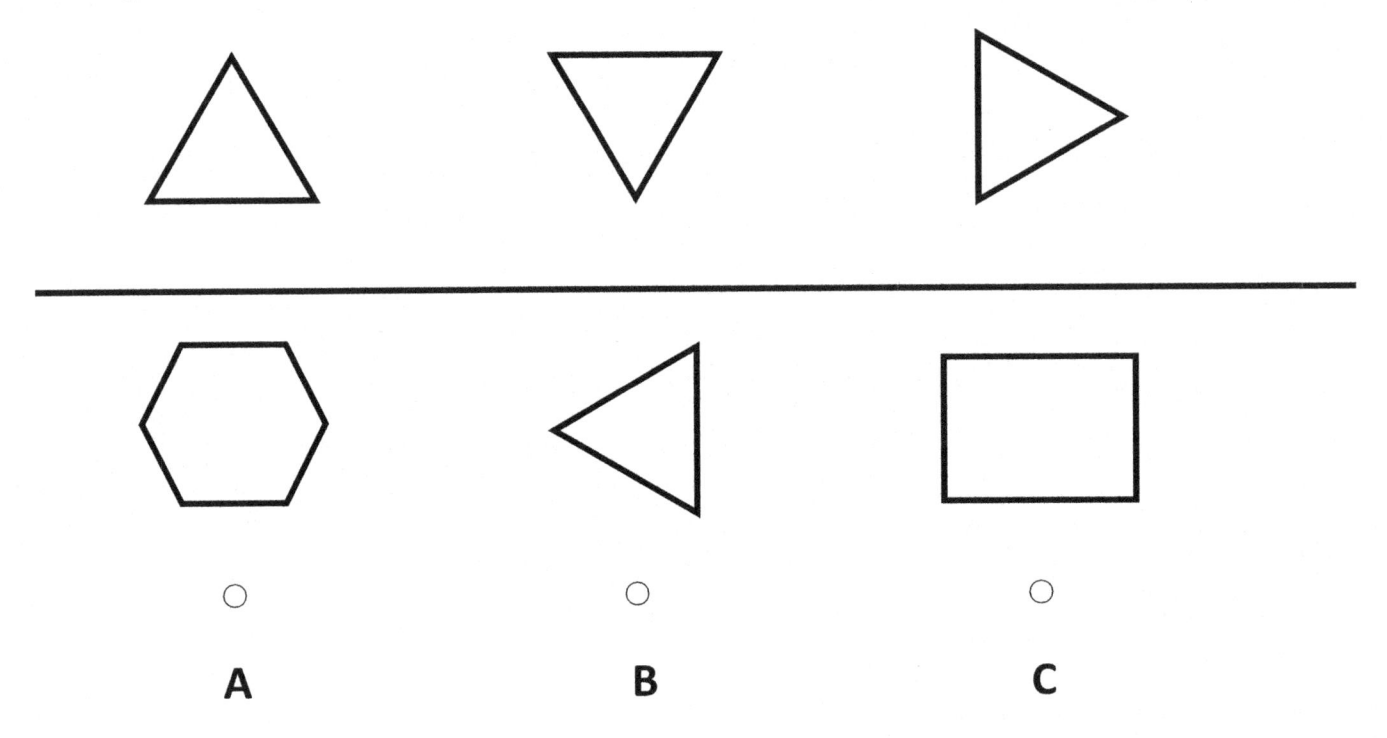

Look at the three pictures on the top. What do these three figures have in common?
You can see three white triangles in the same size.
Now, look at the shapes in the row of the answer choices. Which image matches best the three shapes in the top row?

The image of the answer choice must be a white triangle. The right answer is "B".

68

PRACTICE TEST GRADE 1

Tips for Figure Classification

- Be sure to review all answer choices before selecting one.

- Try to use logic and sequential reasoning.

- Carefully consider the elements of each figure:

1. color
2. form
3. number of sides
4. orientation
5. number of elements inside each figure

- Try to exclude the obviously wrong options to reduce the answer choices.

PRACTICE TEST GRADE 1

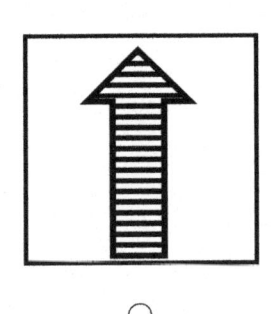

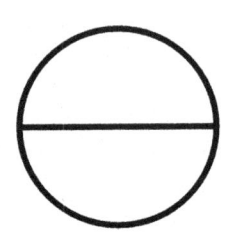

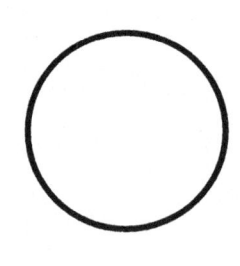

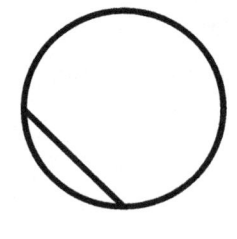

1.

2.

70

PRACTICE TEST GRADE 1

3.

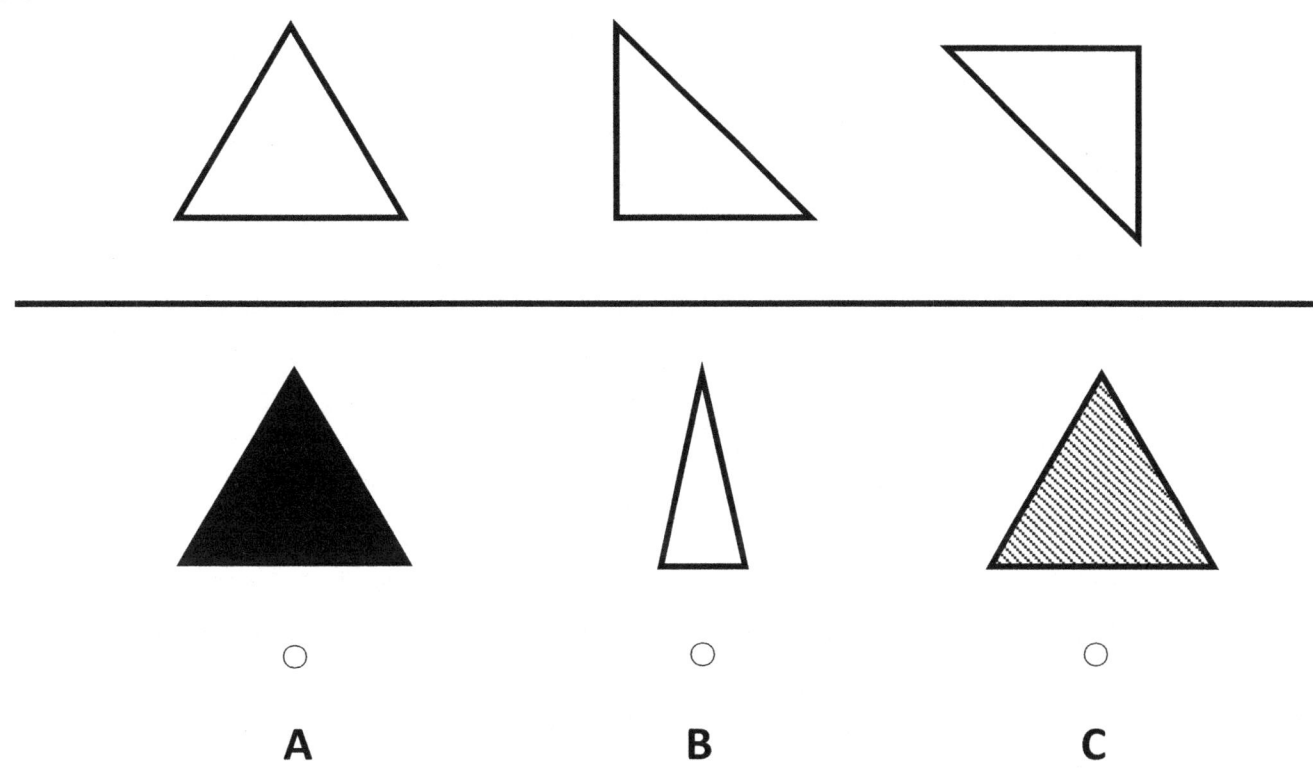

○
A

○
B

○
C

4.

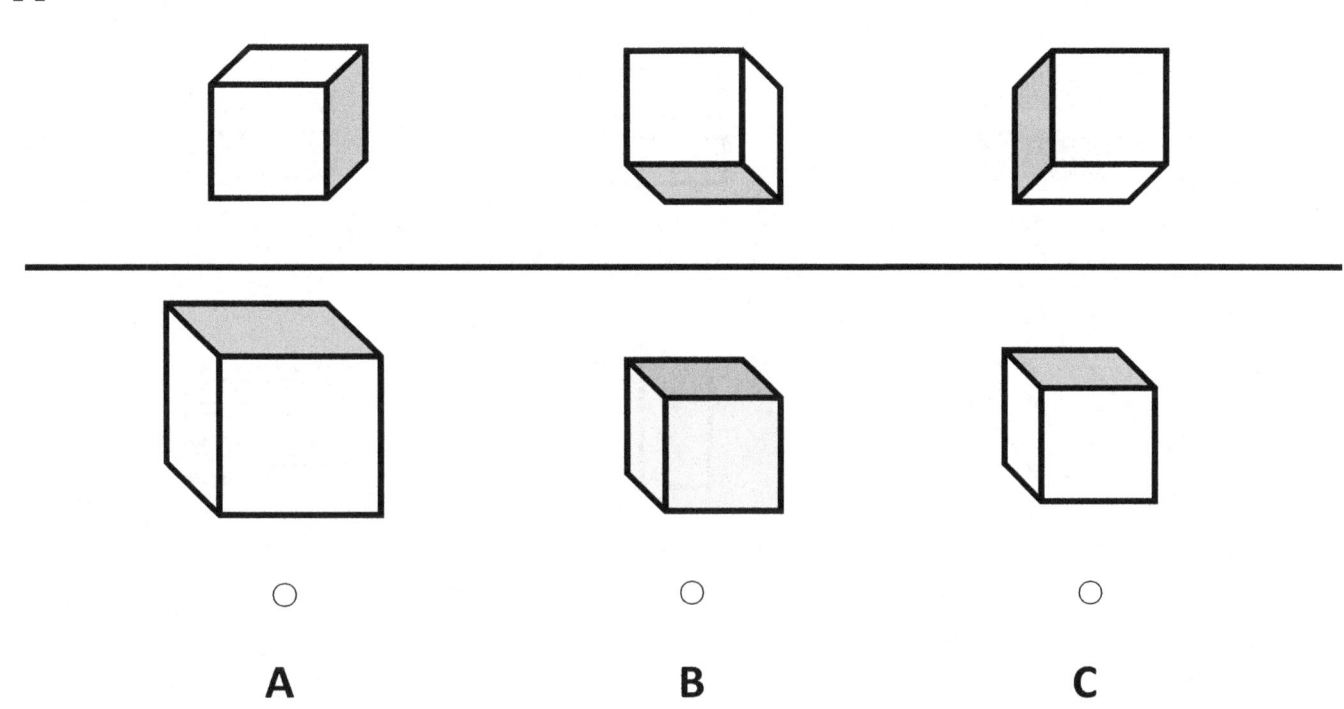

○
A

○
B

○
C

71

PRACTICE TEST GRADE 1

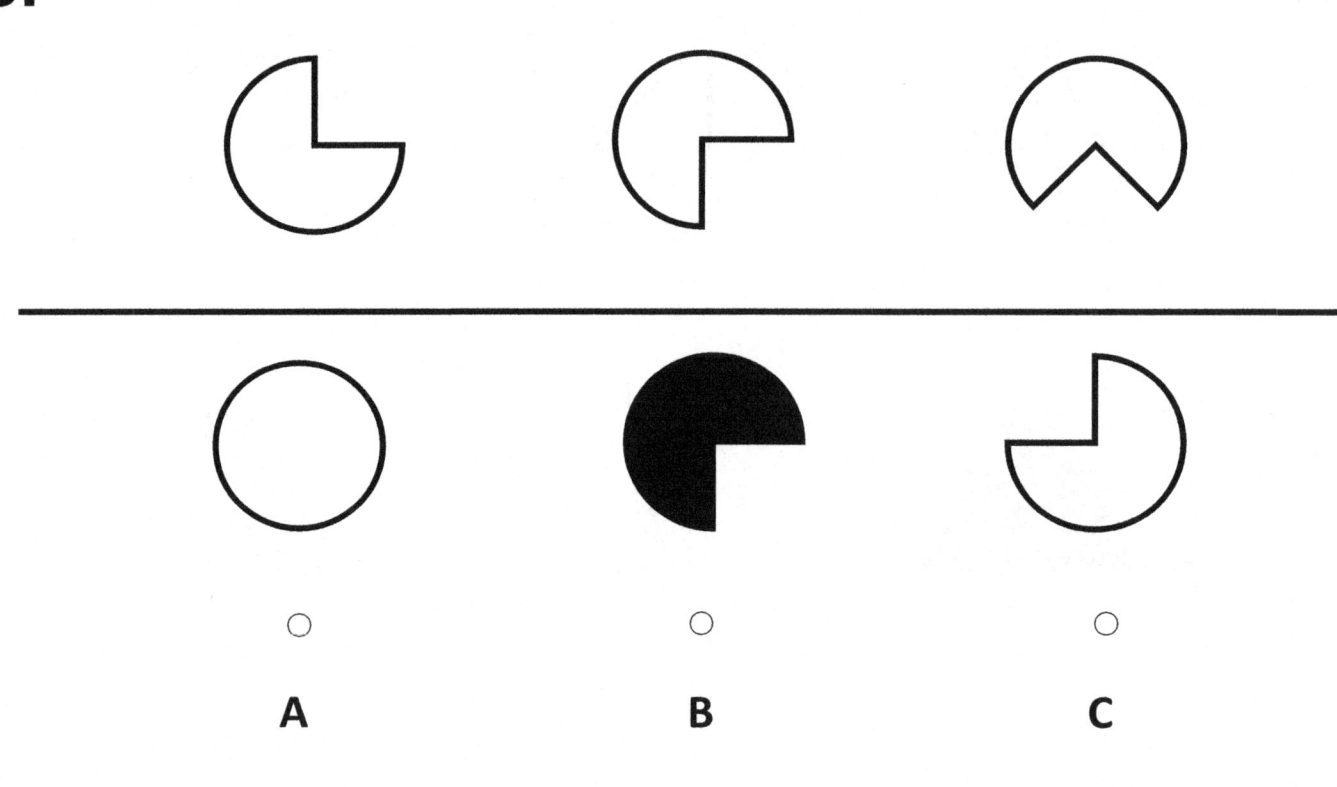

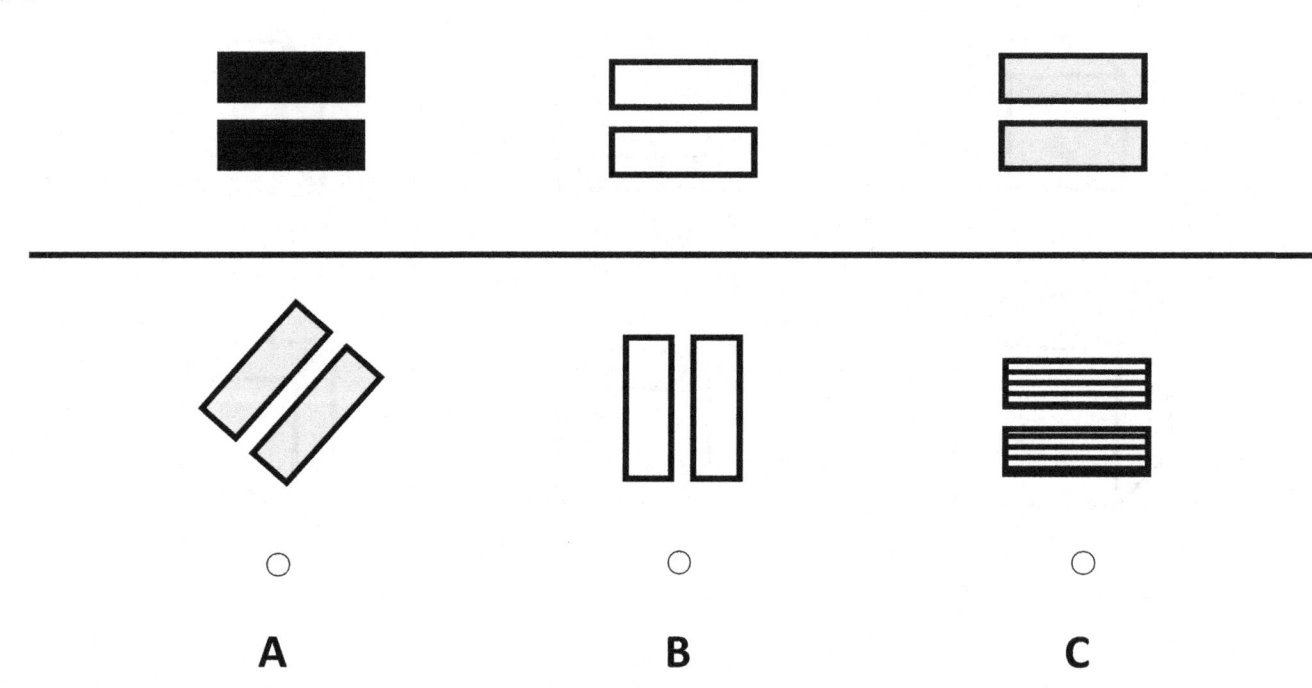

5.

6.

72

PRACTICE TEST GRADE 1

7.

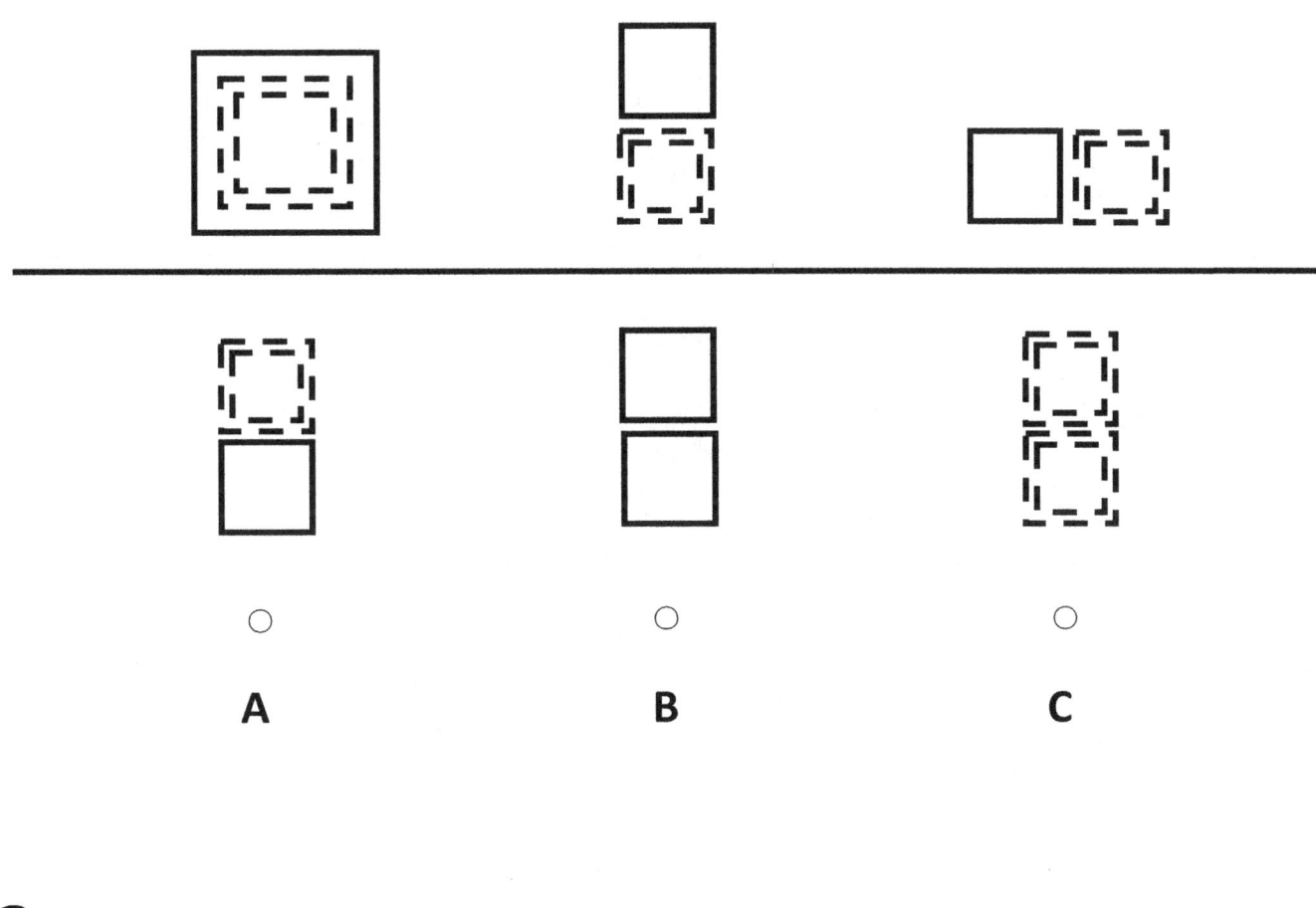

A B C

8.

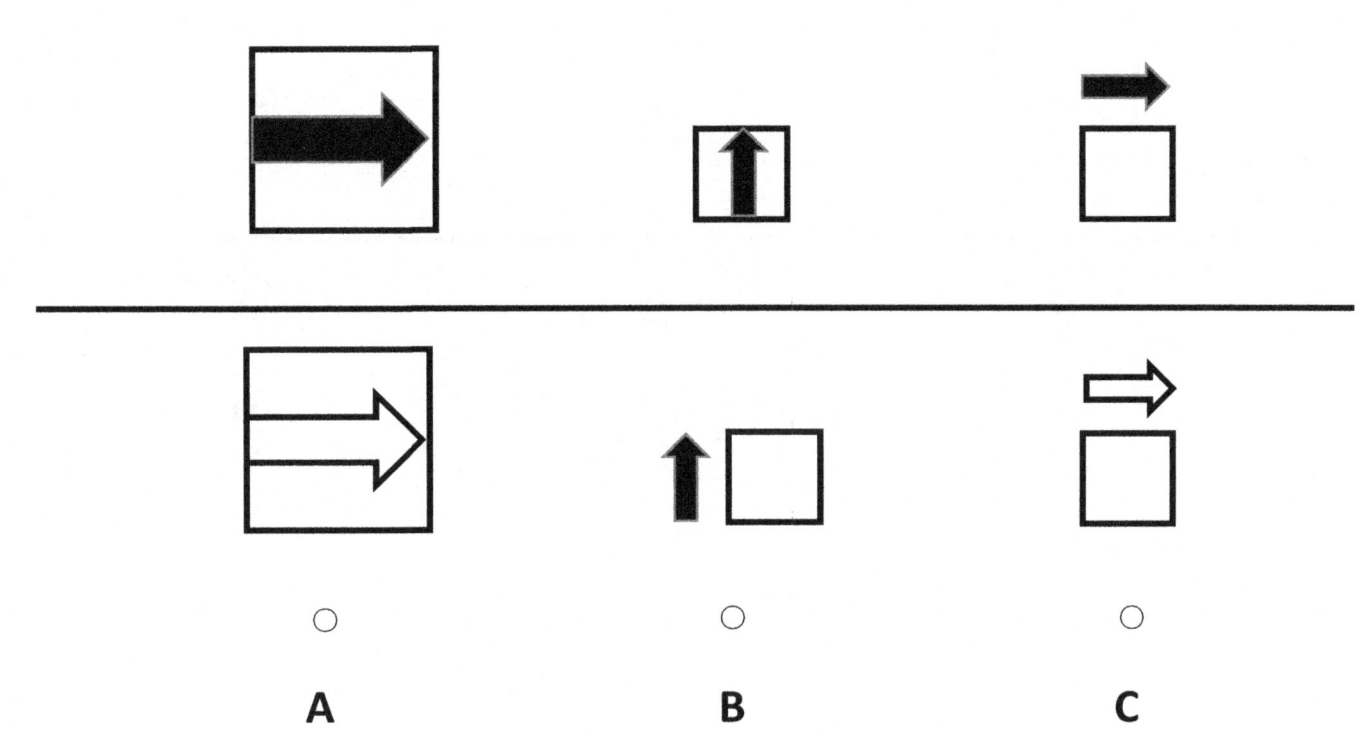

A B C

PRACTICE TEST GRADE 1

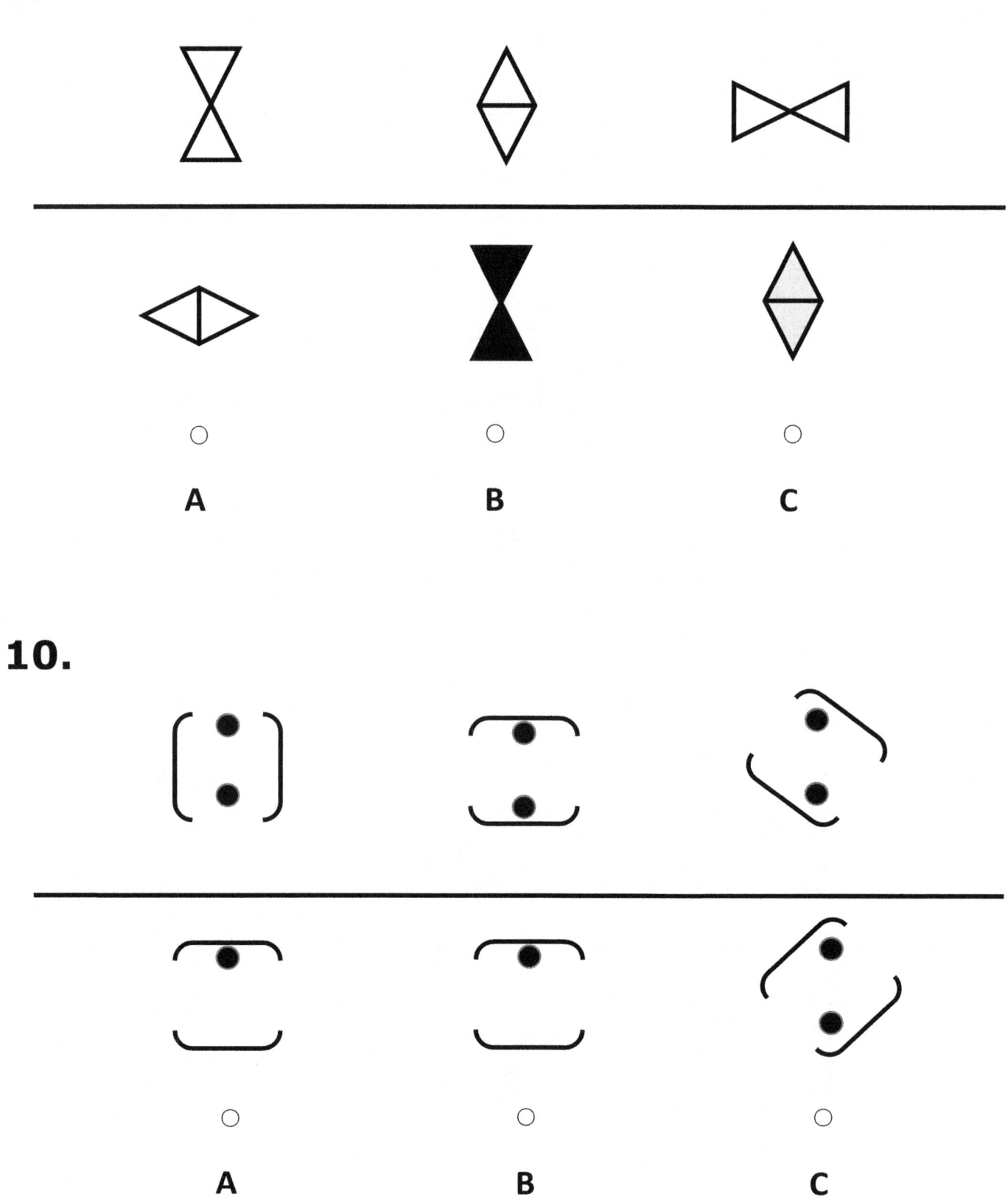

9.

10.

74

PRACTICE TEST GRADE 1

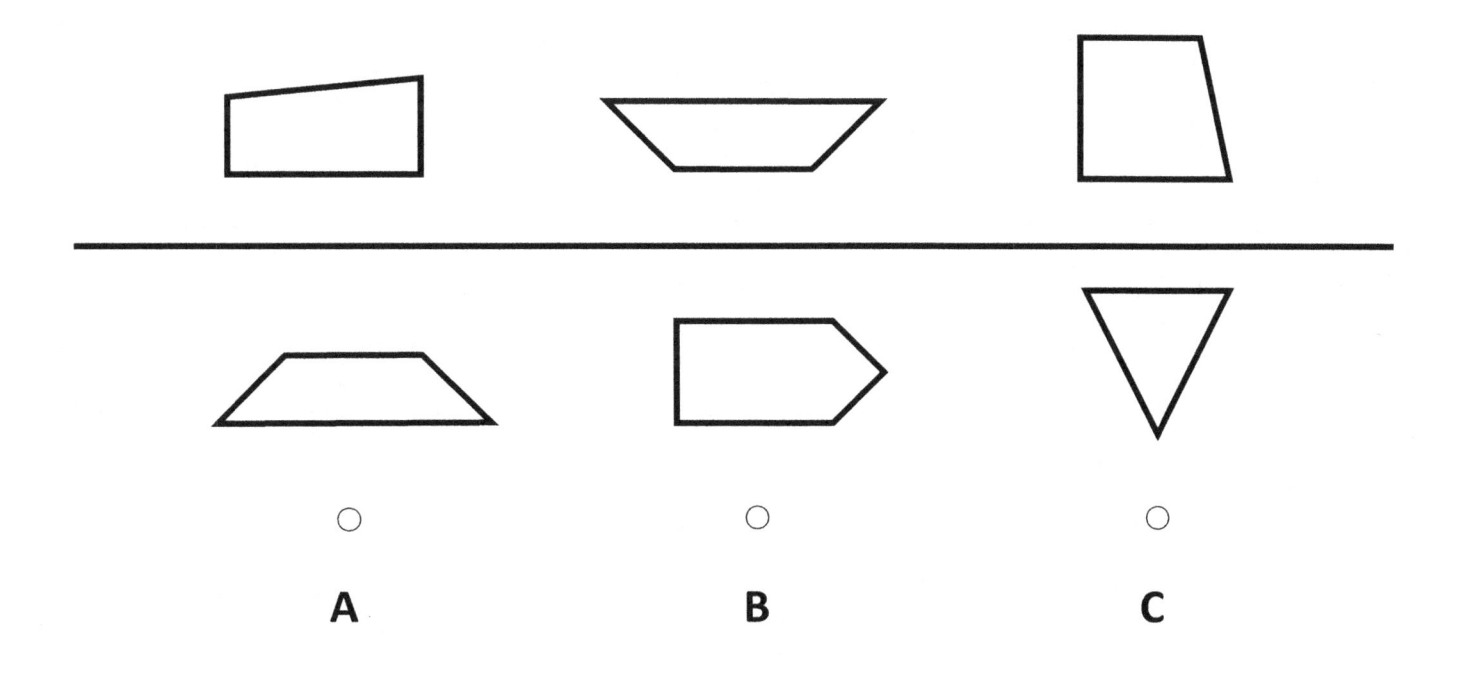

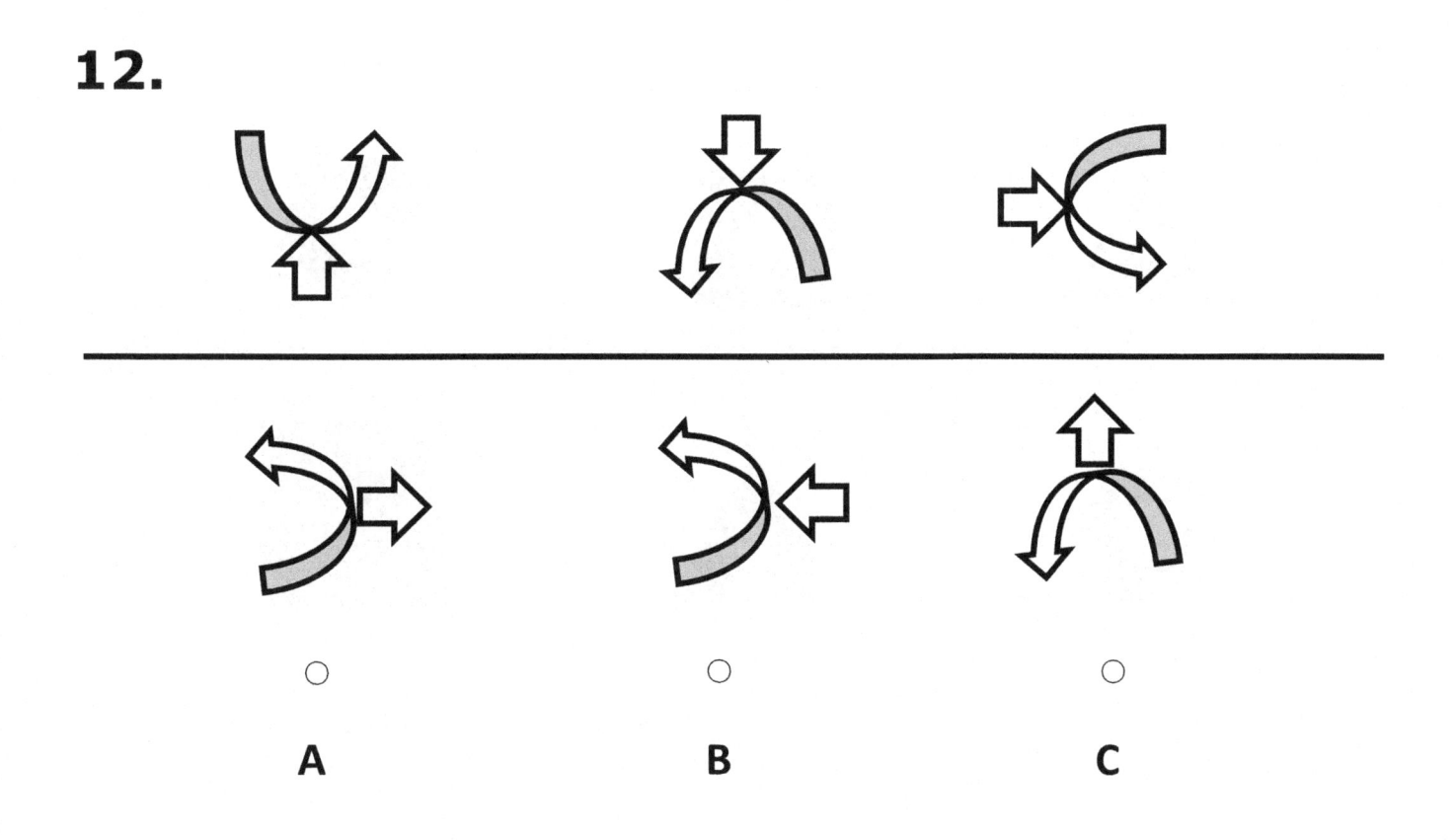

11.

12.

75

PRACTICE TEST GRADE 1

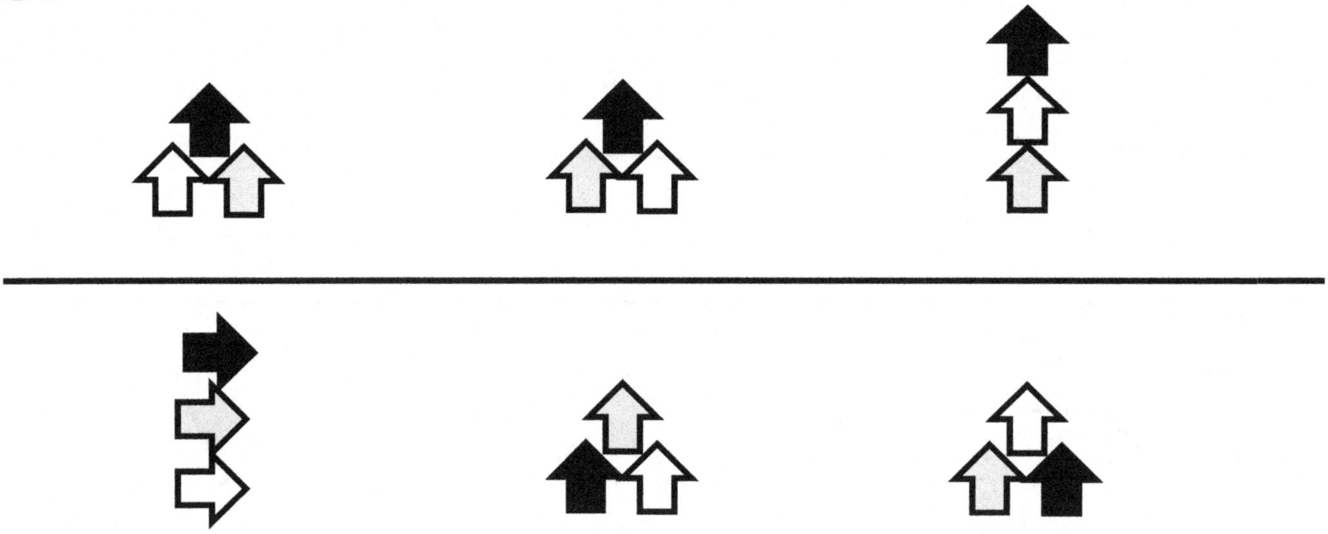

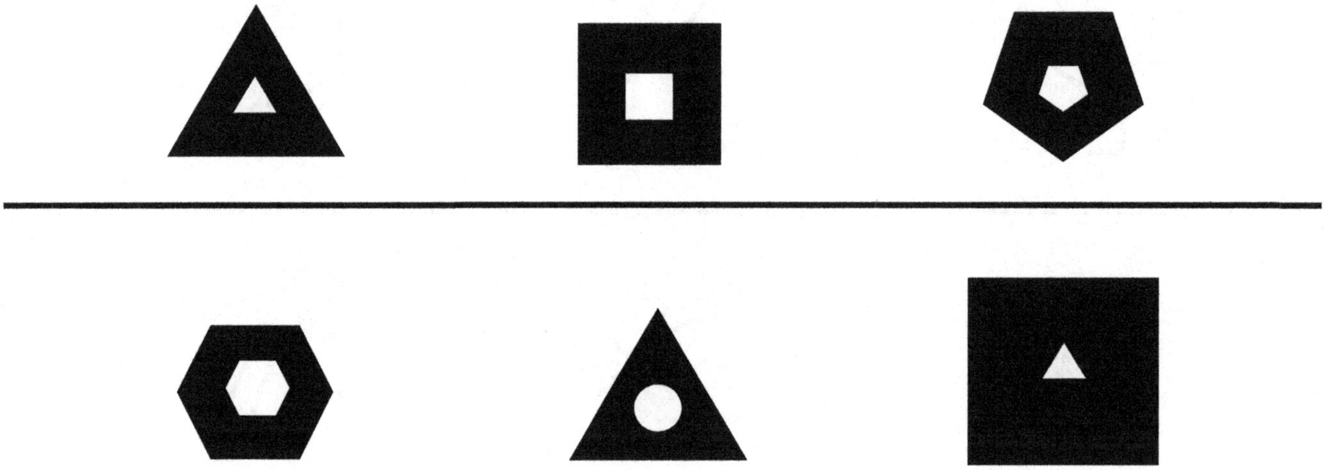

13.

14.

76

PRACTICE TEST GRADE 1

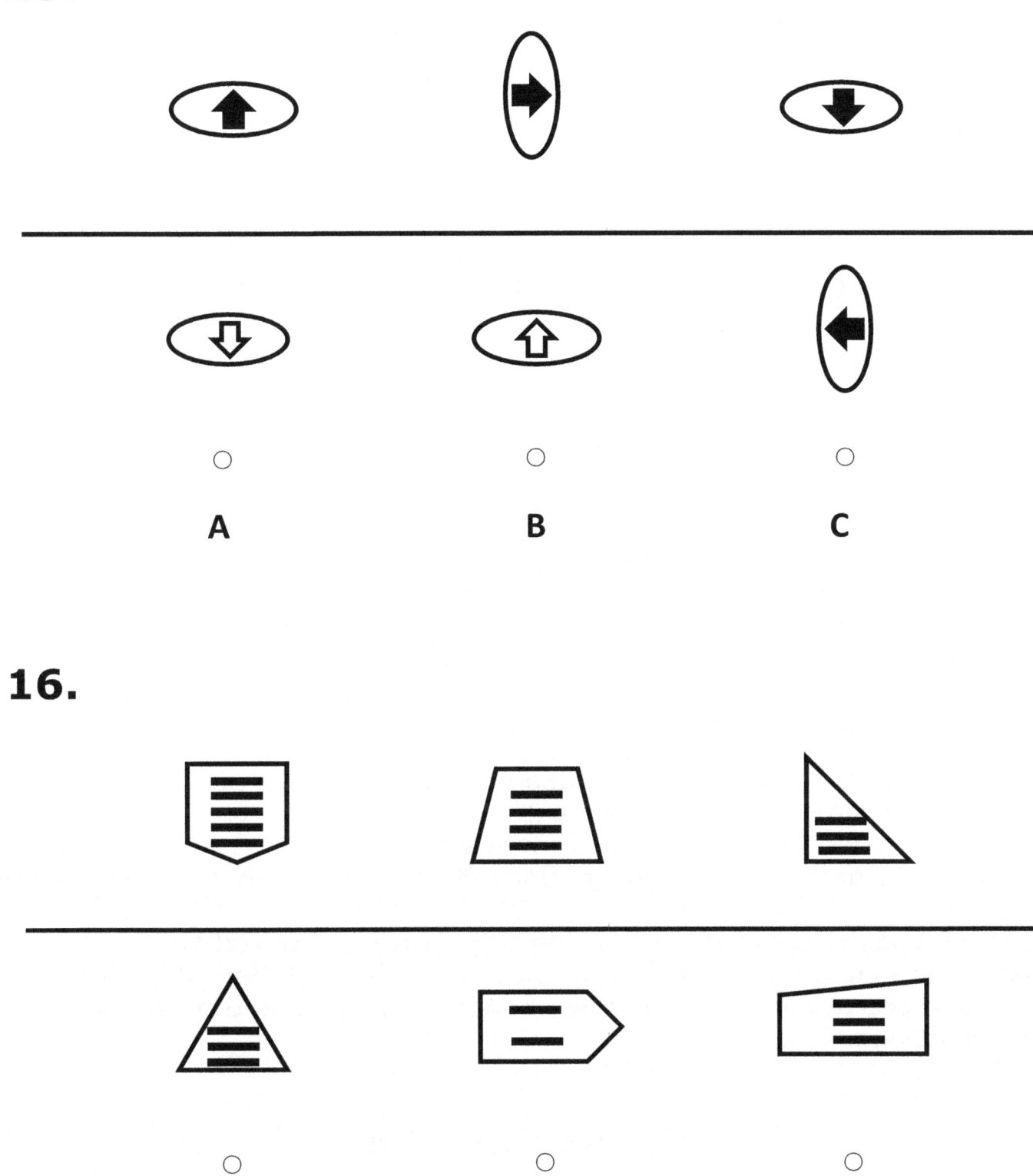

15.

16.

77

PRACTICE TEST GRADE 1

Paper Folding

Children need to determine the appearance of a perforated and folded sheet of paper, once opened.

Example

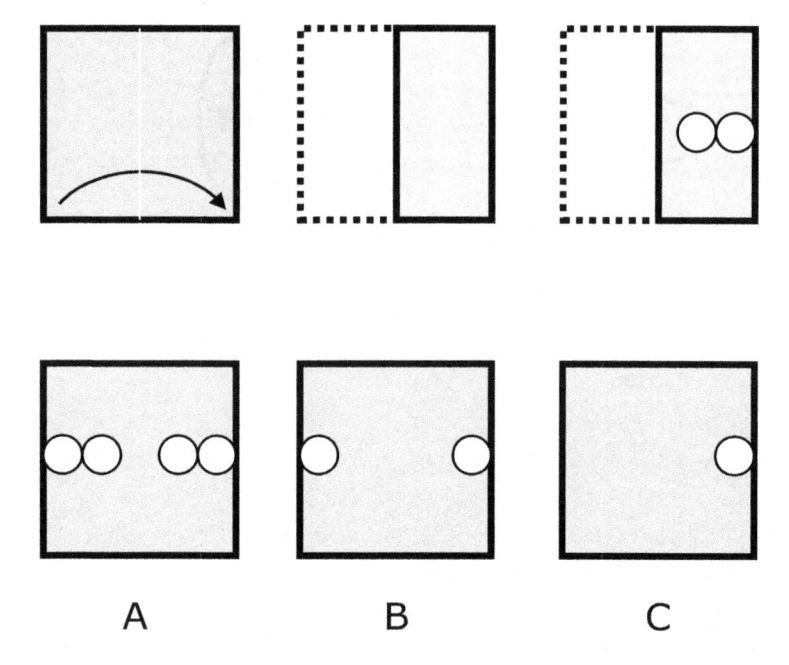

A   B   C

The figures at the top represent a square piece of paper being folded, and the last of these figures has two holes on it.
One of the lower three figures shows where the perforations will be when the paper is fully unfolded. You have to understand which of these images is the right one.
First, the paper was folded horizontally, from left to right.
Then, two holes was punched out. Therefore, when the paper is unfolded the holes will mirror on the left and right side of the sheet. The right answer is "A".

Tips for Paper Folding

The best way to get ready for these challenging questions is to practice. The patterns that show up on the test can confuse students, so the demonstration of folding and unfolding real paper can be very helpful.

PRACTICE TEST GRADE 1

1.

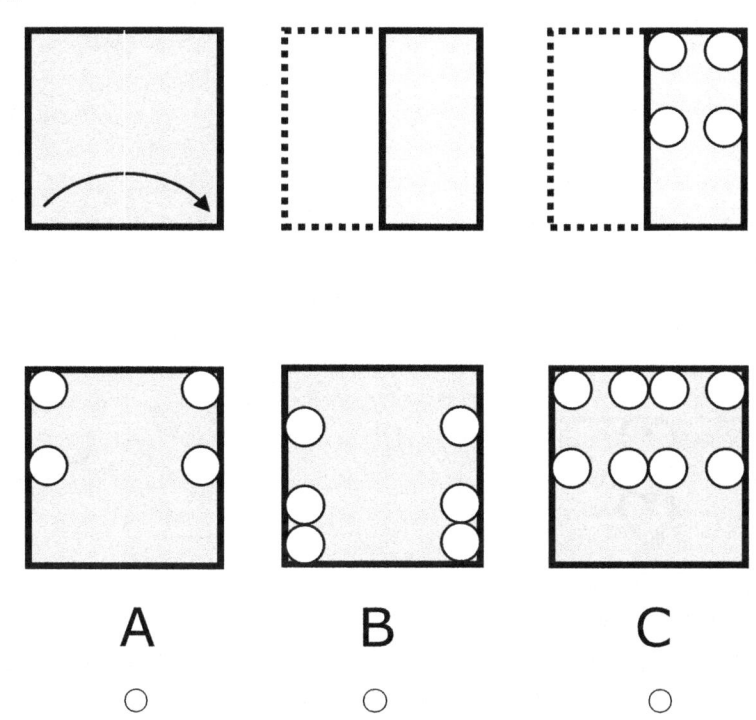

A B C

2.

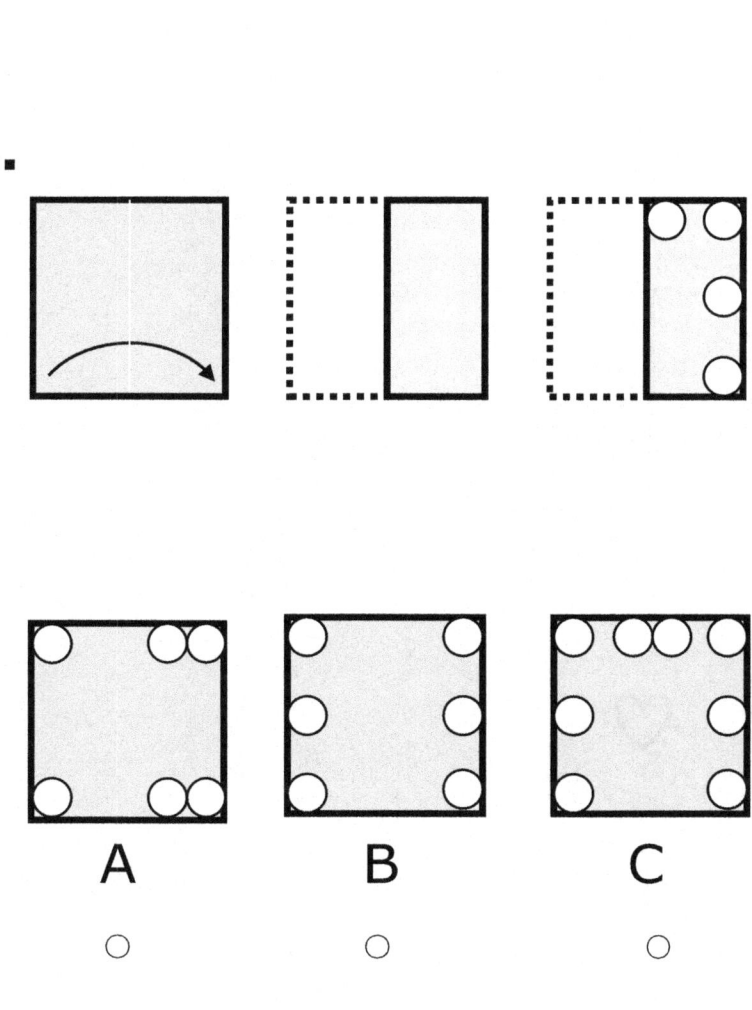

A B C

79

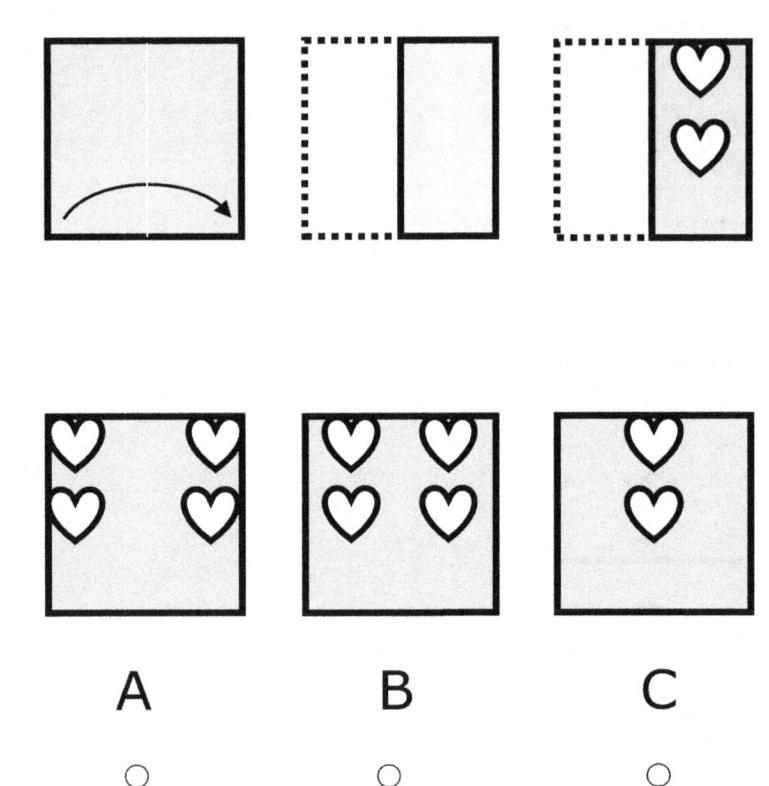

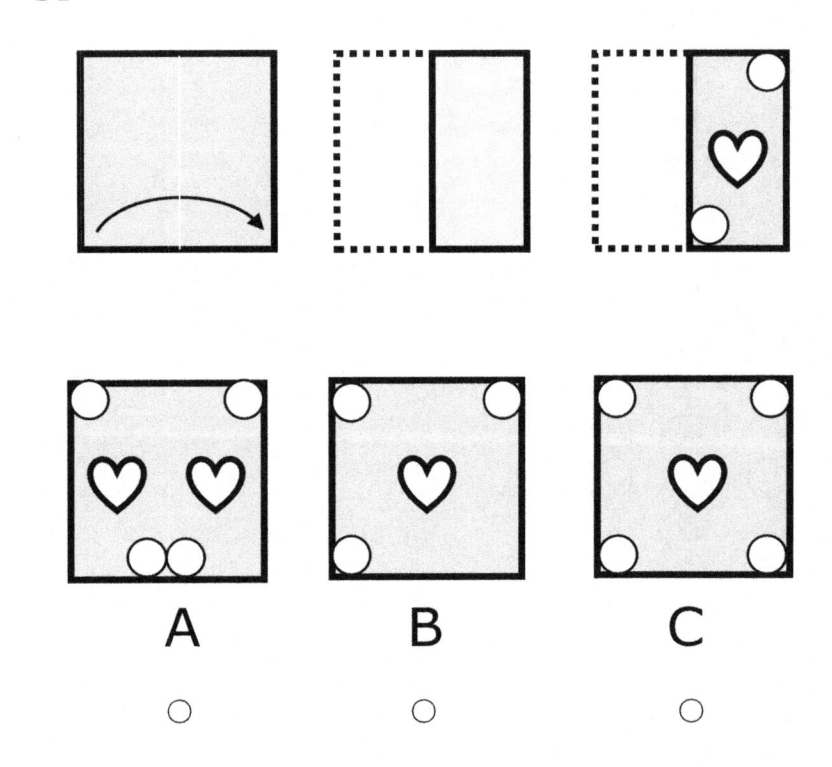

PRACTICE TEST GRADE 1

3.

4.

80

PRACTICE TEST GRADE 1

5.

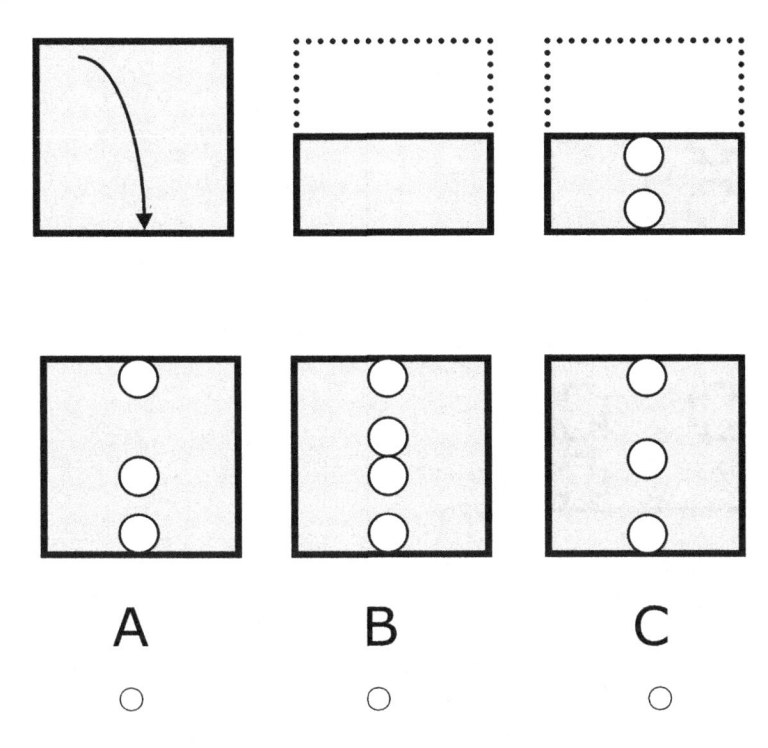

A   B   C

6.

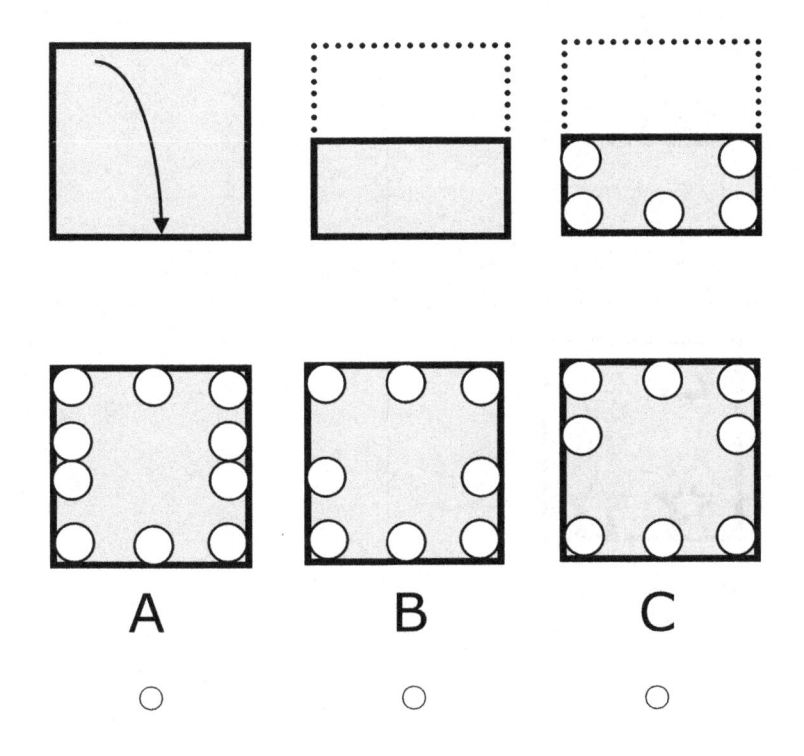

A   B   C

81

PRACTICE TEST GRADE 1

7.

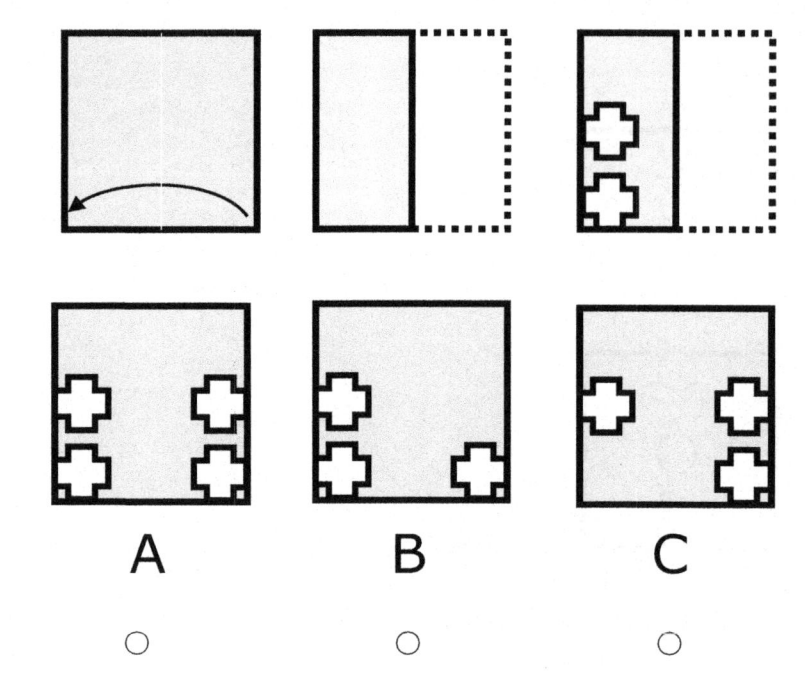

A   B   C
○   ○   ○

8.

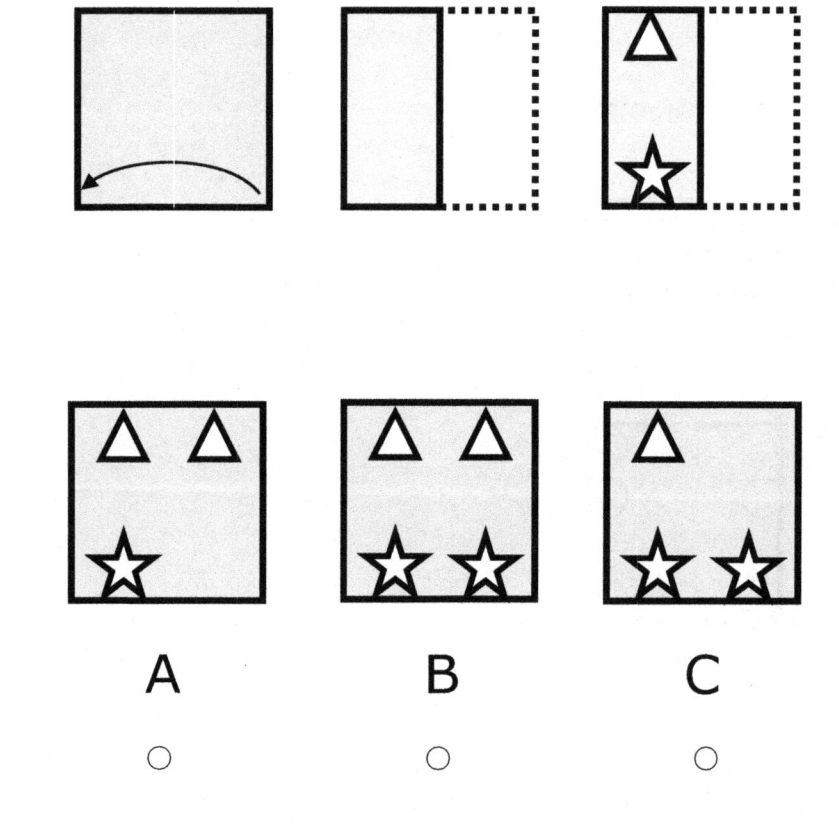

A   B   C
○   ○   ○

82

PRACTICE TEST GRADE 1

9.

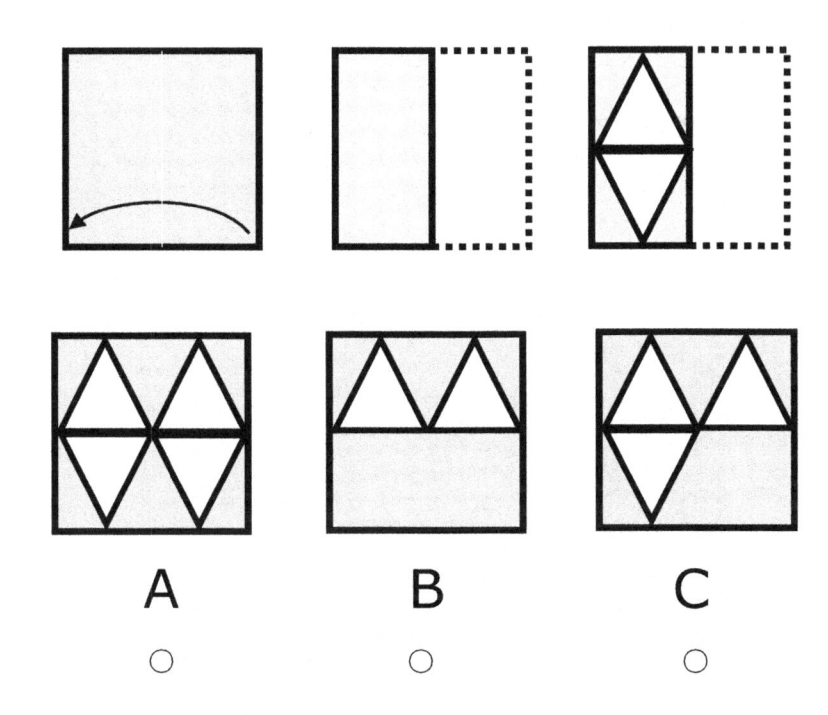

A B C
○ ○ ○

10.

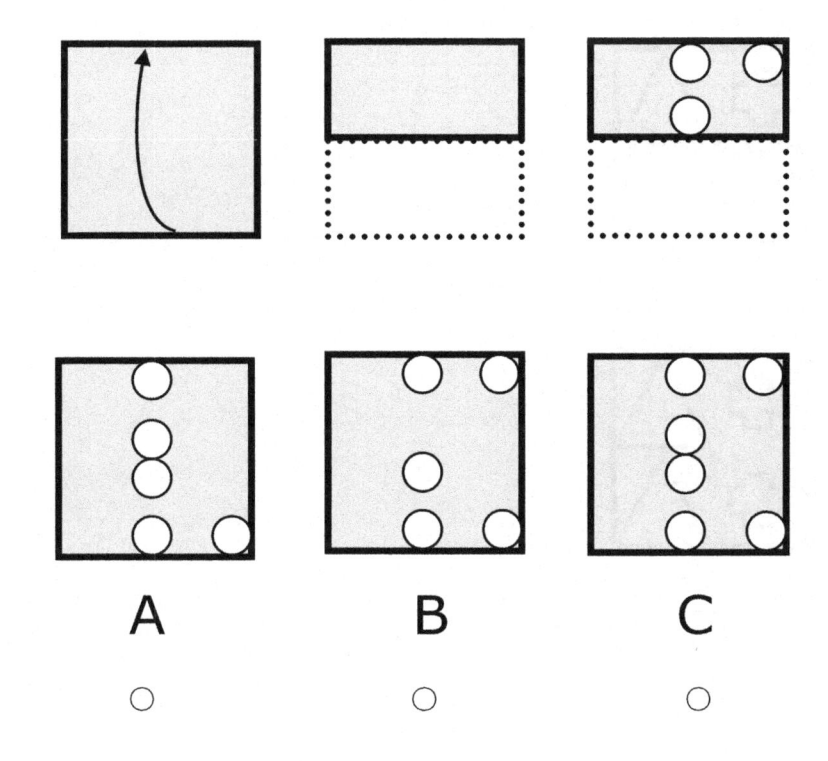

A B C
○ ○ ○

83

PRACTICE TEST GRADE 1

11.

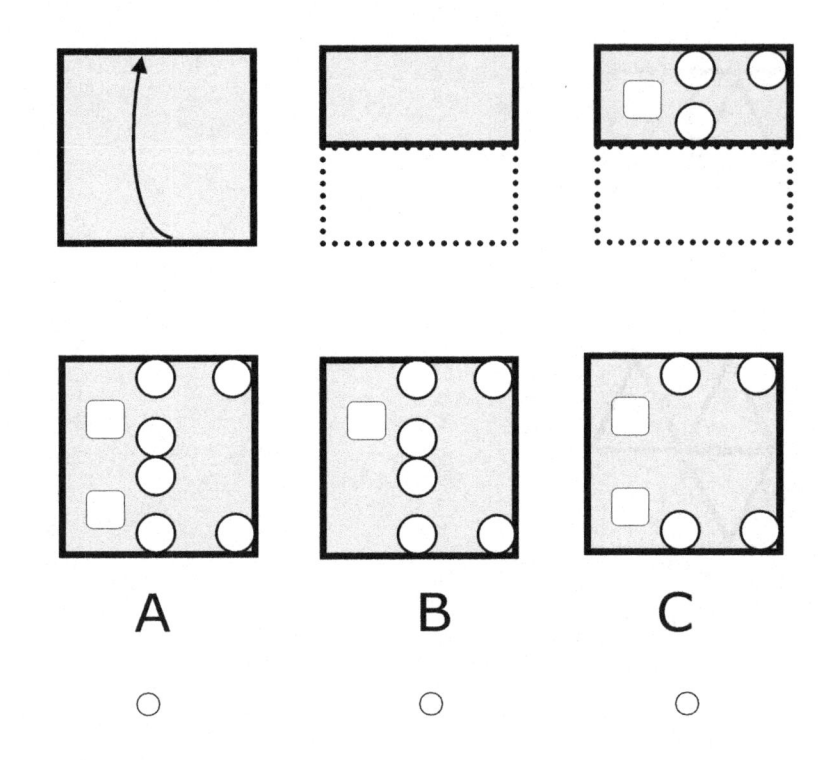

A   B   C

12.

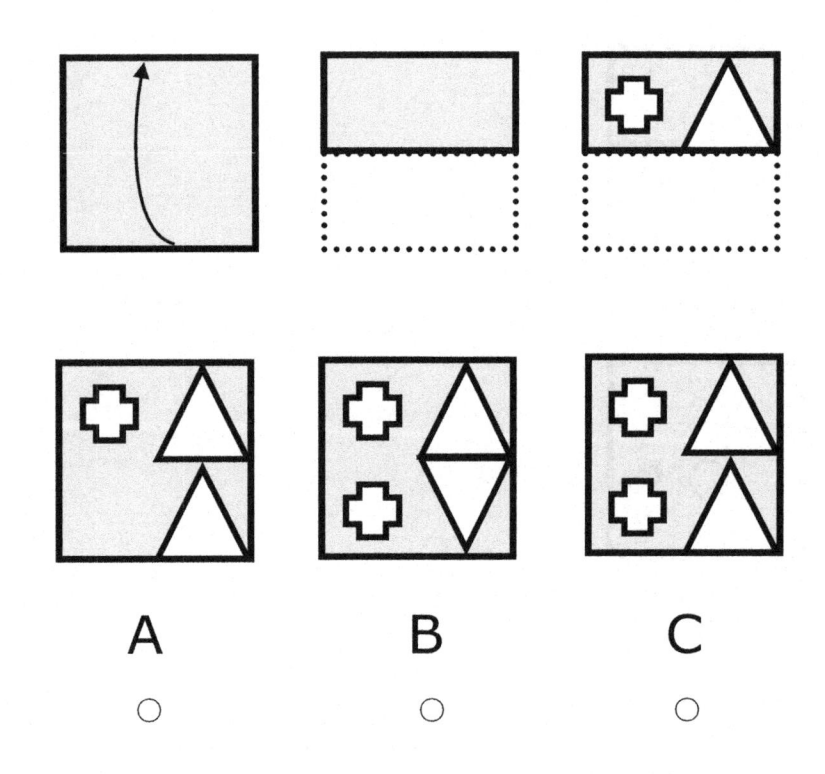

A   B   C

84

PRACTICE TEST GRADE 1

PRACTICE TEST QUANTITATIVE BATTERY

This section introduces abstract reasoning and problem-solving skills to learners and is one of the most challenging sections in the test.

PRACTICE TEST GRADE 1

Number Puzzle

Children see two trains. They must choose the answer picture that makes the second train carrying an equal number of things as the first one.

Example

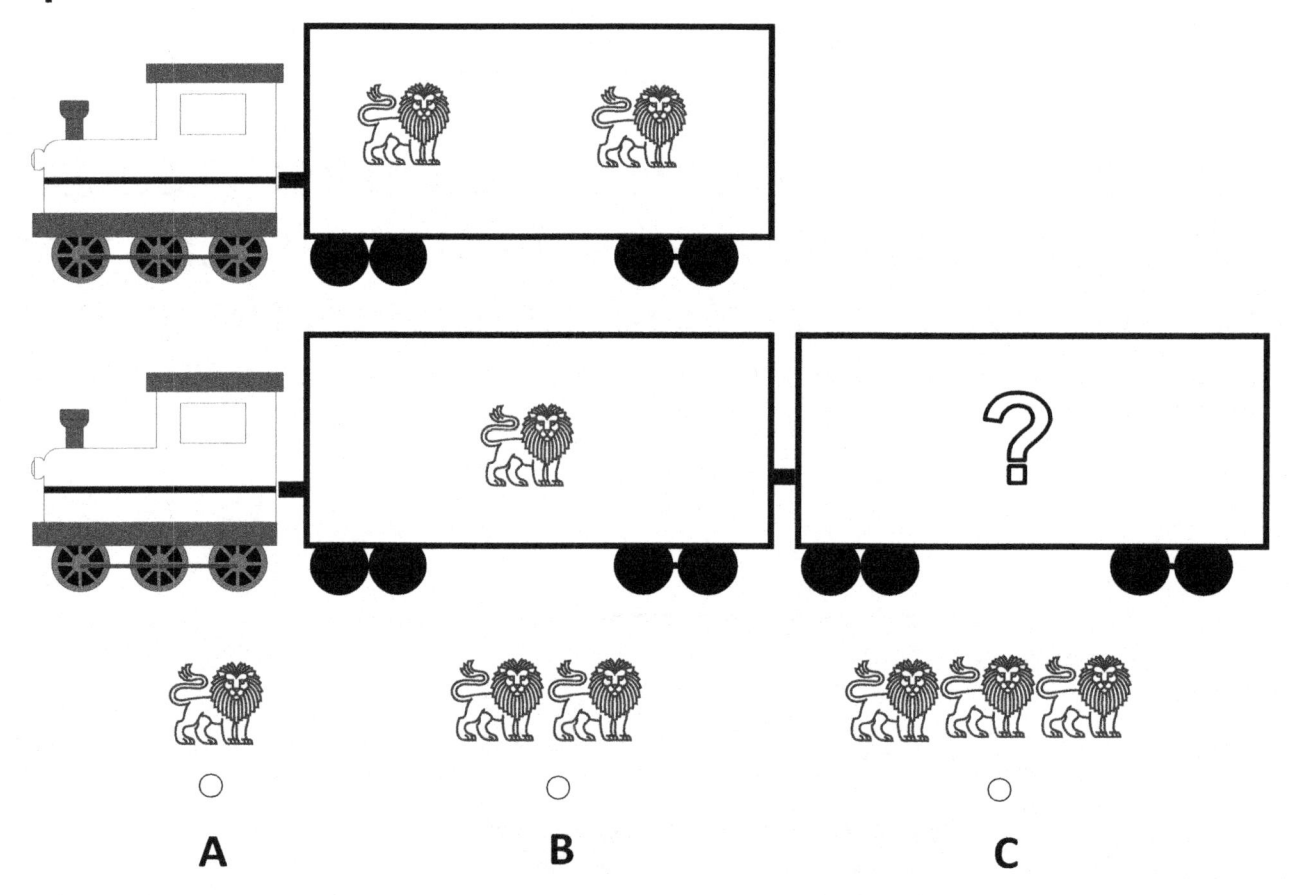

- Look at the train in the top row. In this train, there are 2 lions. In the train on the bottom row, there are 1 lion in one wagon.
- How many lions are needed in the wagon with the question mark, so that both trains have the same amount of lions?
- 1 lion is needed to make a total of 2 lions in the bottom train.
- The correct answer is A

Tips for Number Puzzle

- Try to fully understand the meaning of "equal", as the purpose is to provide the missing items that will make the 2 trains carry the same number of objects.
- Train yourself to solve simple additions and subtractions.
- Work with real objects to understand the concepts.

PRACTICE TEST GRADE 1

1.

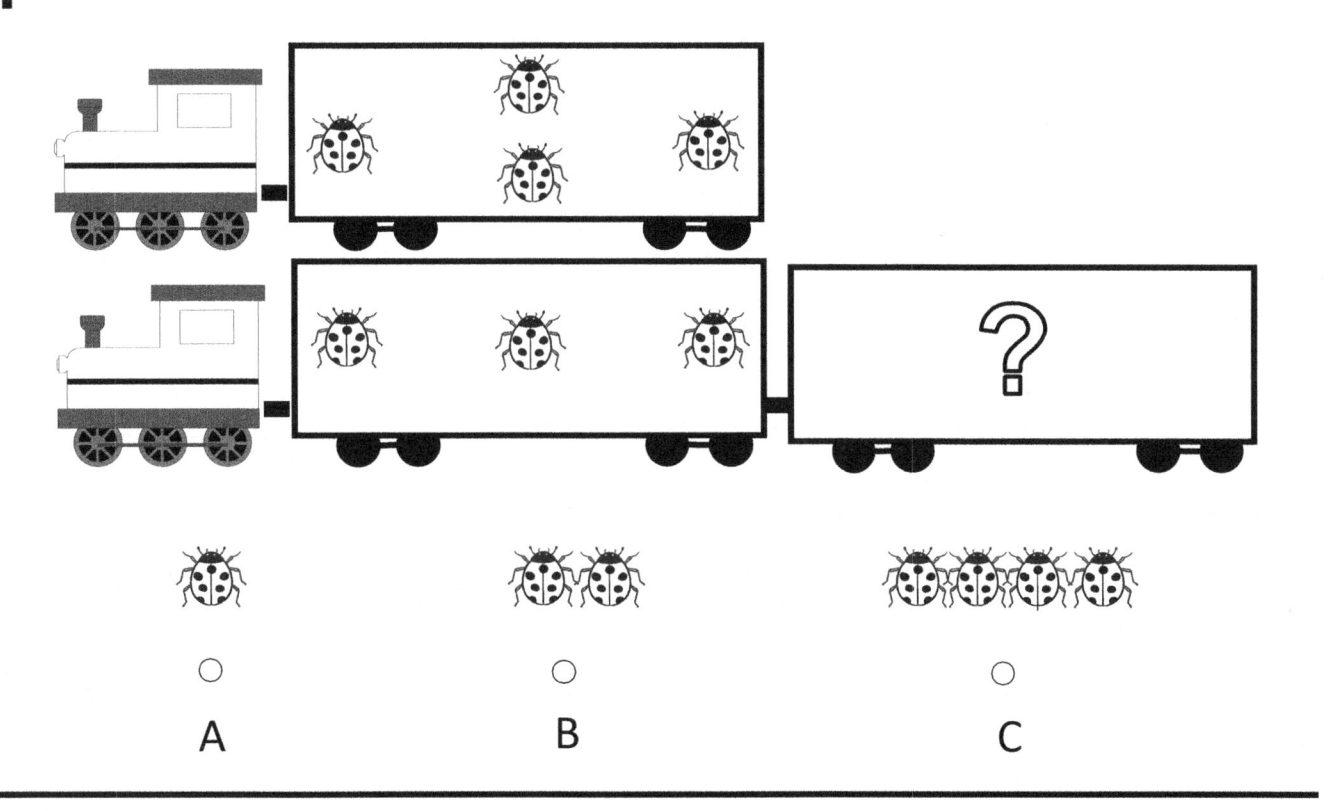

A   B   C

2.

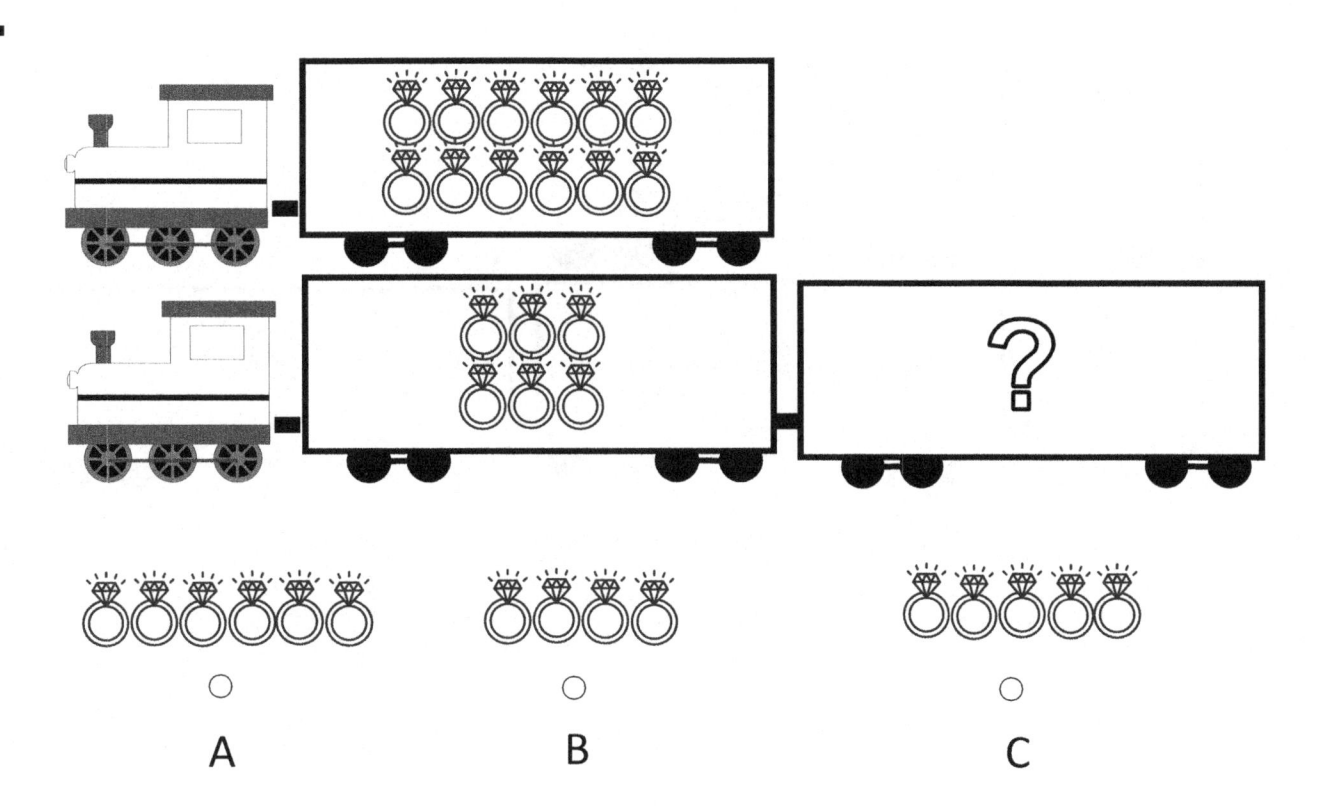

A   B   C

87

PRACTICE TEST GRADE 1

3.

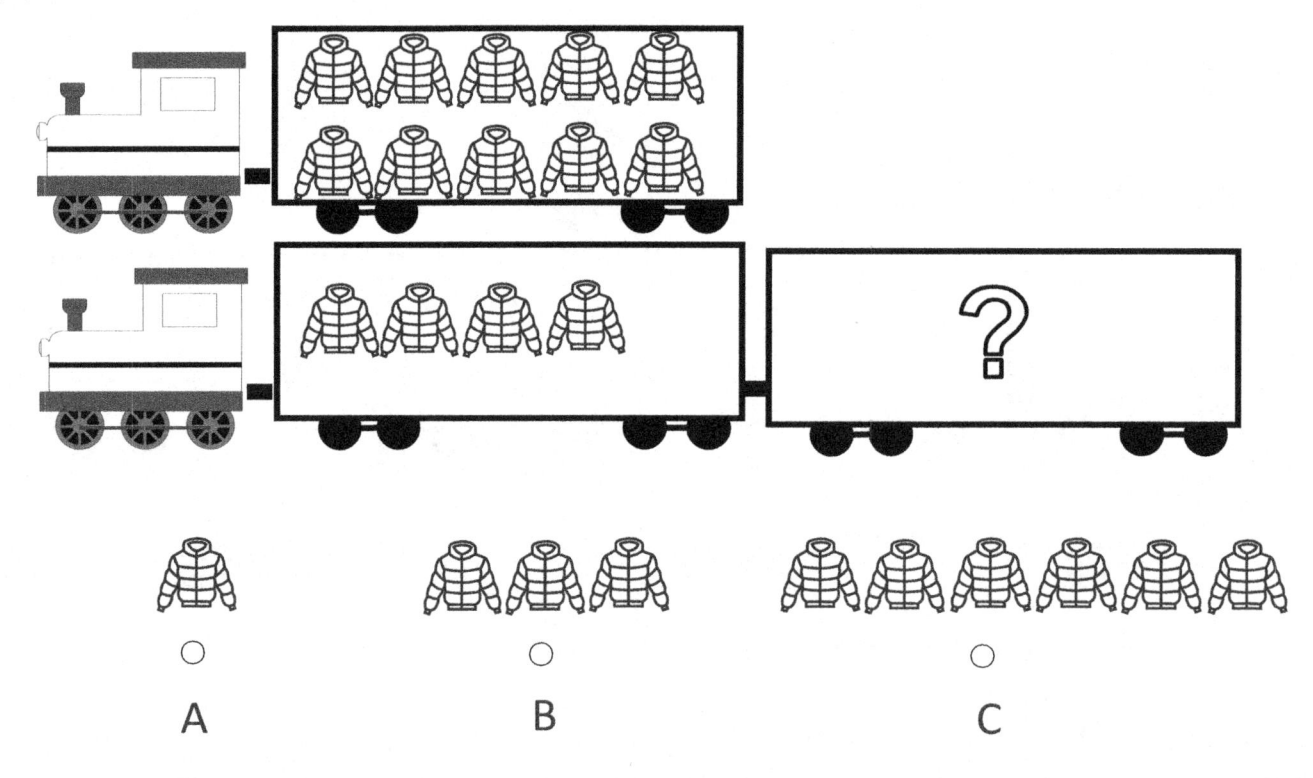

A   B   C

4.

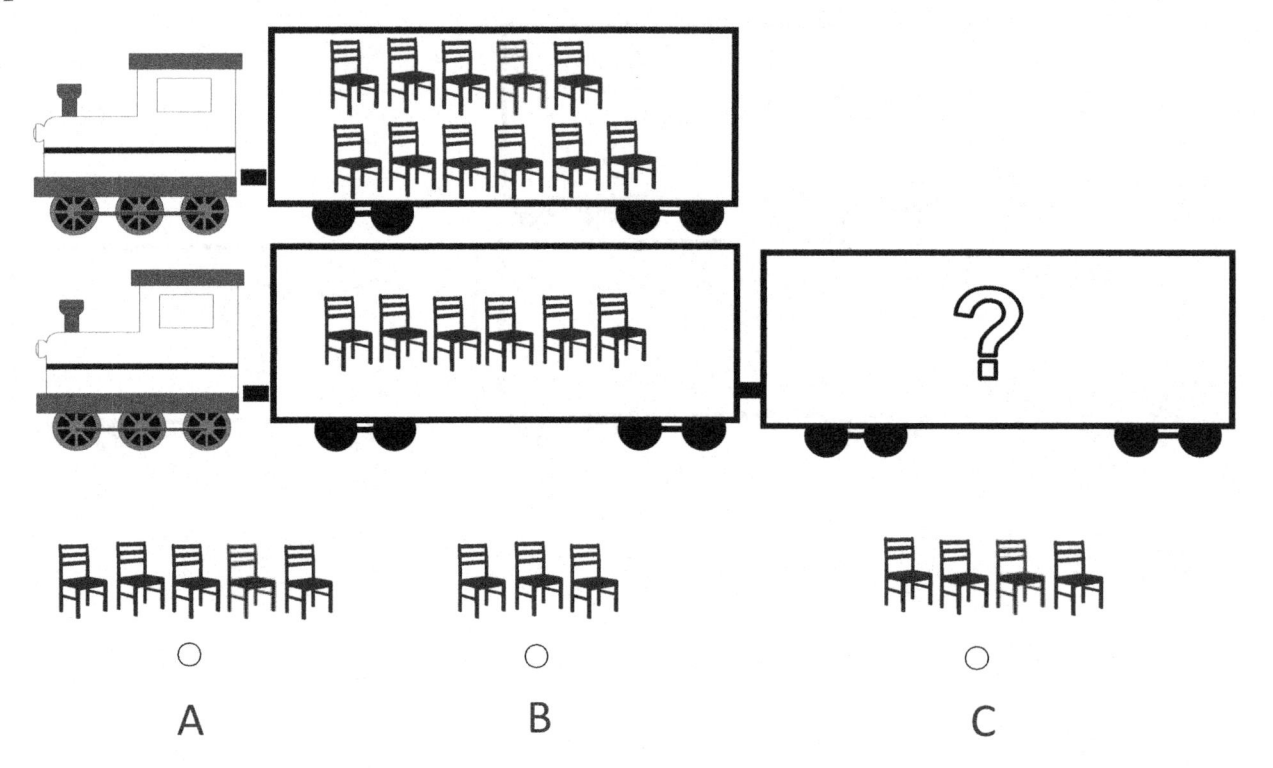

A   B   C

88

PRACTICE TEST GRADE 1

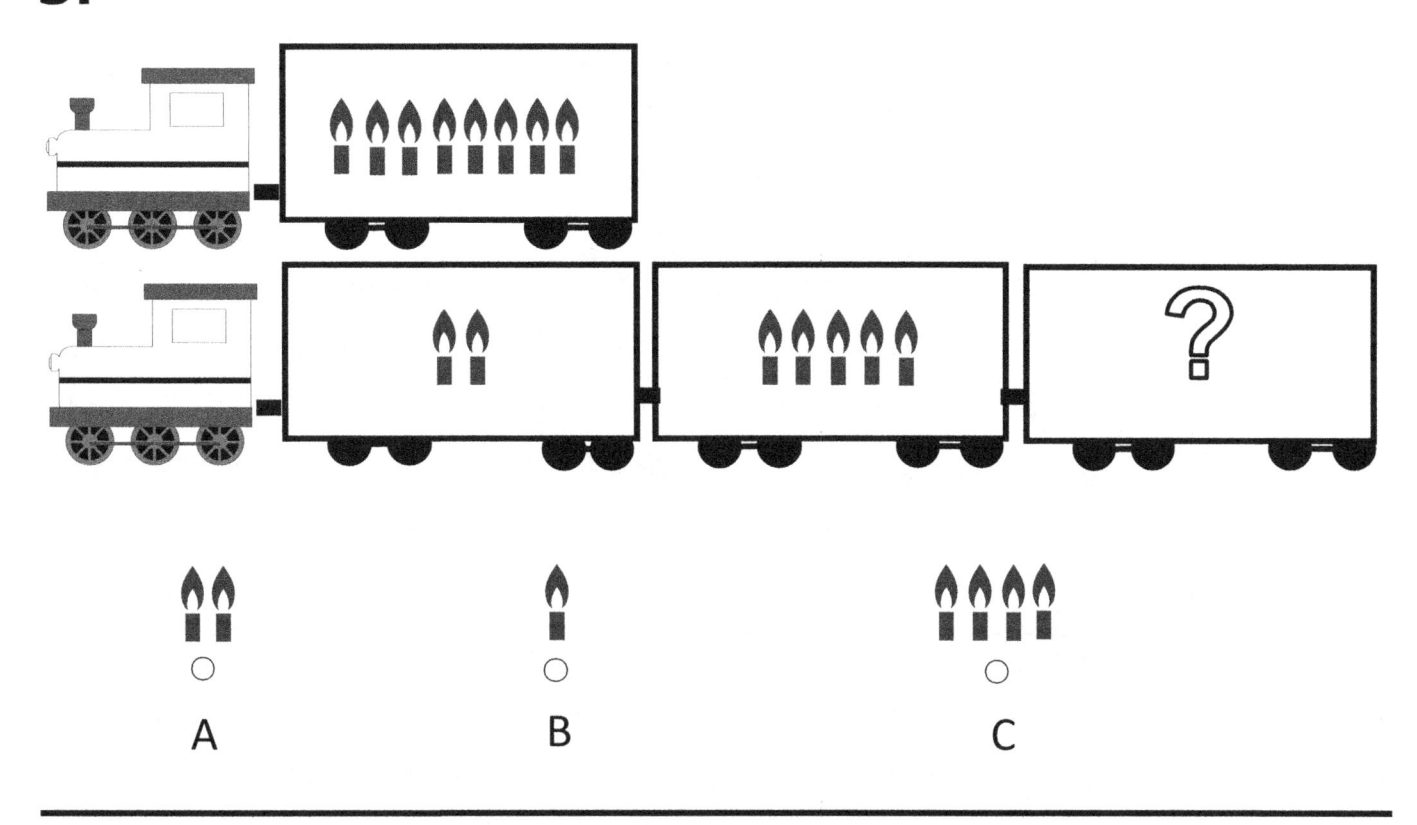

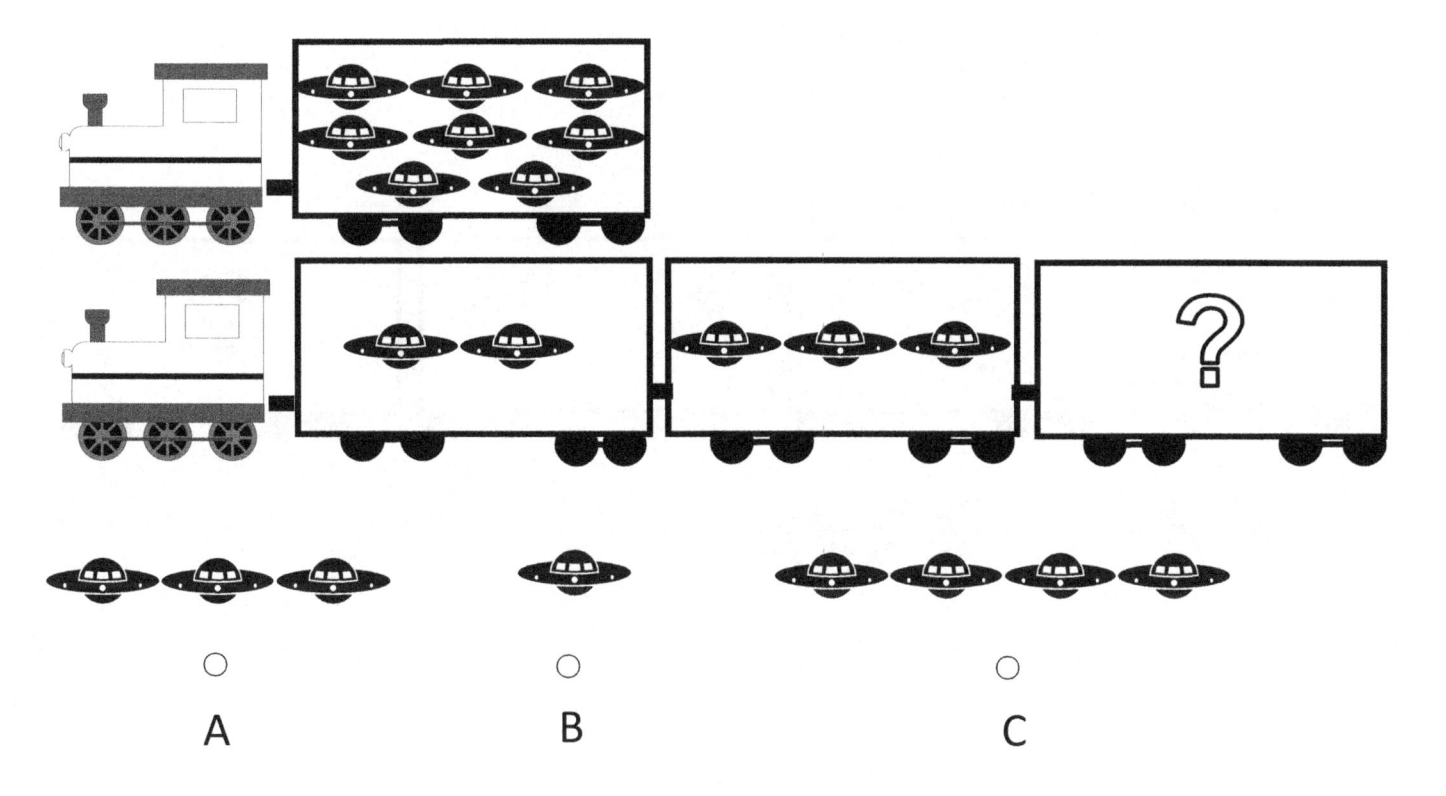

5.

6.

89

PRACTICE TEST GRADE 1

7.

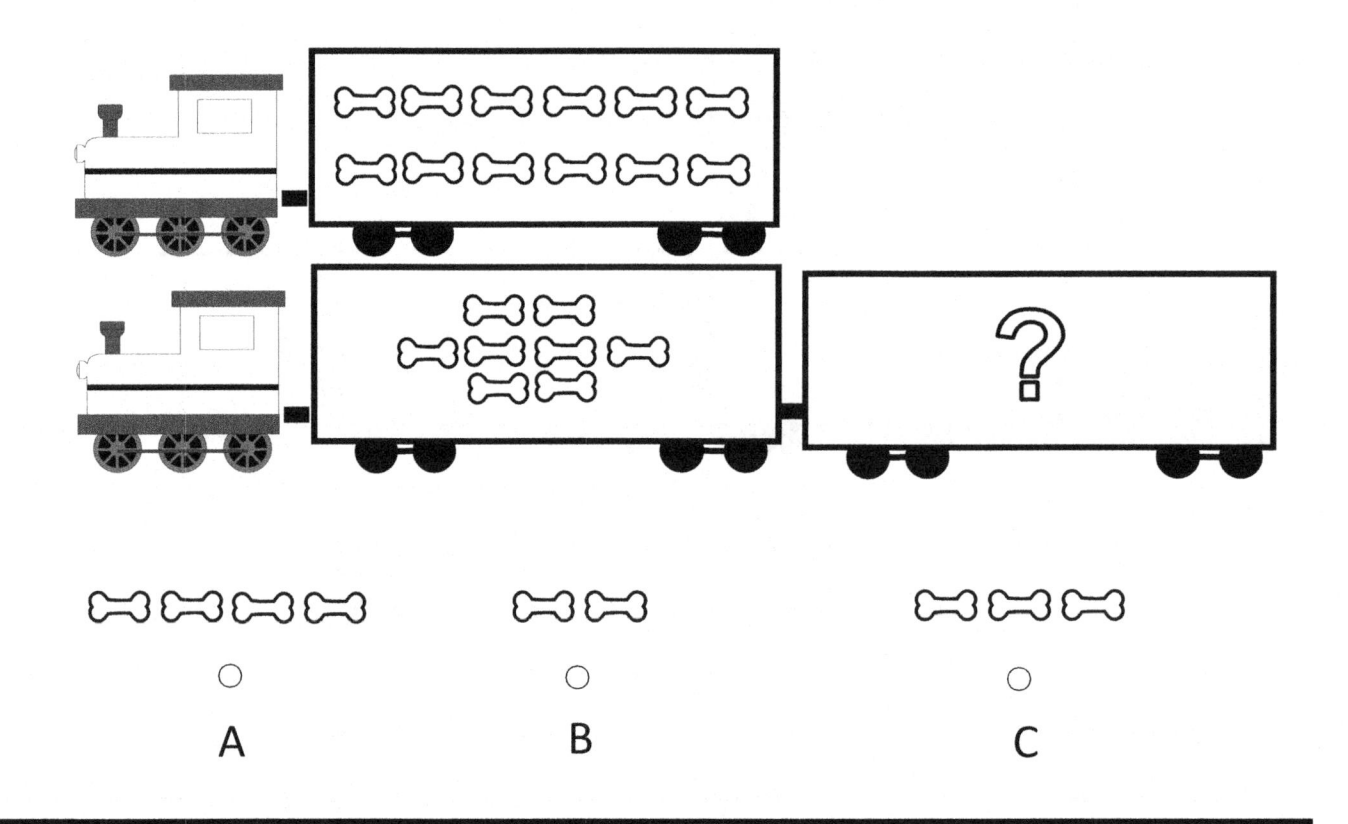

A   B   C

8.

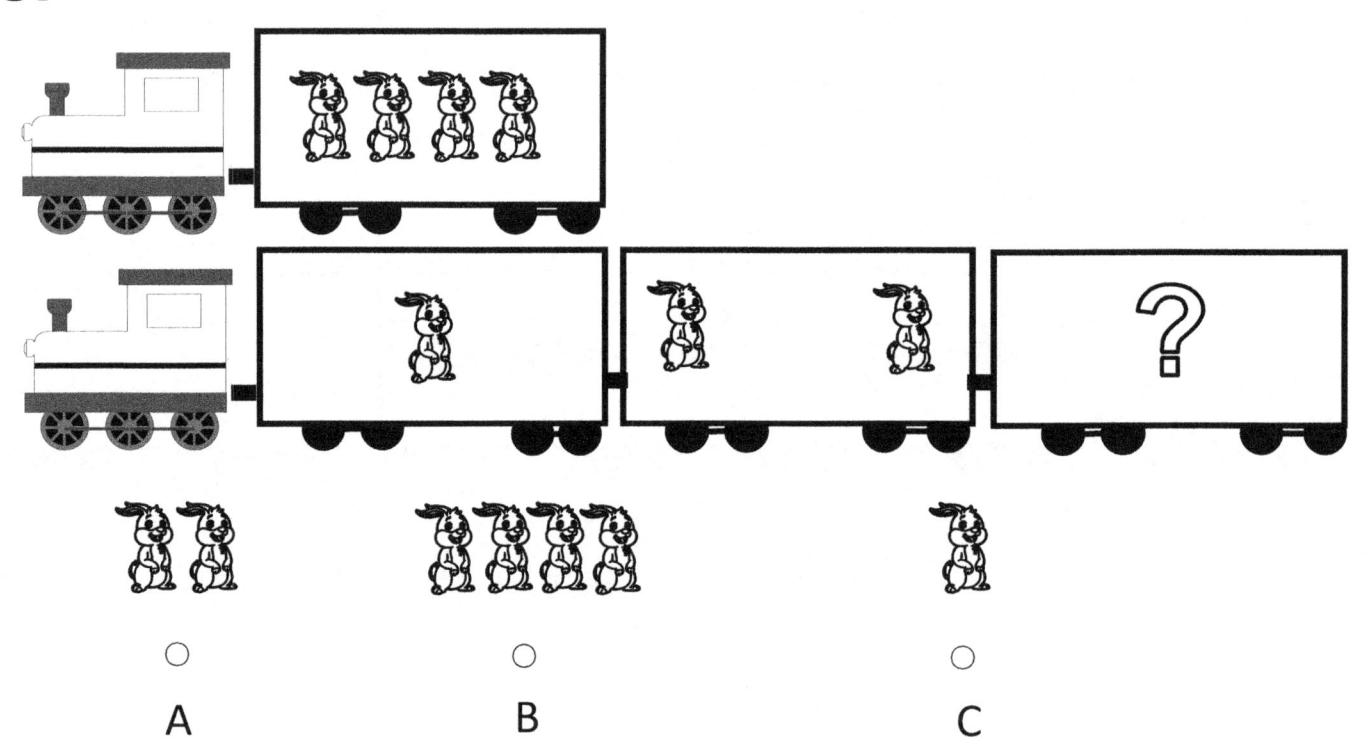

A   B   C

90

PRACTICE TEST GRADE 1

9.

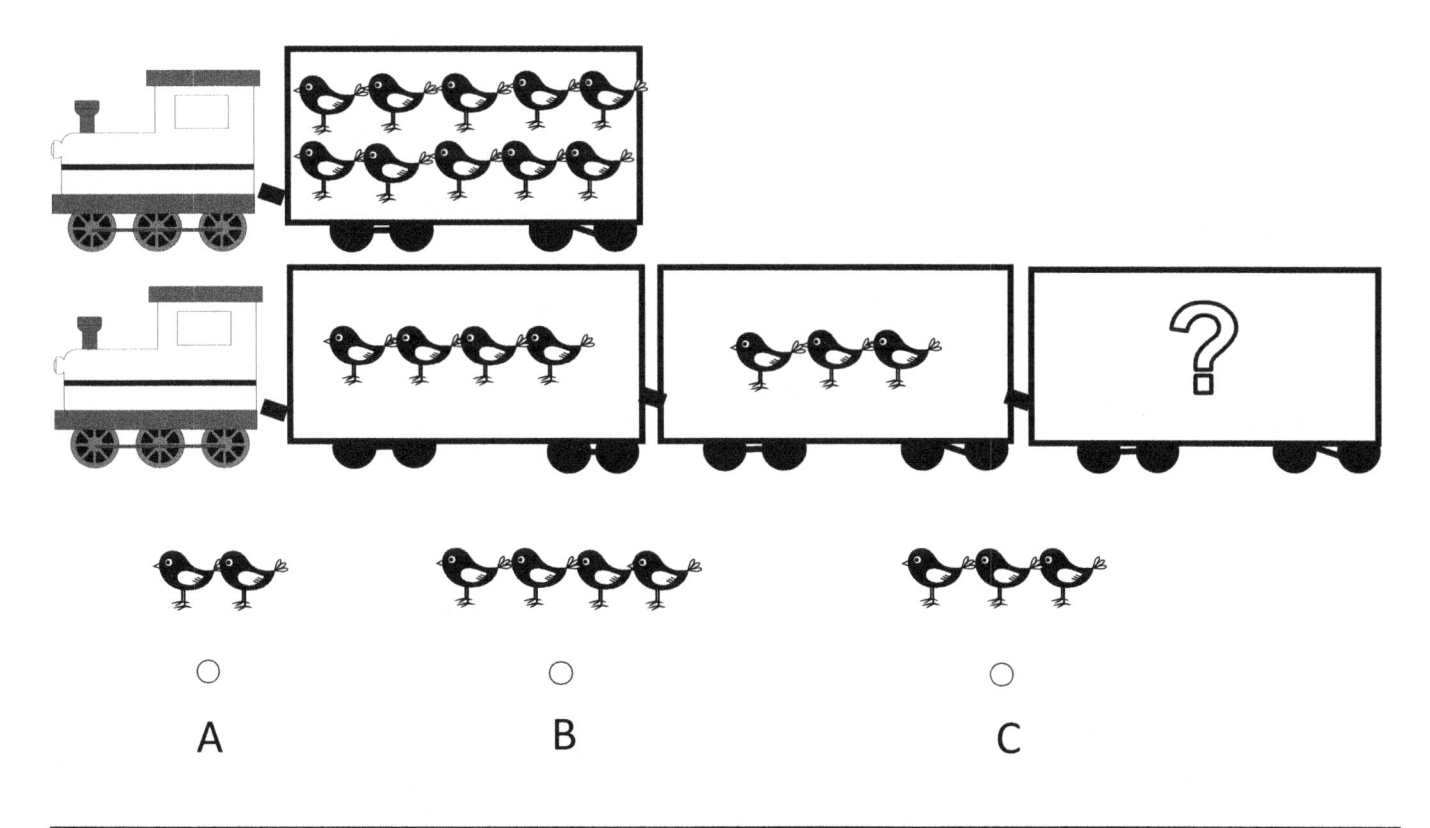

A B C

10.

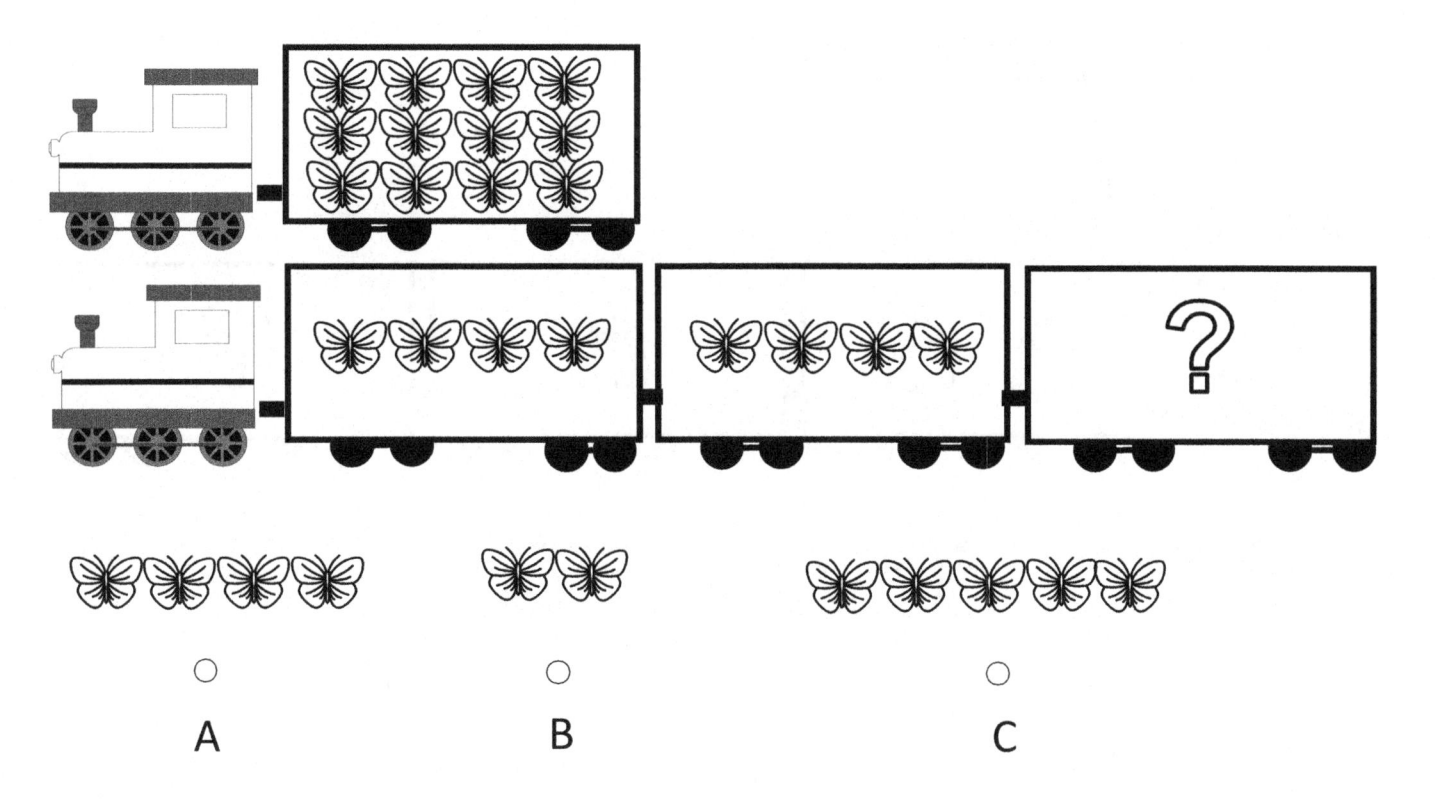

A B C

91

PRACTICE TEST GRADE 1

11.

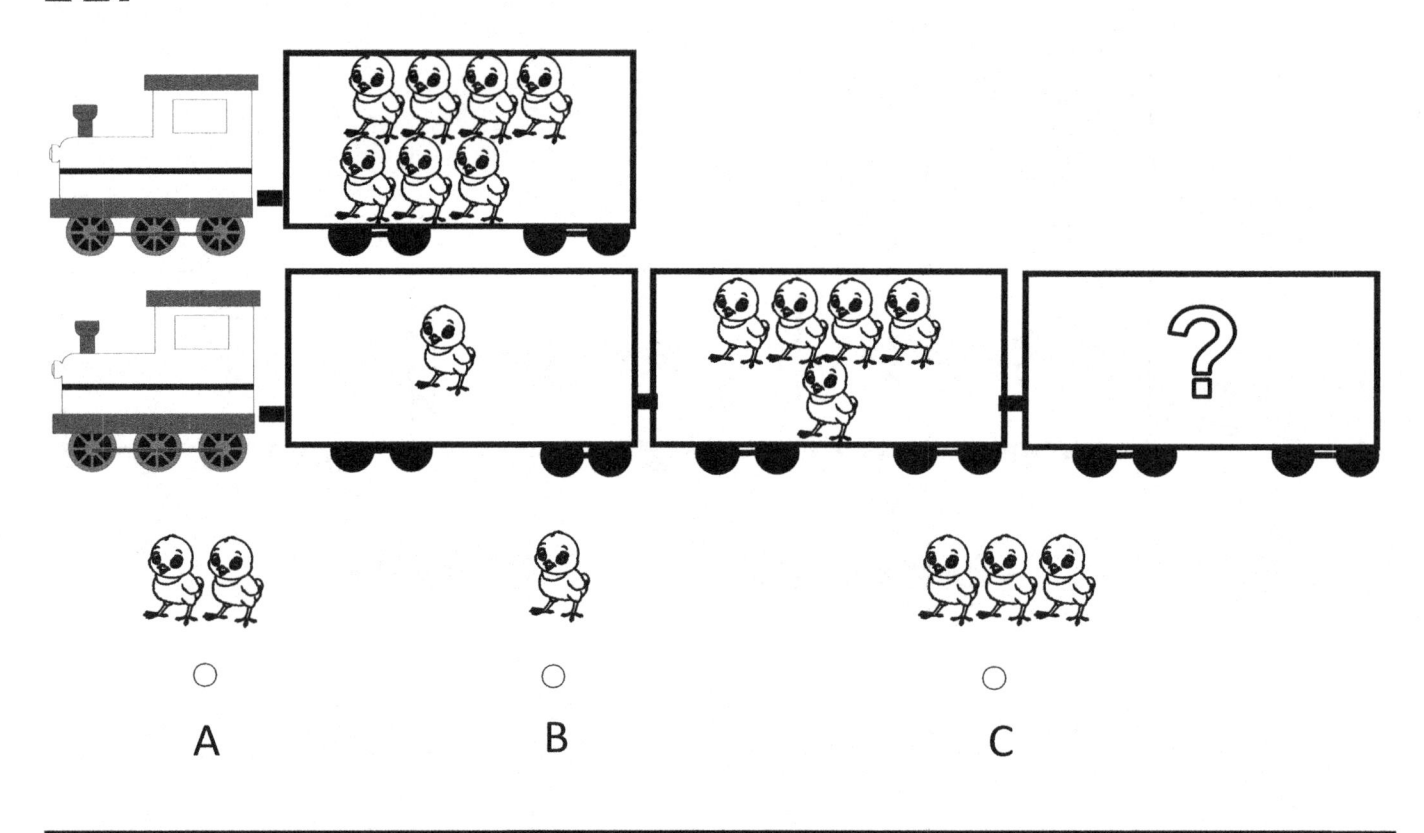

A   B   C

12.

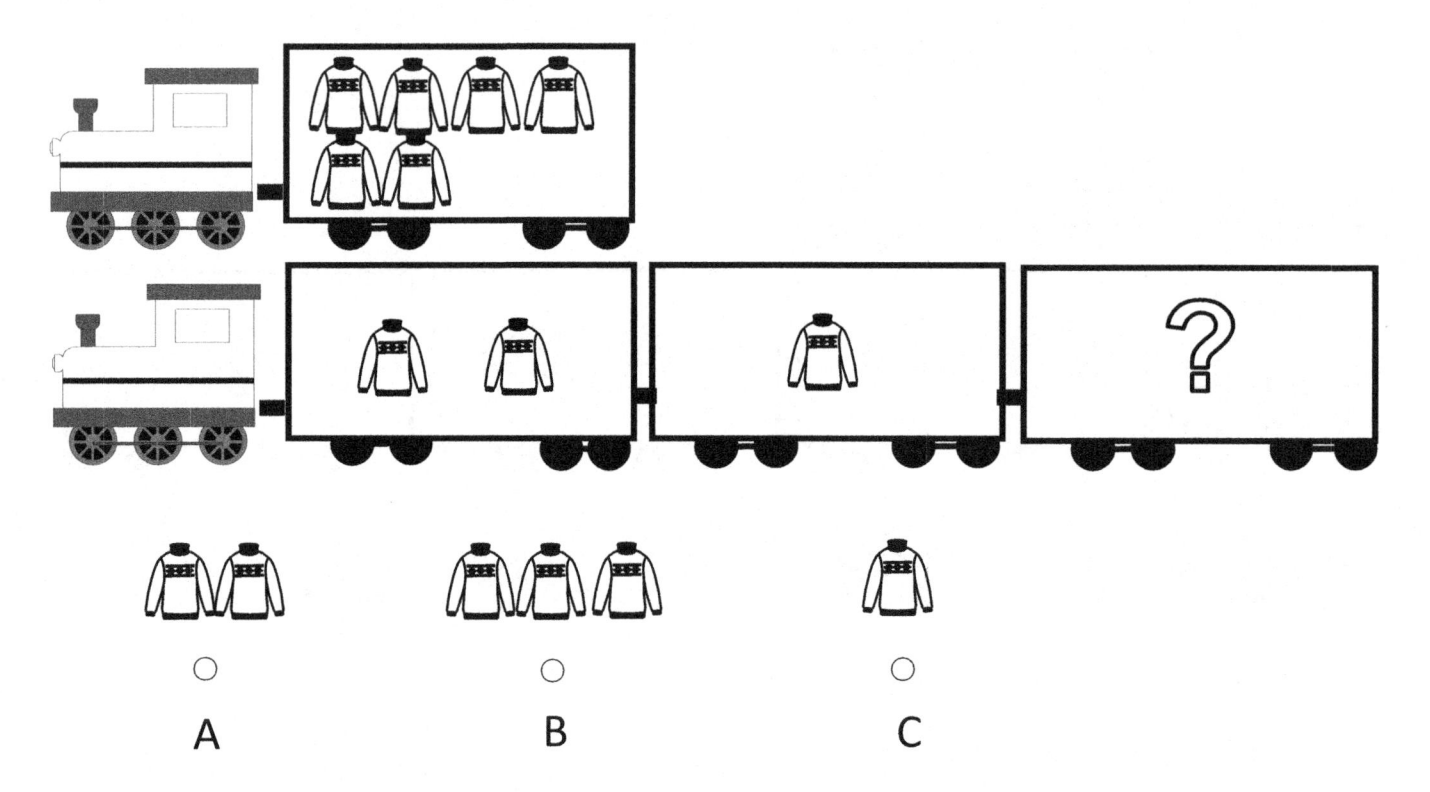

A   B   C

92

PRACTICE TEST GRADE 1

Number Analogies

Children will be provided with 2x2 basic matrices. Each box of the matrices contains a certain number of objects. In the lower row, the child must identify the same relationship as in the upper row and select the answer option that best fits the box with the question mark.

Example

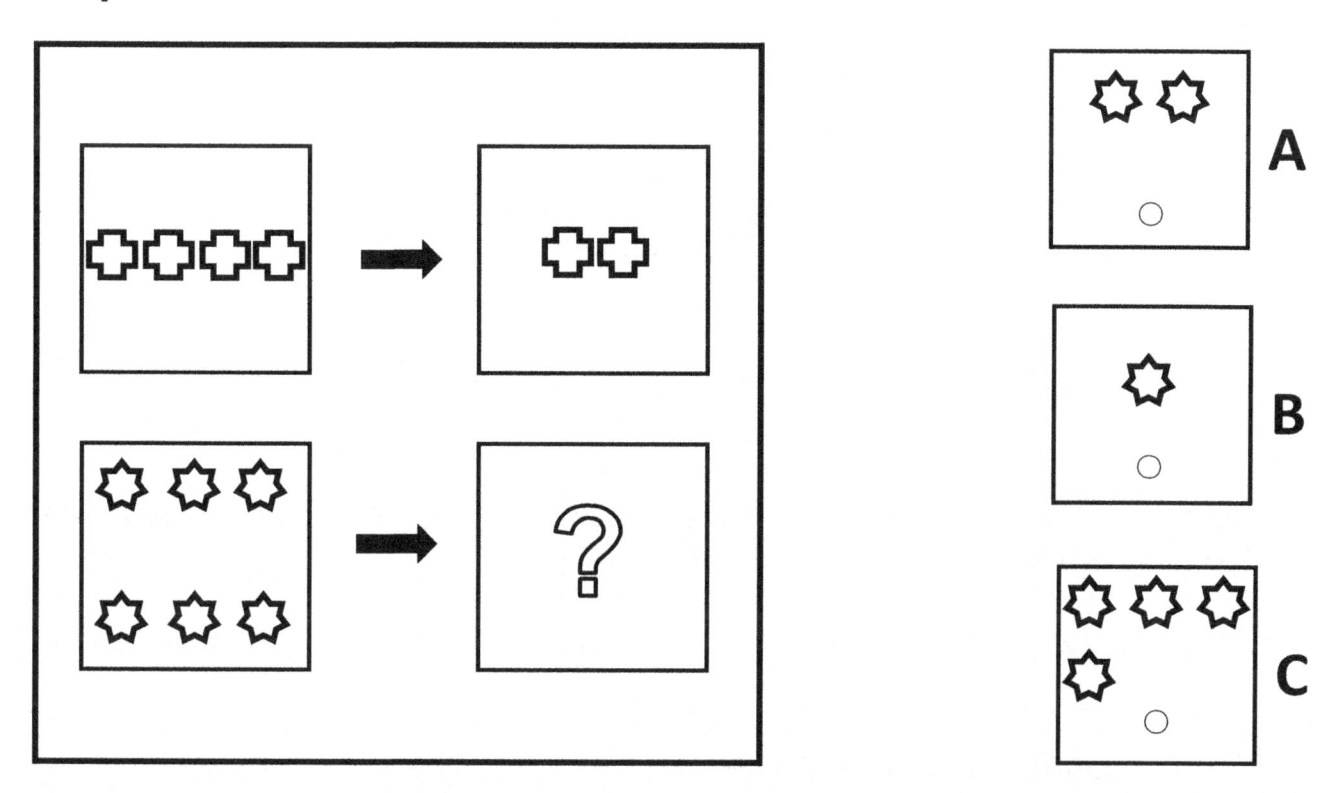

- First, identify the relationship between the objects in the upper squares.

    What is the relationship between "4 cross" and "2 cross"?

    4 is greater than 2 by 2 (4-2=2).

- Now, look at the objects in the lower squares. In the left box we have 6 stars.
- Which of the possible choices follows the previous rule?

    In the right box, we should have 2 less stars. Therefore, the correct answer is C (6-2=4).

93

Tips for Number Analogies

- Step 1: Acquire all the information from the two given pairs (relationships, sums, subtractions, etc.).

- Step 2: Apply the same rules, relations, formulas that you correctly identified in step 1.

- Step 3: Double-check that the rule has been properly applied.

- Train yourself to solve simple additions and subtractions.

- Work with real objects to understand the concepts.

- Start with simple numerical analogies and gradually increase the level of complexity.

PRACTICE TEST GRADE 1

1.

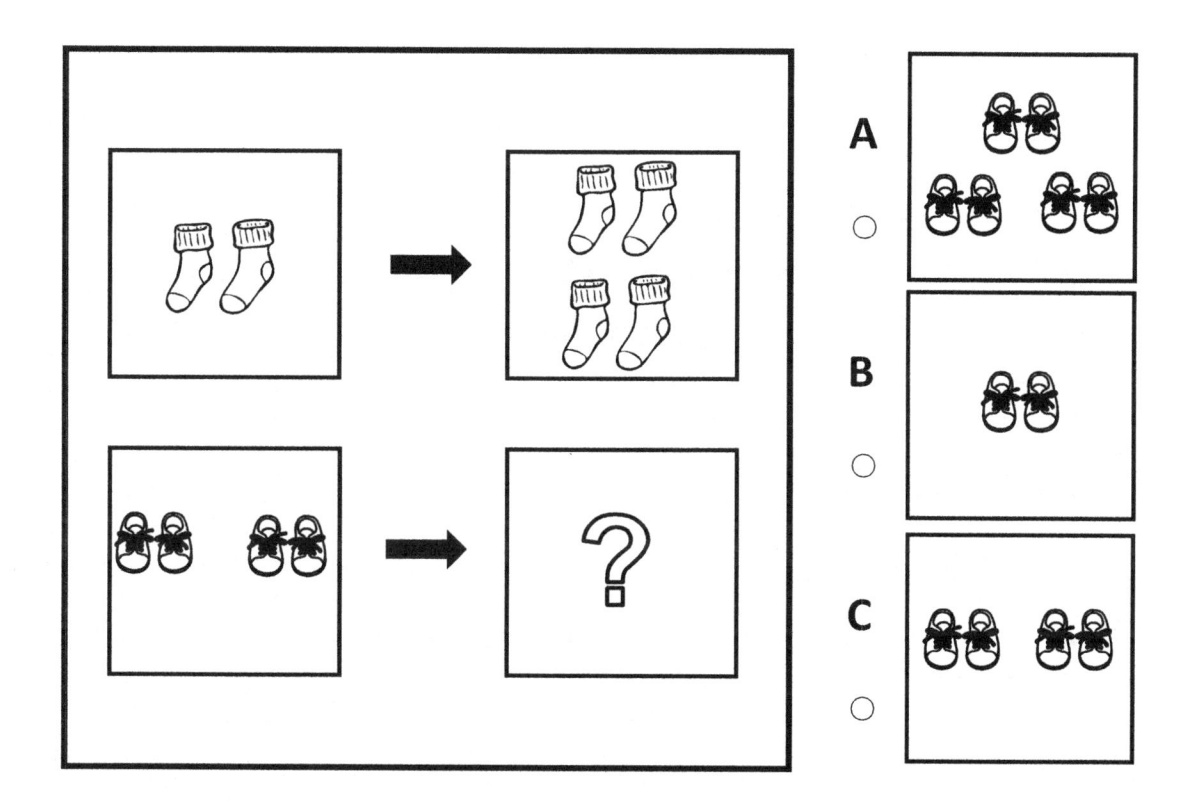

2.

95

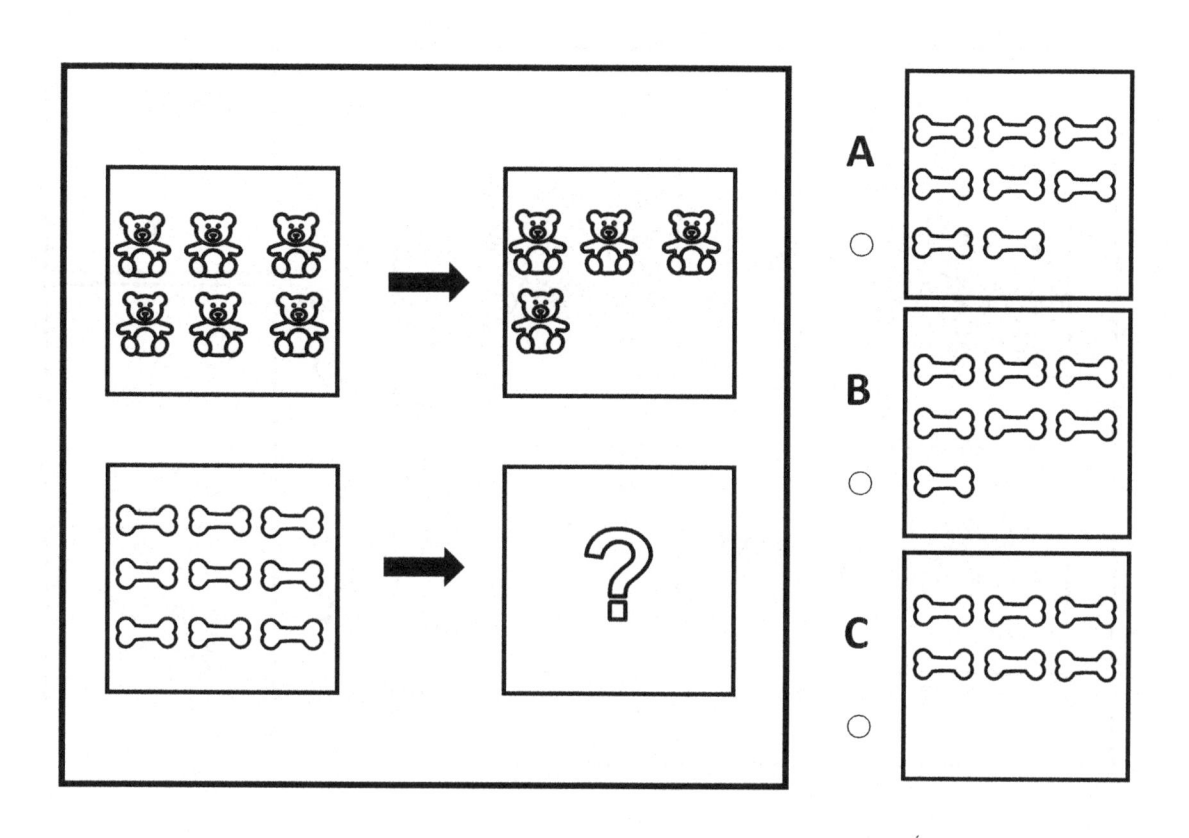

PRACTICE TEST GRADE 1

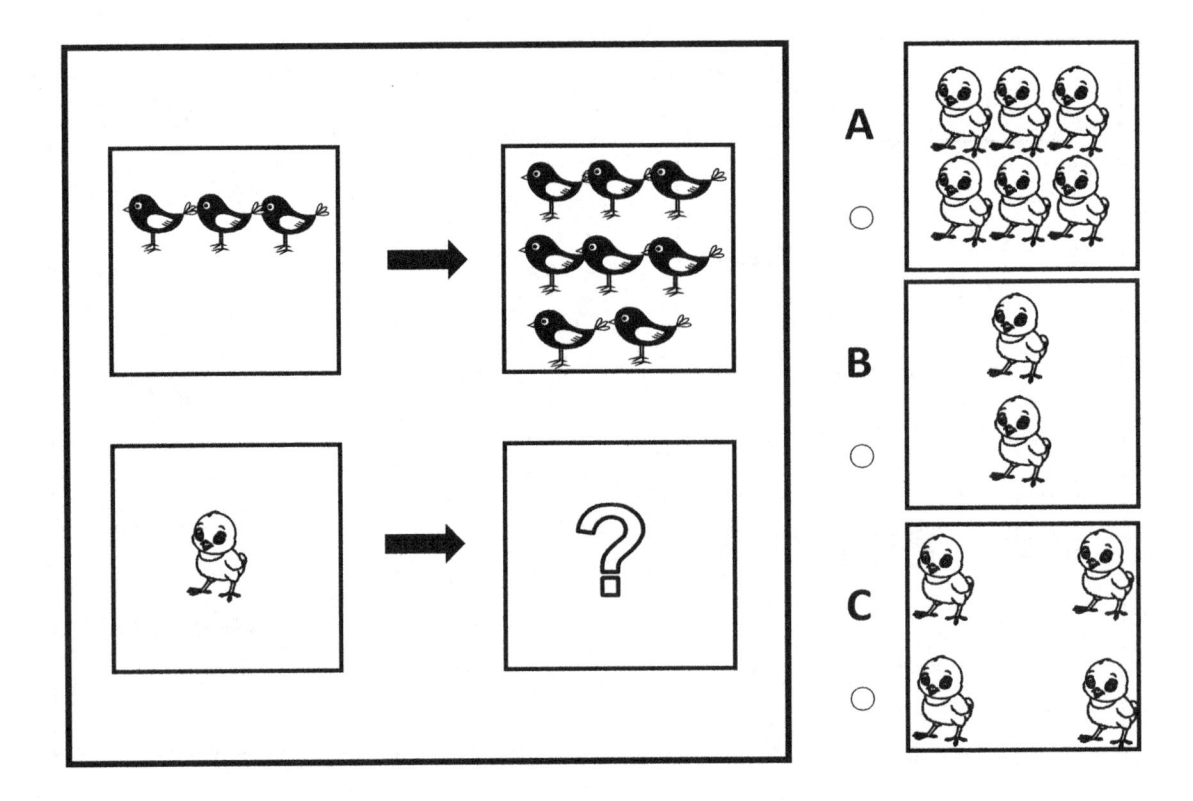

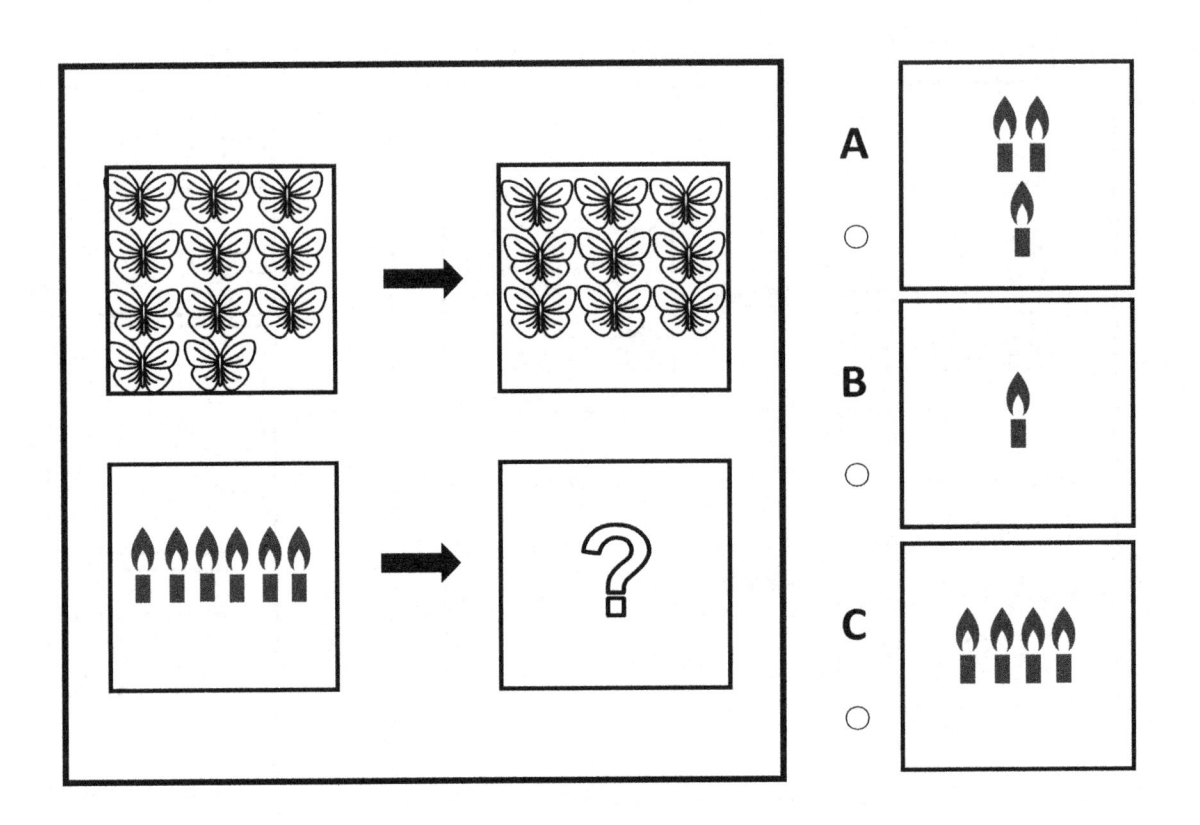

3.

4.

96

PRACTICE TEST GRADE 1

5.

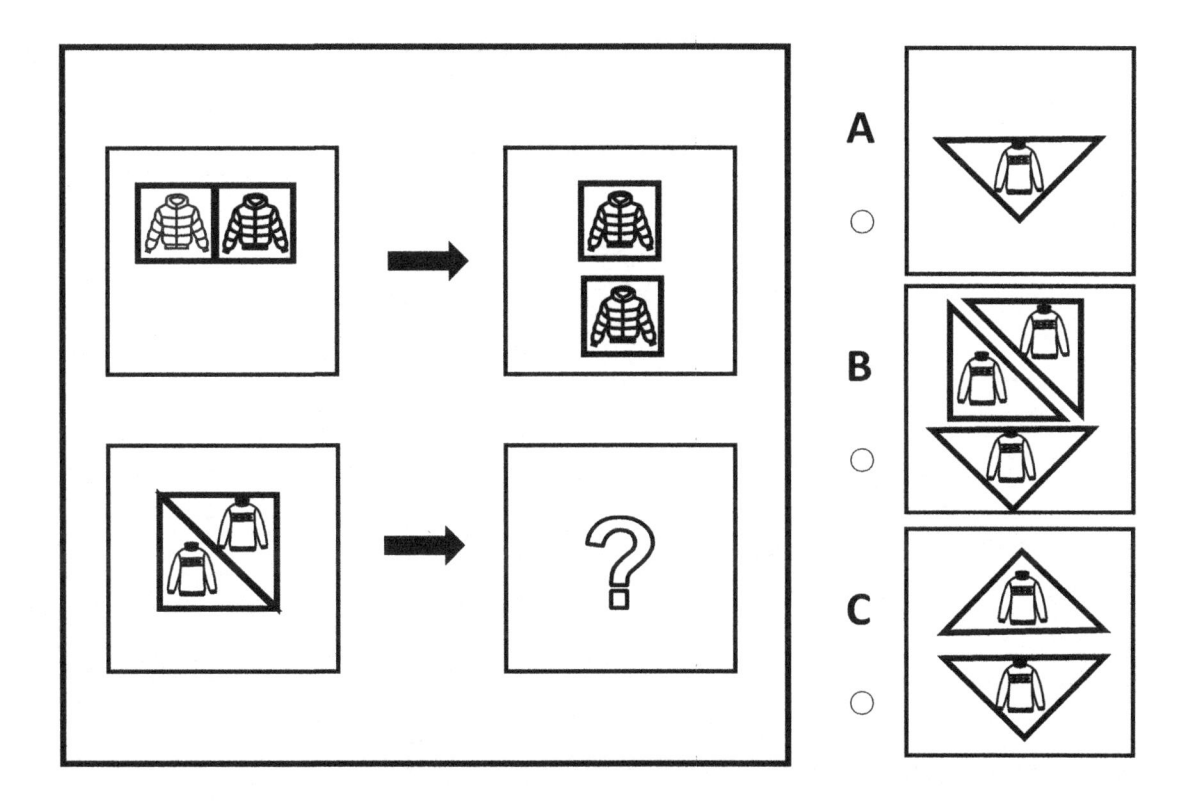

6.

97

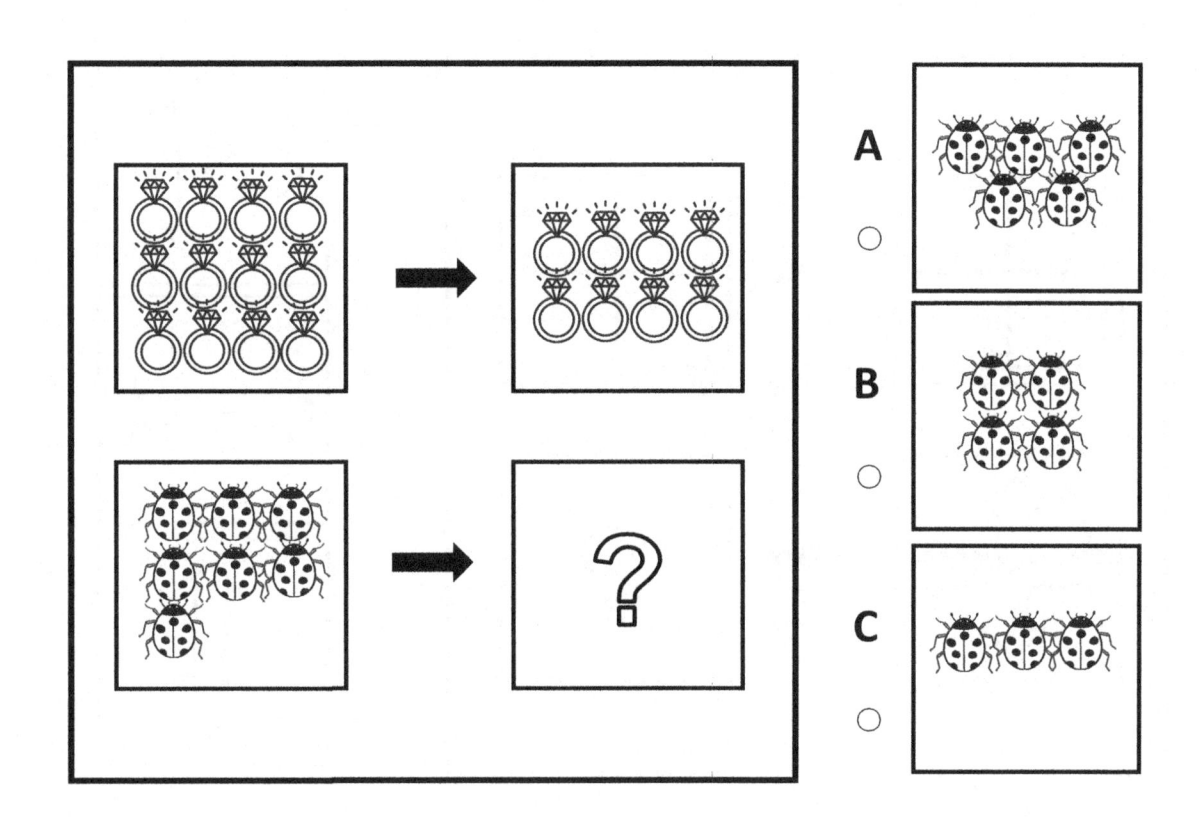

PRACTICE TEST GRADE 1

7.

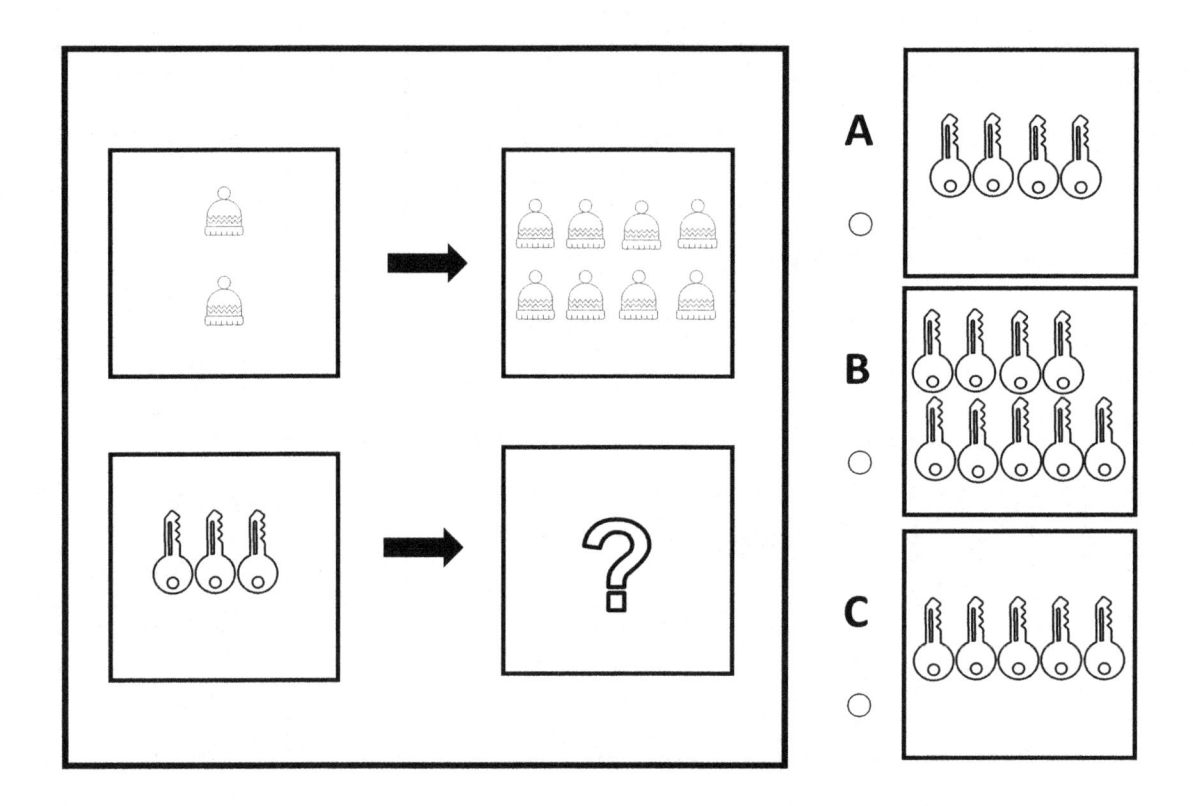

8.

98

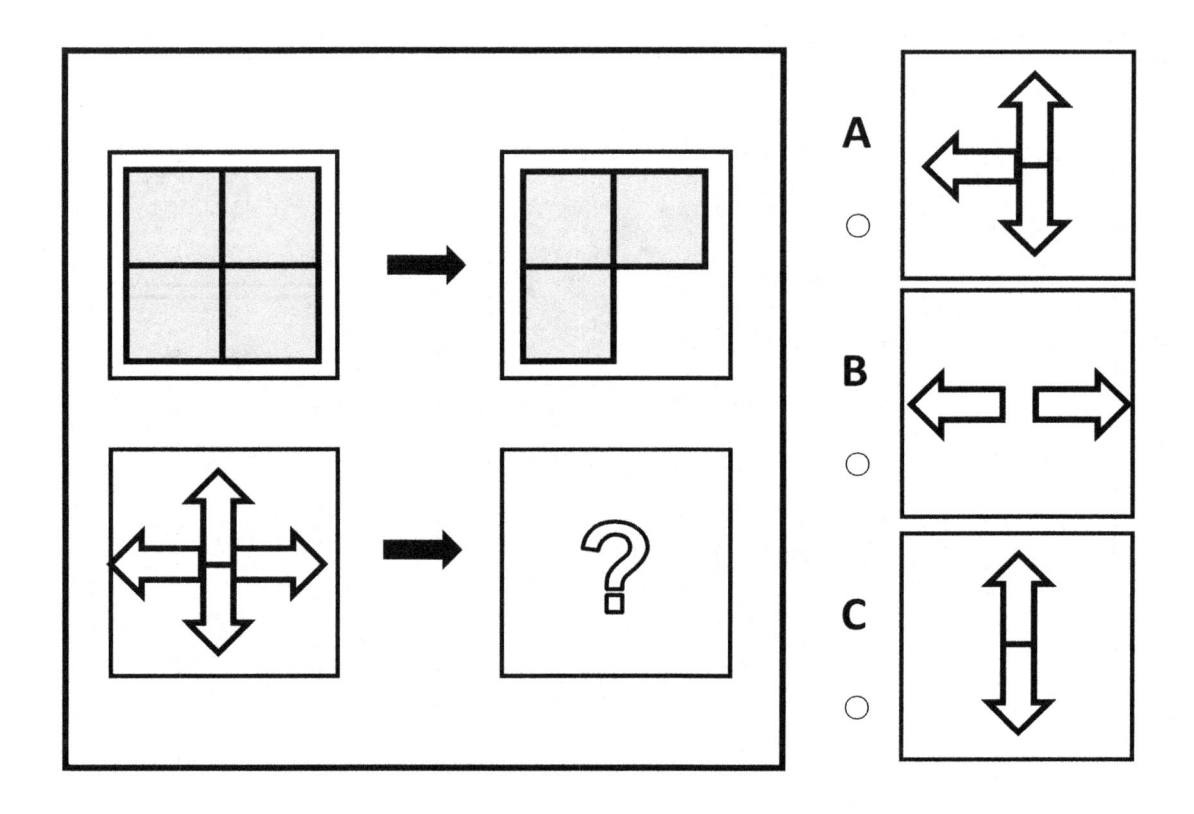

PRACTICE TEST GRADE 1

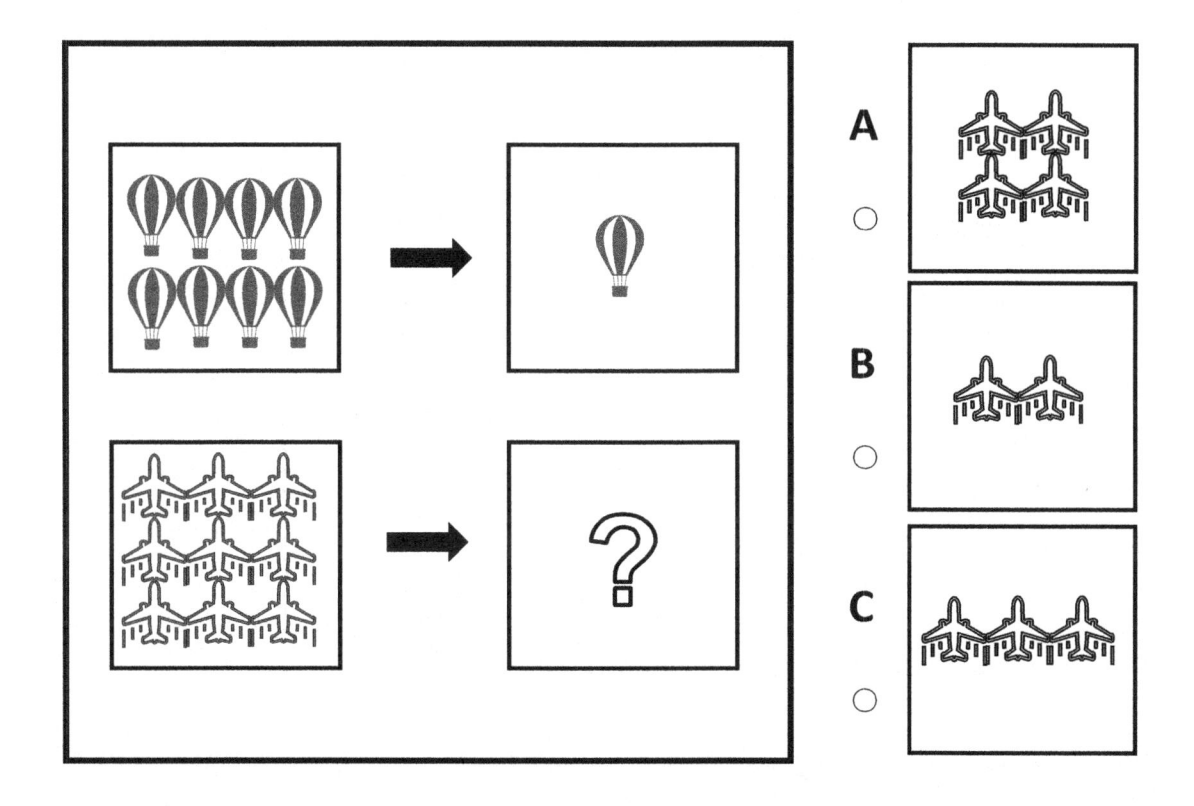

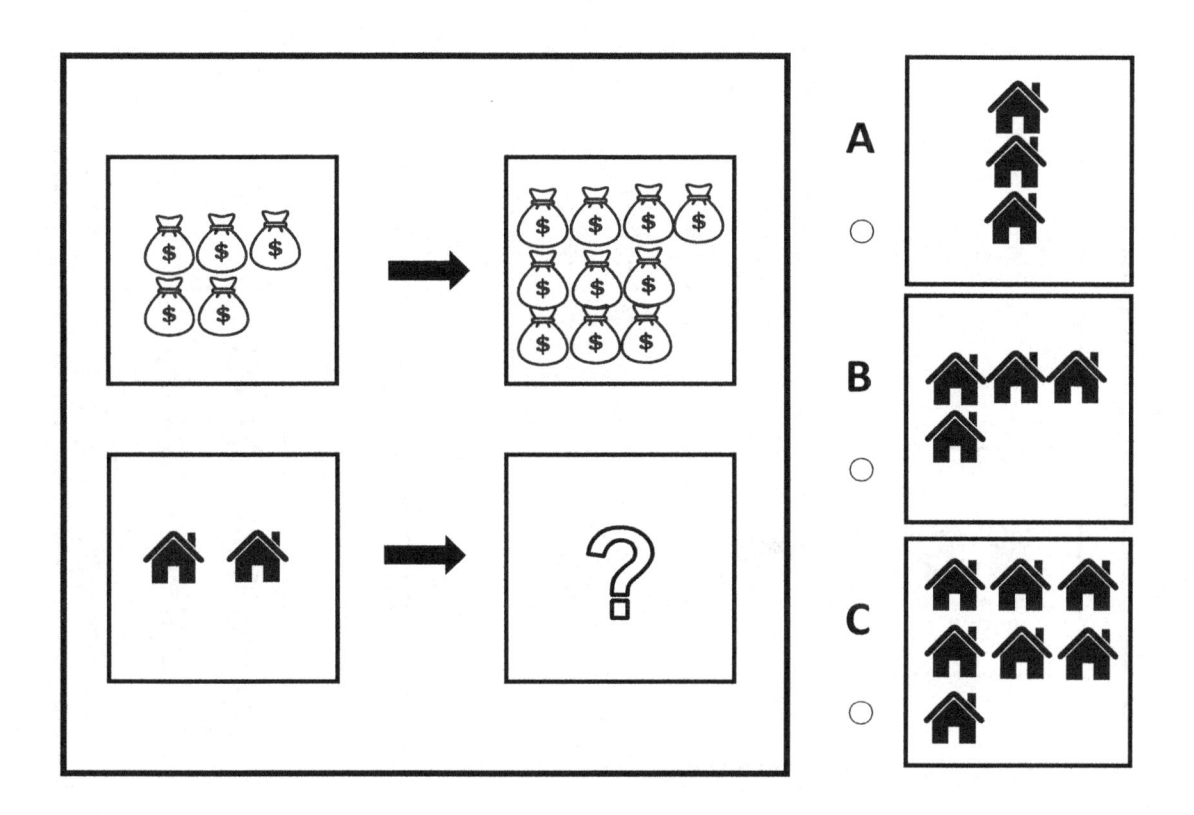

9.

10.

99

PRACTICE TEST GRADE 1

11.

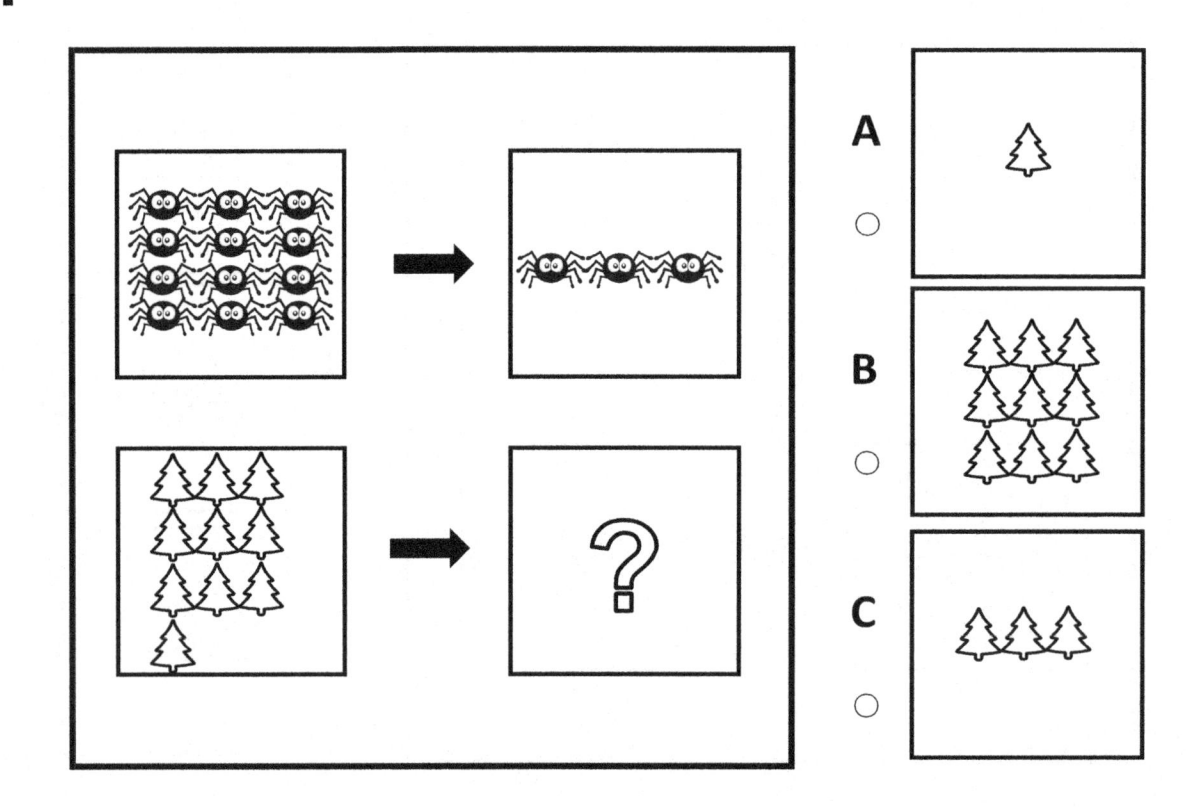

12.

100

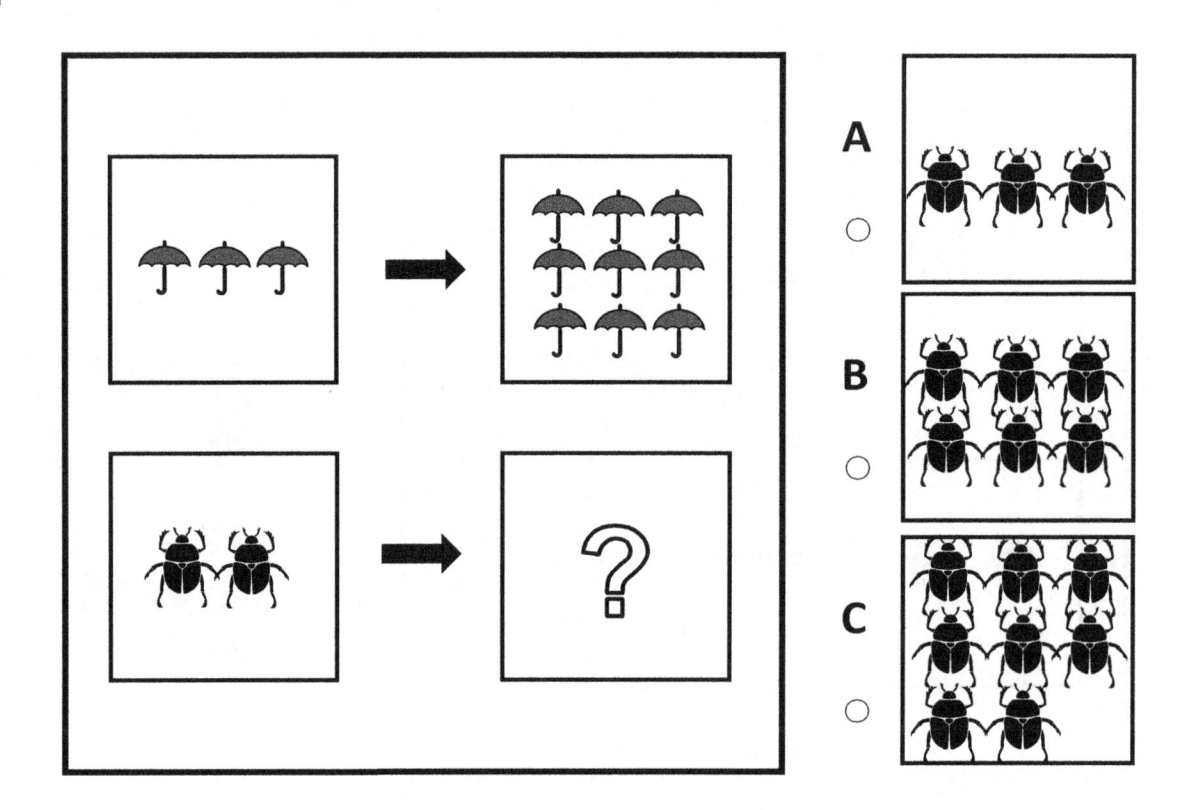

PRACTICE TEST GRADE 1

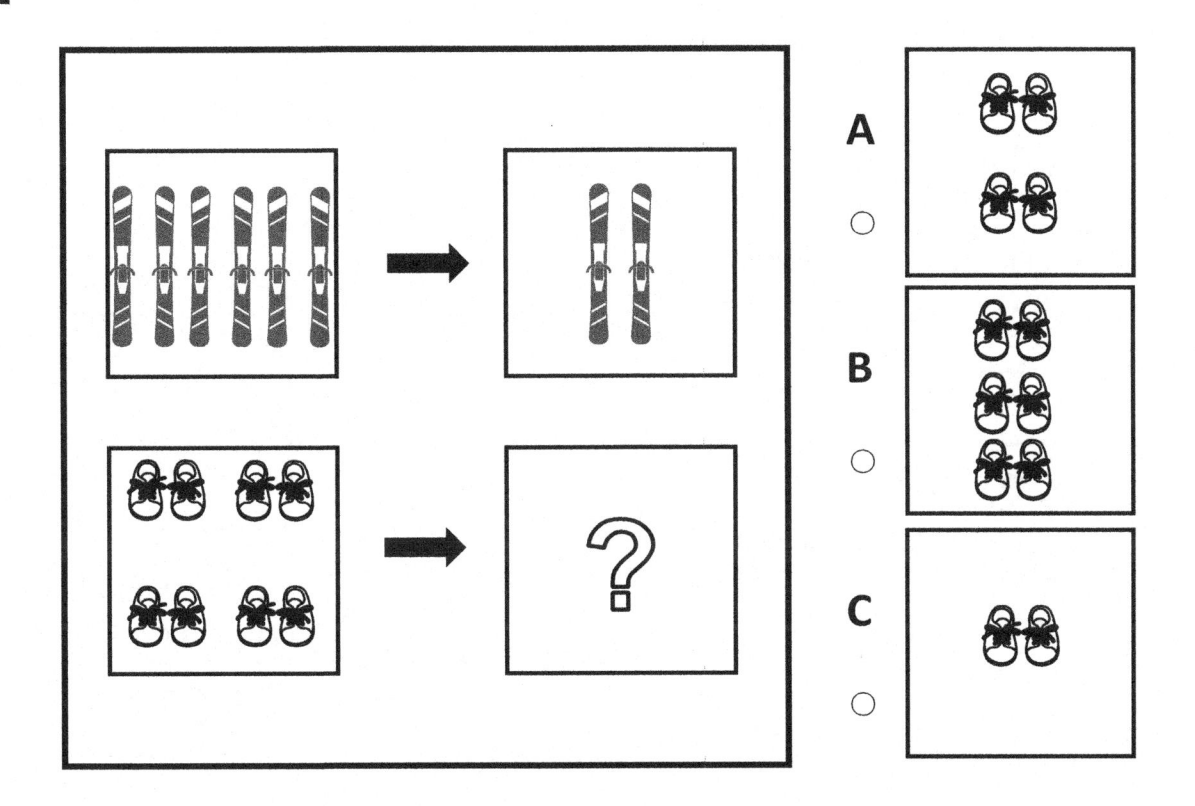

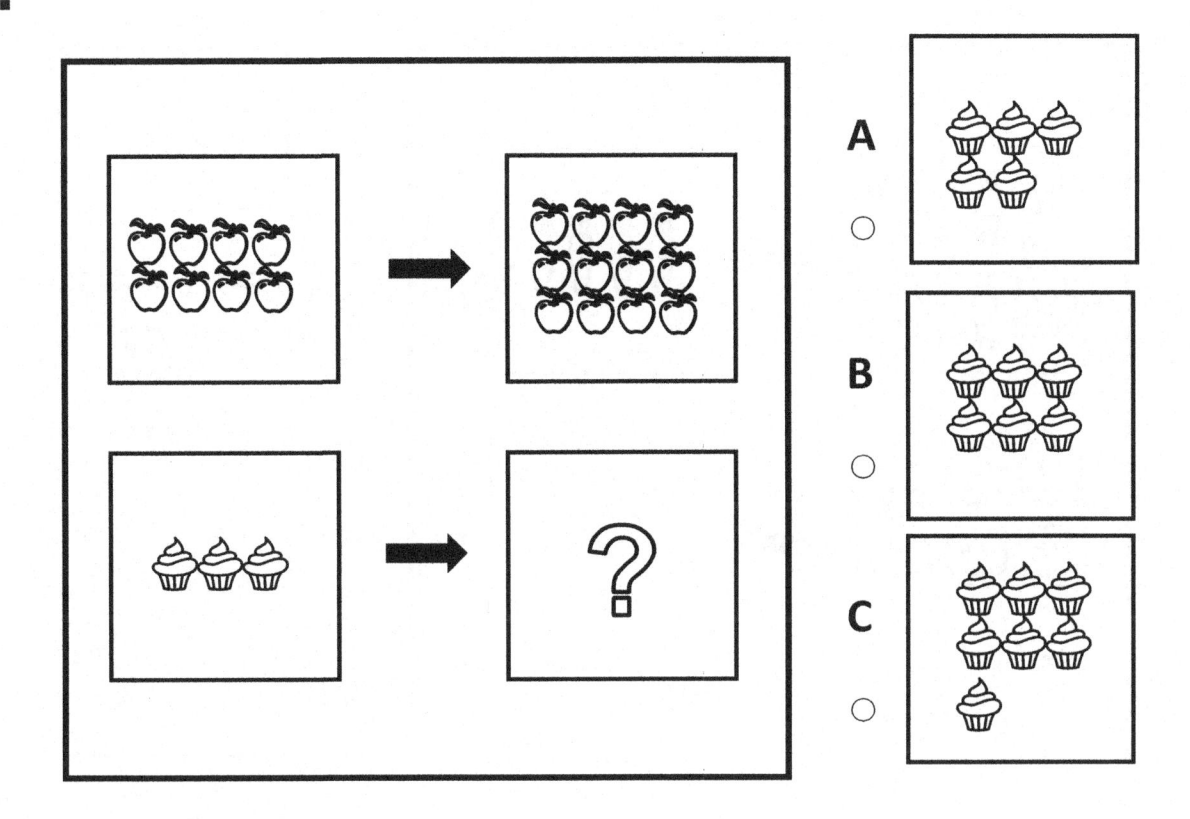

13.

14.

101

PRACTICE TEST GRADE 1

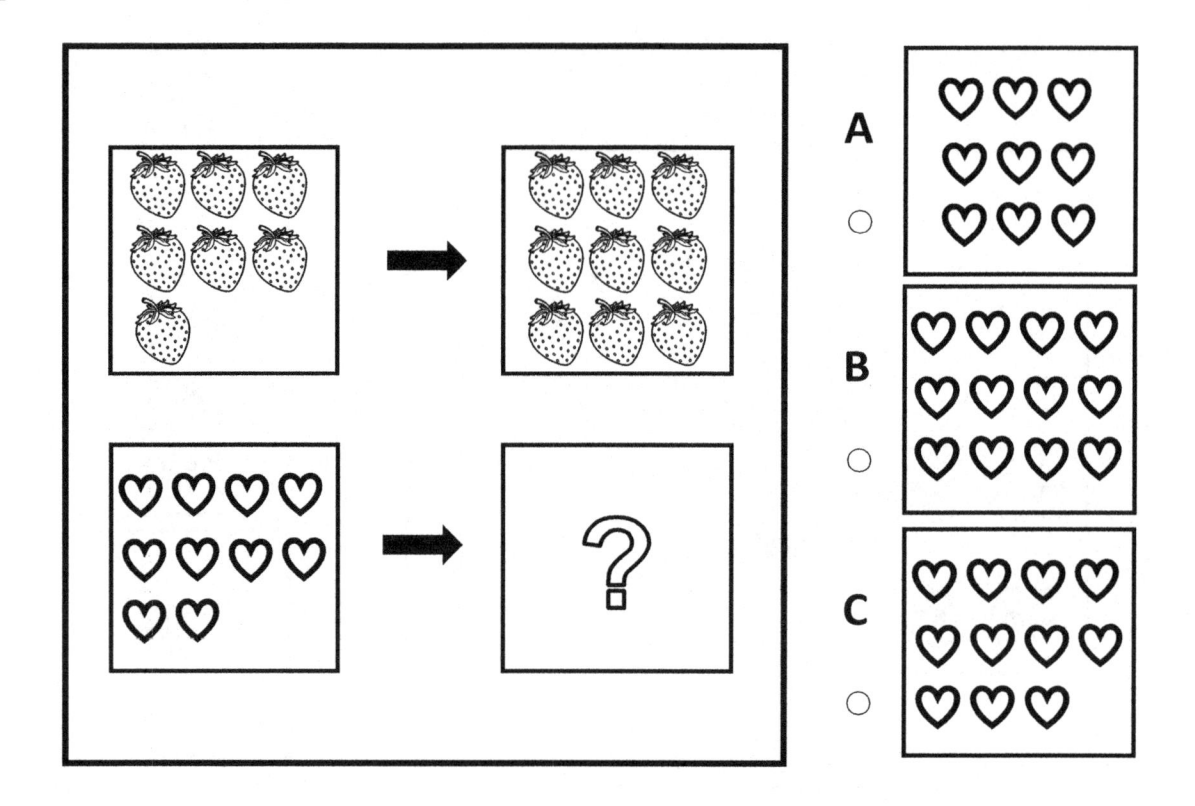

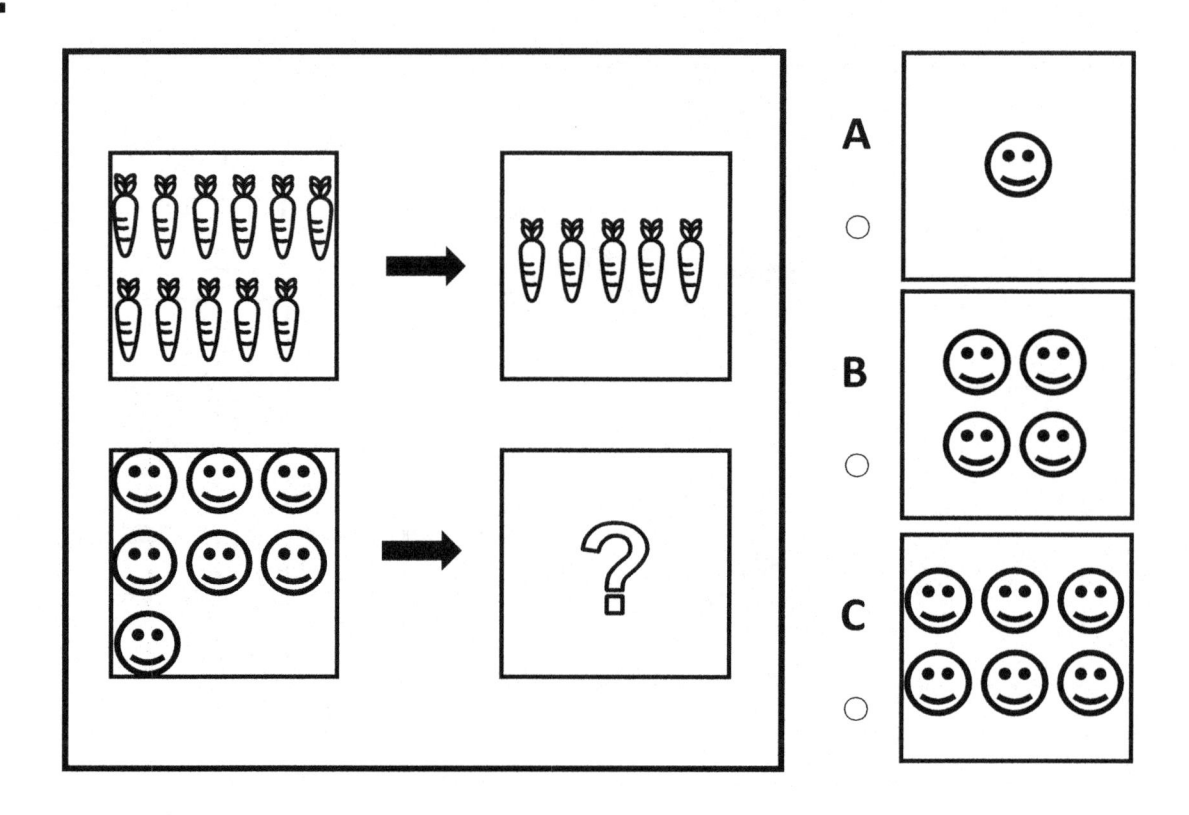

15.

16.

102

PRACTICE TEST GRADE 1

Number Series

Children are required to determine which string of beads is needed to complete a sequence that follows a specific pattern by observing an abacus.

Example 1

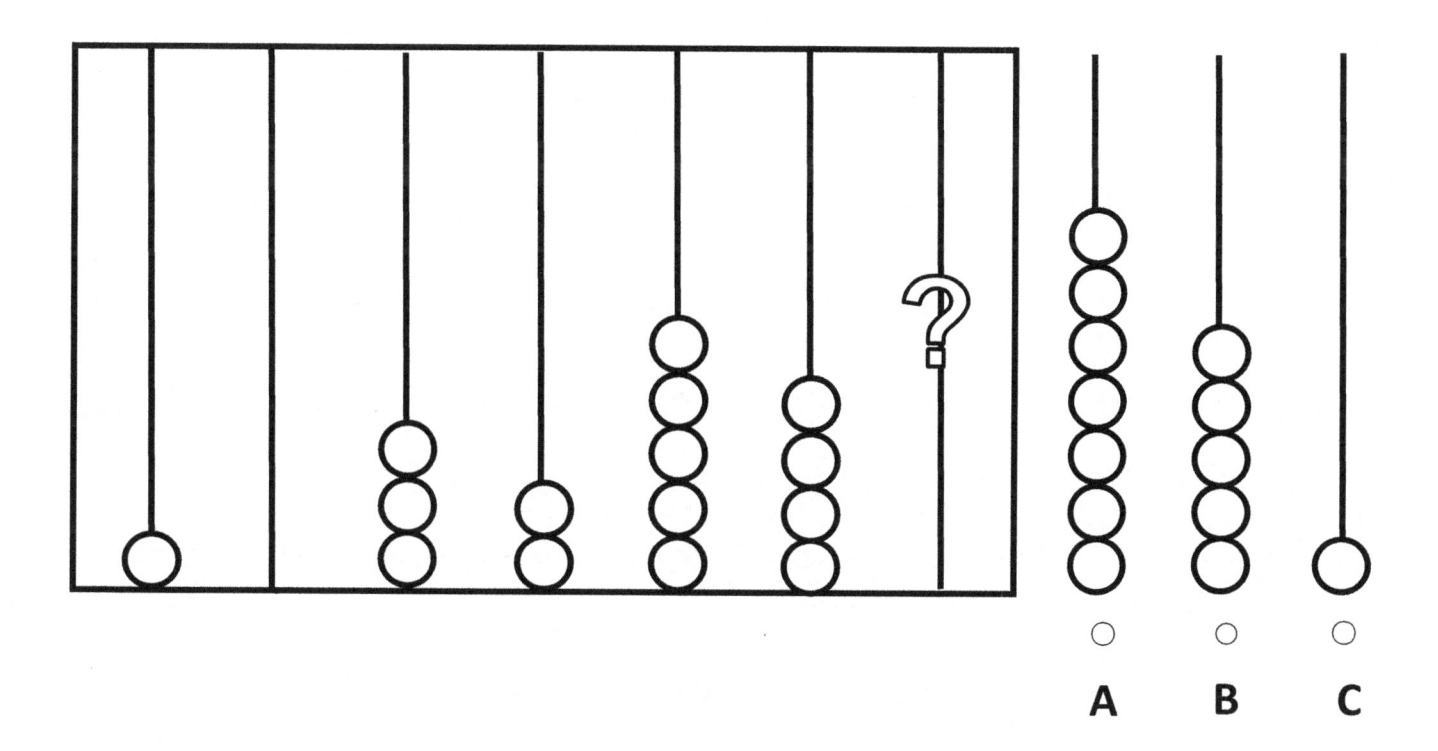

- The numbers on the strings are: 1 0 3 2 5 4 ?
- **1-1=0; 0+3=3; 3-1=2; 2+3=5; 5-1=4; etc.**
- It's easy to realize that the sequence is **-1, +3, -1, +3, -1, etc.**
- Apply the same rule to the number 4.

4 + 3 = 7 The right answer is "A"

PRACTICE TEST GRADE 1

Example 2

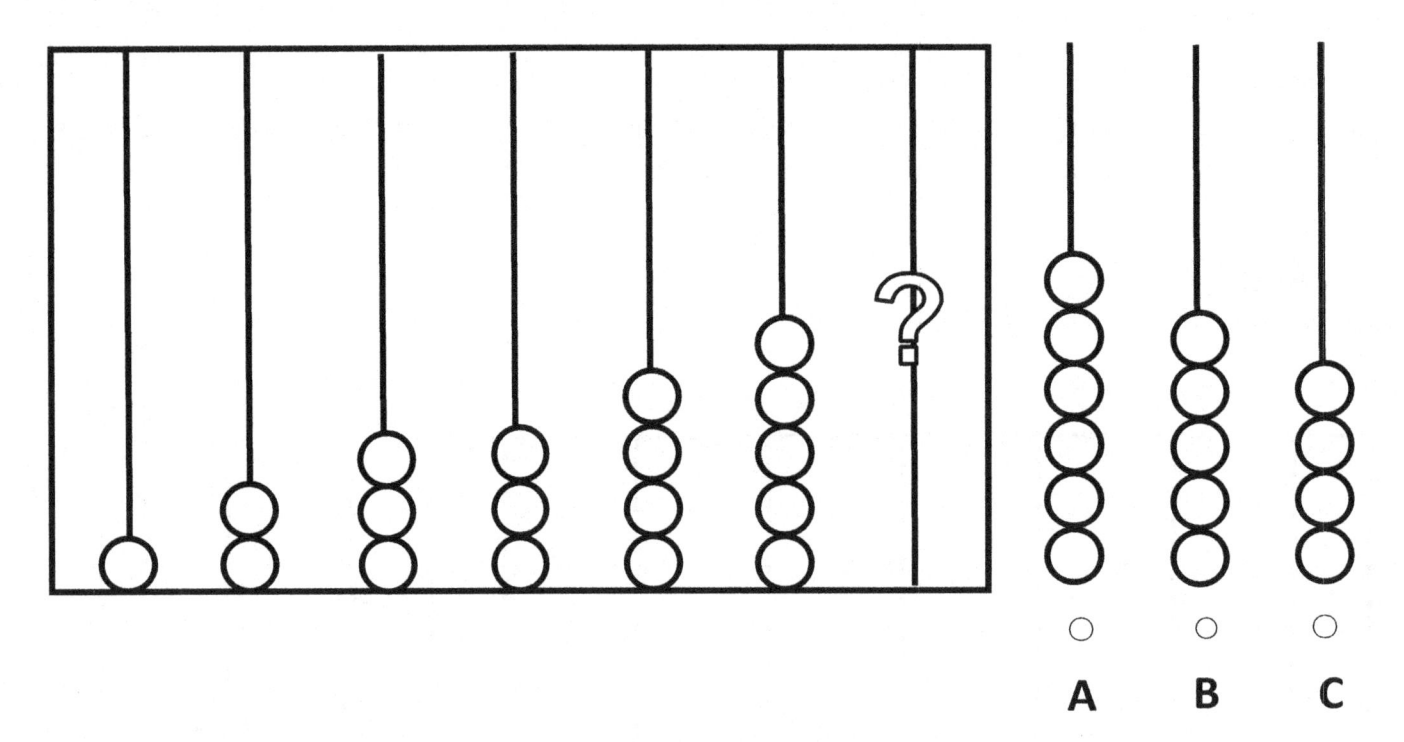

- The numbers on the strings are: 1   2   3   3   4   5   ?
- 1+**1**=2; 2+**1**=3; 3+**0**=3; 3+**1**=4; 4+**1**=5 etc.
- It's easy to realize that the sequence is: +1, +1, 0, +1, +1, 0, etc.
- Apply the same rule to the number 5.

5+0=5 The right answer is "B"

Tips for Number Series

To answer these questions, children will need to be able to identify the pattern in a sequence of numbers and provide the missing item. Therefore, it is necessary to perform as many exercises as possible, moving from the easiest to the hardest.

In the beginning, to make the logic of the sequences easier, it is useful to work with real objects.

PRACTICE TEST GRADE 1

1

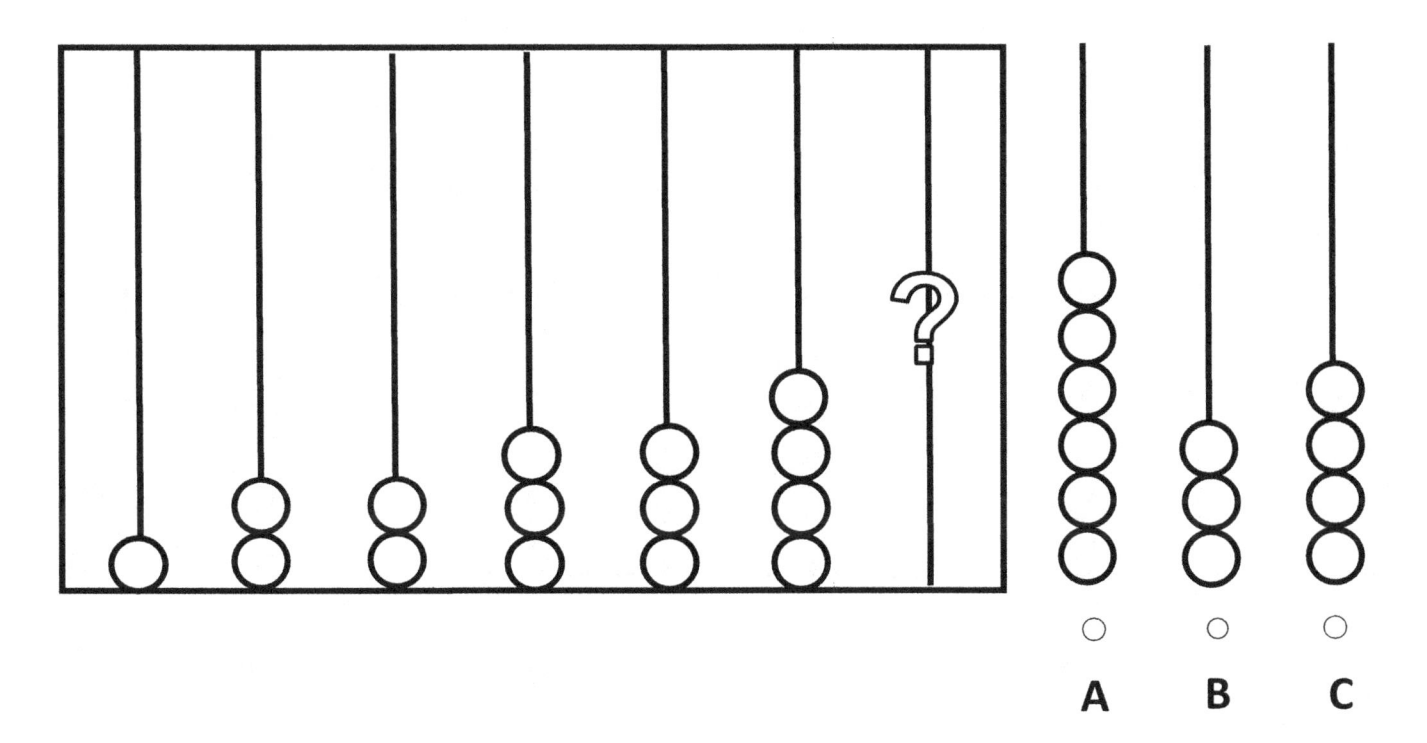

A B C

2.

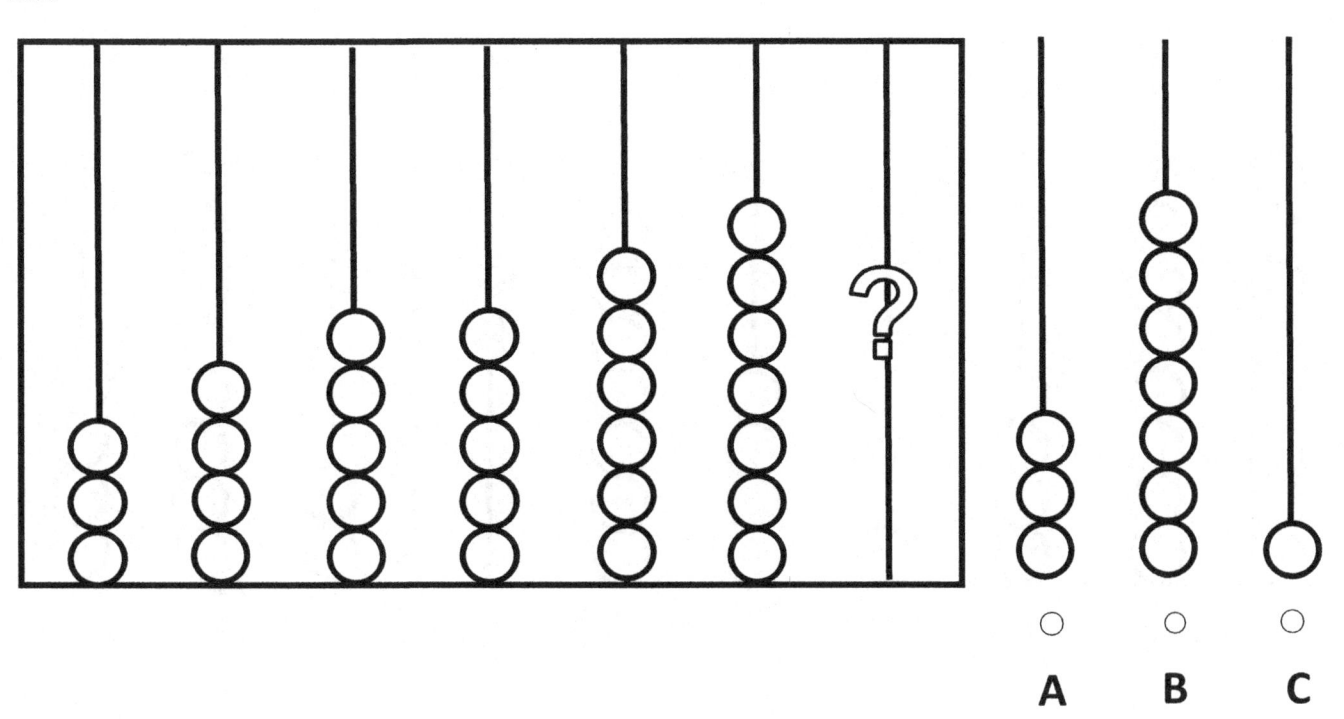

A B C

105

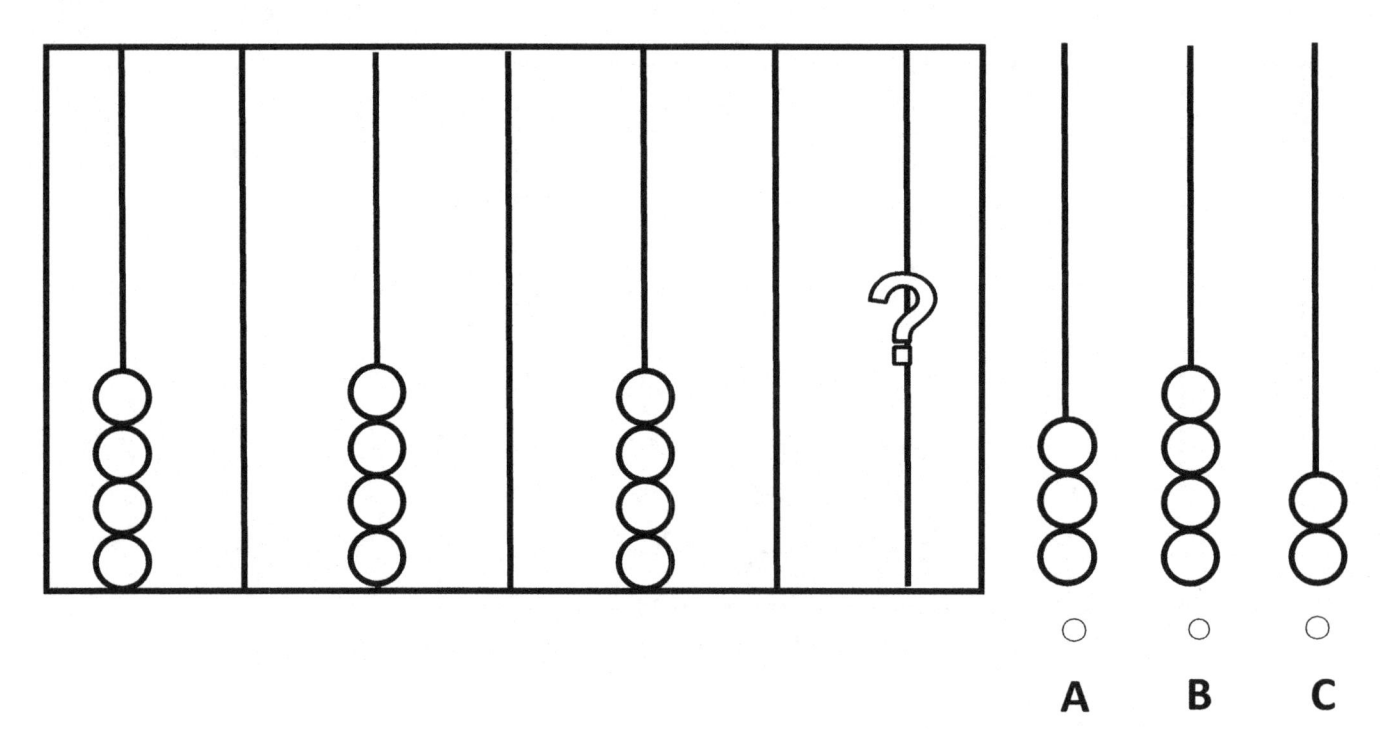

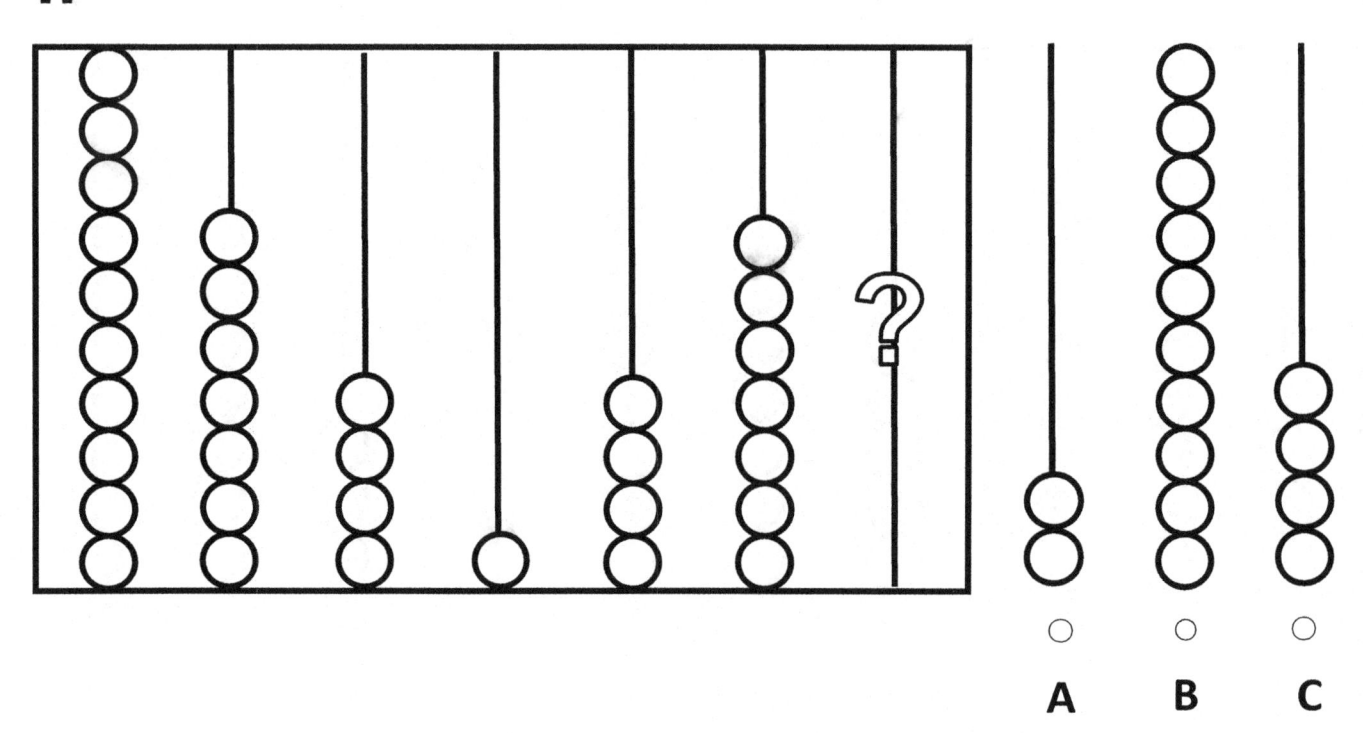

PRACTICE TEST GRADE 1

3.

4.

106

PRACTICE TEST GRADE 1

5.

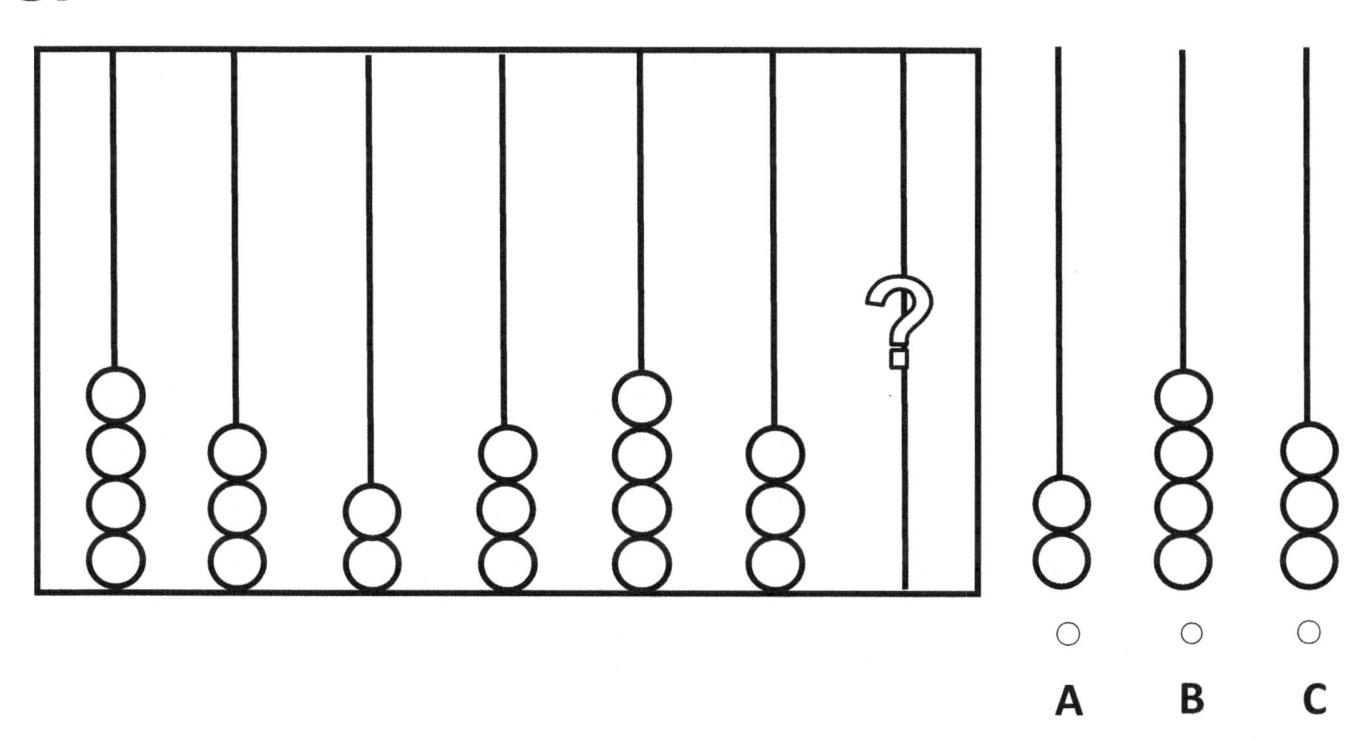

○   ○   ○
A   B   C

6.

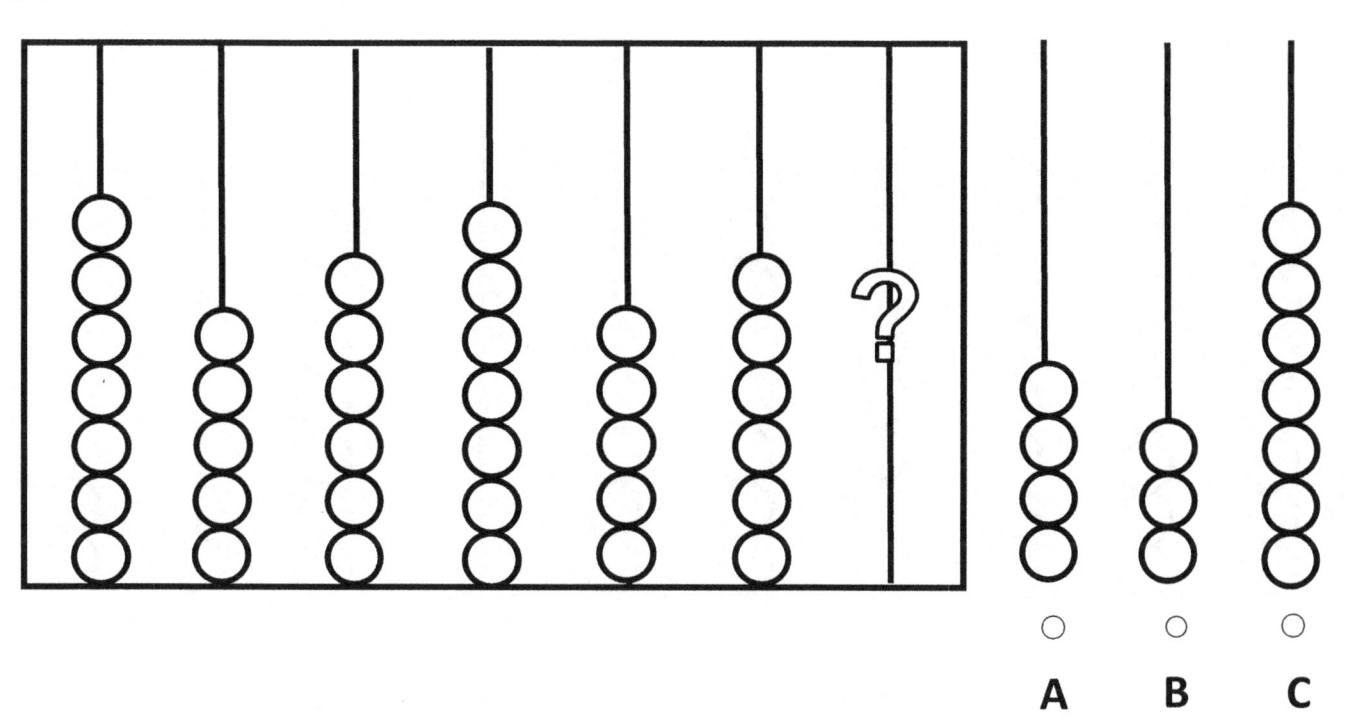

○   ○   ○
A   B   C

107

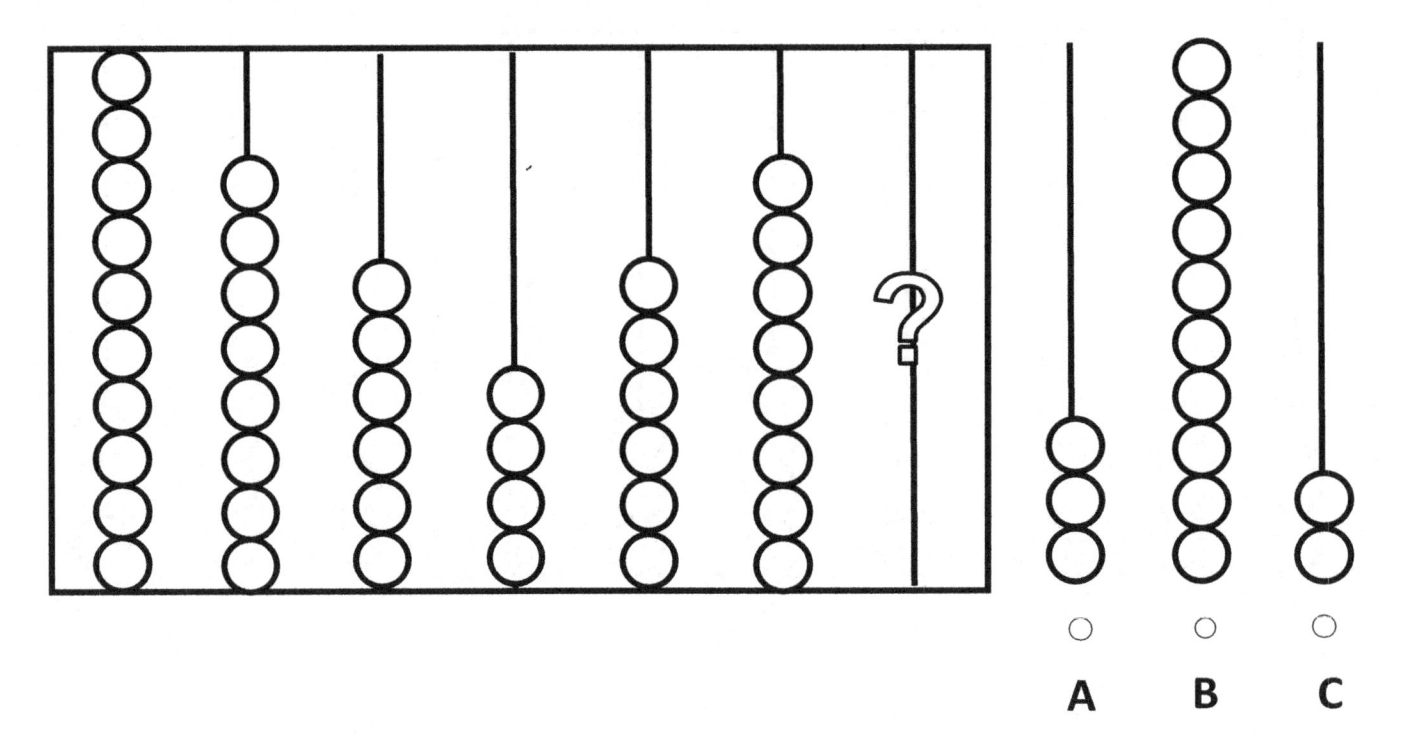

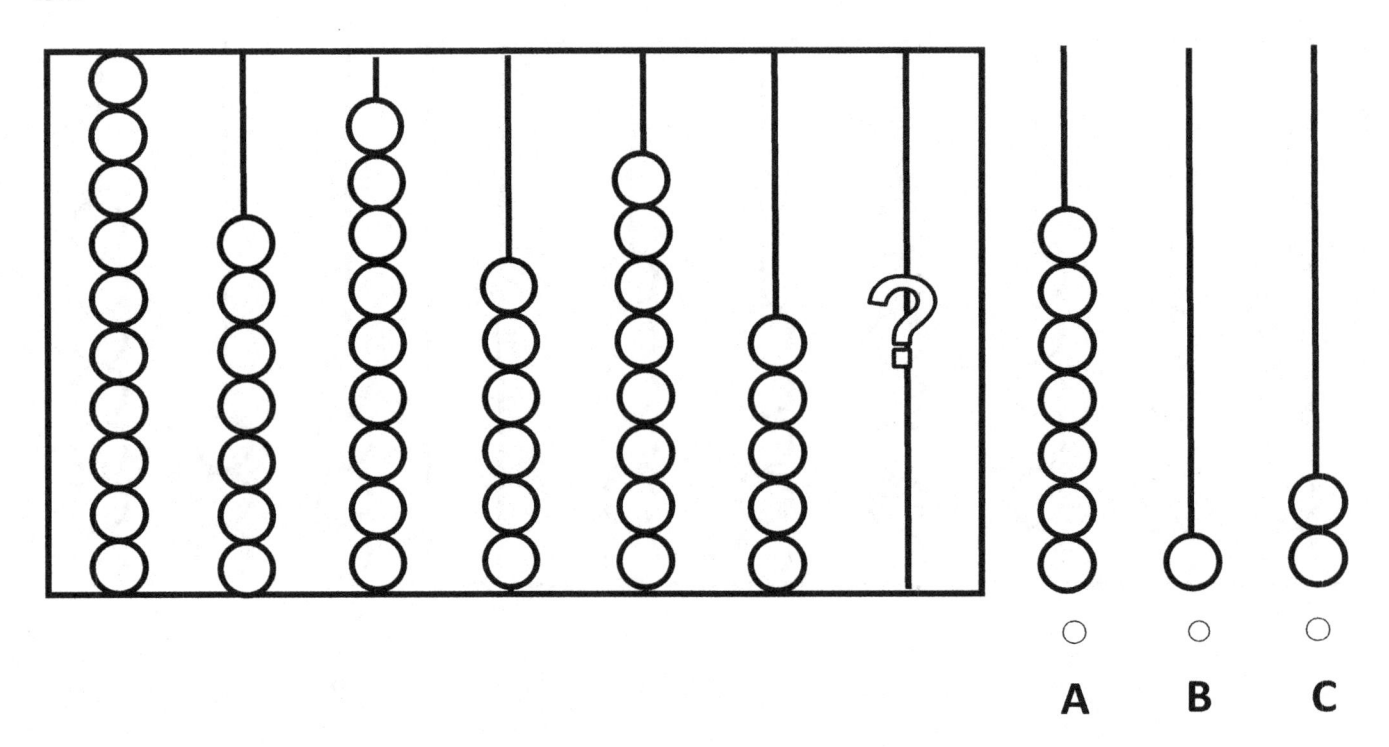

PRACTICE TEST GRADE 1

7.

8.

108

PRACTICE TEST GRADE 1

9.

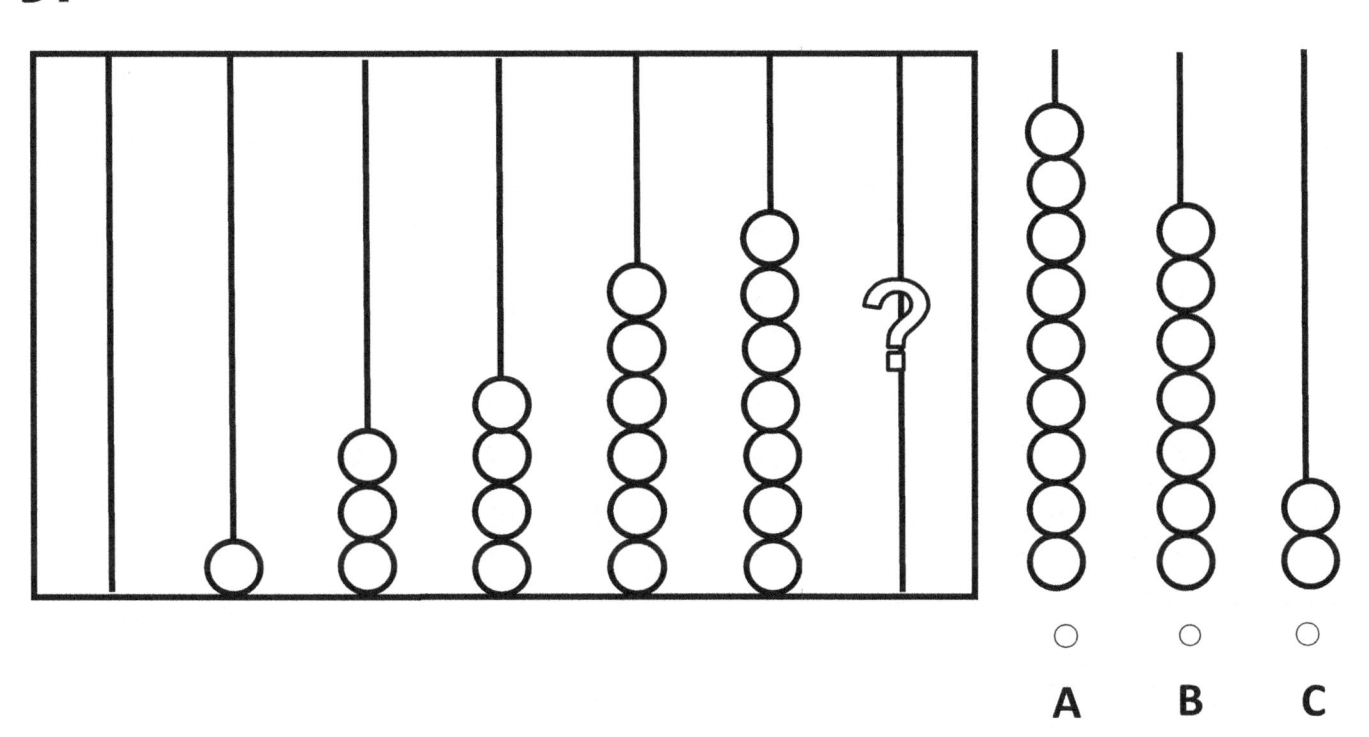

10.

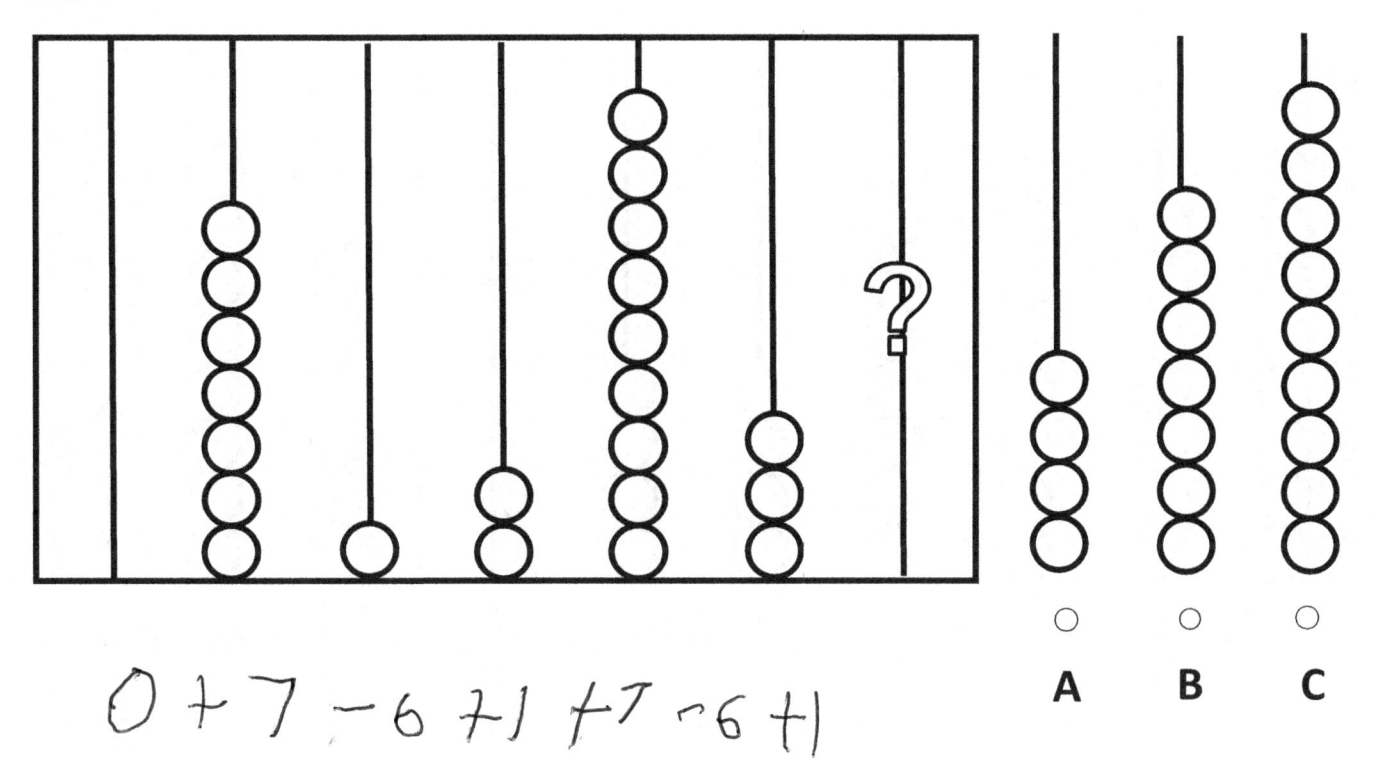

0 +7 -6 +1 +7 -6 +1

109

PRACTICE TEST GRADE 1

11.

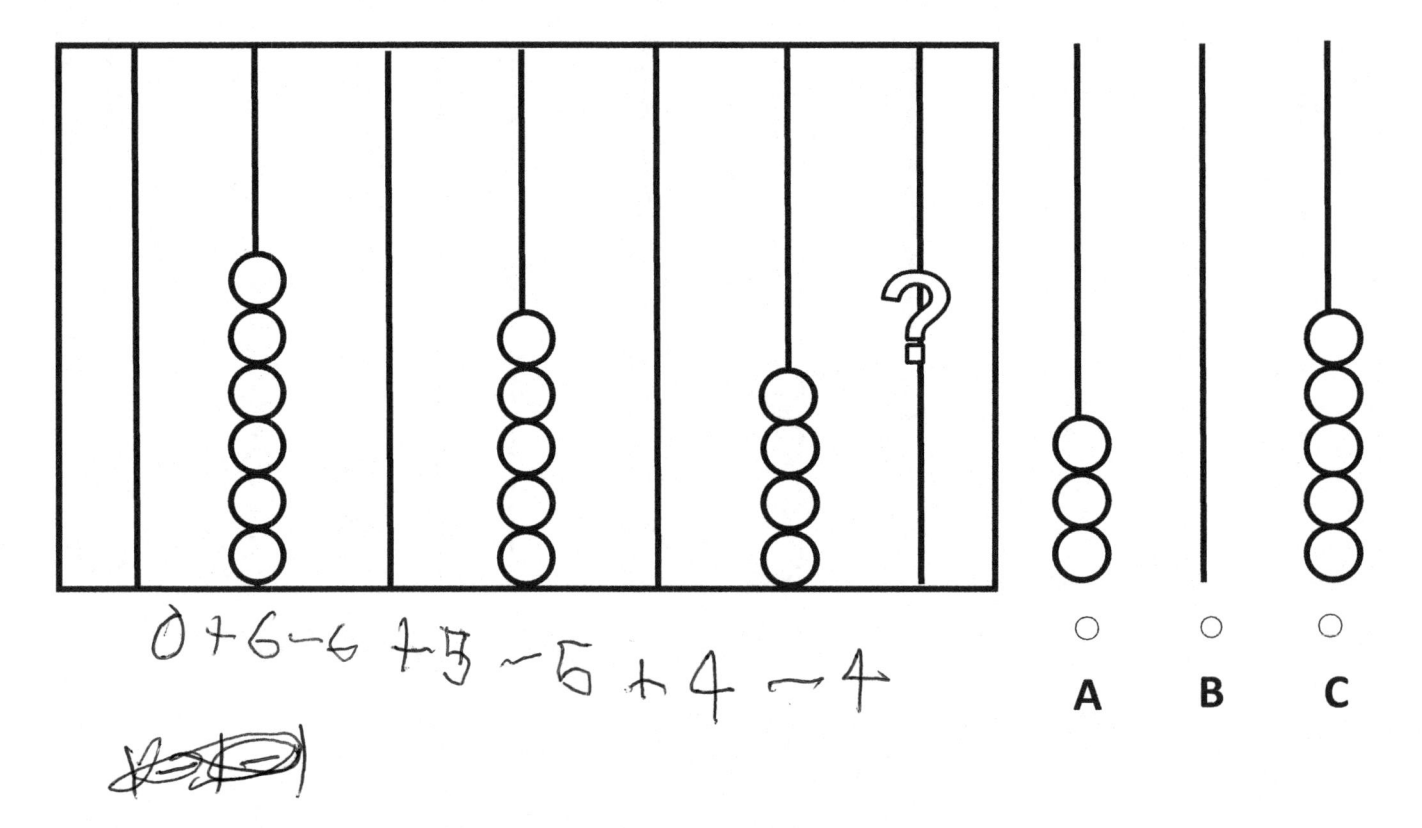

0+6-6 +5 -5 +4 -4

12.

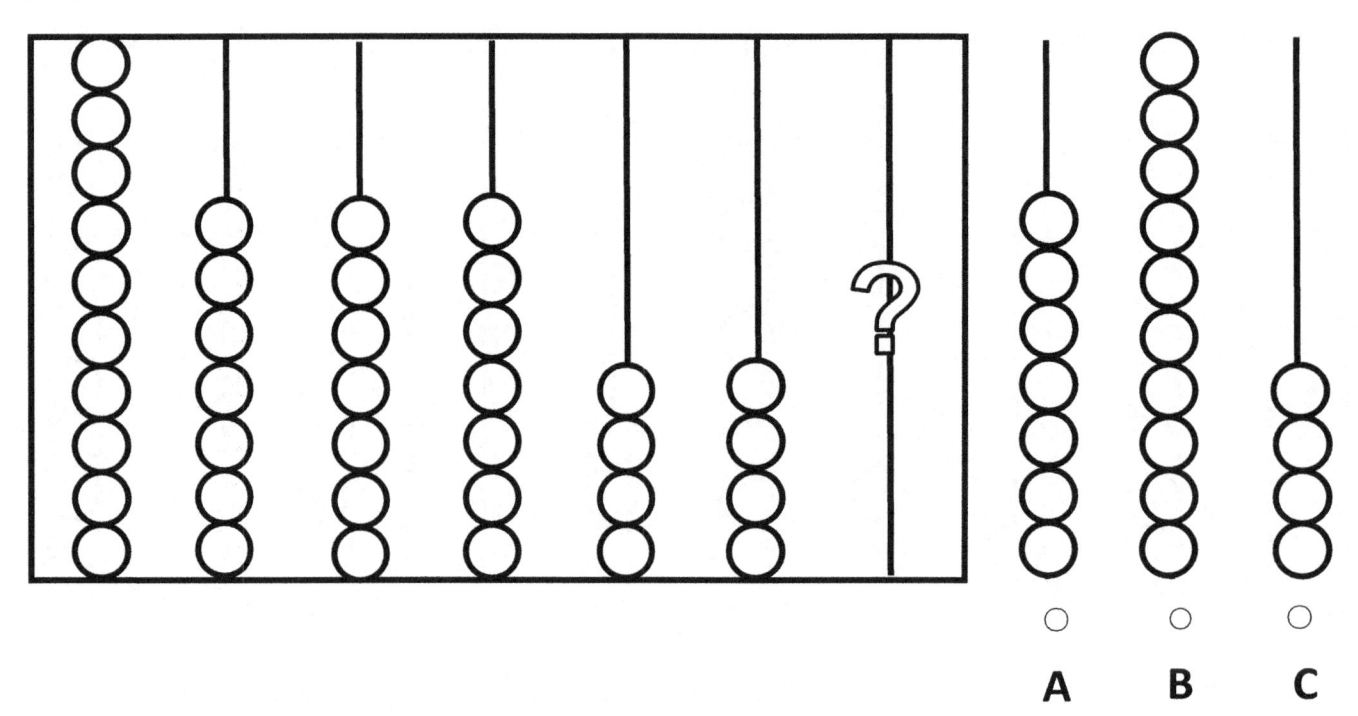

PRACTICE TEST GRADE 1

13.

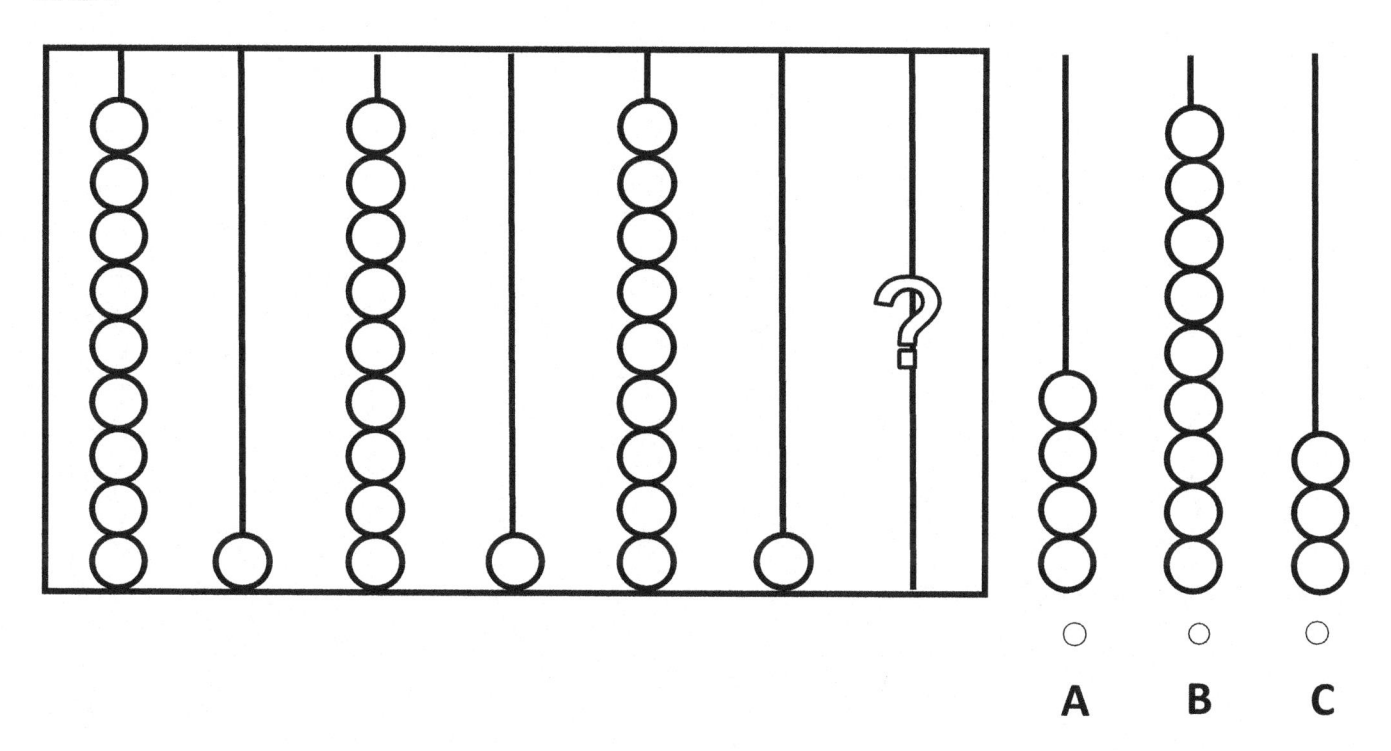

14.

111

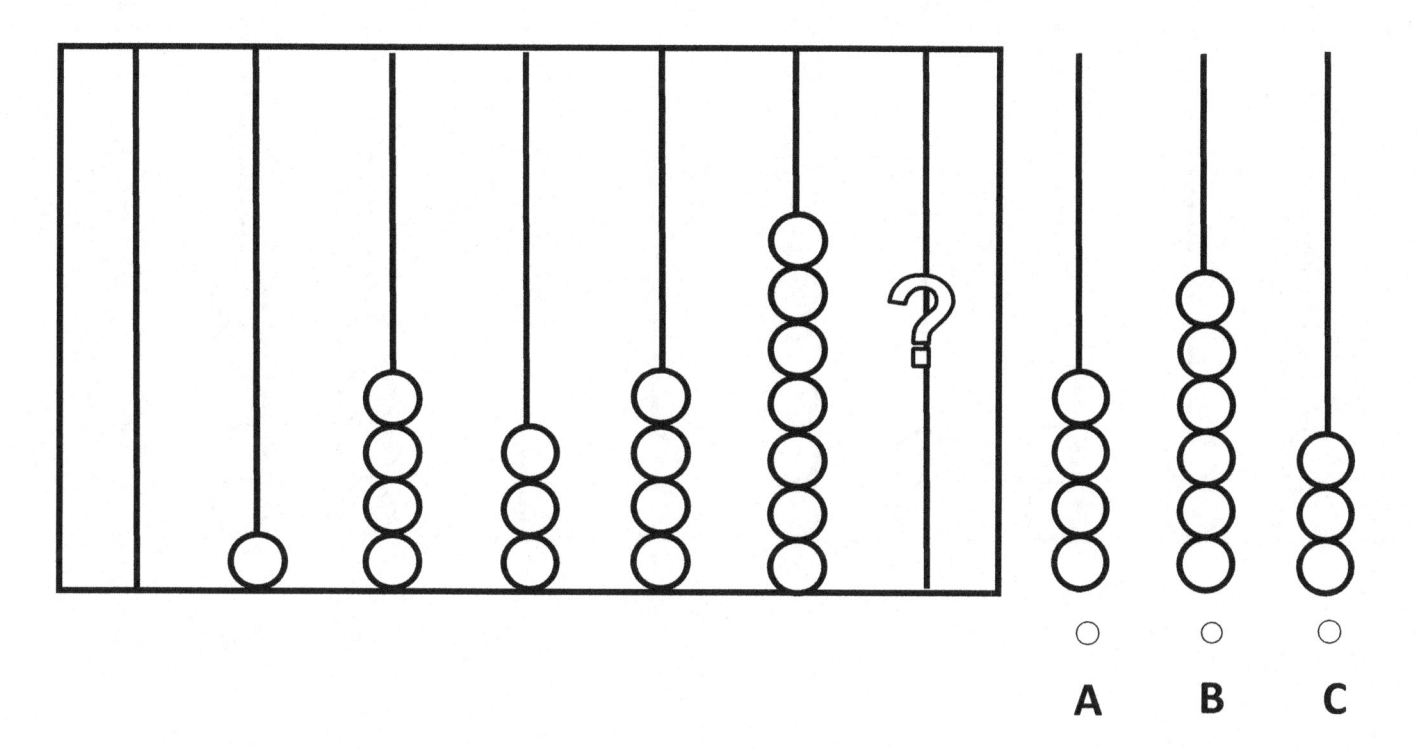

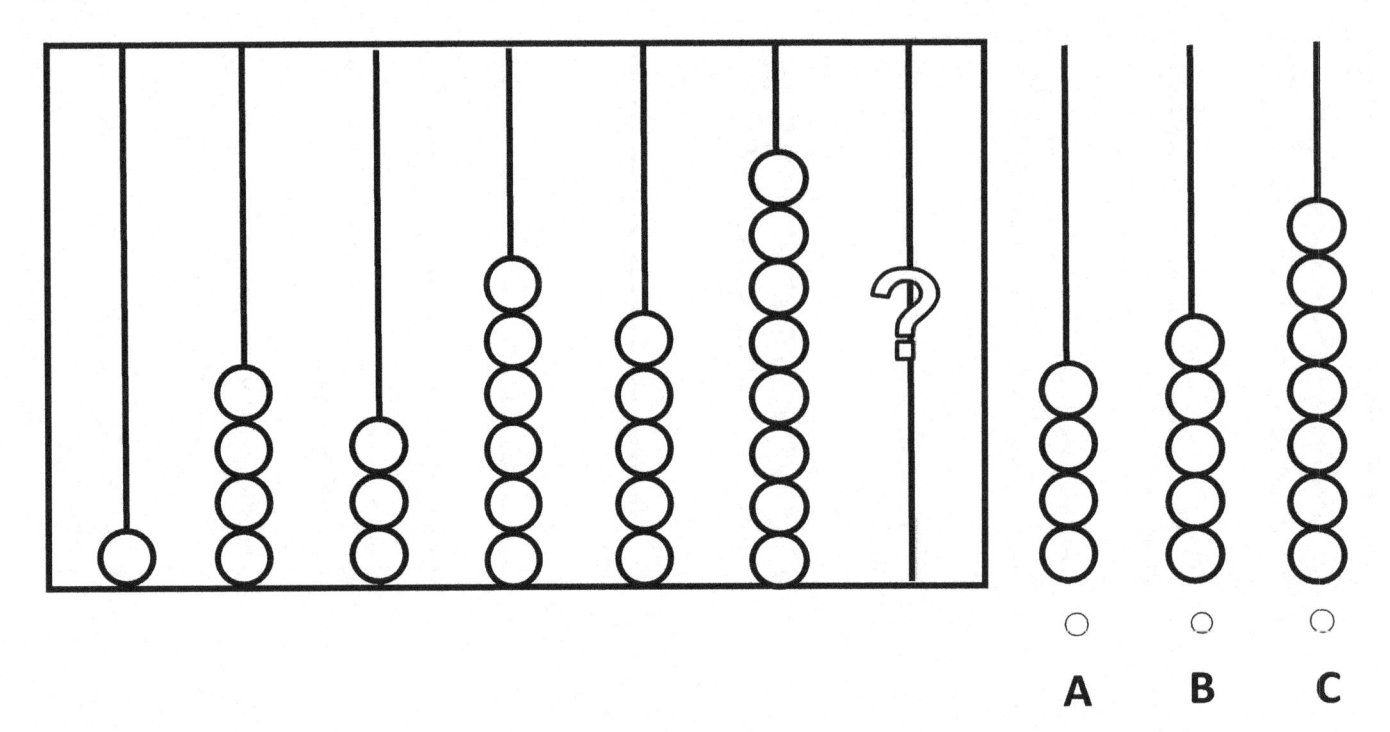

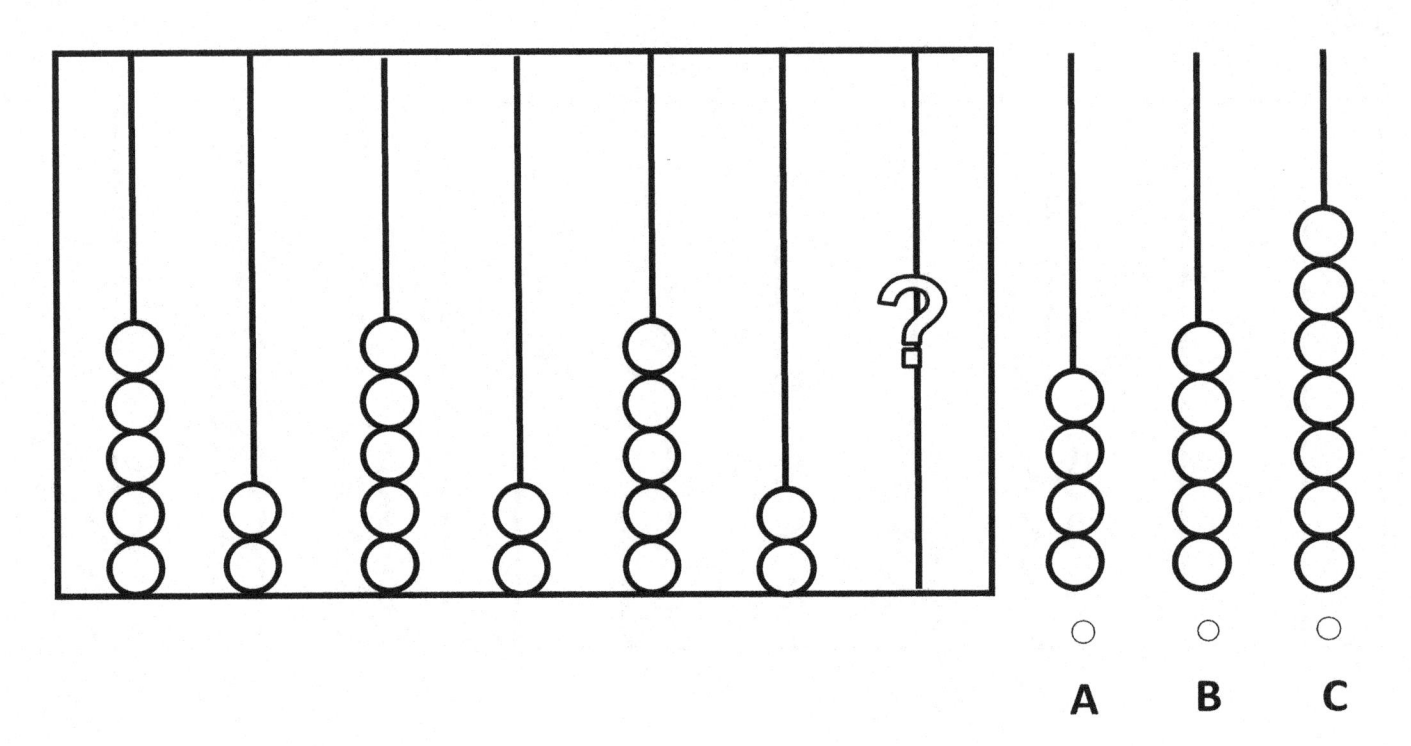

PRACTICE TEST GRADE 1

15.

16.

112

ANSWER KEY GRADE 1

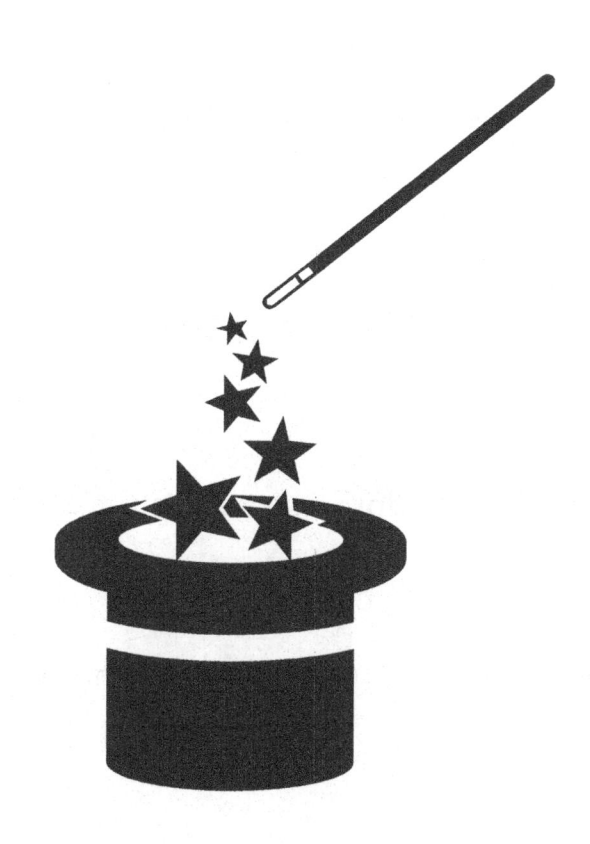

ANSWER KEY GRADE 1

Picture Analogies Practice Test
p.20

1.
Answer: option B
Explanation: T-Rex was a carnivorous dinosaur; Apatosaurus was an herbivorous dinosaur.

2.
Answer: option C
Explanation: Guns throw bullets; bows throw arrows.

3.
Answer: option B
Explanation: The Moon rotates around the Earth; the Earth rotates around the Sun.

4.
Answer: option A
Explanation: The figures on the left rotate by 90 degrees counterclockwise.

5.
Answer: option B
Explanation: Lipstick is for lips; mascara is for eyes.

6.
Answer: option A
Explanation: The remote control is used for the television; the mouse is used for the computer.

7.
Answer: option B
Explanation: Trains move on the rails; cars move on the road.

8.
Answer: option C
Explanation: To wash your hands, you use soap; to brush your teeth, you use toothpaste.

ANSWER KEY GRADE 1

9.
Answer: option B
Explanation: Fins are used to the sea; skis are used in the mountains.

10.
Answer: option B
Explanation: Dogs love bones; rabbits love carrots.

11.
Answer: option A
Explanation: Snowmen are made of snow; sweaters are made of wool.

12.
Answer: option A
Explanation: Doctors use stethoscopes; cooks use knives.

13.
Answer: option B
Explanation: Books are put in libraries; money is put in strongboxes.

14.
Answer: option A
Explanation: The basic shape of the Pyramid is the triangle; the basic shape of the cube is the square.

15.
Answer: option A
Explanation: The vehicle of an alien is the flying saucer; the vehicle of an astronaut is the rocket.

16.
Answer: option B
Explanation: The plug must be inserted into the socket; the key must be inserted into the lock.

ANSWER KEY GRADE 1

Picture Classification Practice Test
p.30

1.
Answer: option B
Explanation: Swimsuit, flippers, swimming goggles and life buoy are used at the sea.

2.
Answer: option C
Explanation: Helicopters, airplanes, rockets, and hot air balloons fly in the sky.

3.
Answer: option A
Explanation: Teddy bear, rocking horse, block cube, and spinning top are children's toys.

4.
Answer: option C
Explanation: Steering wheel, tire, car key, and wiper are parts of a car.

5.
Answer: option A
Explanation: Football helmet, baseball hat, woolen hat, and chef's hat are all headgear.

6.
Answer: option B
Explanation: Eyeglasses, telescopes, cameras, and microscopes are used with the eyes.

7.
Answer: option B
Explanation: Hands, eyes, ears, and feet are parts of the body.

8.
Answer: option A
Explanation: Drums, bells, trumpets, and doorbells emit sounds.

ANSWER KEY GRADE 1

9.
Answer: option C
Explanation: Tennis rackets, baseball bats, balls and skis are sports equipment.

10.
Answer: option B
Explanation: The drill, refrigerator, lamp, and television work with electricity.

11.
Answer: option C
Explanation: Chairs, stools, armchairs, and sleds are objects on which you can sit.

12.
Answer: option B
Explanation: Elephants, sheep, cows, and reindeer are herbivorous animals.

13.
Answer: option A
Explanation: Soup, water, milk and wine are liquids.

14.
Answer: option C
Explanation: Spider webs, nests, hives, and anthills are structures created by animals.

15.
Answer: option C
Explanation: Witches, pumpkins, bats, and ghosts are typical characters of the Halloween party.

16.
Answer: option B
Explanation: Eyes, hands, ears, and nose belong to the upper body.

Sentence Completion Practice Test

p.41

1.
Answer: option C
Explanation: Hatchet can be used to cut a log.

2.
Answer: option B
Explanation: The stool is used to sit on.

3.
Answer: option A
Explanation: Toilet paper is not stored in the kitchen.

4.
Answer: option C
Explanation: Tyrannosaurus Rex was a reptile.

5.
Answer: option A
Explanation: Mary will use a leash.

6.
Answer: option B
Explanation: Sheep is not a wild animal.

7.
Answer: option C
Explanation: Image C shows a chef at work.

8.
Answer: option A
Explanation: Image A shows less than 4 fruits. Image C does not show a fruit but a mushroom.

ANSWER KEY GRADE 1

9.
Answer: option B
Explanation: Mommy won't need ham.

10.
Answer: option A
Explanation: Image A shows an apple on a table.

11.
Answer: option A
Explanation: Mike will not need a swimsuit.

12.
Answer: option A
Explanation: Image A does not show a part of a house but a tree.

13.
Answer: option C
Explanation: Oscar will not need television.

14.
Answer: option A
Explanation: The camel is not a jumping animal.

15.
Answer: option C
Explanation: Grape is needed to make wine.

16.
Answer: option A
Explanation: Mary will not meet a reindeer.

ANSWER KEY GRADE 1

Figure Matrices Practice Test
p.60

1.
Answer: option B
Explanation: Larger shapes are removed; inside shapes become white.

2.
Answer: option C
Explanation: Arrows double, rotate by 90 degrees clockwise, and keep the same color as the respective figures on the left.

3.
Answer: option B
Explanation: The figure on the left turns black and a white heart appears above it.

4.
Answer: option A
Explanation: The arrow turns white and moves up over the left figure.

5.
Answer: option C
Explanation: The top circle is removed.

6.
Answer: option B
Explanation: Addiction of a smaller white shape inside the figure on the left

7.
Answer: option A
Explanation: The figure on the right disappears and the figure on the left rotates by 180 degrees clockwise.

8.
Answer: option C
Explanation: The larger figure disappears. The smaller shape rotates by 45 degrees clockwise.

ANSWER KEY GRADE 1

9.
Answer: option A
Explanation: The larger figure becomes the smaller one and vice versa.

10.
Answer: option B
Explanation: The right arrow is removed.

11.
Answer: option C
Explanation: Both figures on the left rotate by 90 degrees clockwise.

12.
Answer: option A
Explanation: The upper shape becomes black; the lower shape becomes white and rotates by 180 degrees clockwise.

13.
Answer: option B
Explanation: The shape on the right is placed above the left one.

14.
Answer: option B
Explanation: The lower figure is removed.

15.
Answer: option C
Explanation: The shape inside the top figure is eliminated. The 2 remaining figures are overturned.

16.
Answer: option A
Explanation: The figure at the top changes place with the figure at the bottom. The figure in the middle does not move.

ANSWER KEY GRADE 1

Figure Classification Practice Test
p.70

1.
Answer: option A
Explanation: Arrows in the same size, pointing down.

2.
Answer: option A
Explanation: Circles are divided into two equal parts.

3.
Answer: option B
Explanation: White triangles.

4.
Answer: option C
Explanation: Cubes of the same size and colors.

5.
Answer: option C
Explanation: ¾ of a circle in white color.

6.
Answer: option C
Explanation: 2 rectangles placed horizontally in the same size.

7.
Answer: option A
Explanation: 2 squares with a dashed outline and 1 square with a regular outline.

8.
Answer: option B
Explanation: Combos of a black arrow and a white square.

9.
Answer: option A
Explanation: Combos of 2 white triangles.

ANSWER KEY GRADE 1

10.
Answer: option C
Explanation: Combos of 2 brackets and 2 black circles.

11.
Answer: option A
Explanation: Four-sided shapes.

12.
Answer: option B
Explanation: Two arrows pointing in the same direction.

13.
Answer: option A
Explanation: Three arrows, black, grey and white. The black arrow is always on the top.

14.
Answer: option A
Explanation: Two figures of the same type, one inside the other. The white shape is smaller.

15.
Answer: option C
Explanation: Combos of an oval shape and a black arrow.

16.
Answer: option A
Explanation: The number of lines equals the number of sides.

ANSWER KEY GRADE 1

Paper Folding Practice Test
p.79

1.
Answer: option C

2.
Answer: option C

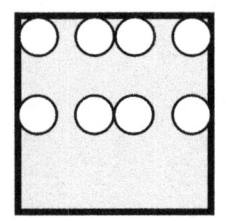

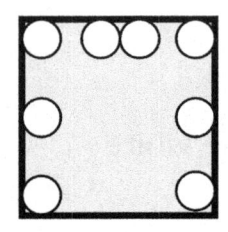

3.
Answer: option B

4.
Answer: option A

ANSWER KEY GRADE 1

5.
Answer: option B

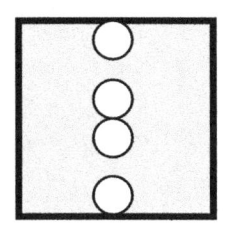

6.
Answer: option A

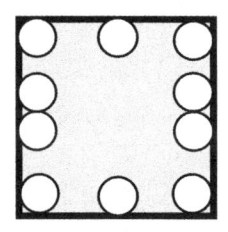

7
Answer: option A

8.
Answer: option B

9.
Answer: option A

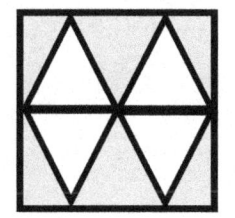

ANSWER KEY GRADE 1

10.
Answer: option C

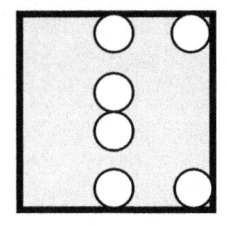

11.

Answer: option A

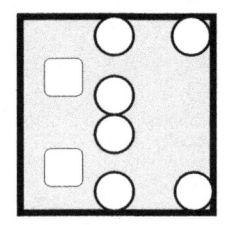

12.

Answer: option B

Number Puzzle Practice Test

p.87

1.
Answer: option A
Explanation: 3+1=4

2.
Answer: option A
Explanation: 6+6=12

3.
Answer: option C
Explanation: 4+6=10

4.
Answer: option A
Explanation: 6+5=11

5.
Answer: option B
Explanation: 2+5+1=8

6.
Answer: option A
Explanation: 2+3+3=8

7.
Answer: option A
Explanation: 8+4=12

8.
Answer: option C
Explanation: 1+2+1=4

ANSWER KEY GRADE 1

9.
Answer: option C
Explanation: 4+3+3=10

10.
Answer: option A
Explanation: 4+4+4=12

11.
Answer: option B
Explanation: 1+5+1=7

12.
Answer: option B
Explanation: 2+1+3=6

ANSWER KEY GRADE 1

Number Analogies Practice Test
p.95

1.
Answer: option A
Explanation: 1 pairs of shoes more (2 shoes more).

2.
Answer: option B
Explanation: 2 less.

3.
Answer: option A
Explanation: 5 more.

4.
Answer: option C
Explanation: 2 less.

5.
Answer: option C
Explanation: Same number of objects.

6.
Answer: option C
Explanation: 4 less.

7.
Answer: option B
Explanation: 6 more.

8.
Answer: option A
Explanation: 1 less.

9.
Answer: option B
Explanation: 7 less.

ANSWER KEY GRADE 1

10.
Answer: option C
Explanation: 5 more.

11.
Answer: option A
Explanation: 9 less.

12.
Answer: option C
Explanation: 6 more.

13.
Answer: option A
Explanation: 2 pairs of shoes less (4 shoes less).

14.
Answer: option C
Explanation: 4 more.

15.
Answer: option B
Explanation: 2 more.

16.
Answer: option A
Explanation: 6 less.

Number Series Practice Test
p.105

1.
Answer: option C
Explanation: +1 +0, +1, +0, +1, +0, etc.
1+1=2; 2+0=2; 2+1=3; 3+0=3; 3+1=4; 4+0=4

2.
Answer: option B
Explanation: +1, +1, +0, +1, +1, +0, etc.

3.
Answer: option B
Explanation: -4,+4,-4,+4,-4,+4, etc.

4.
Answer: option B
Explanation: -3, -3, -3, +3, +3, +3, etc.

5.
Answer: option A
Explanation: -1, -1, +1, +1, -1, -1, etc.

6.
Answer: option C
Explanation: -2, +1, +1, -2, +1, +1, etc.

7.
Answer: option B
Explanation: -2, -2, -2, +2, +2, +2, etc.

8.
Answer: option A
Explanation: -3, +2, -3, +2, -3, +2, etc.

9.
Answer: option A
Explanation: +1, +2, +1, +2, +1, +2, etc.

ANSWER KEY GRADE 1

10.
Answer: option A
Explanation: +7, -6, +1, +7, -6, +1, etc.

11.
Answer: option B
Explanation: +6, -6, +5, -5, +4, -4, etc.

12.
Answer: option C
Explanation: -3, +0, +0, -3, +0, +0, etc.

13.
Answer: option B
Explanation: -8, +8, -8, +8, -8, +8, etc.

14.
Answer: option B
Explanation: +1, +3, -1, +1, +3, -1 etc.

15.
Answer: option C
Explanation: +3, -1, +3, -1, +3, -1, etc.

16.
Answer: option B
Explanation: -3, +3, -3, +3, -3, +3 etc.

THANK YOU PAGE GRADE 1

HOW TO DOWNLOAD 54 BONUS QUESTIONS

Thank you for reading this book, we hope you really enjoyed it and found it very helpful.

PLEASE LEAVE US A REVIEW ON THE WEBSITE WHERE YOU PURCHASED THIS BOOK!

By leaving a review, you give us the opportunity to improve our work.

A GIFT FOR YOU!

FREE ONLINE ACCESS TO 54 BONUS PRACTICE QUESTIONS.

Follow this link:

⬇

| https://www.skilledchildren.com/free-download-cogat-test-prep-grade-1.php |
| You will find a PDF to download: please insert this PASSWORD: 140228 |

Nicole Howard and the SkilledChildren.com Team

www.skilledchildren.com

PRACTICE TEST GRADE 2

COGAT®GRADE 2 TEST PREP

PRACTICE TEST GRADE 2

PRACTICE TEST VERBAL BATTERY

This section of the CogAT® test assesses the child's use of language, particularly the skill in identifying the correlation between words. These questions often involve the use of analogy.

137

PRACTICE TEST GRADE 2

Picture Analogies

A picture analogy traces a similarity between a pair of objects and another pair of objects.

Example

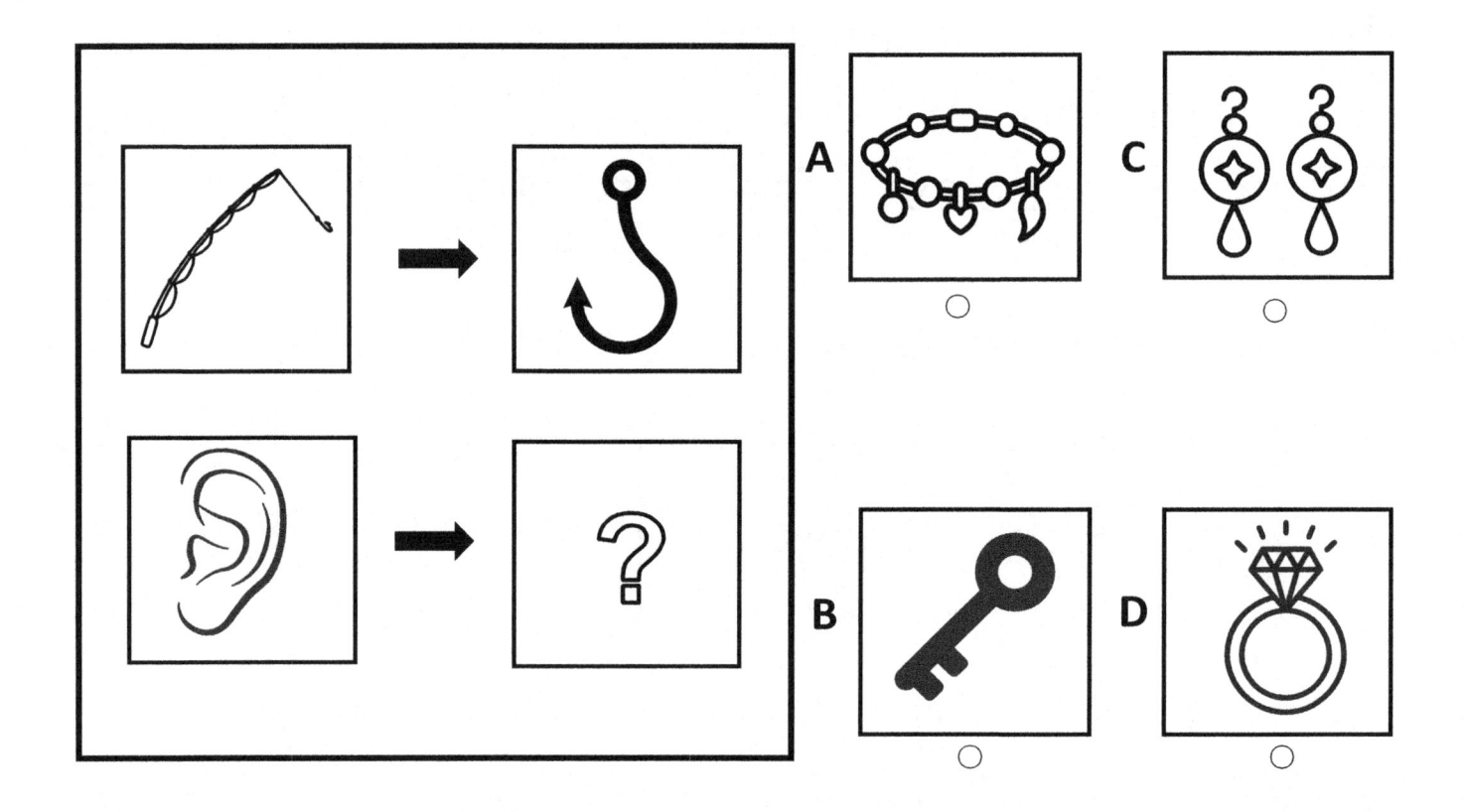

- First, identify the relationship between the first pair of objects.
- How do the objects "fishing rod" and "fishing hook" go together?

- **The fishing hook is attached to the fishing rod.**

- Now, look at the object "ear".
- Which of the possible choices follows the previous rule?

  Earrings are attached to the ear, so the correct answer is C.

Tips for Solving Picture Analogies

- Try to identify the correlation between the first two pictures.

- Review all answers before you make a choice.

- The best approach to answering questions that might seem difficult is to proceed by elimination. Only one of the given answers will be correct. In case of doubt, find out which choice is less likely to be the correct one and eliminate it. This way of proceeding will leave fewer options and make it easier to find the right one.

- Evaluate the possible alternative uses of the objects.

- Try to transform analogies into sentences that have a logical meaning.

- Finally, the best way to improve the resolution of verbal analogies is through practice.

PRACTICE TEST GRADE 2

1.

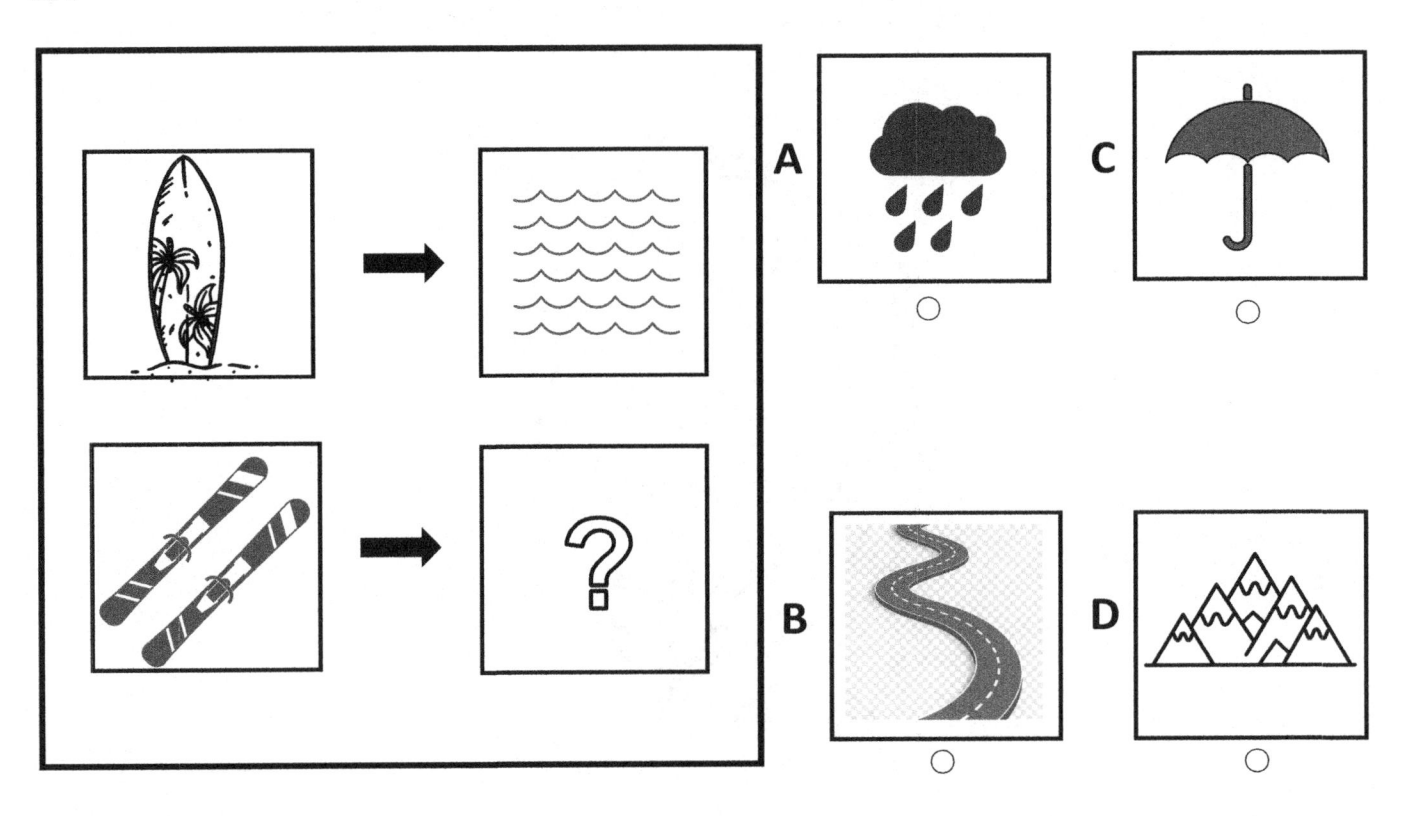

2.

140

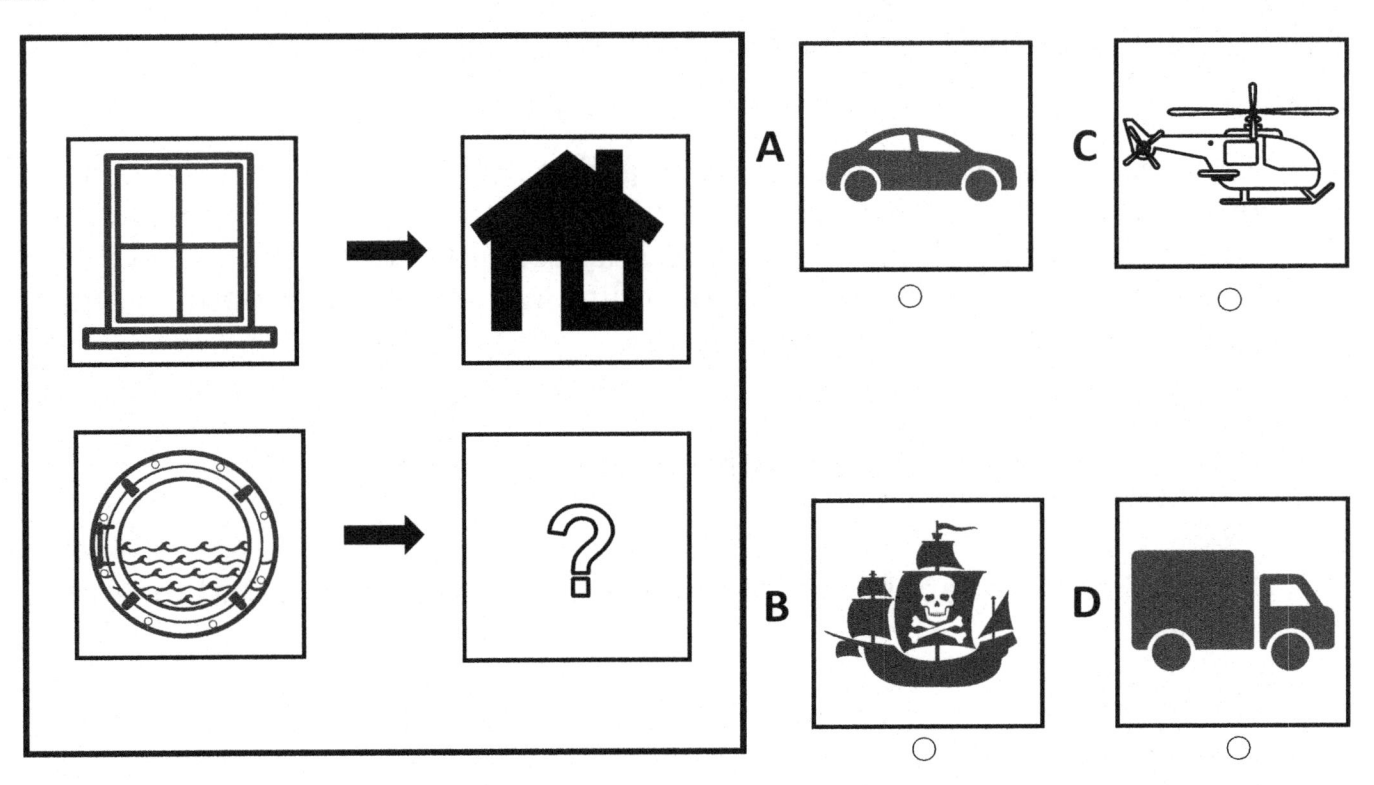

PRACTICE TEST GRADE 2

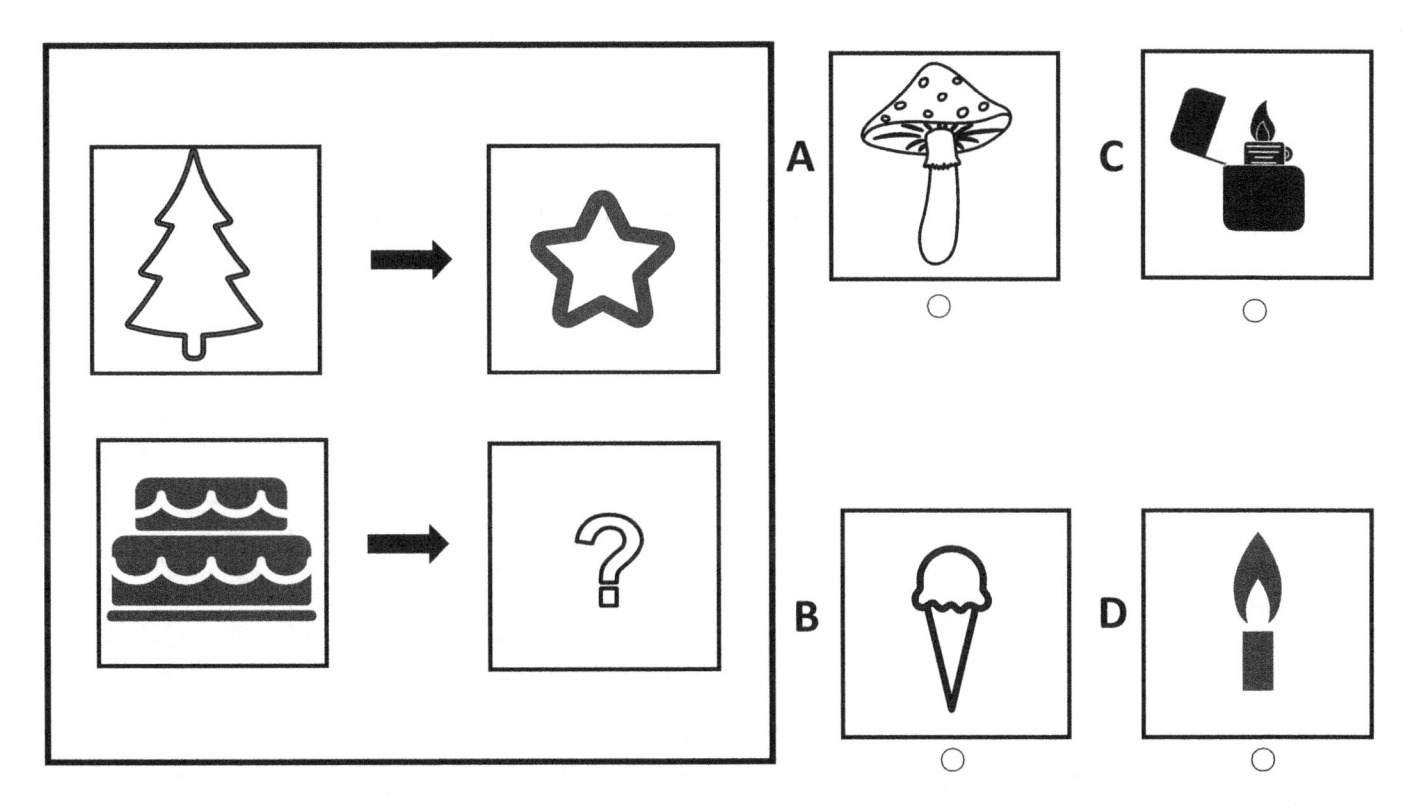

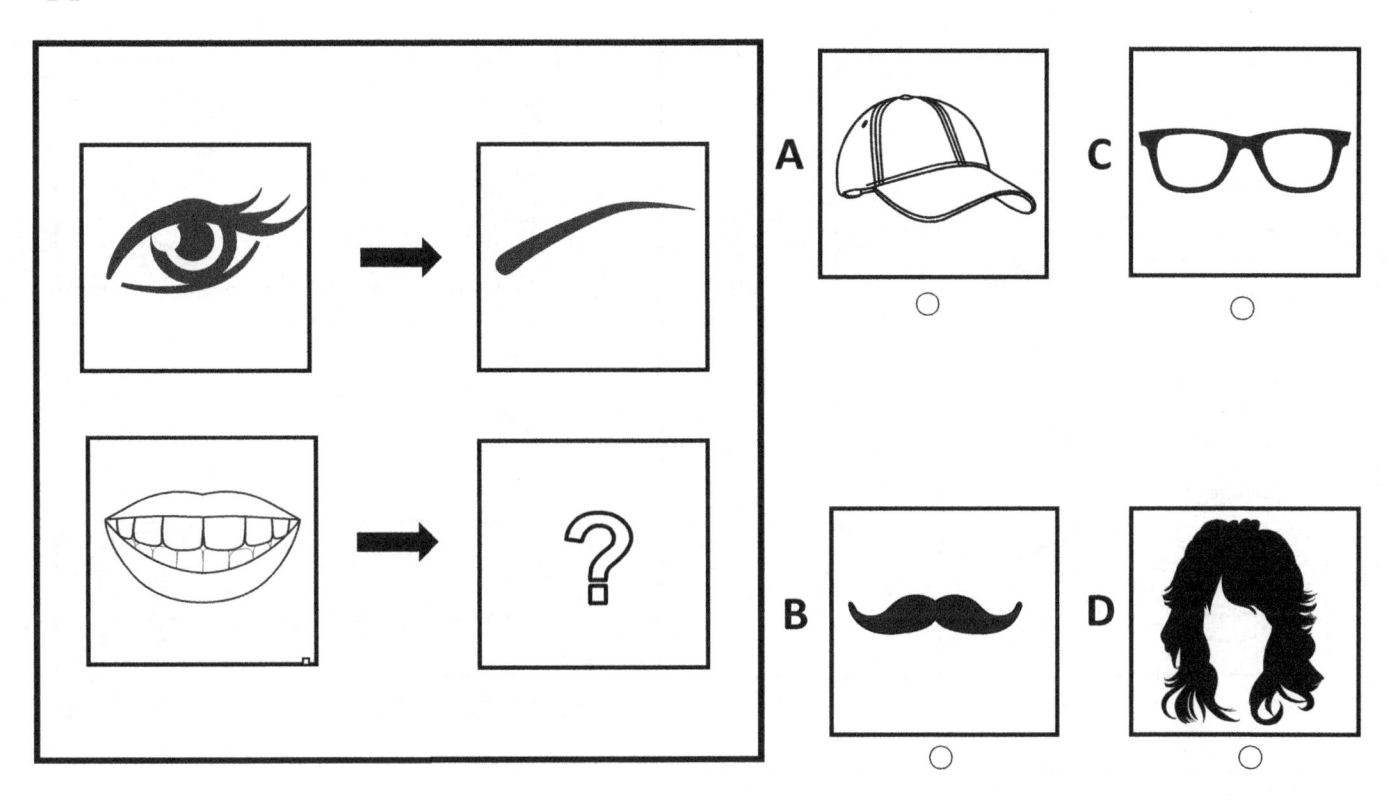

3

4.

141

PRACTICE TEST GRADE 2

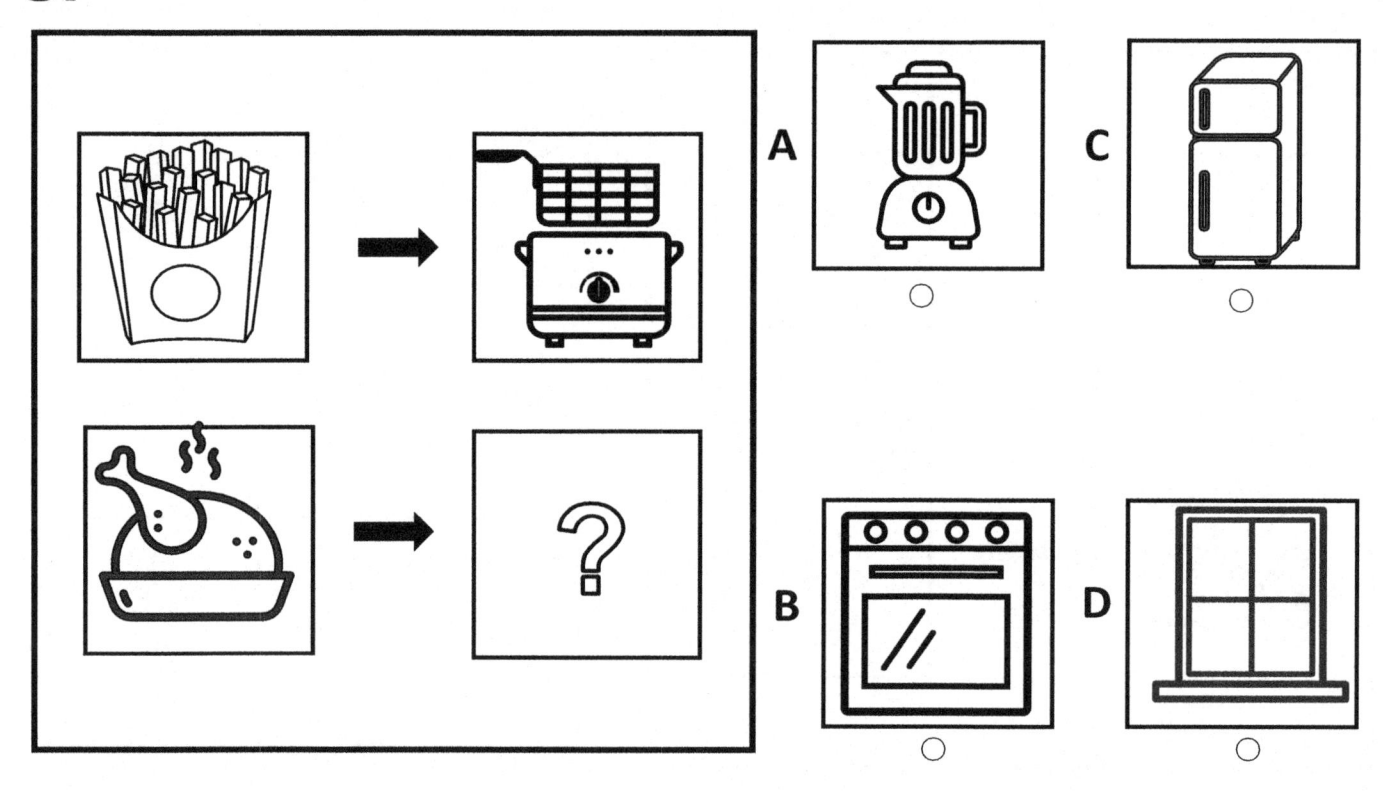

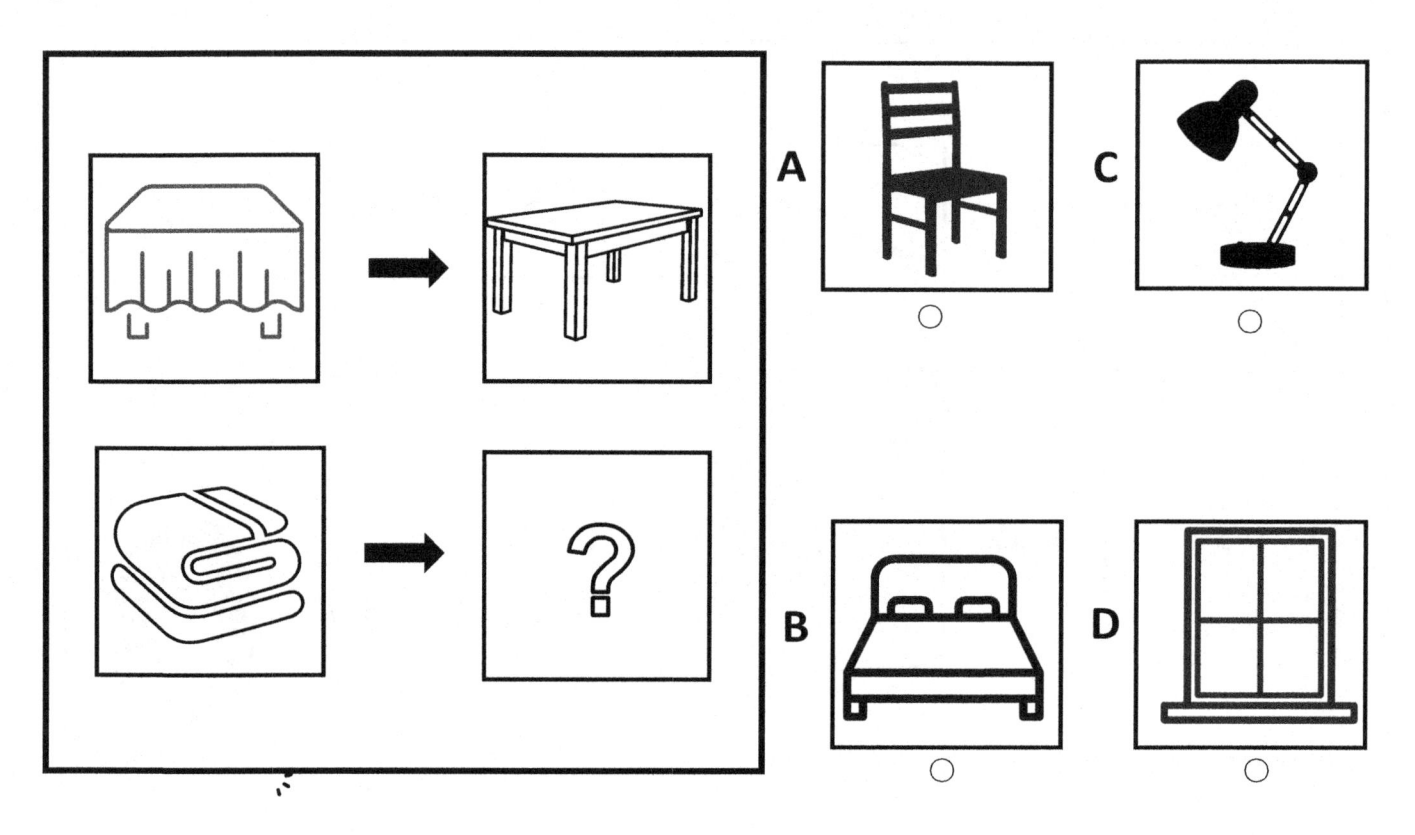

5.

6.

142

PRACTICE TEST GRADE 2

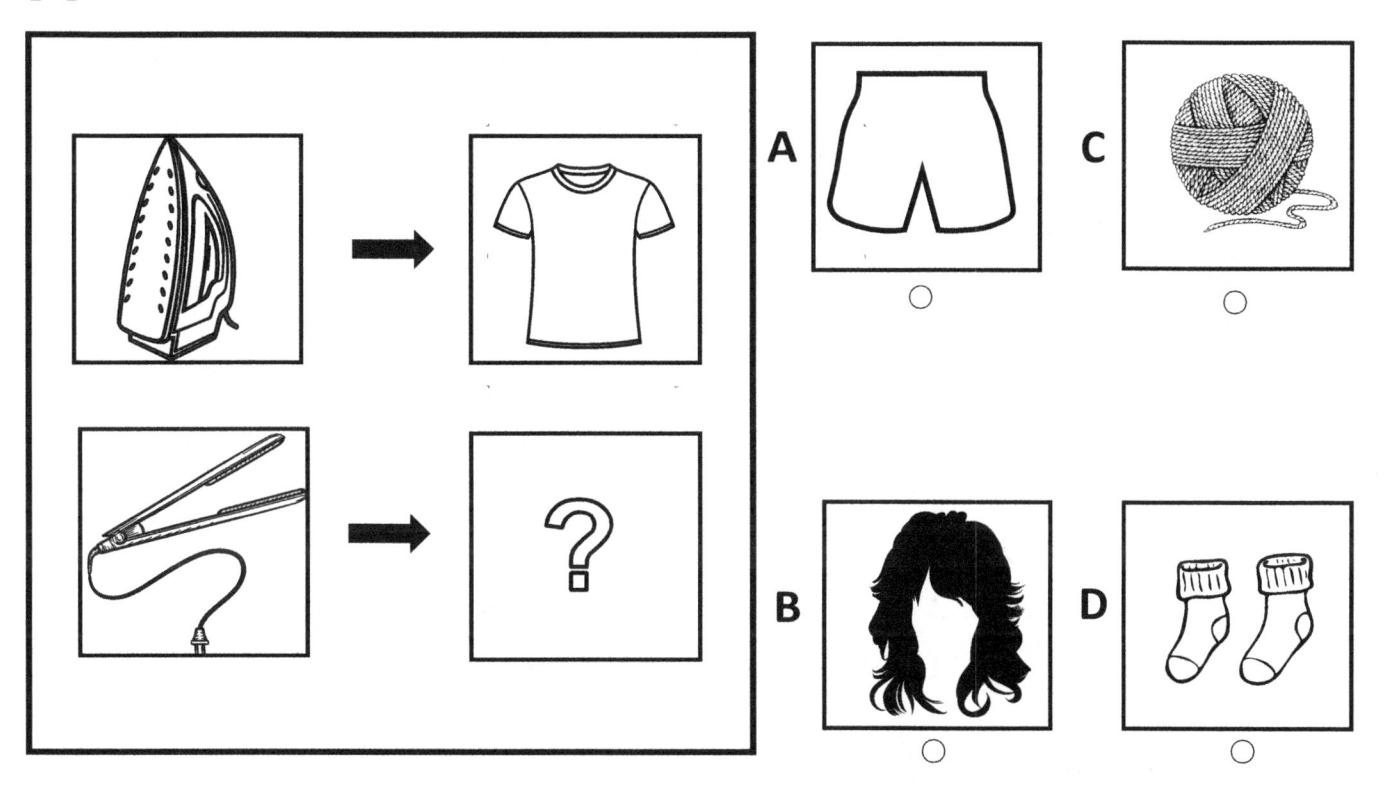

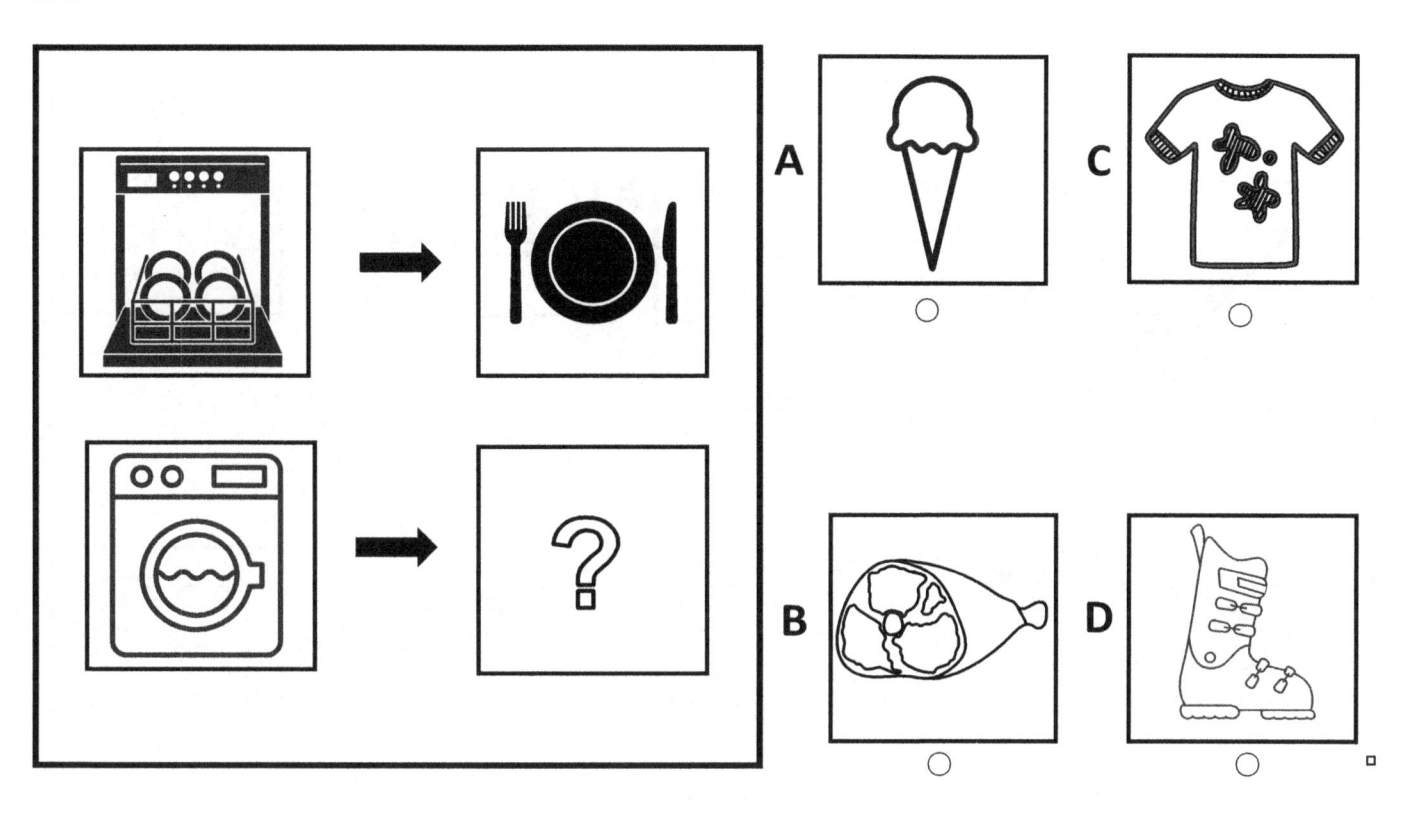

7.

8.

143

PRACTICE TEST GRADE 2

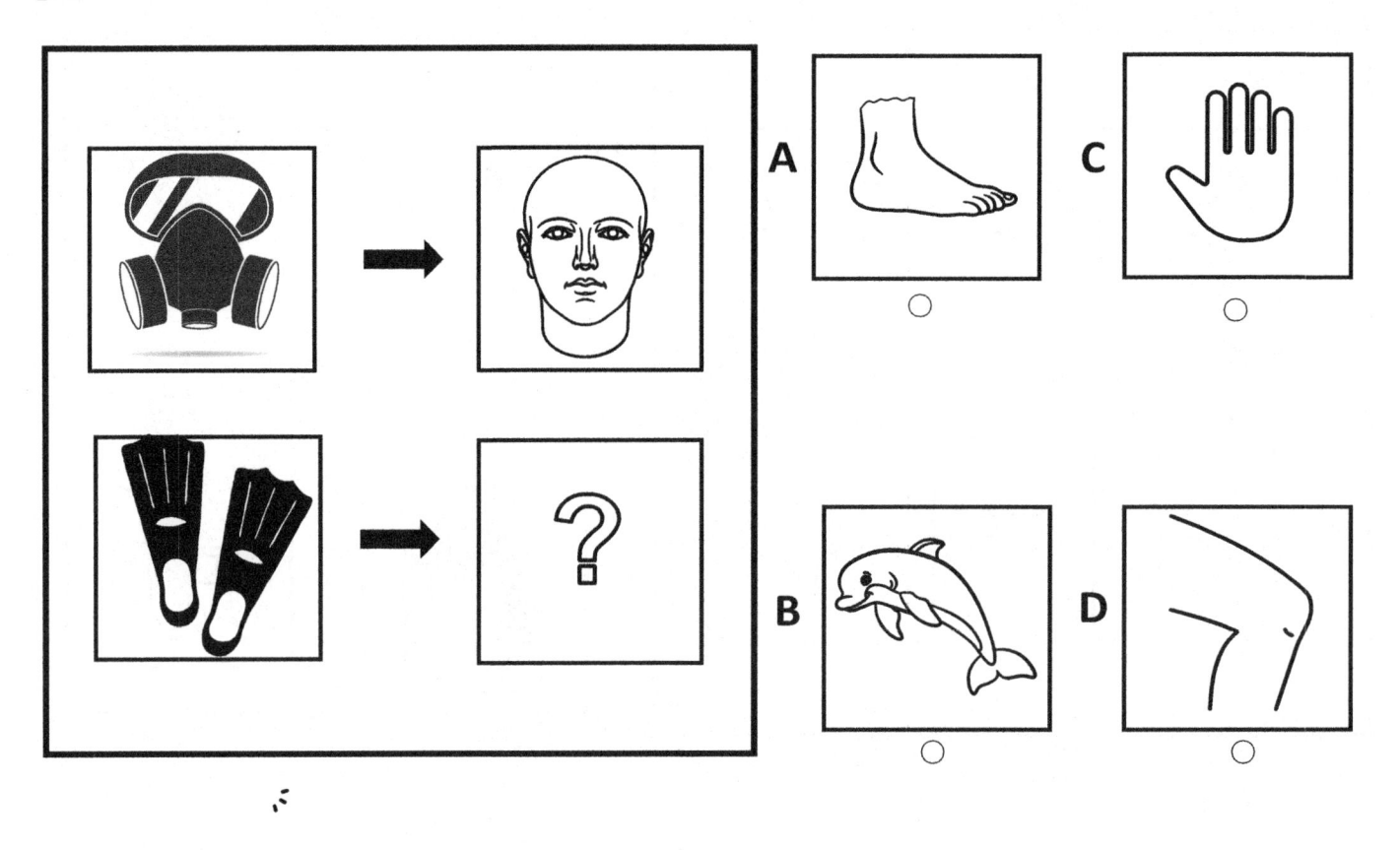

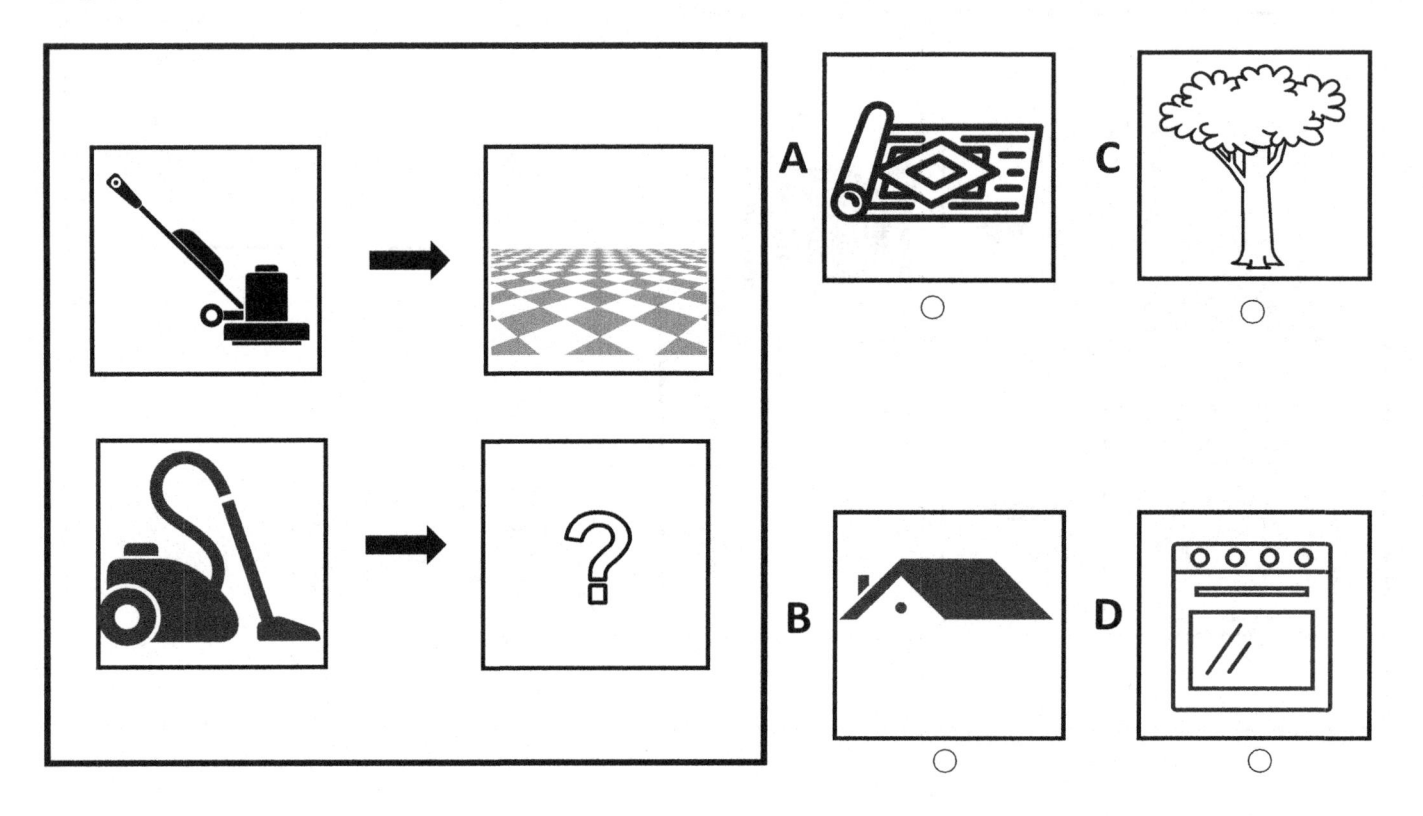

9.

10.

144

PRACTICE TEST GRADE 2

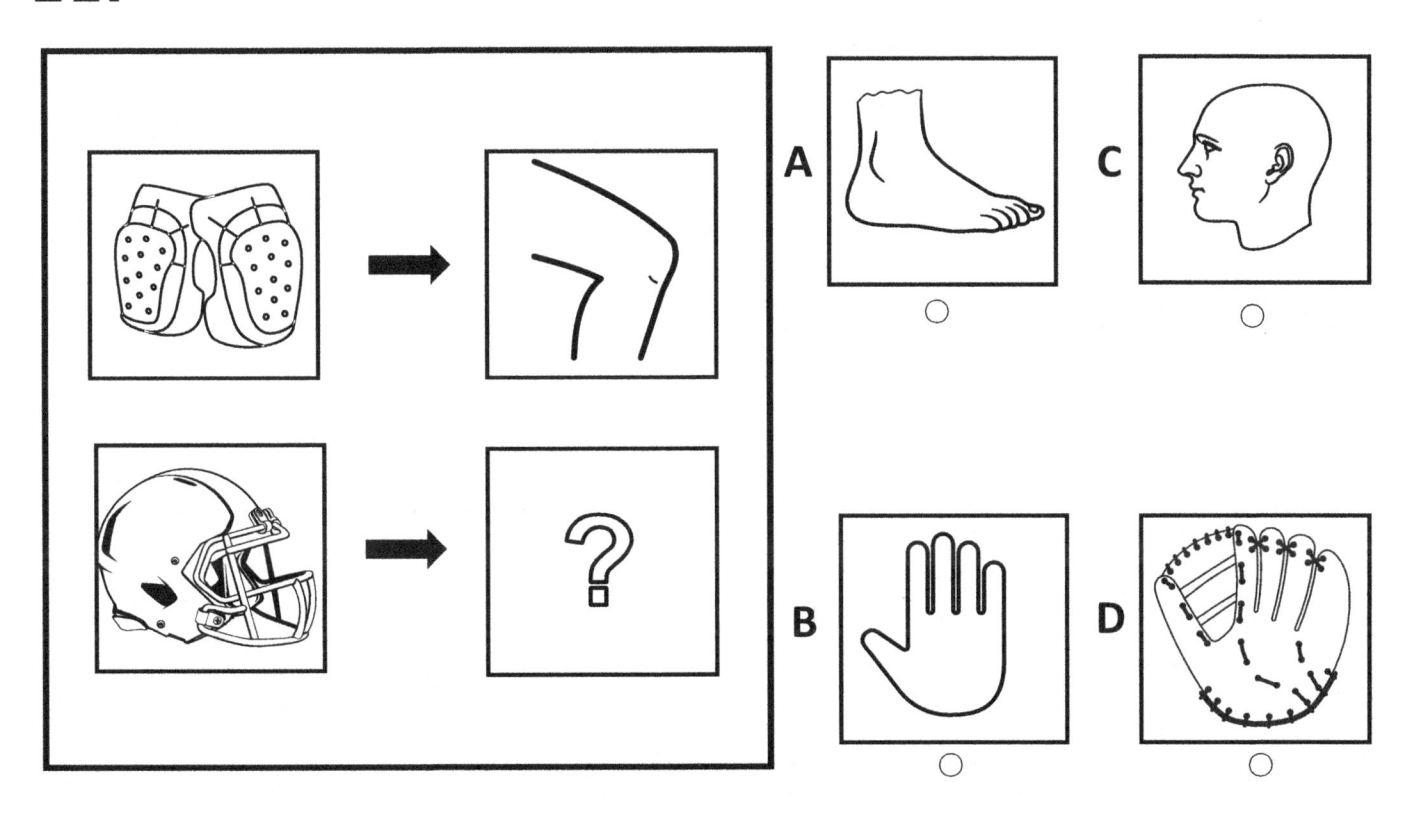

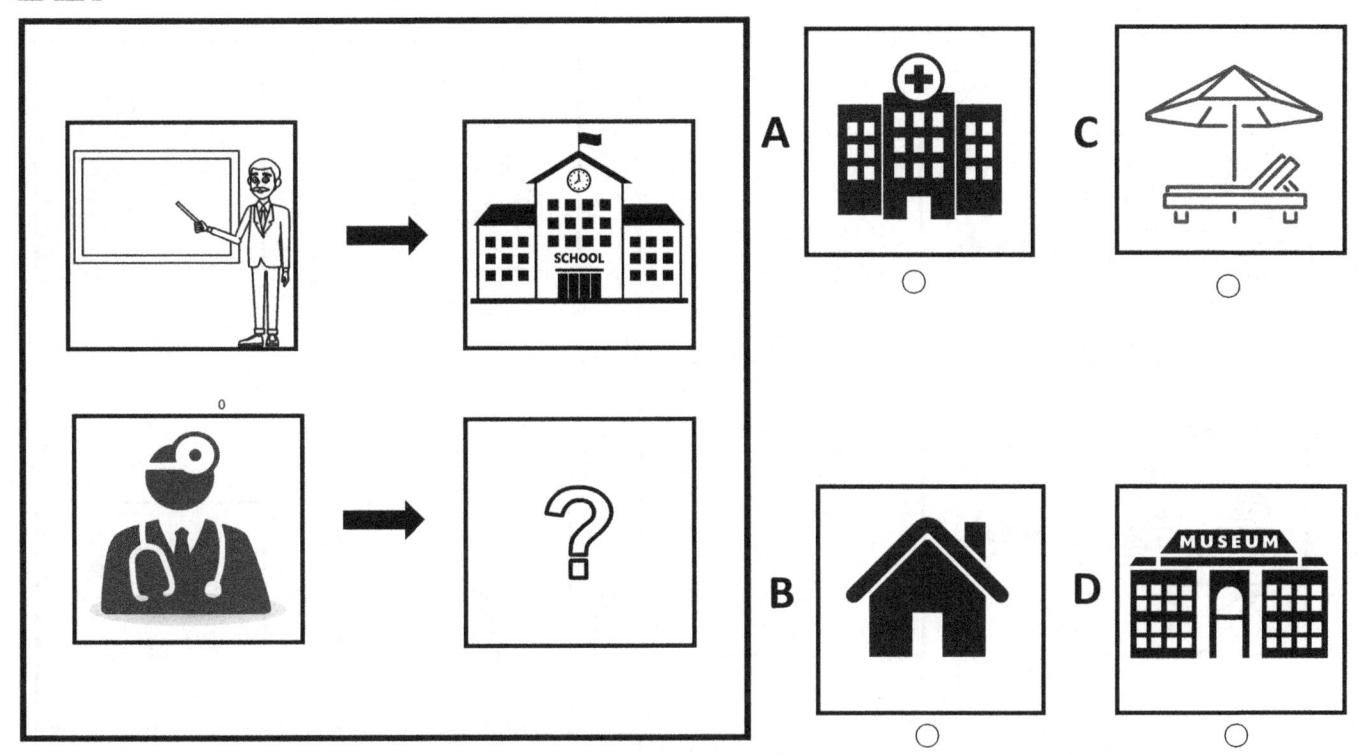

11.

12.

145

PRACTICE TEST GRADE 2

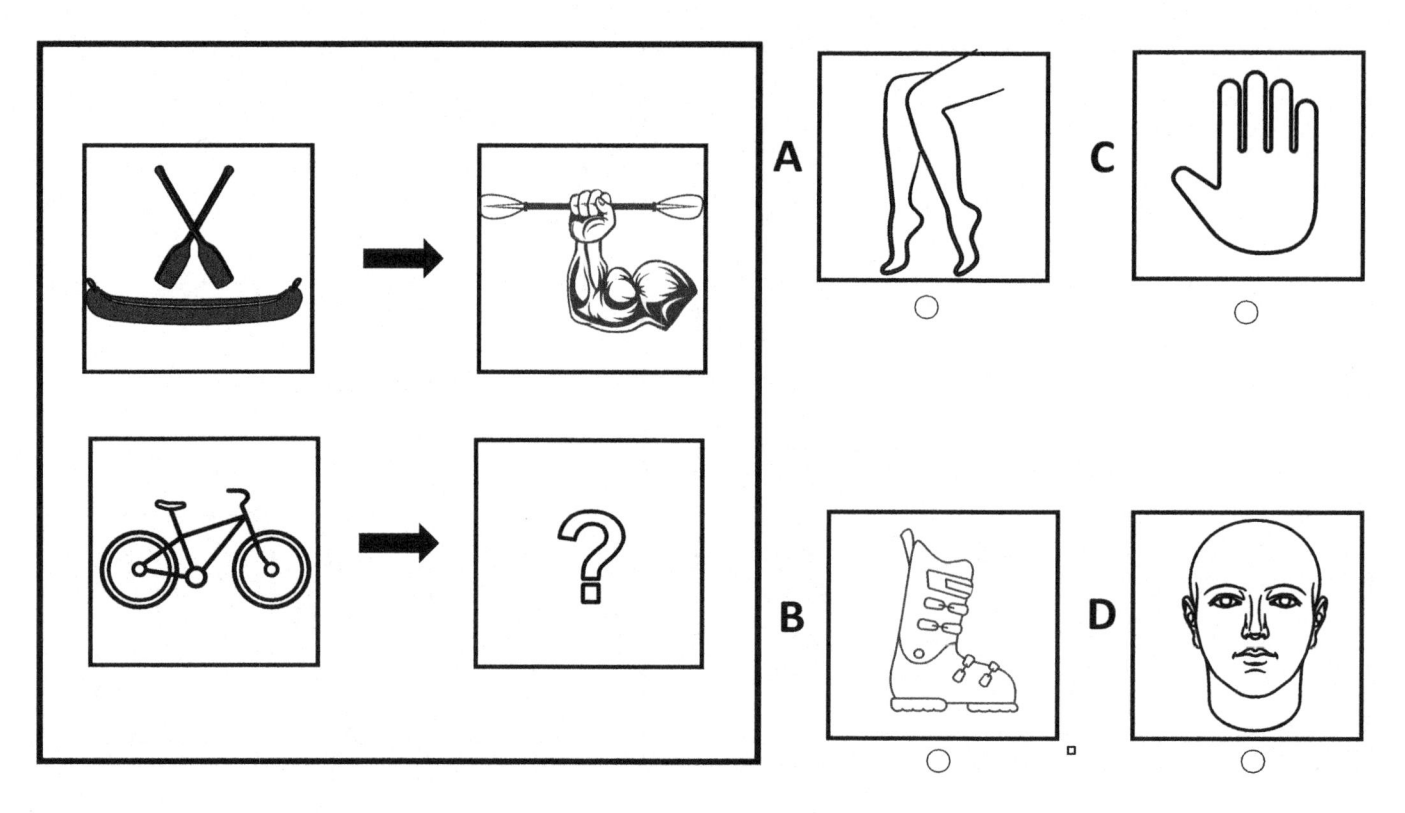

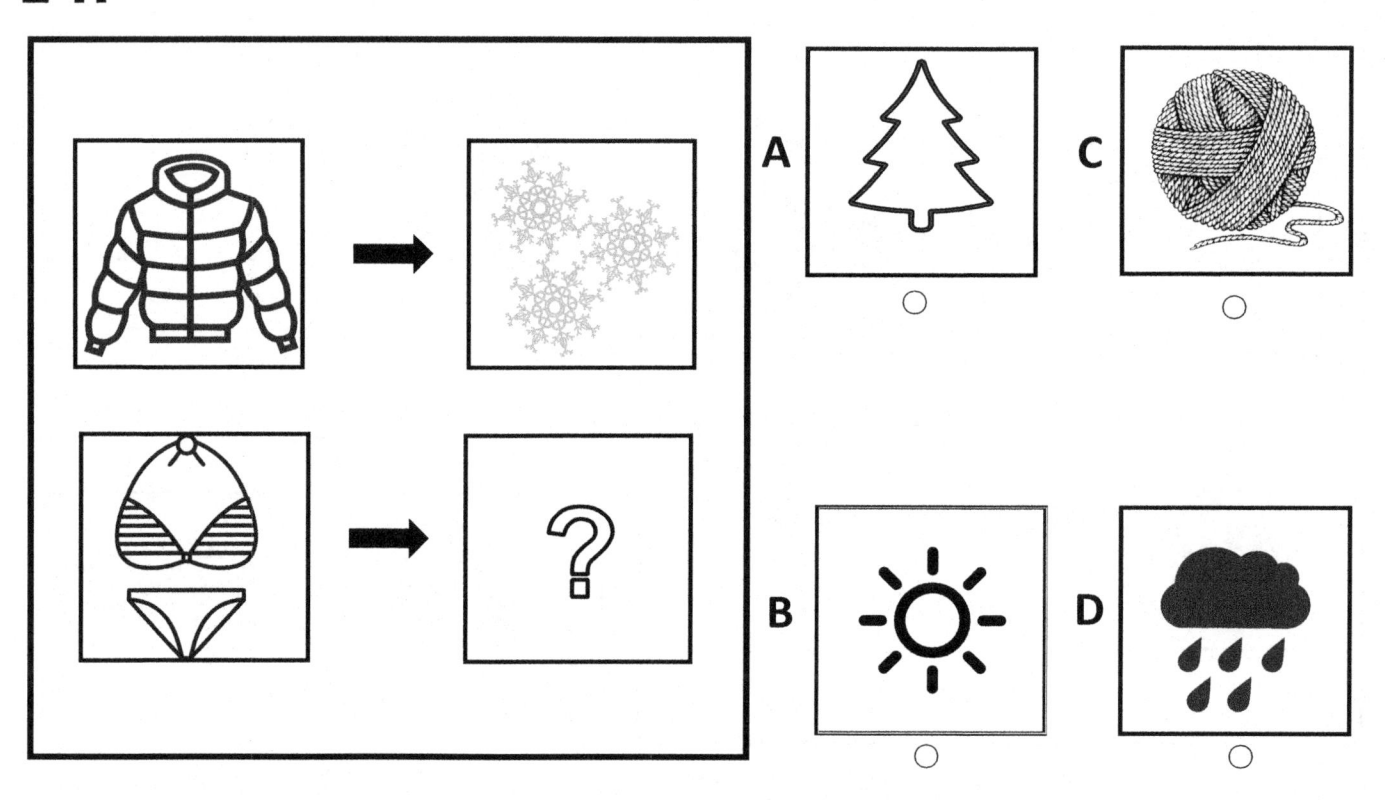

13.

14.

146

PRACTICE TEST GRADE 2

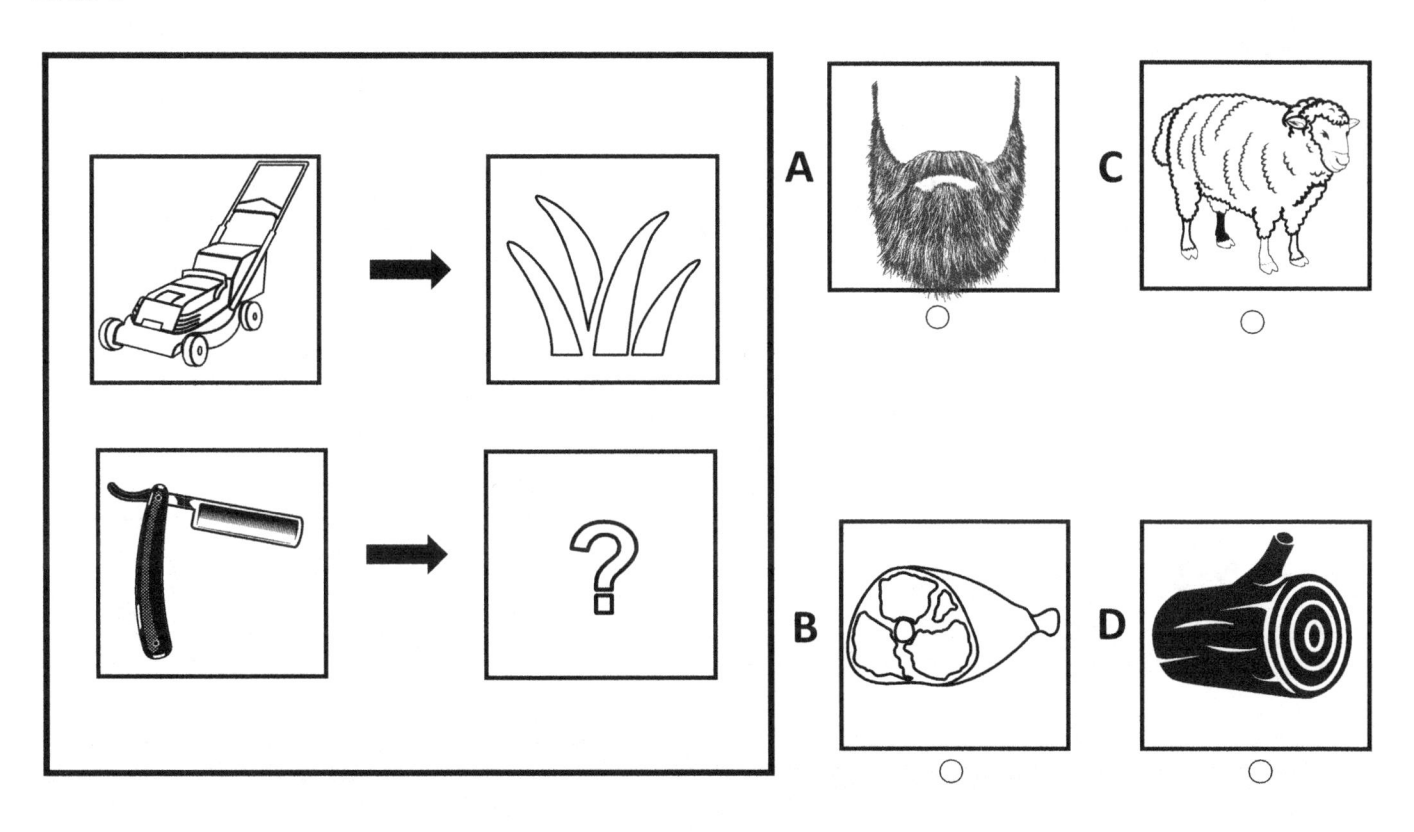

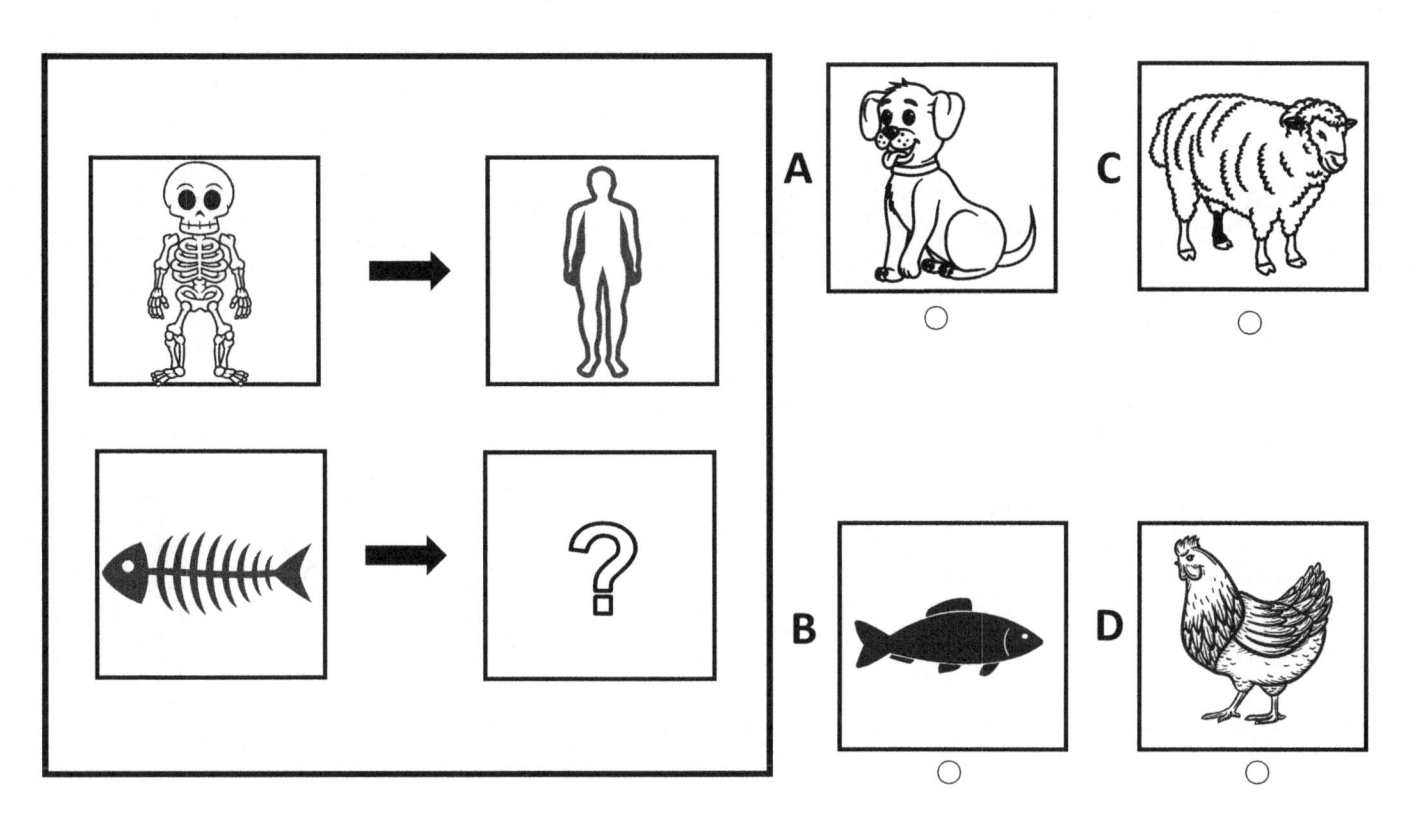

15.

16.

147

PRACTICE TEST GRADE 2

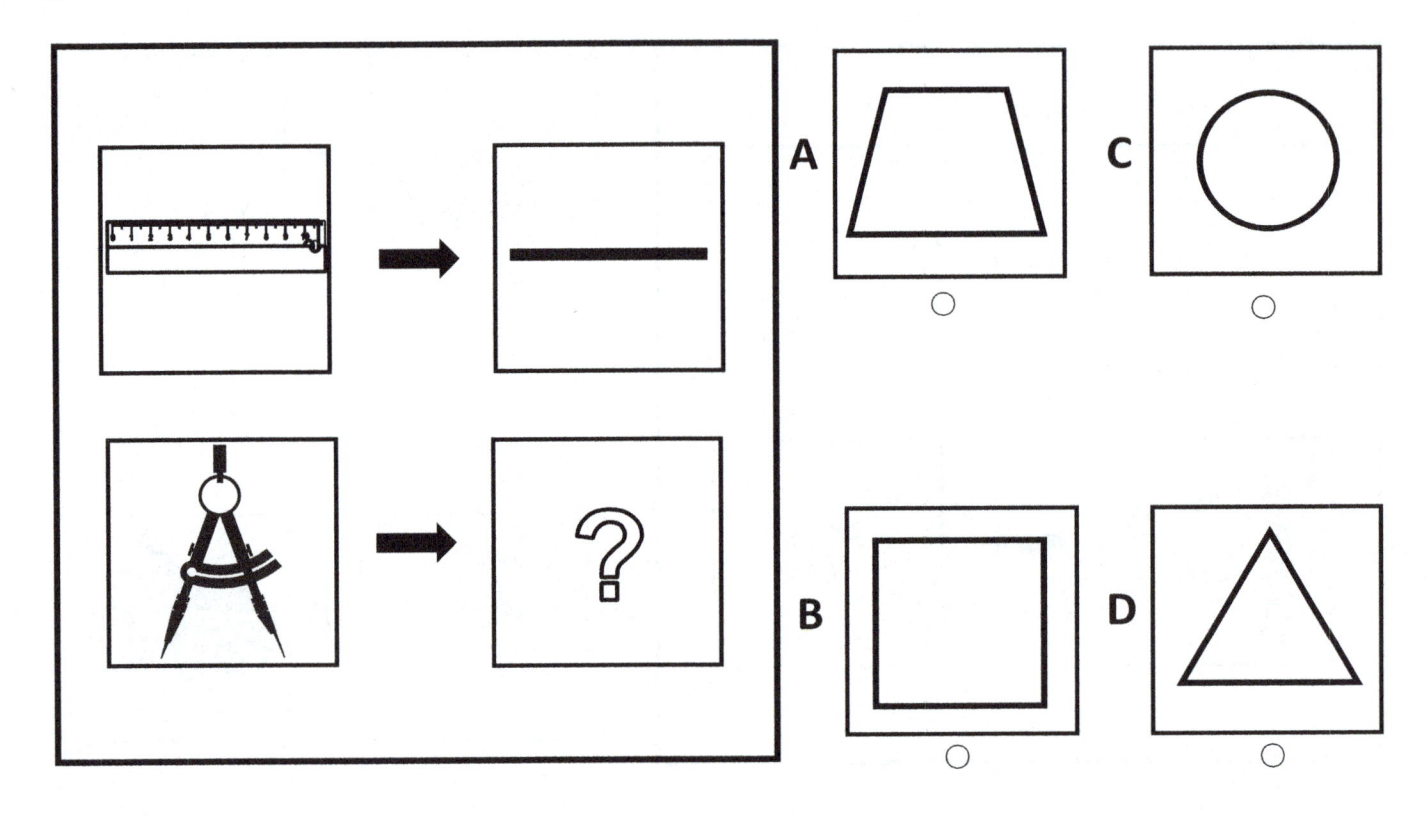

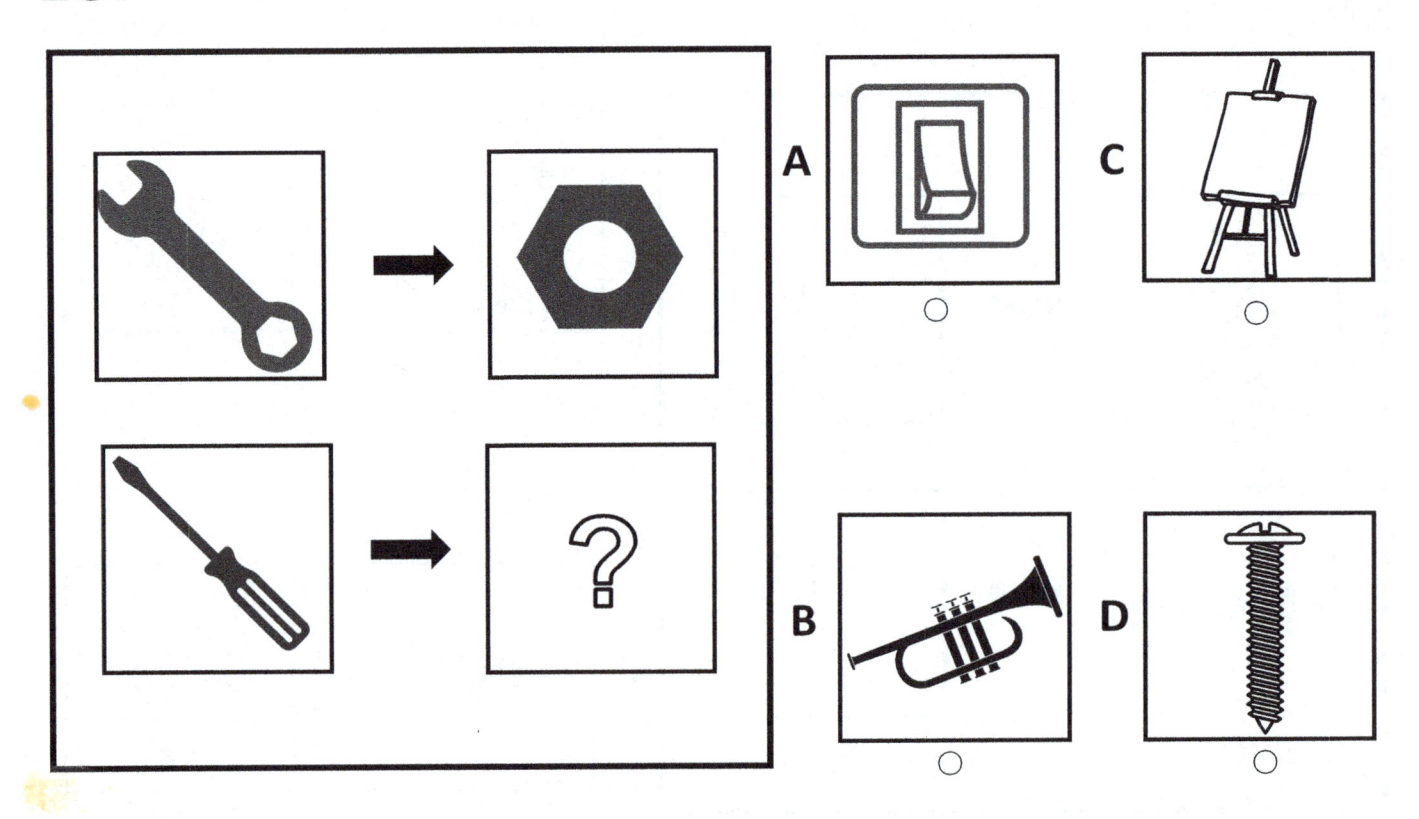

17.

18.

148

PRACTICE TEST GRADE 2

Picture Classification

Picture classification questions ask the student to choose the picture that belongs to a group of three images.

Example

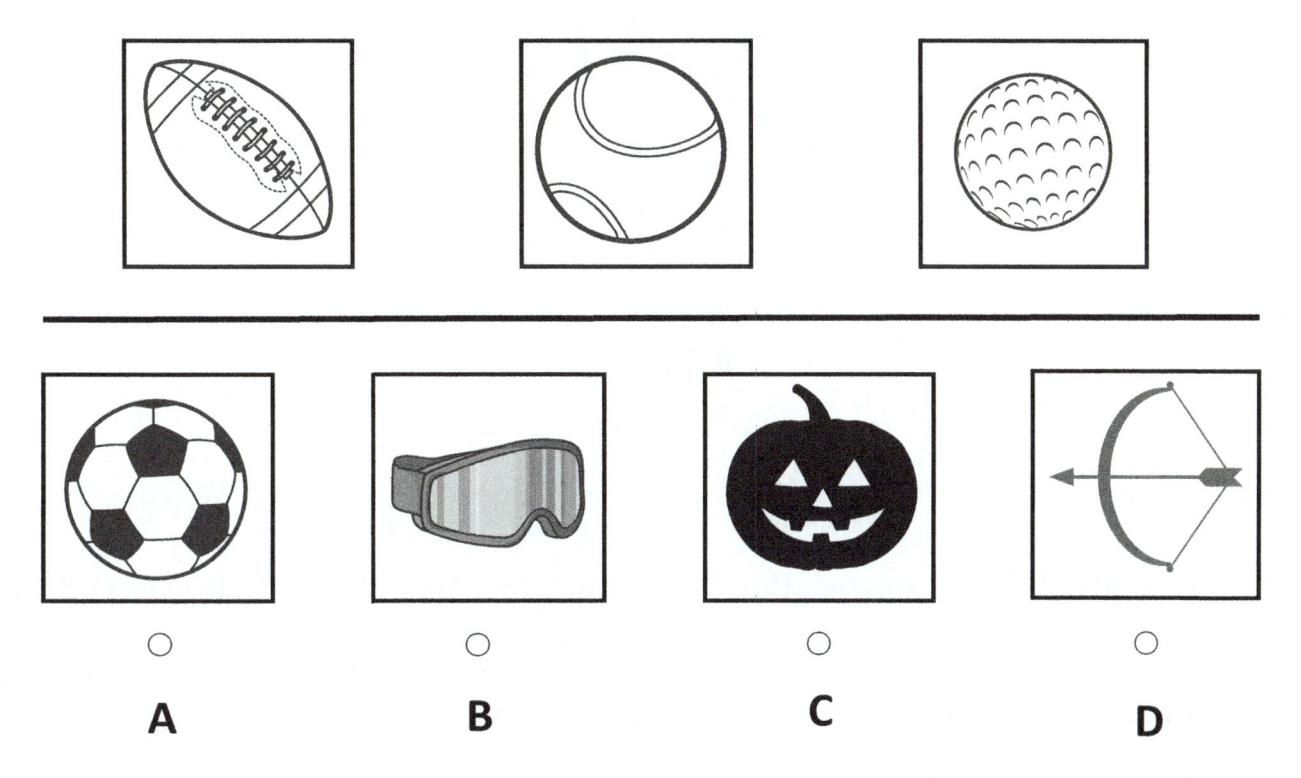

- First, identify the relationship between the three pictures in the first row.
- What do the objects "football ball", "tennis ball", and "golf ball" have in common?

Football ball, tennis ball, and golf ball are all equipment related to sports that make use of different types of balls.

- Now, look at the three pictures in the lower row: soccer ball, ski glasses, pumpkin, and bow with arrow. Which picture goes best with the three images in the top row?

Soccer ball, obviously, so the correct answer is A.

Tips for Solving Picture Classification Questions

- Try to identify the correlation between the three pictures in the top row.

- Review all answers before you make a choice.

- Remove the pictures in the answers that don't have any kind of relationship with the three pictures in the top row.

- When you work on questions, always dedicate some time to review the incorrect answers. You will learn more from them than from the correct answers.

- Encourage your child to learn how to classify and sort toys, leaves, fruits or other objects into "similar" groups.

PRACTICE TEST GRADE 2

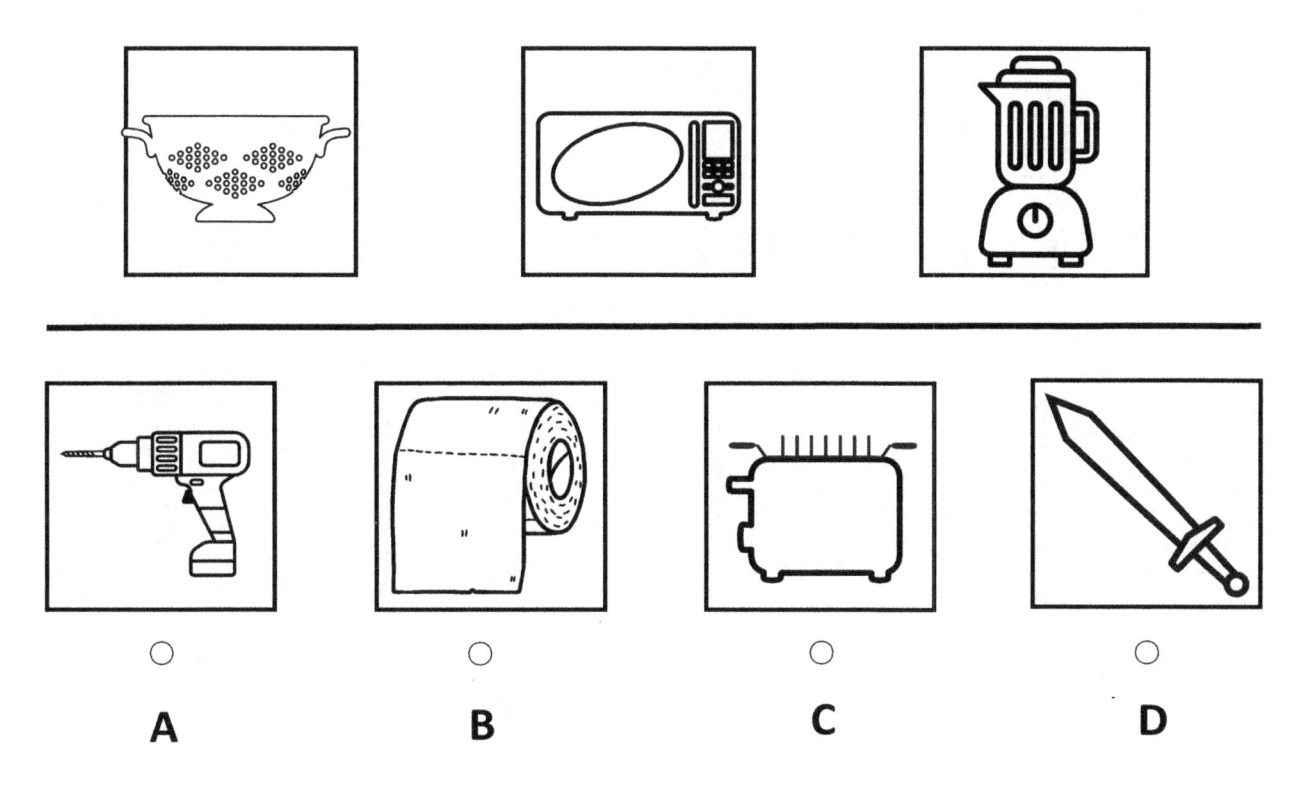

1.

A   B   C   D

2.

A   B   C   D

151

PRACTICE TEST GRADE 2

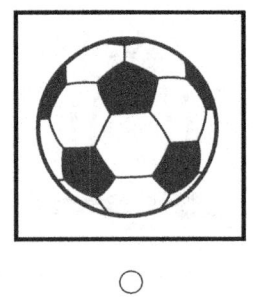

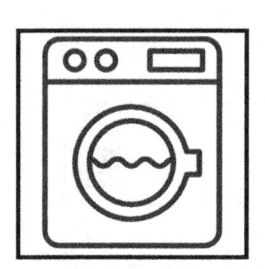

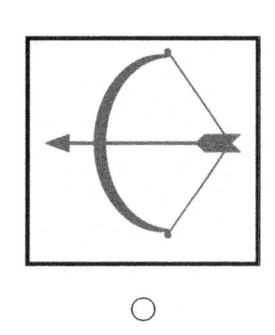

3.

4.

152

PRACTICE TEST GRADE 2

5.

6.

153

PRACTICE TEST GRADE 2

7.

○ A  ○ B 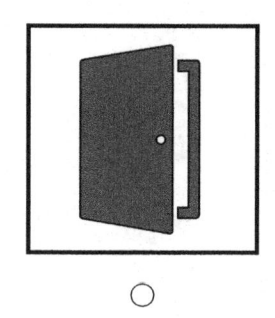 ○ C  ○ D

8.

○ A  ○ B 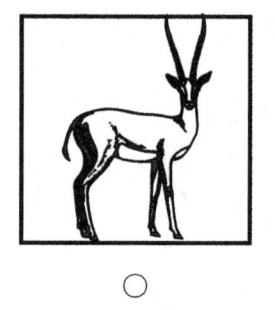 ○ C  ○ D

154

PRACTICE TEST GRADE 2

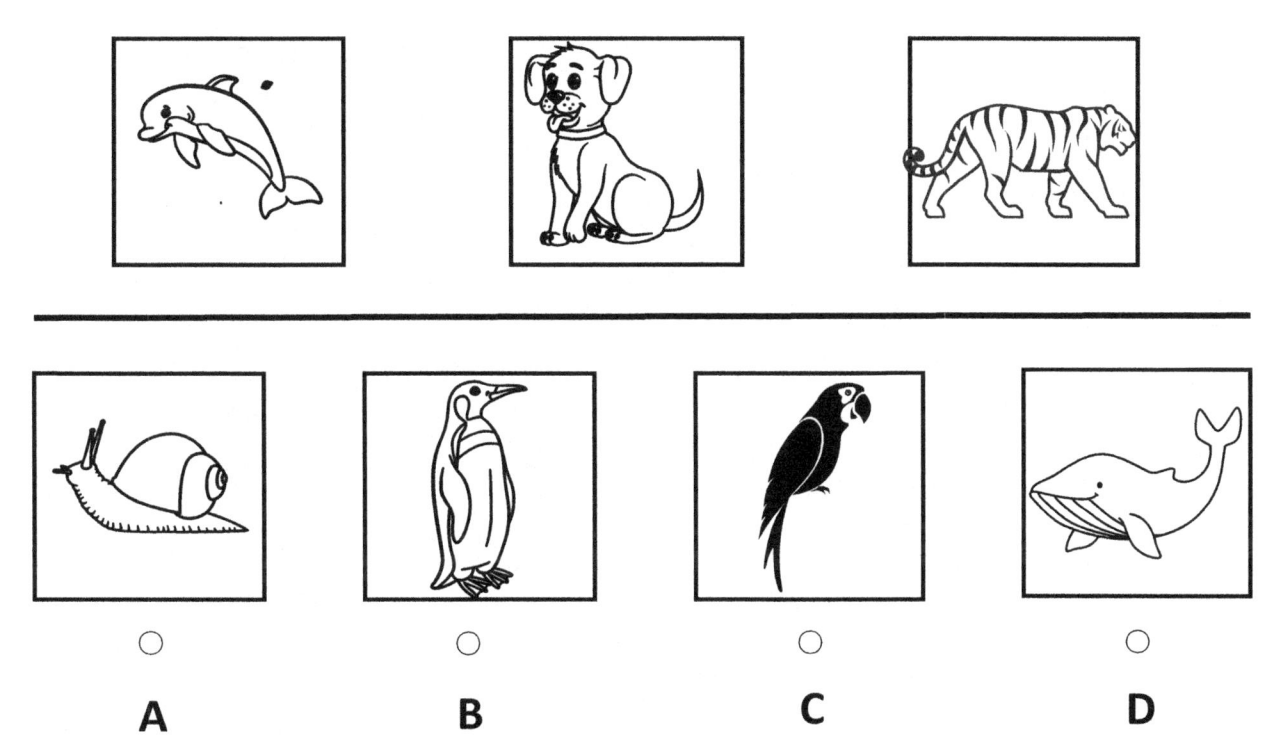

9.

○ A   ○ B   ○ C   ○ D

10.

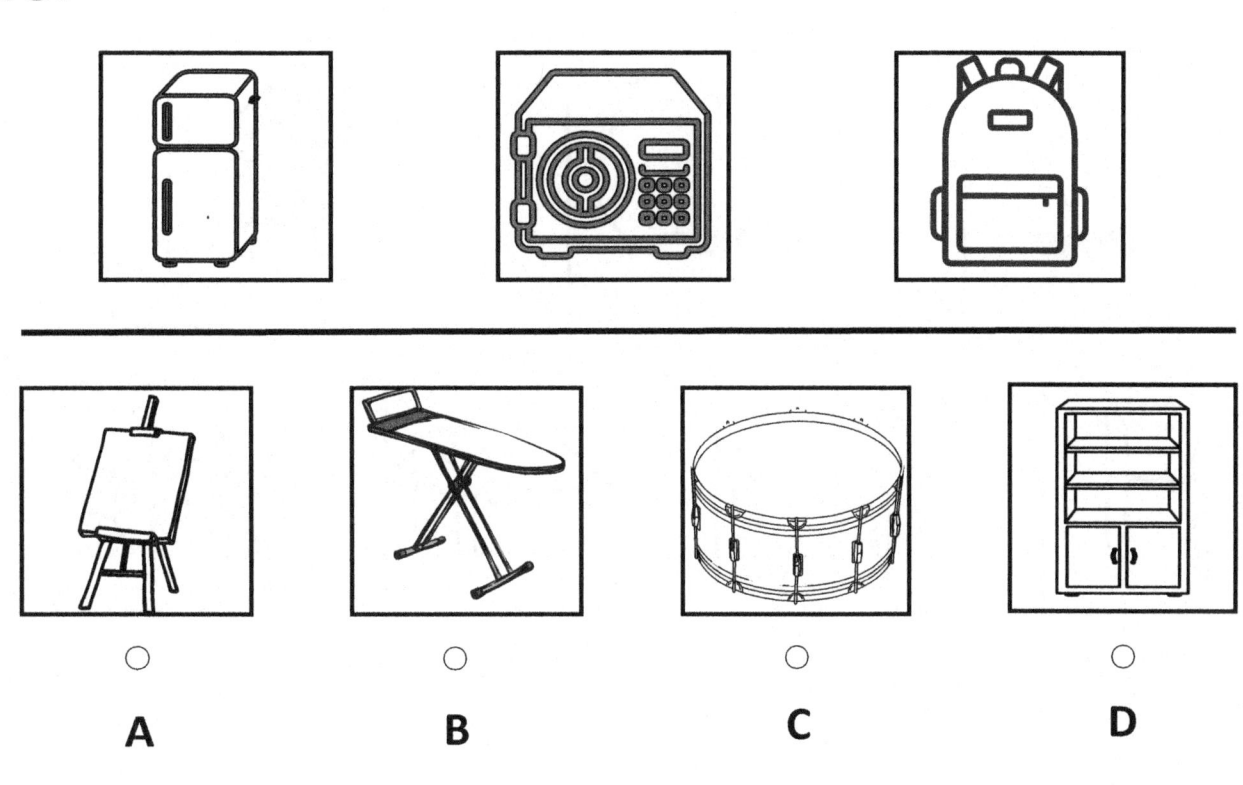

○ A   ○ B   ○ C   ○ D

PRACTICE TEST GRADE 2

11.

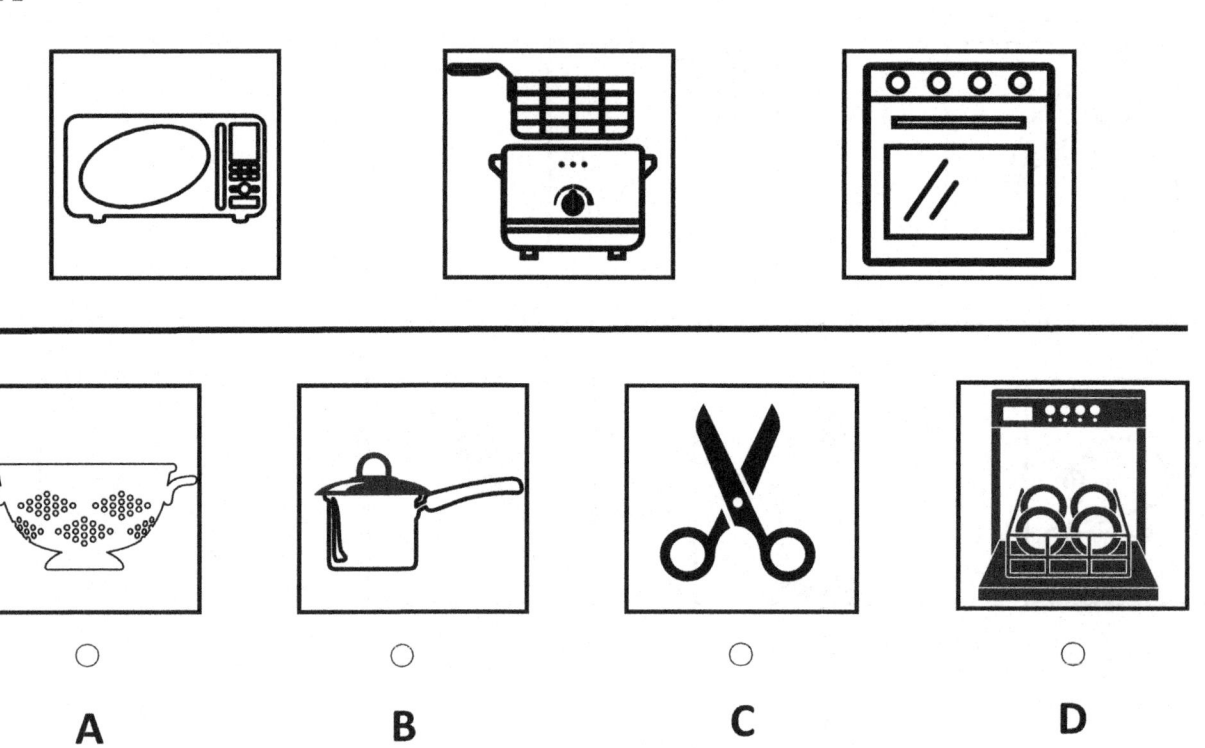

○ A   ○ B   ○ C   ○ D

12.

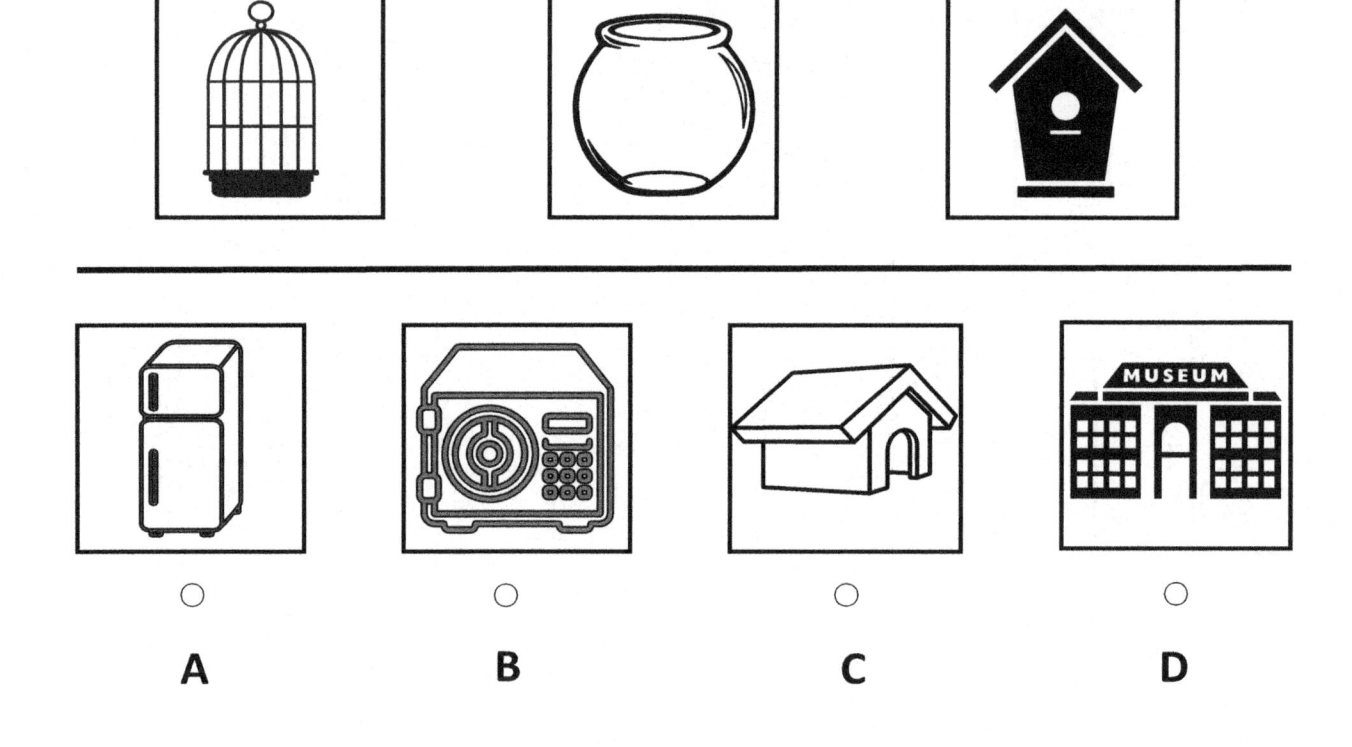

○ A   ○ B   ○ C   ○ D

156

PRACTICE TEST GRADE 2

13.

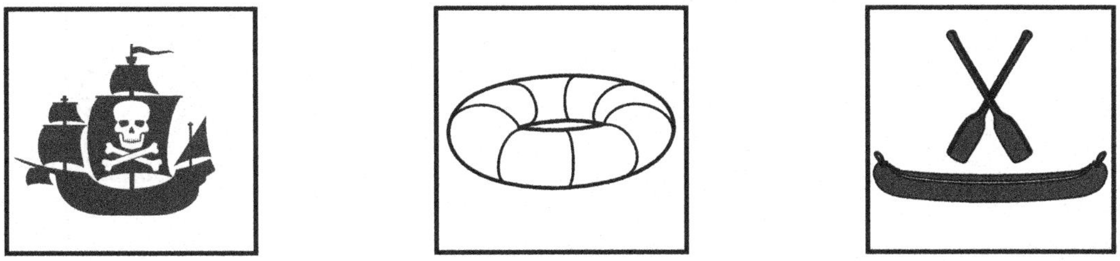

A	B	C	D

14.

A	B	C	D

157

PRACTICE TEST GRADE 2

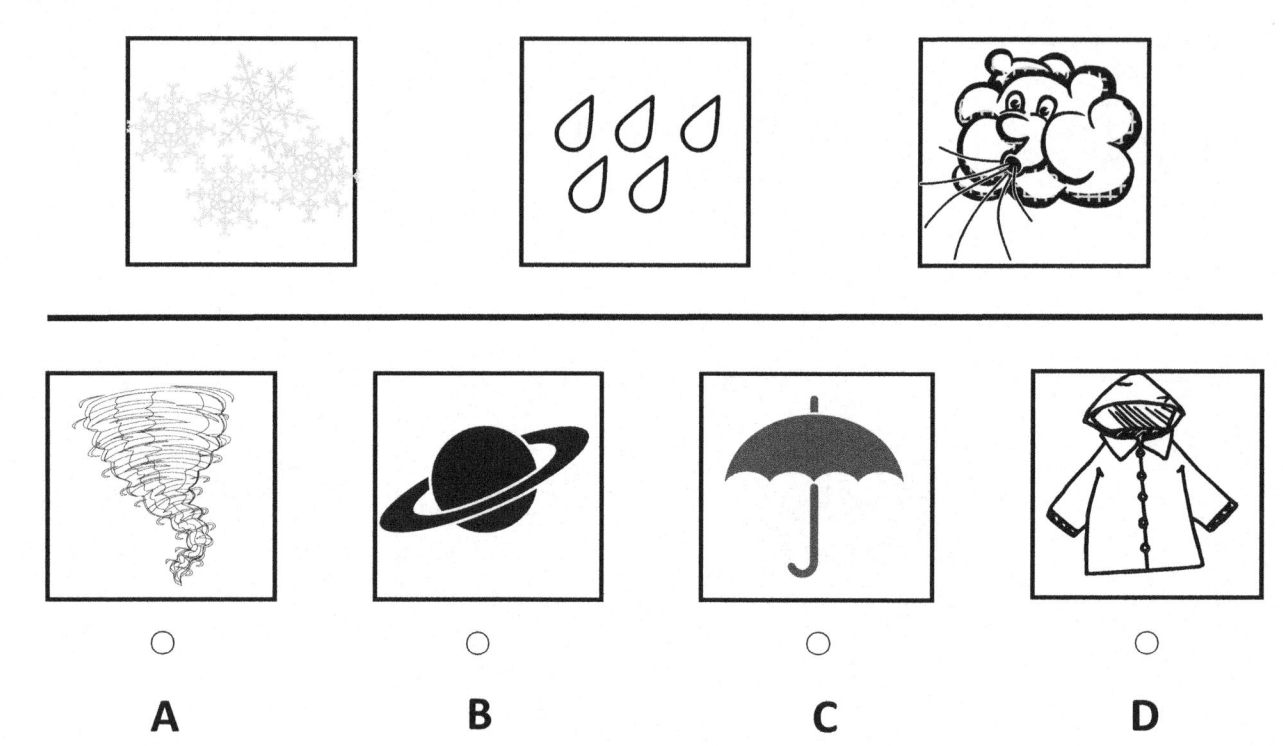

15.

A B C D

16.

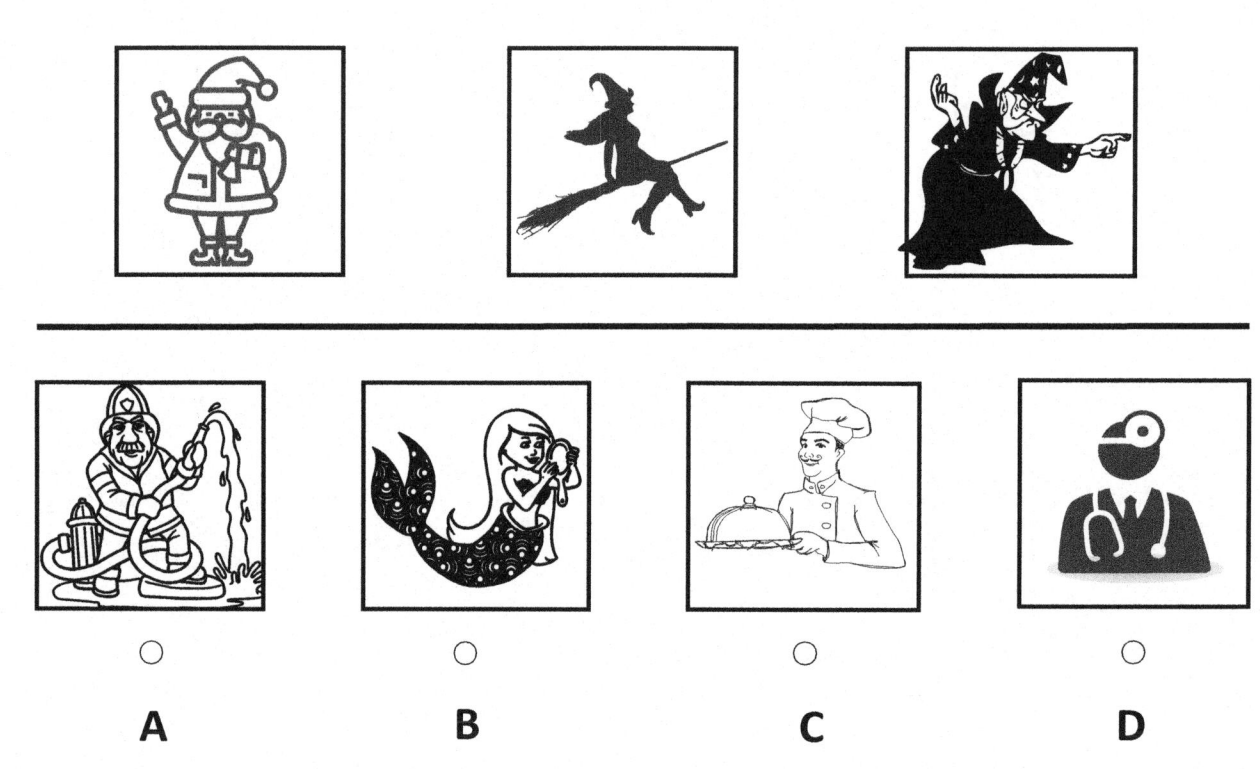

A B C D

158

PRACTICE TEST GRADE 2

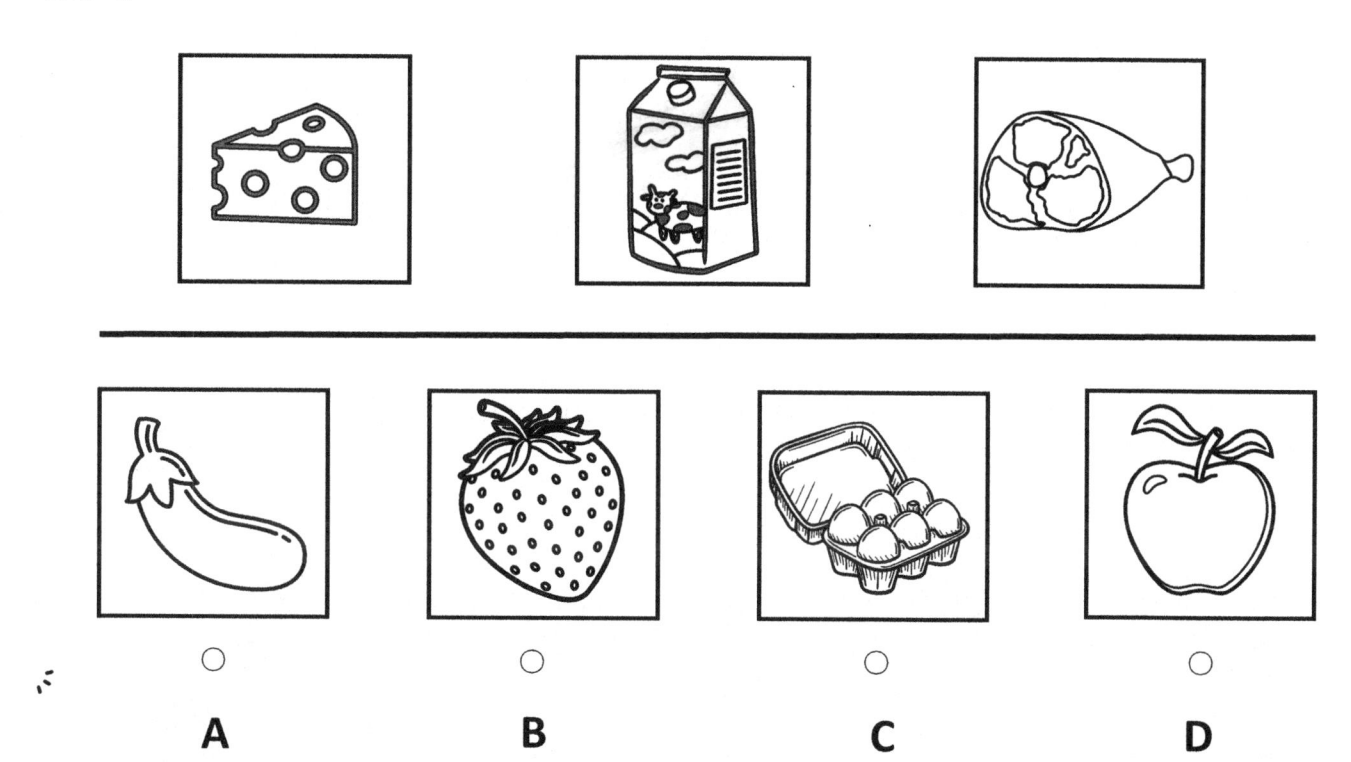

17.

A   **B**   **C**   **D**

18.

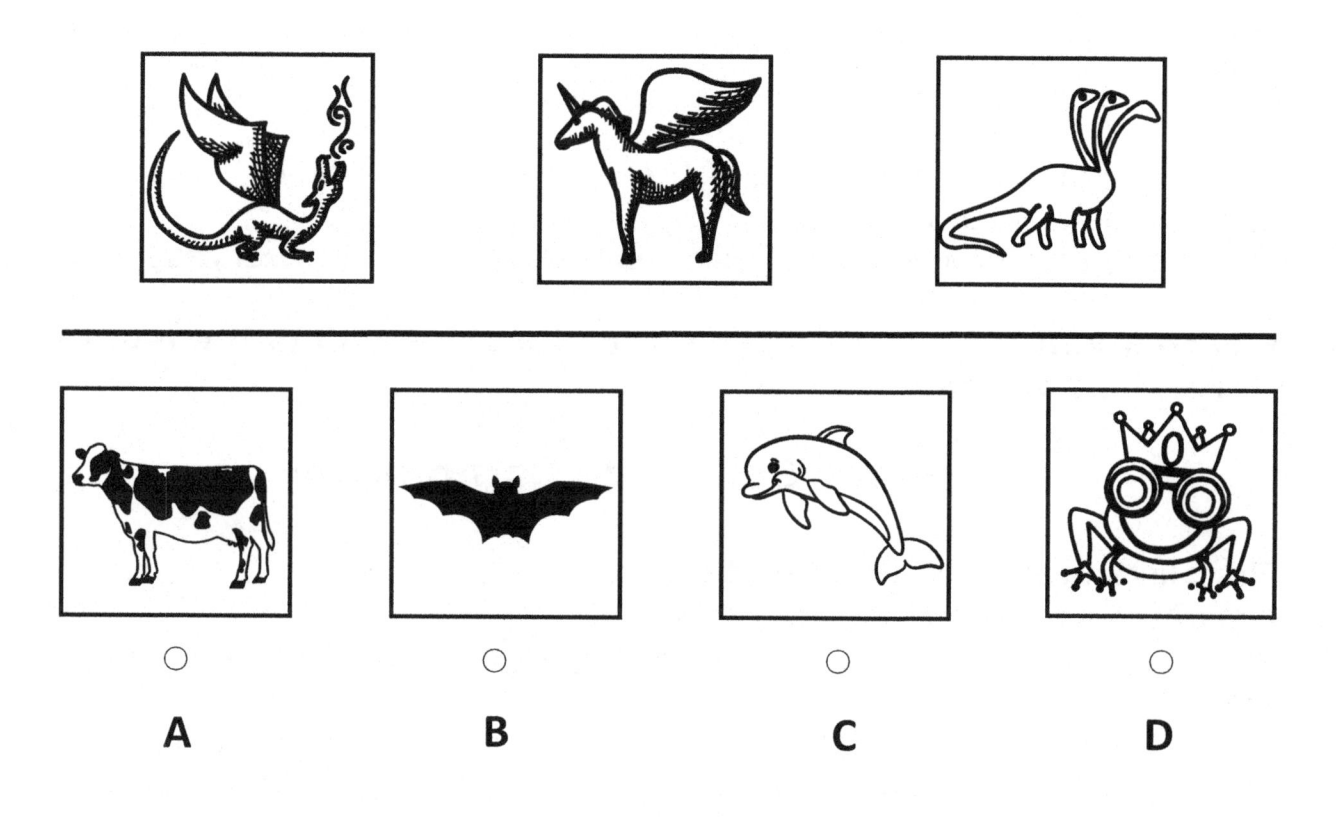

A   **B**   **C**   **D**

PRACTICE TEST GRADE 2

Sentence Completion

The teacher reads aloud a question and does not repeat it a second time. Children must choose the picture that best answers the question in a complete, logical way.
To answer correctly, the child must be very focused on the meaning of the sentence as a whole.

Example

Which tool is needed to drive pitons into the wall?

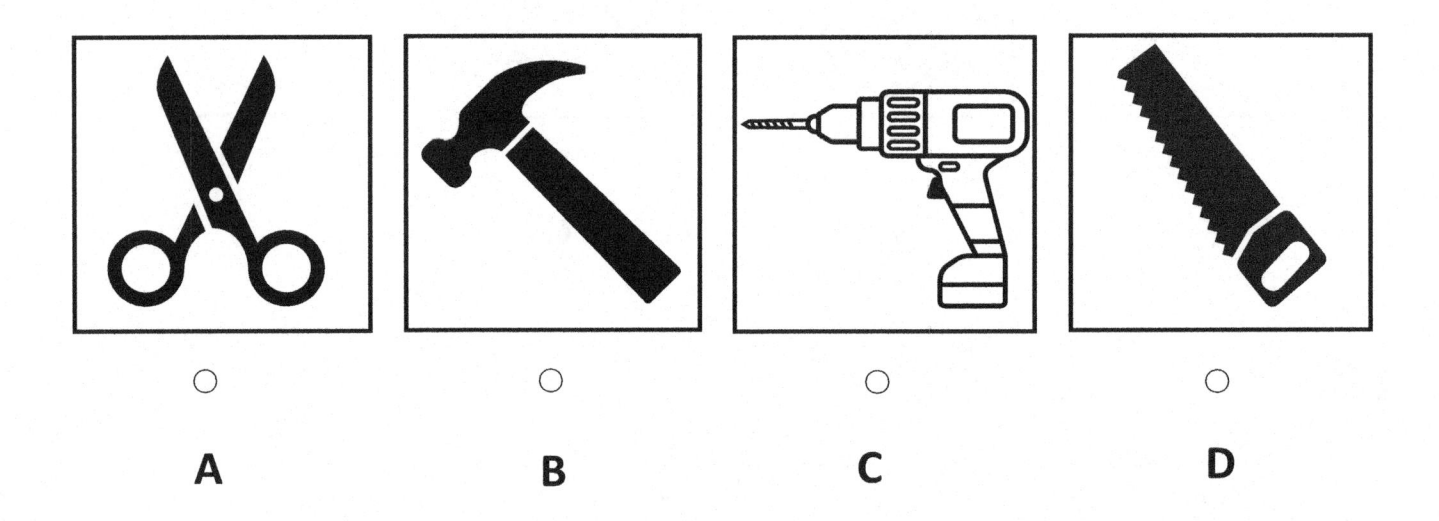

| A | B | C | D |

- First, think about the meaning of the sentence as a whole.
- Look at the answer choices.
- Try to see these tools in your mind as they are used in everyday life.

The only tool you can use to drive pitons into the wall is the hammer. Therefore, the right choice is "B".

Tips for Sentence Completion

- First, listen carefully to the sentence.
- Look at the three pictures in the answer row.
- Remove the pictures that don't have any kind of relationship with the main sentence.
- Try to see objects with your mind, placing them in the real world.

Directions for Sentence Completion

- **On each page, you will find two questions.**
- **Read aloud the first question to your child.**
- **Turn the page and show him the possible choices.**
- **Proceed with the next question.**

PRACTICE TEST GRADE 2

1.

Which animal is classified as bird?

2.

Which of these objects does not protect against the cold?

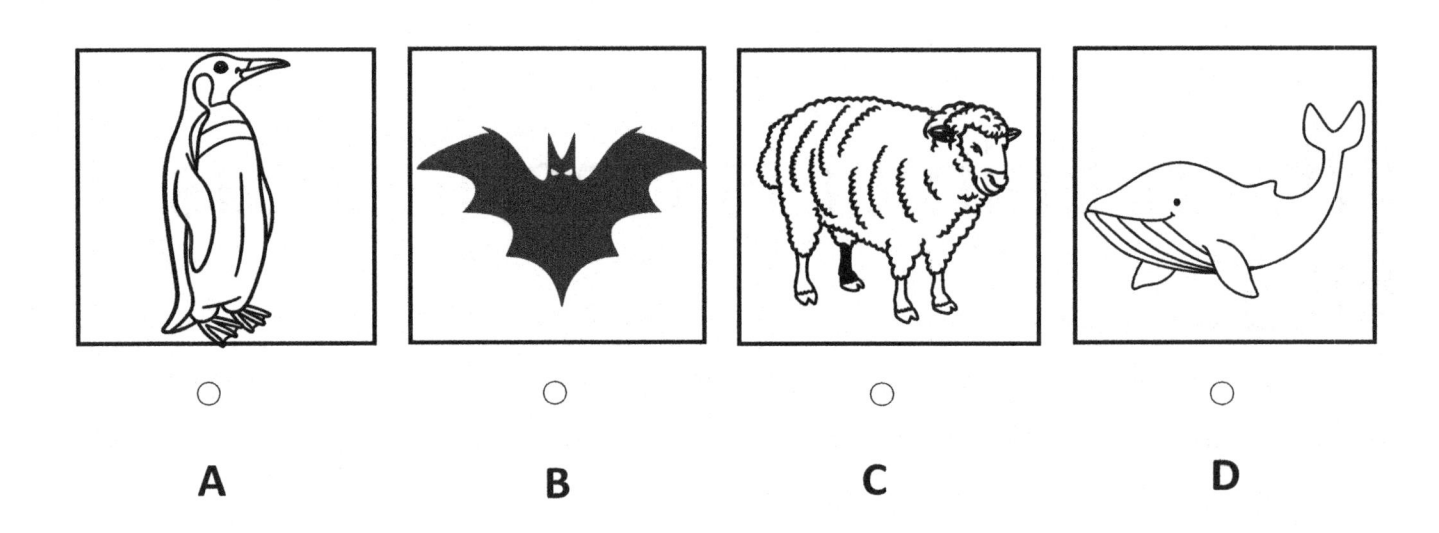

PRACTICE TEST GRADE 2

1.

A B C D

2.

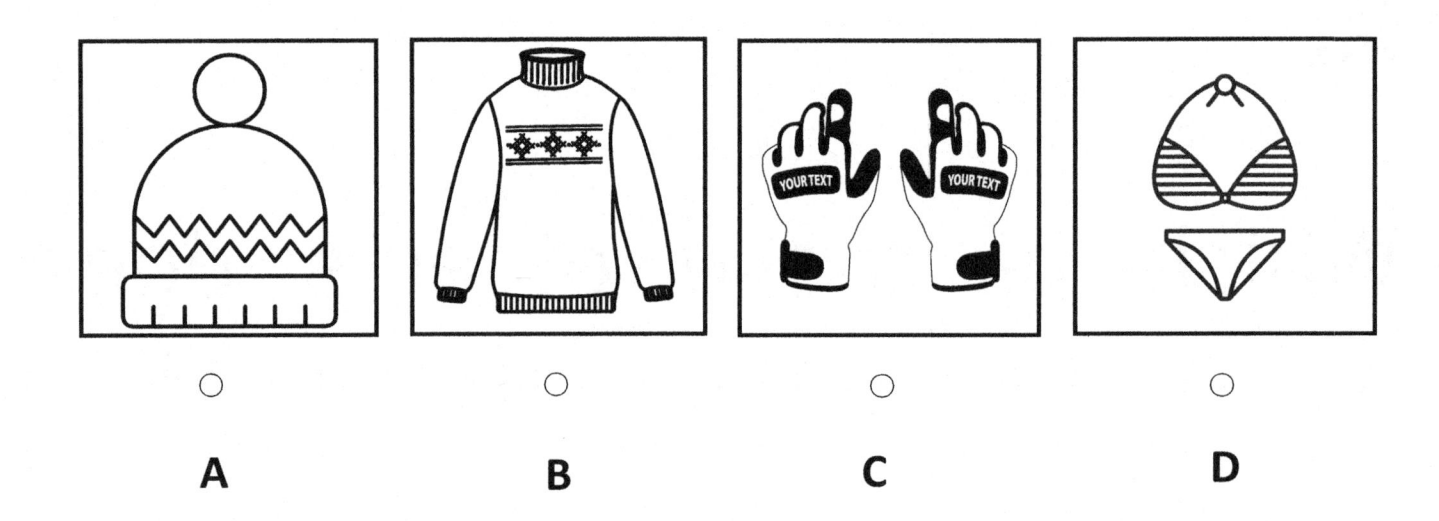

A B C D

3.

Which of these objects will not be found in the garden?

4.

Which image shows a mammal?

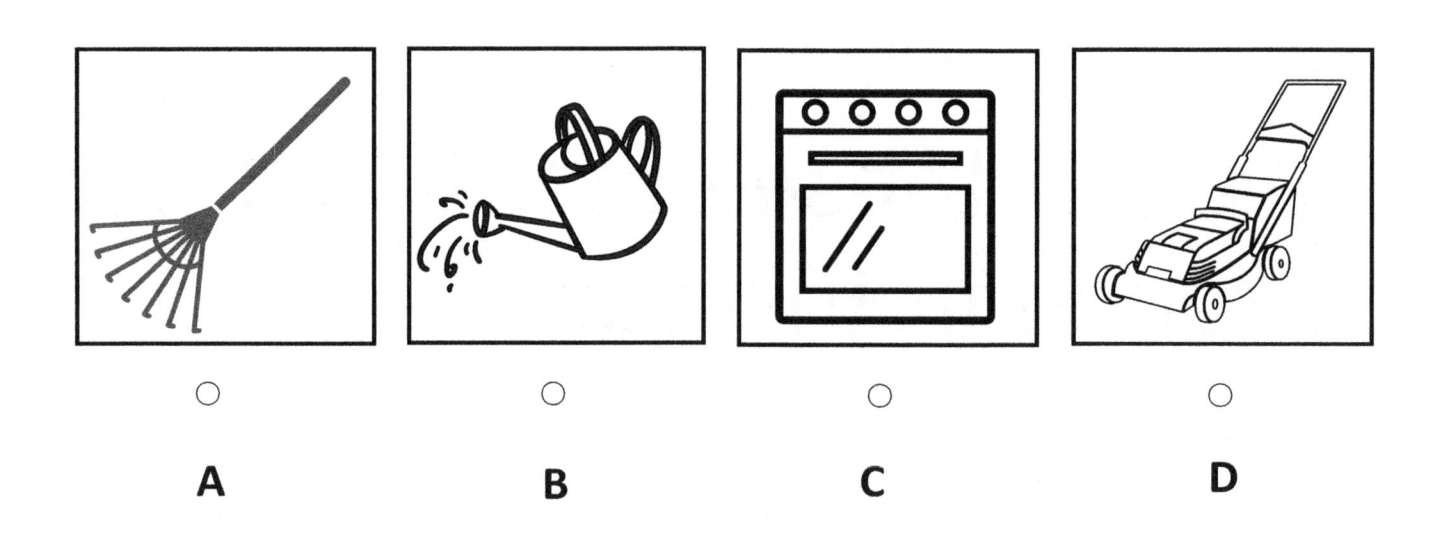

PRACTICE TEST GRADE 2

3.

    A   B   C   D

4

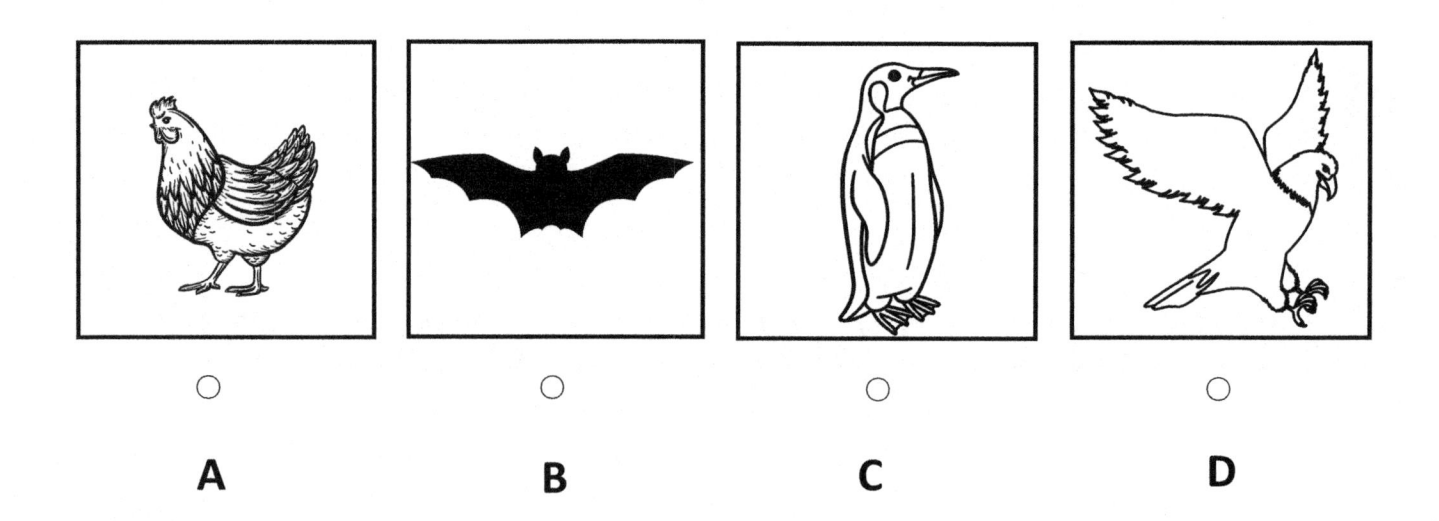

    A   B   C   D

PRACTICE TEST GRADE 2

5.

John wants to play tennis. Which one of these objects will he use?

6.

Which one of these pictures does not show an insect?

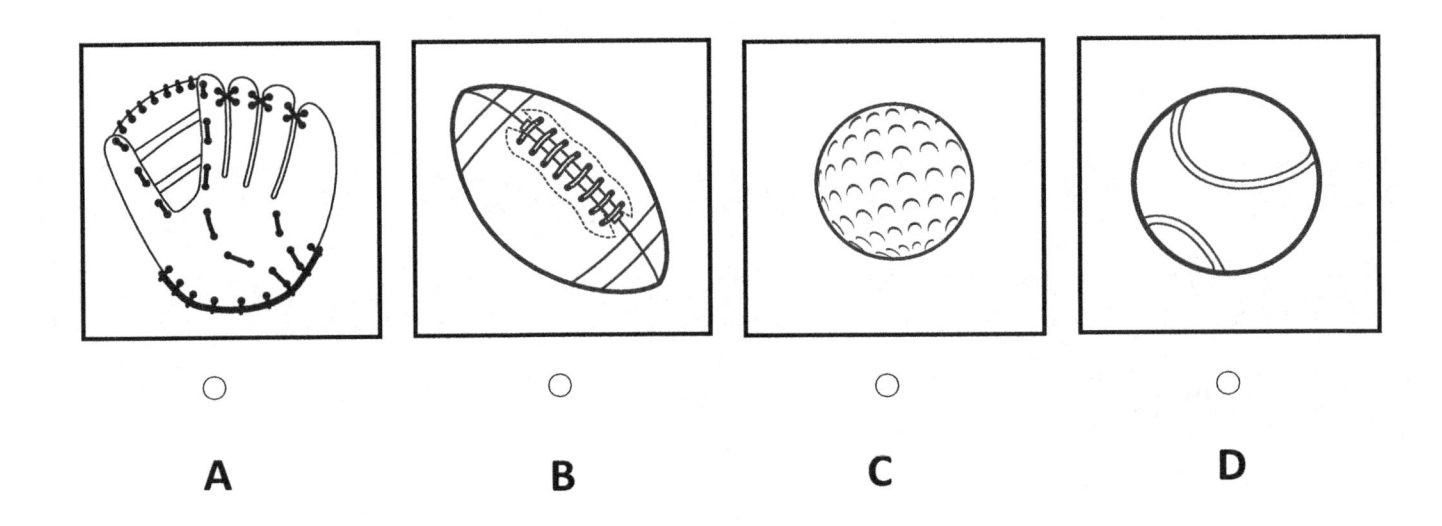

PRACTICE TEST GRADE 2

5.

| A | B | C | D |

6.

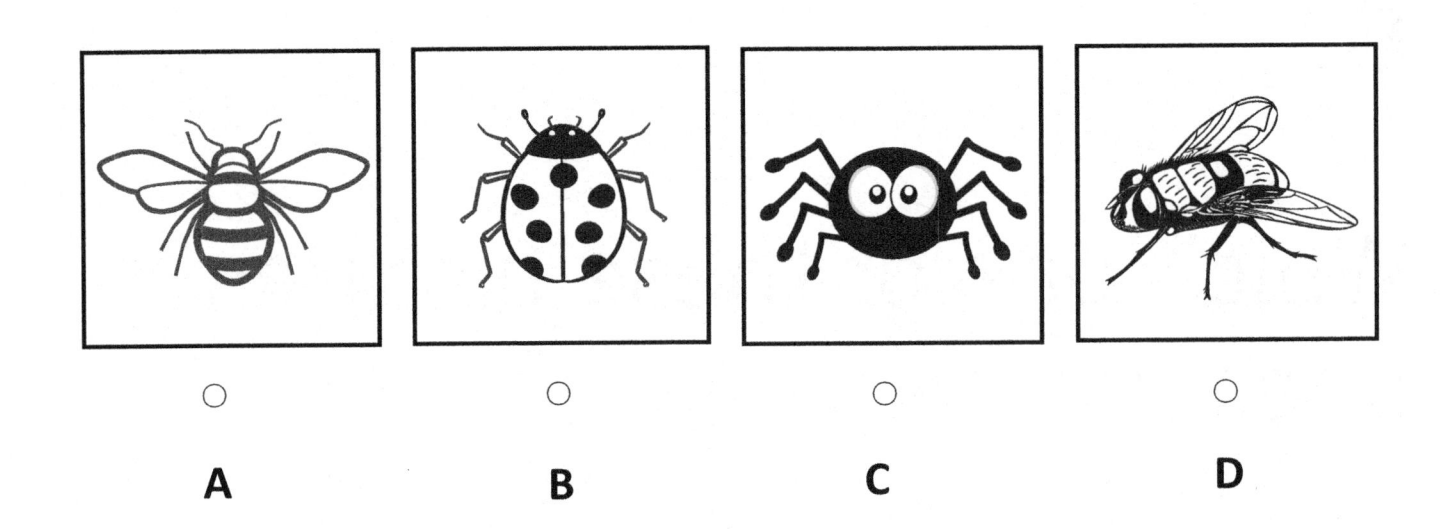

| A | B | C | D |

168

7.

Which of the following body parts contains a human organ?

8.

Which of the following images does not show a vehicle without wheels?

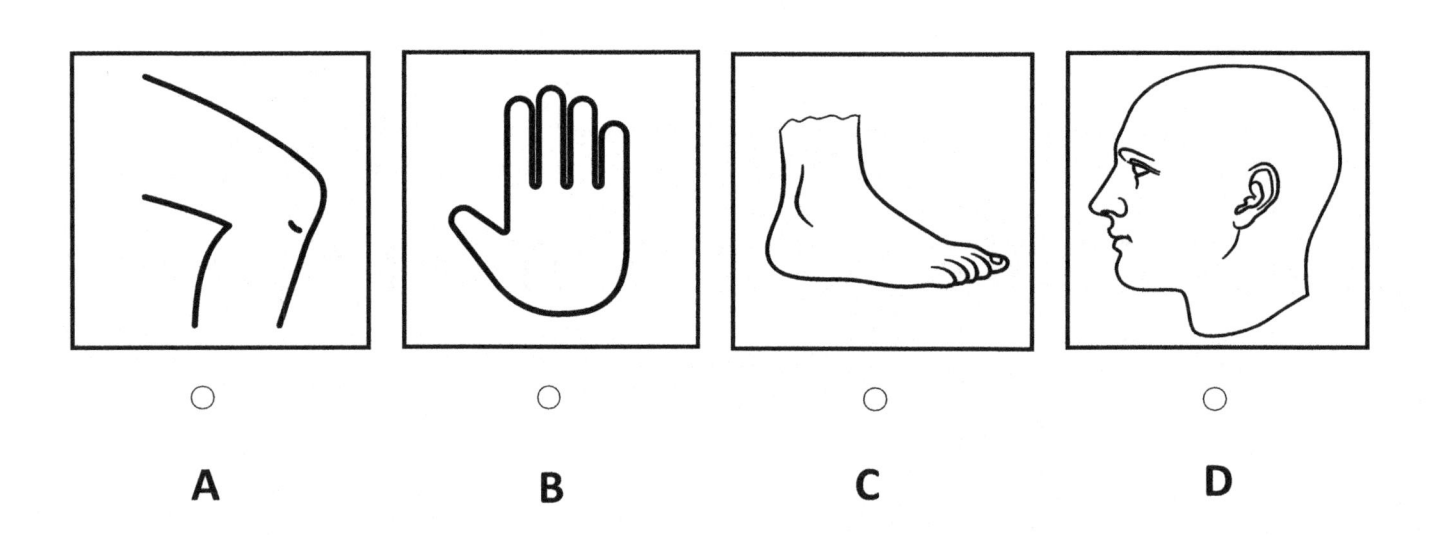

PRACTICE TEST GRADE 2

7.

A	B	C	D

8.

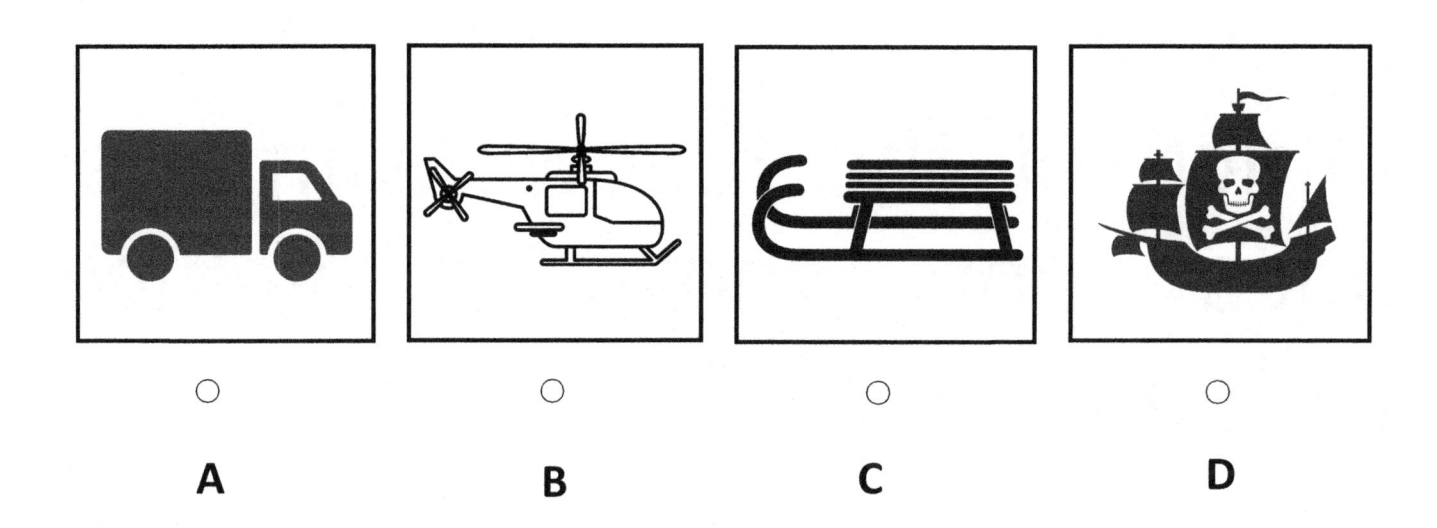

A	B	C	D

170

9.

Which object do you need to observe a star in the sky?

10.

During a big snowstorm, the power went out. Which object could you use as a light source?

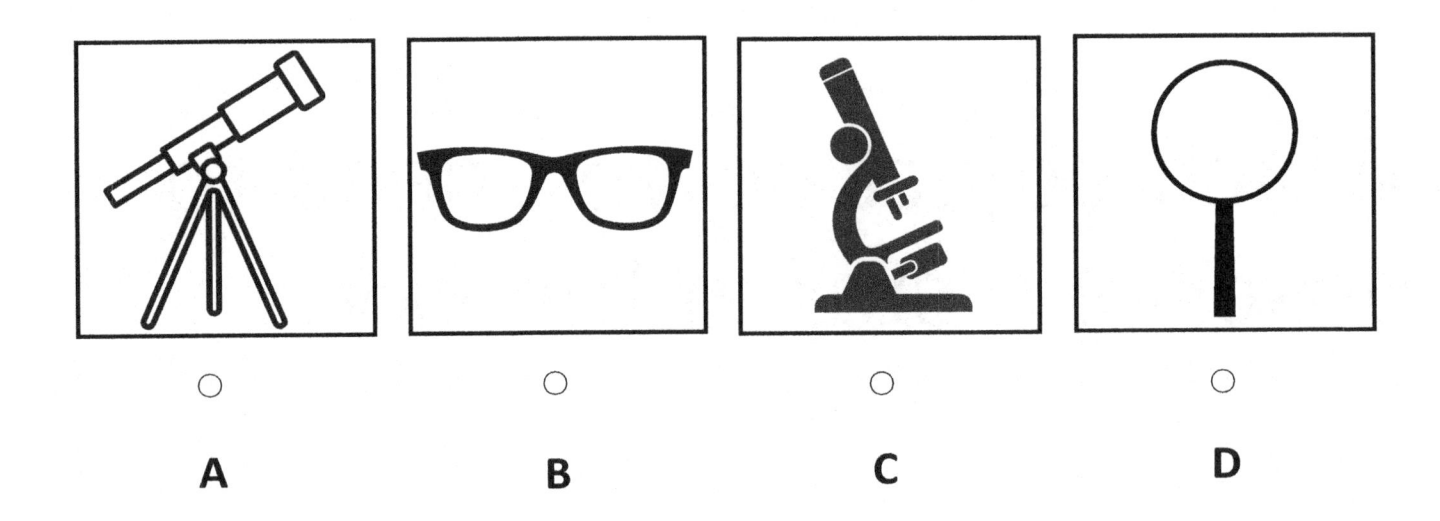

PRACTICE TEST GRADE 2

9.

A	B	C	D
○	○	○	○

10.

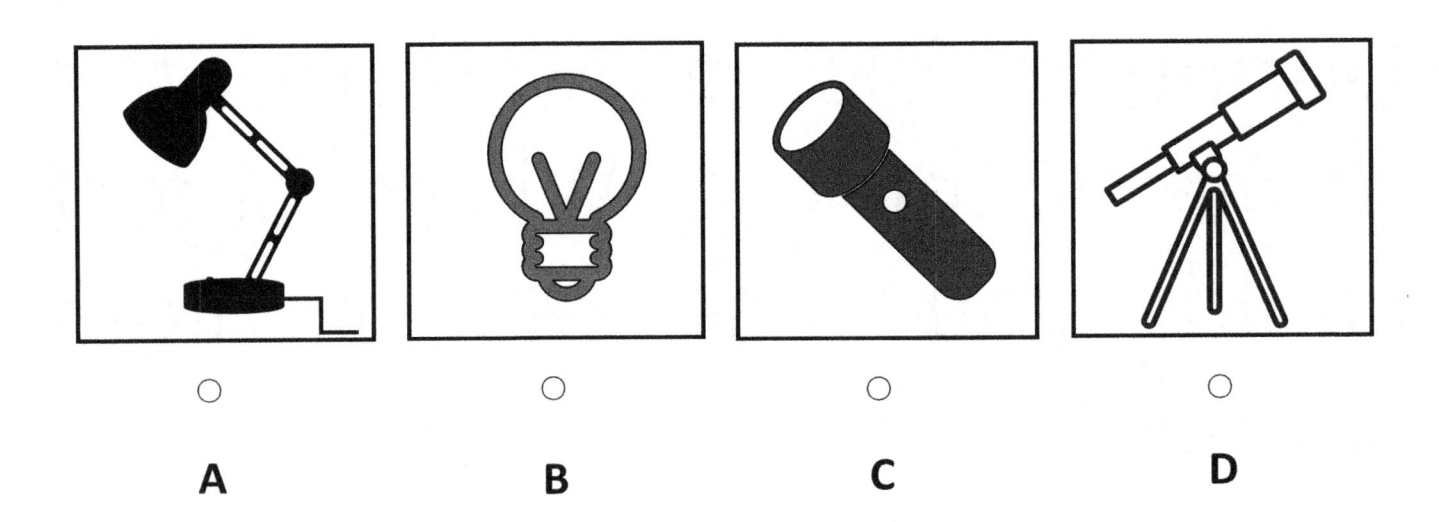

A	B	C	D
○	○	○	○

172

PRACTICE TEST GRADE 2

11.

Which of the following foods does not contain sugar?

12.

Which of the following objects does not grow on a tree?

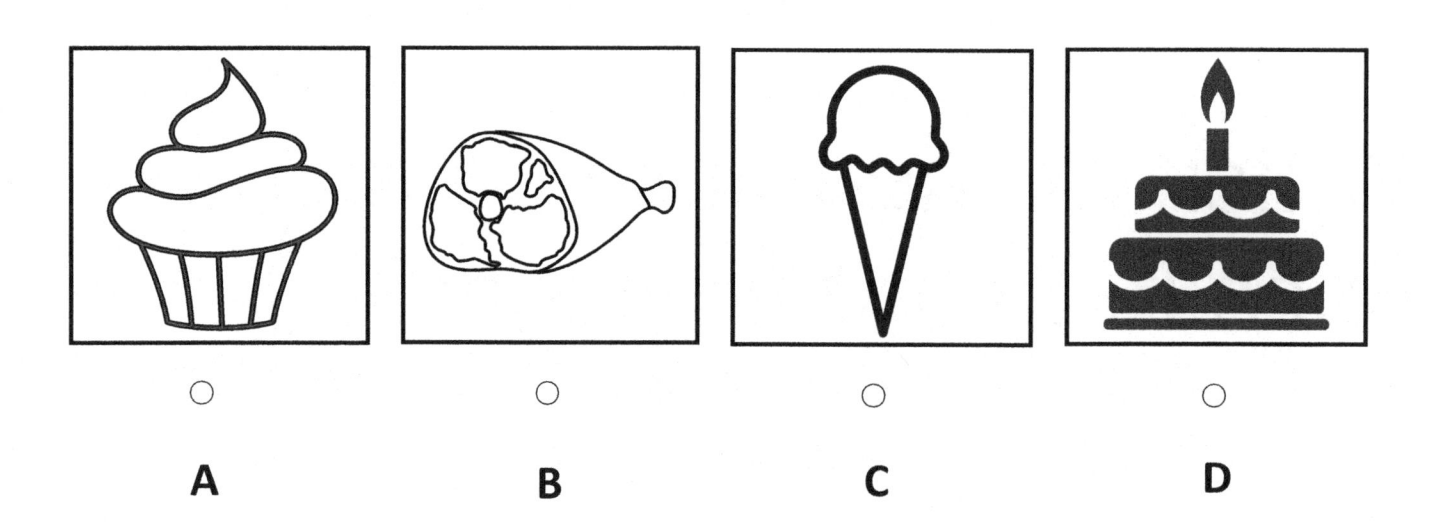

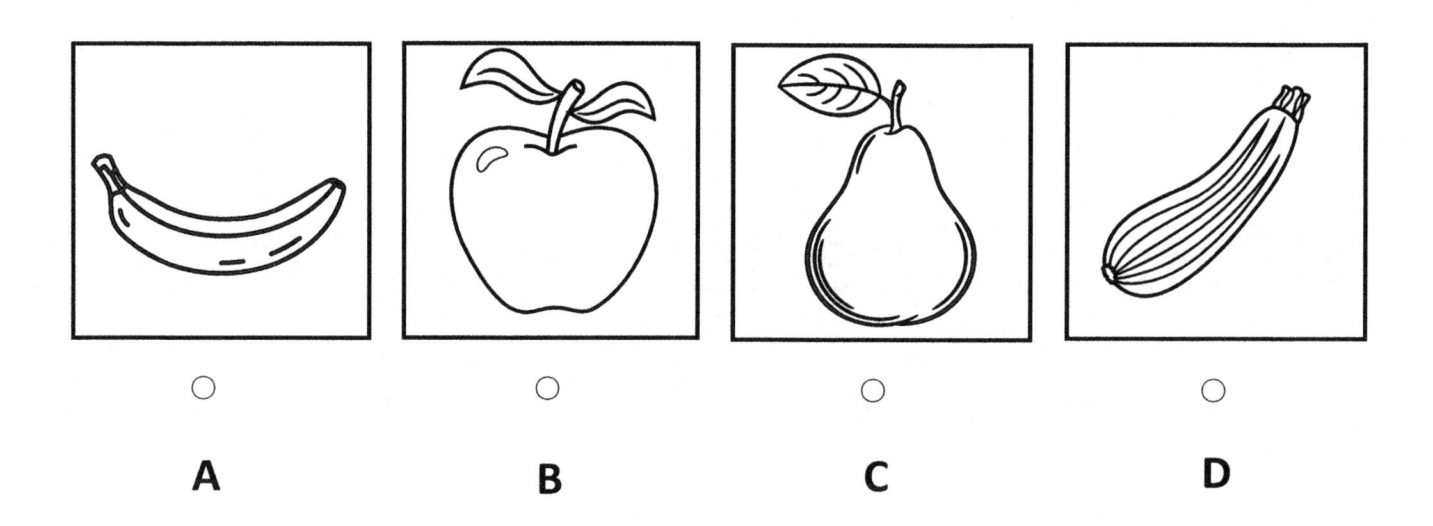

PRACTICE TEST GRADE 2

11.

A	B	C	D
cupcake	ham	ice cream cone	birthday cake

12.

A	B	C	D
banana	apple	pear	zucchini

174

13.

Which of the following objects never stands still?

14.

Which of the following objects do you generally not find in the laundry room?

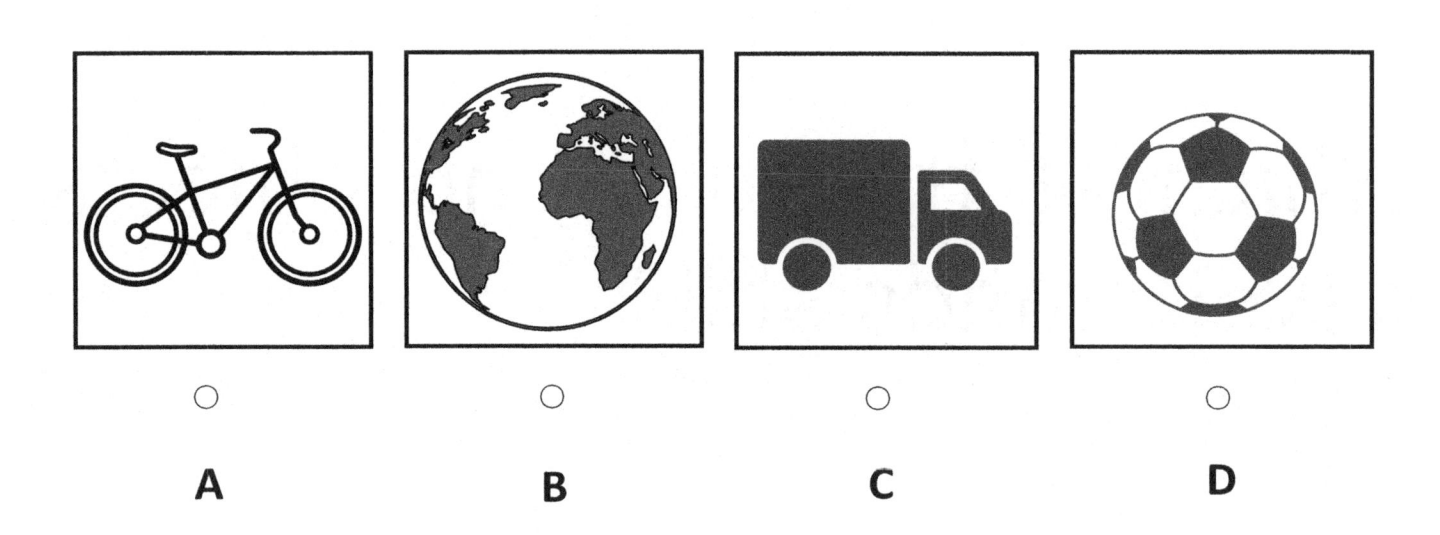

PRACTICE TEST GRADE 2

13.

| A | B | C | D |

14.

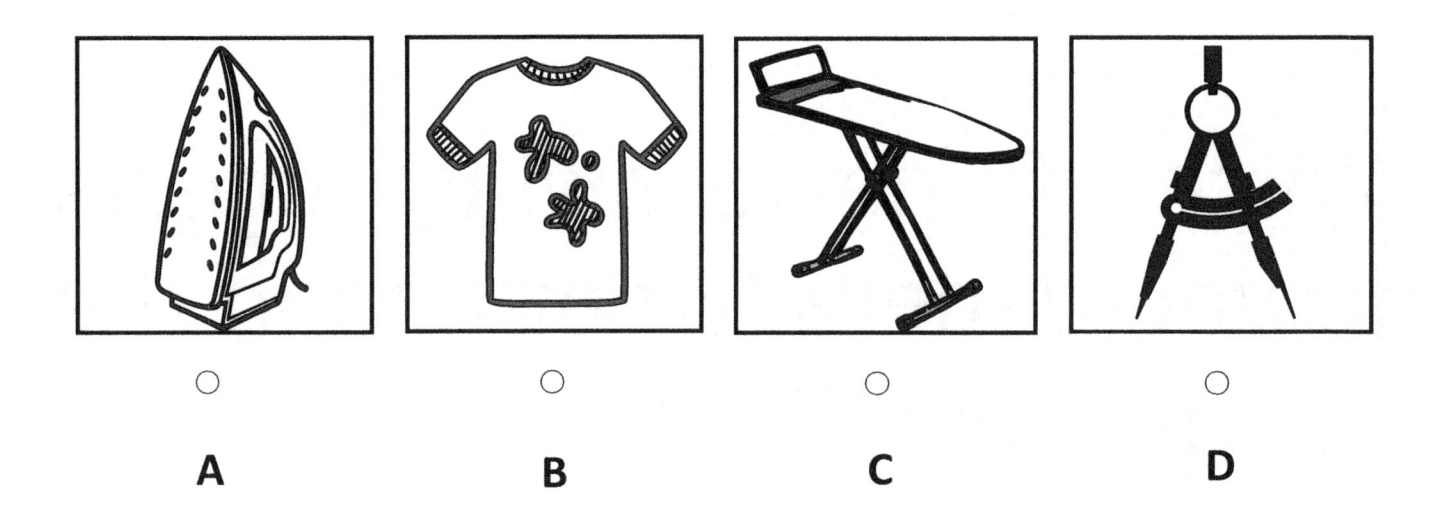

| A | B | C | D |

176

15.

Which of the following foods cannot be given to a horse?

16.

Which of the following objects works with batteries?

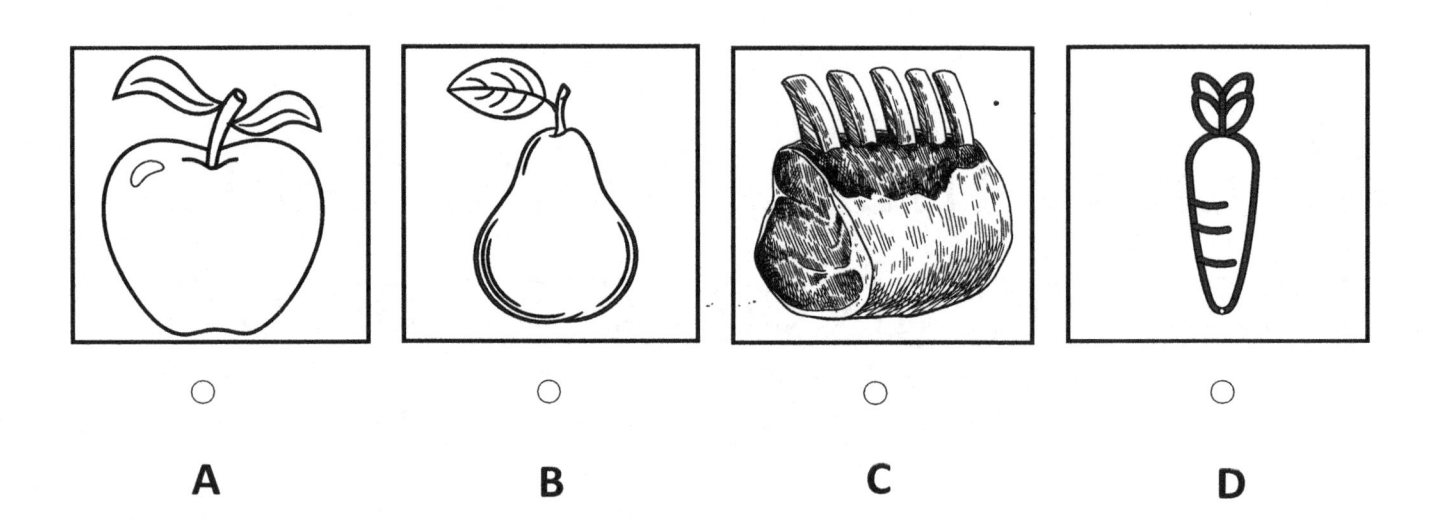

PRACTICE TEST GRADE 2

15.

○ A ○ B ○ C ○ D

16.

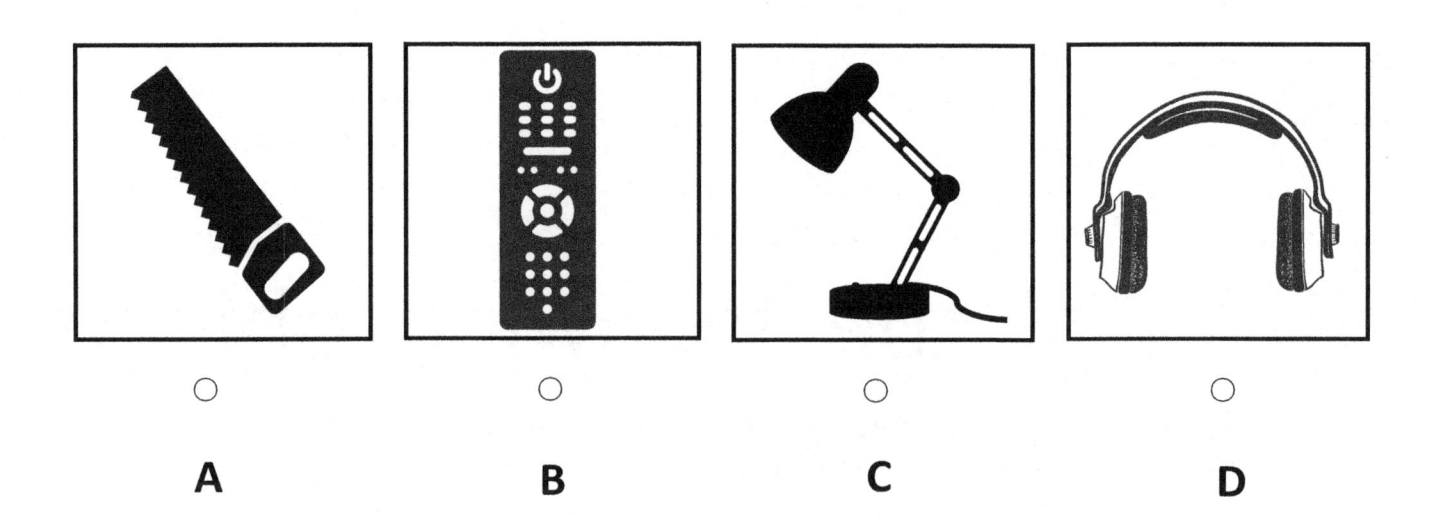

○ A ○ B ○ C ○ D

17.

Which of the following animals does not lay eggs?

18.

Your friend's mother is a seamstress. Which tool doesn't she use for her work?

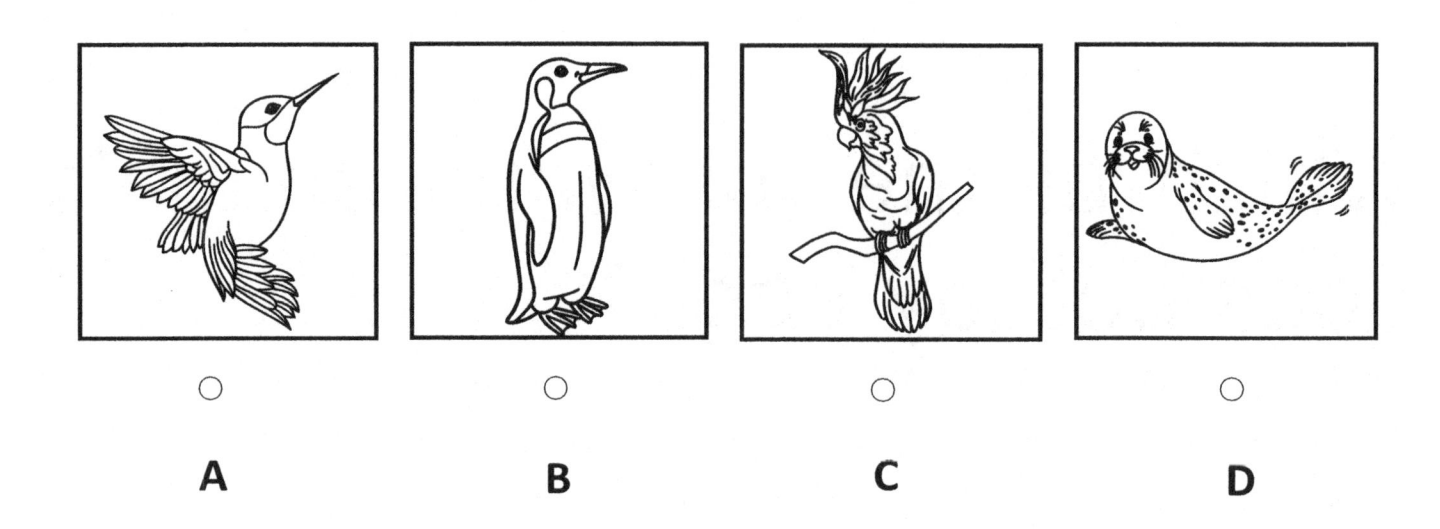

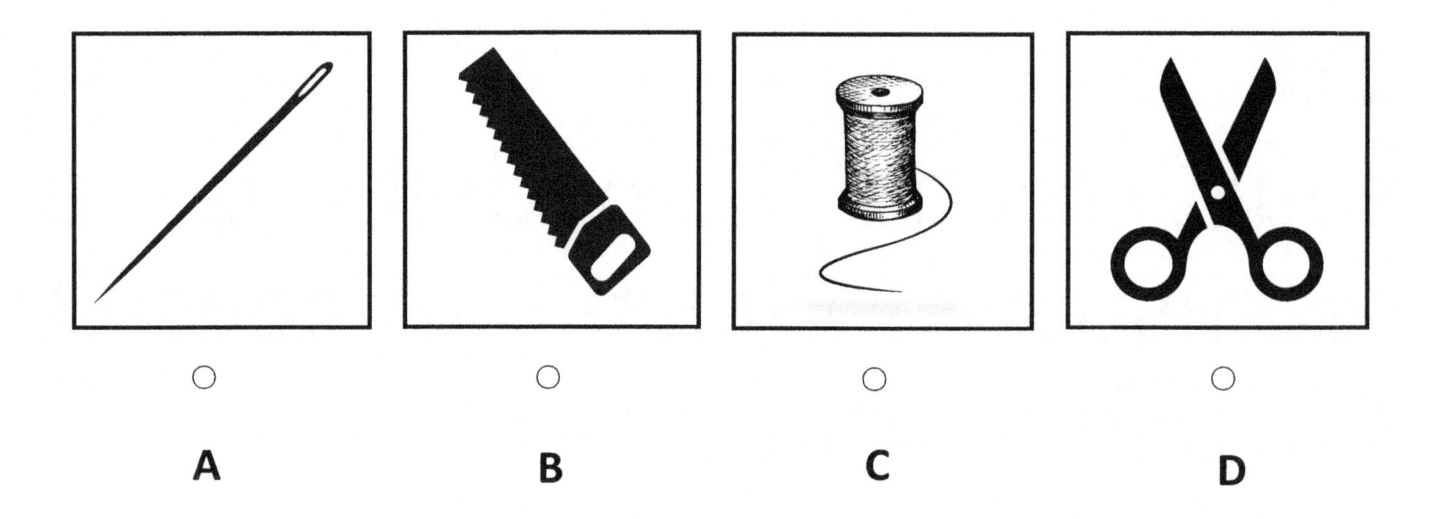

PRACTICE TEST GRADE 2

17.

A	B	C	D

18.

A	B	C	D

180

PRACTICE TEST GRADE 2

PRACTICE TEST NON VERBAL BATTERY

This section is designed to assess a student's ability to reason and think beyond what they've already been taught. This section includes geometric shapes and figures that aren't normally seen in the classroom.

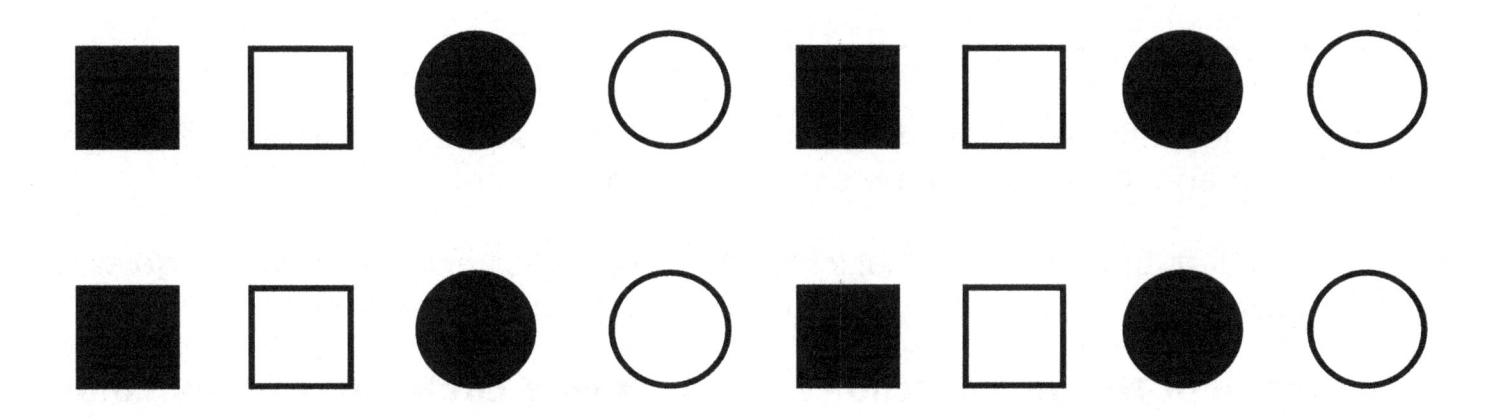

PRACTICE TEST GRADE 2

Figure Matrices

Children are provided with a 2X2 matrix with the image missing in one cell. They have to identify the relationship between the two spatial shapes in the upper line and find a fourth image that has the same correlation with the left shape in the lower line.

Example

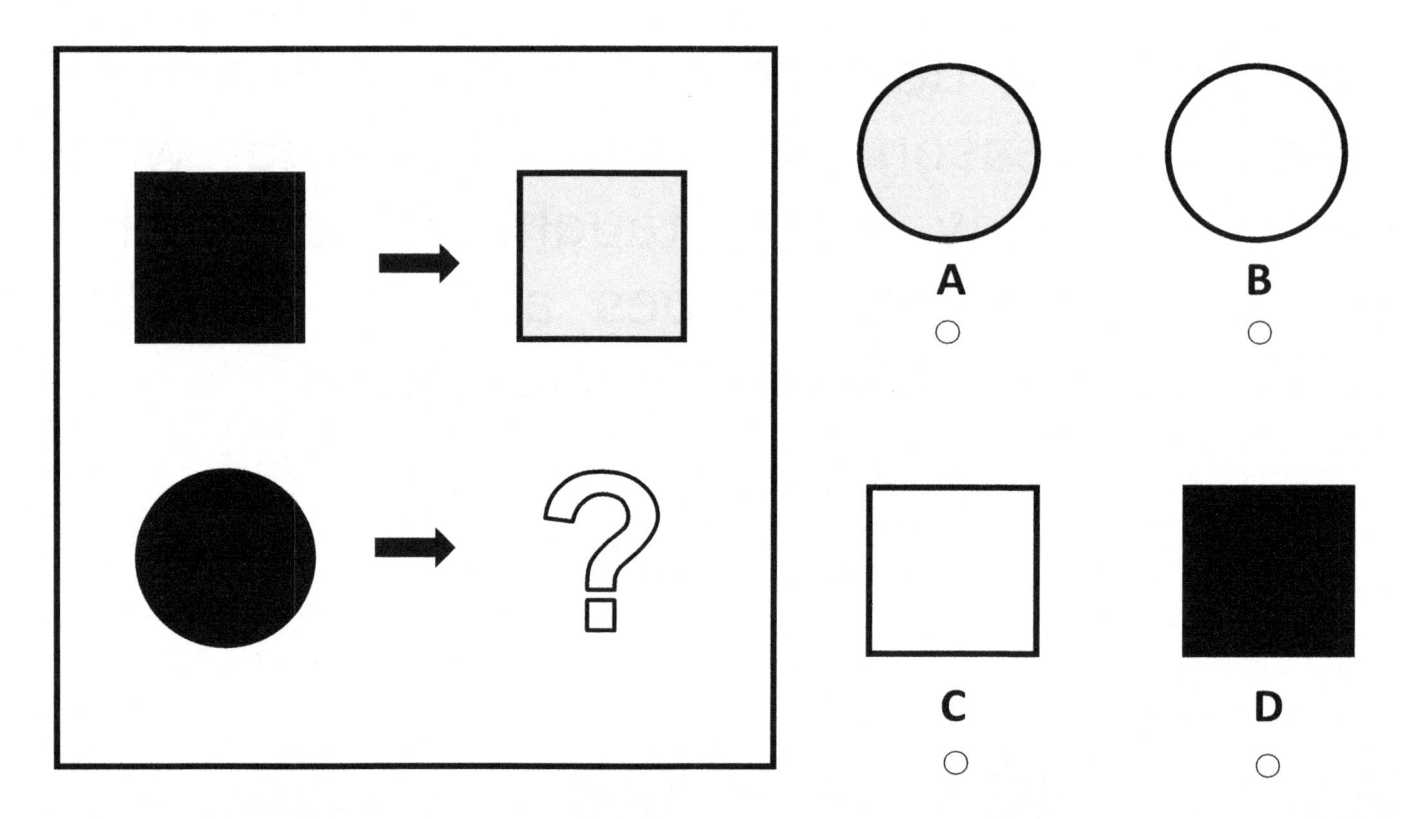

In the upper left box, the image shows a black square. In the upper right box, the image shows the same square, but in grey color.

The lower left box shows a black circle. Which answer choice would go with this image in the same way as the upper images go together?

**The image of the answer choice must show a circle but in grey color, following the same logic of the upper shapes.
The right answer is "A".**

Tips for Figure Matrices

- Consider all the answer choices before selecting one.

- Try to use logic and sequential reasoning.

- Eliminate the logically wrong answers to restrict the options.

- Train yourself to decipher the relationship between different figures and shapes.

- Try to use real objects.

PRACTICE TEST GRADE 2

1.

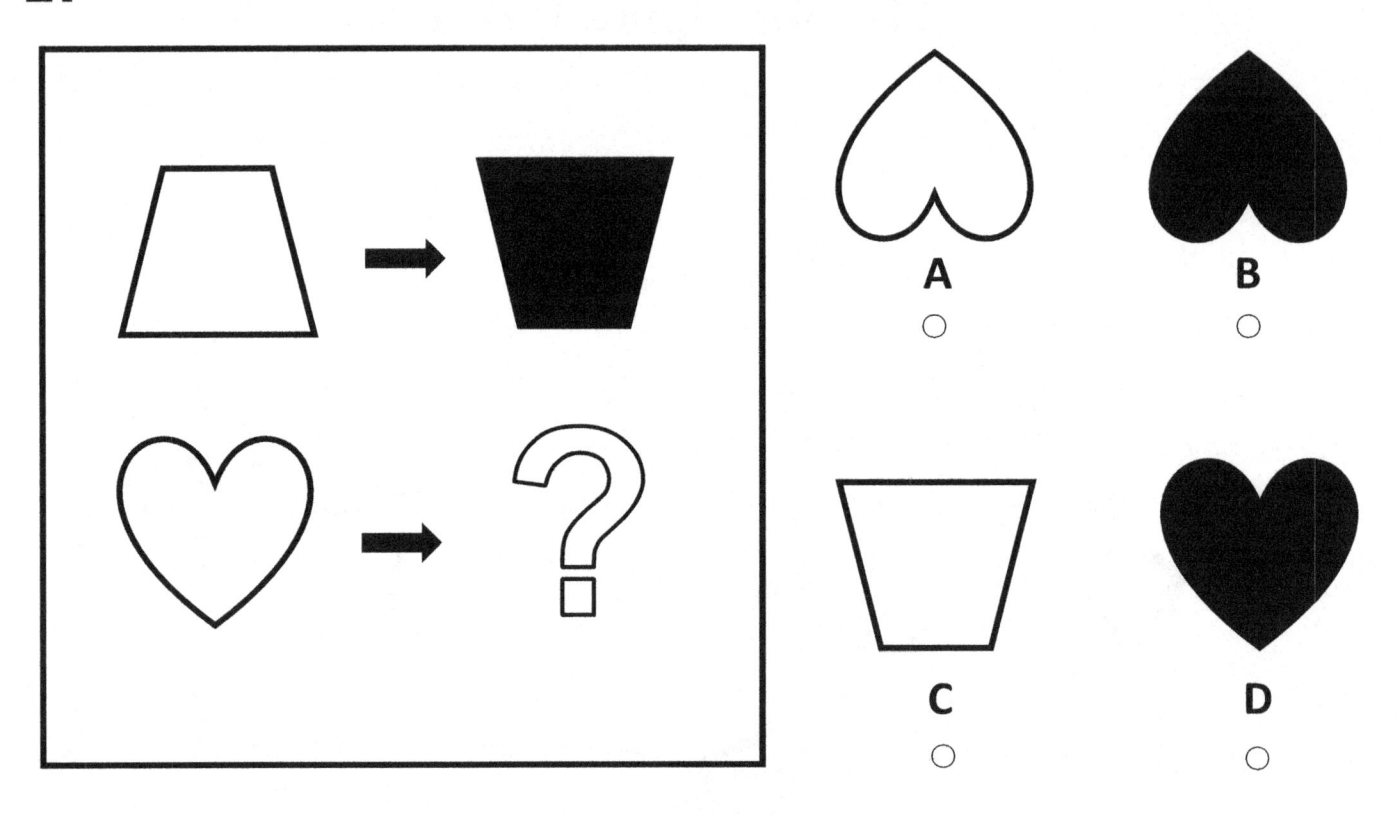

A
B
C
D

2.

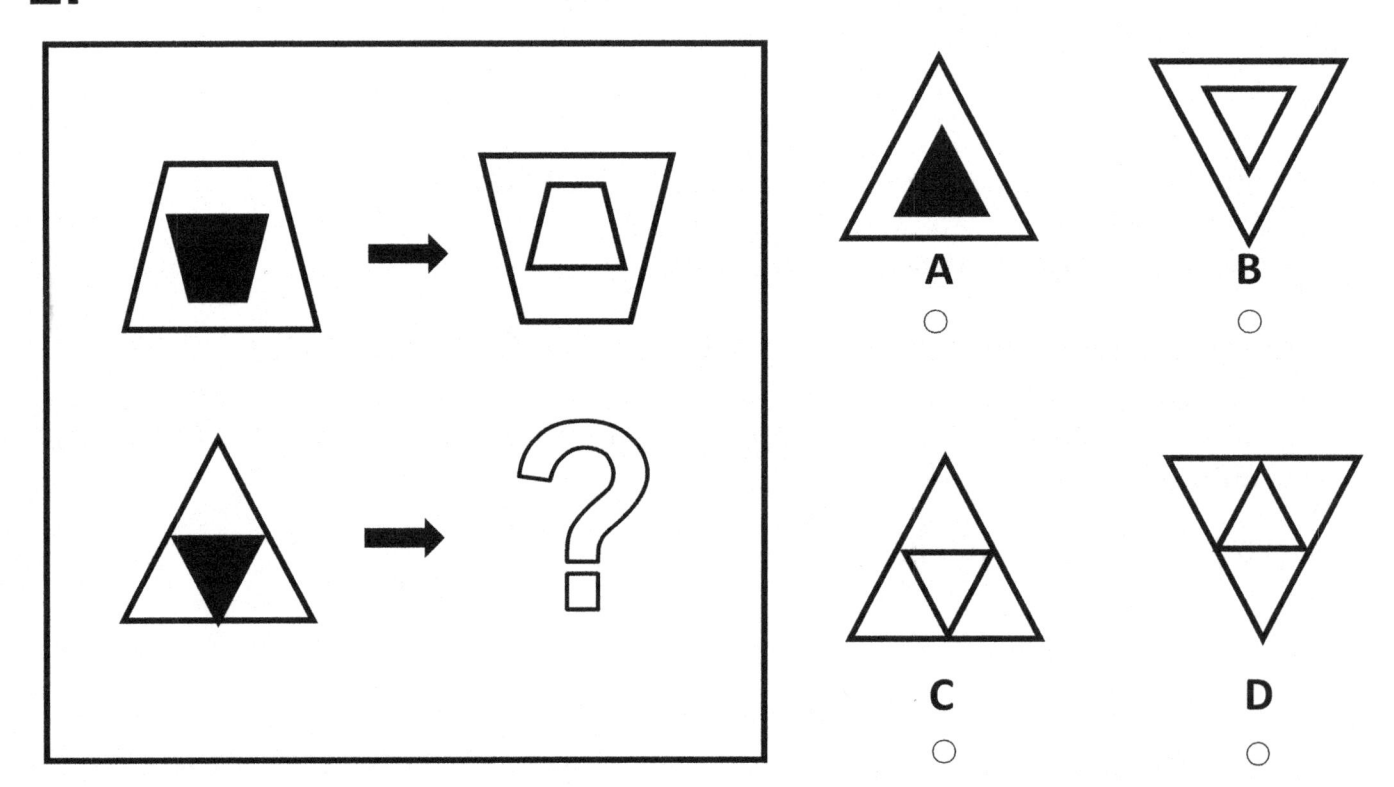

A
B
C
D

184

PRACTICE TEST GRADE 2

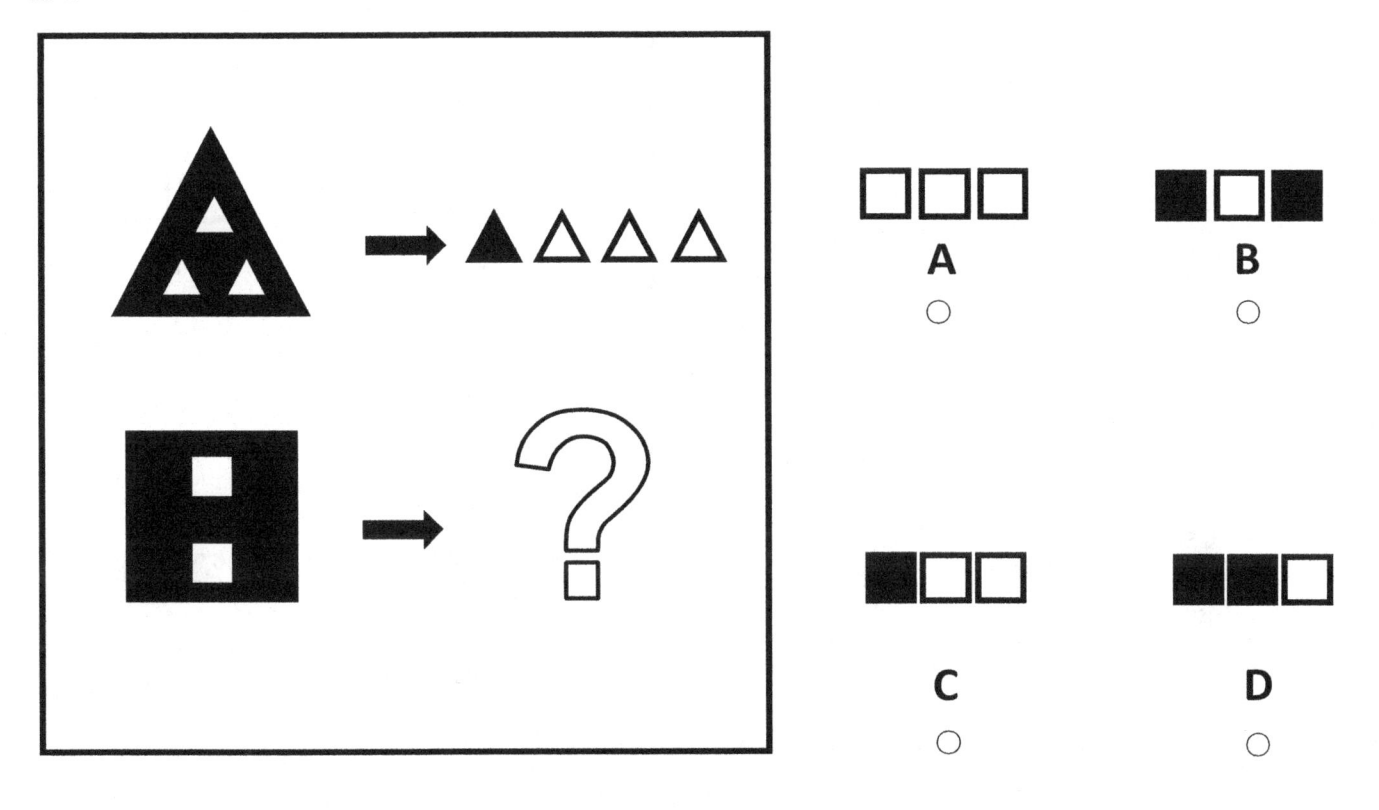

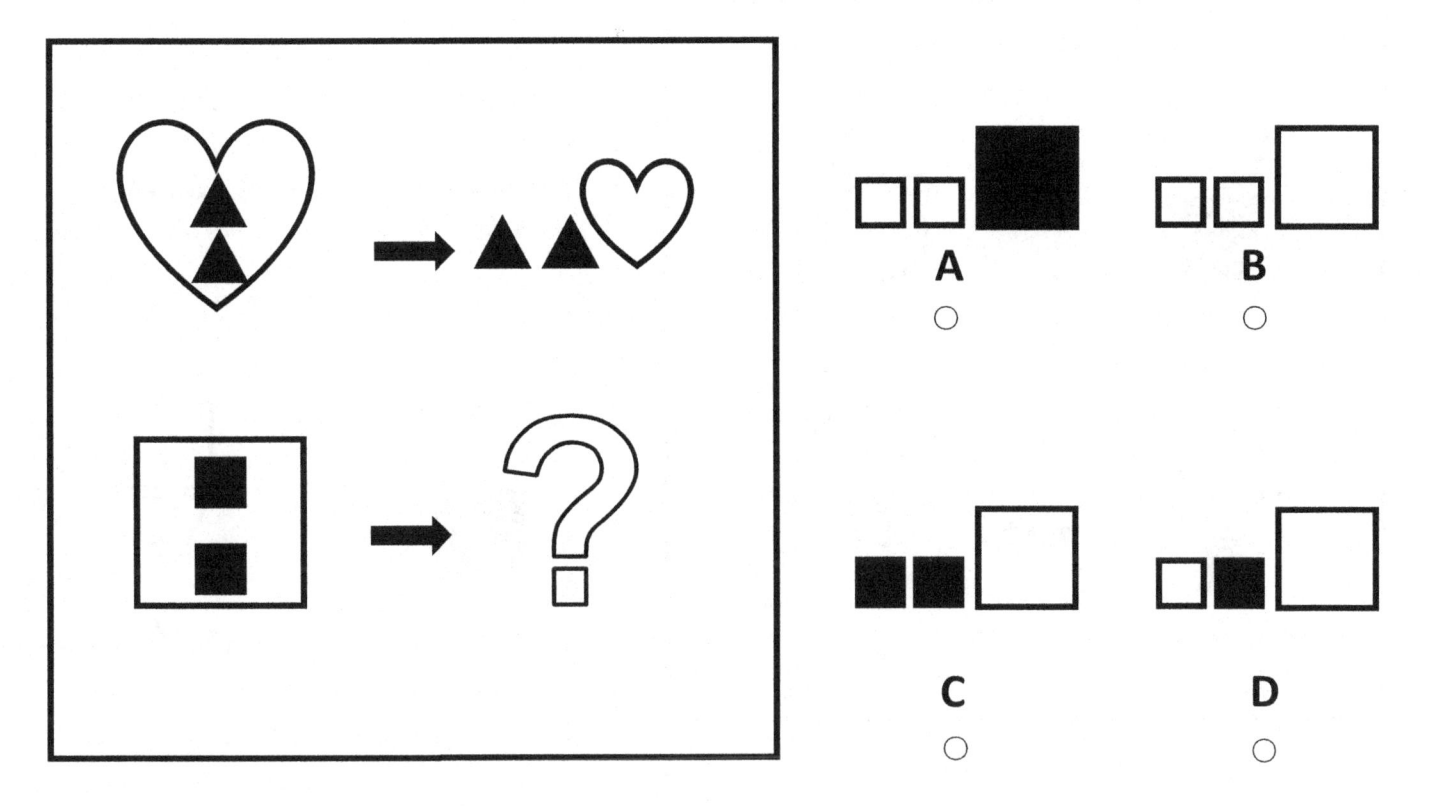

3.

4.

185

PRACTICE TEST GRADE 2

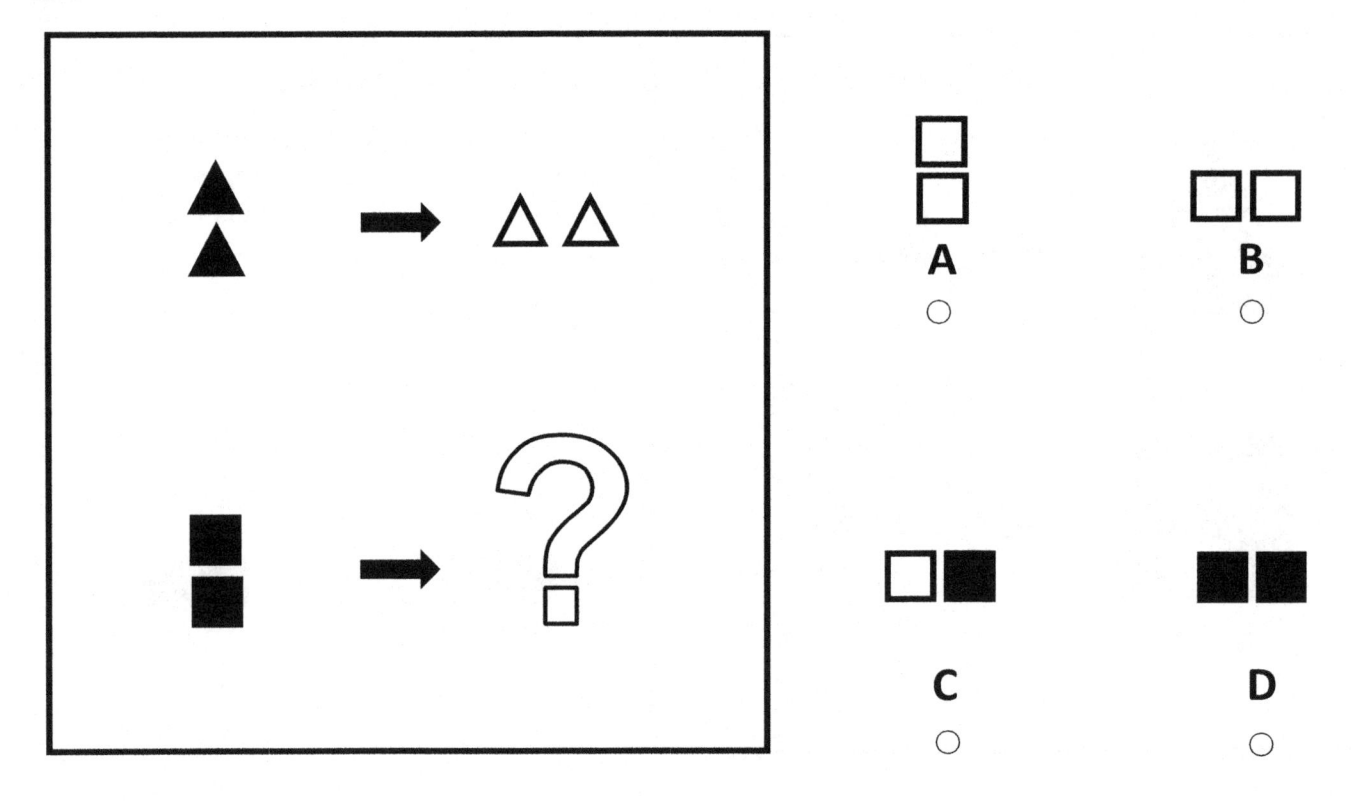

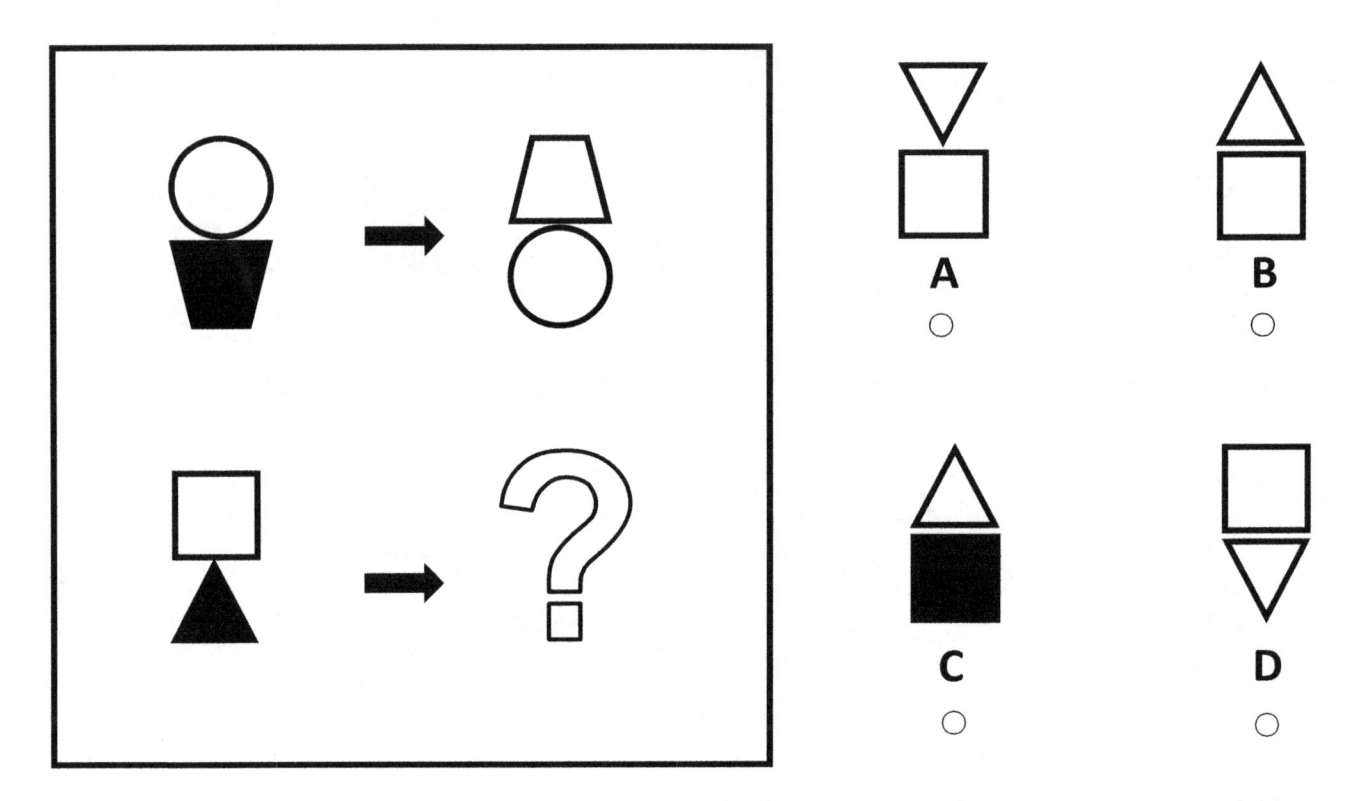

5.

6.

186

PRACTICE TEST GRADE 2

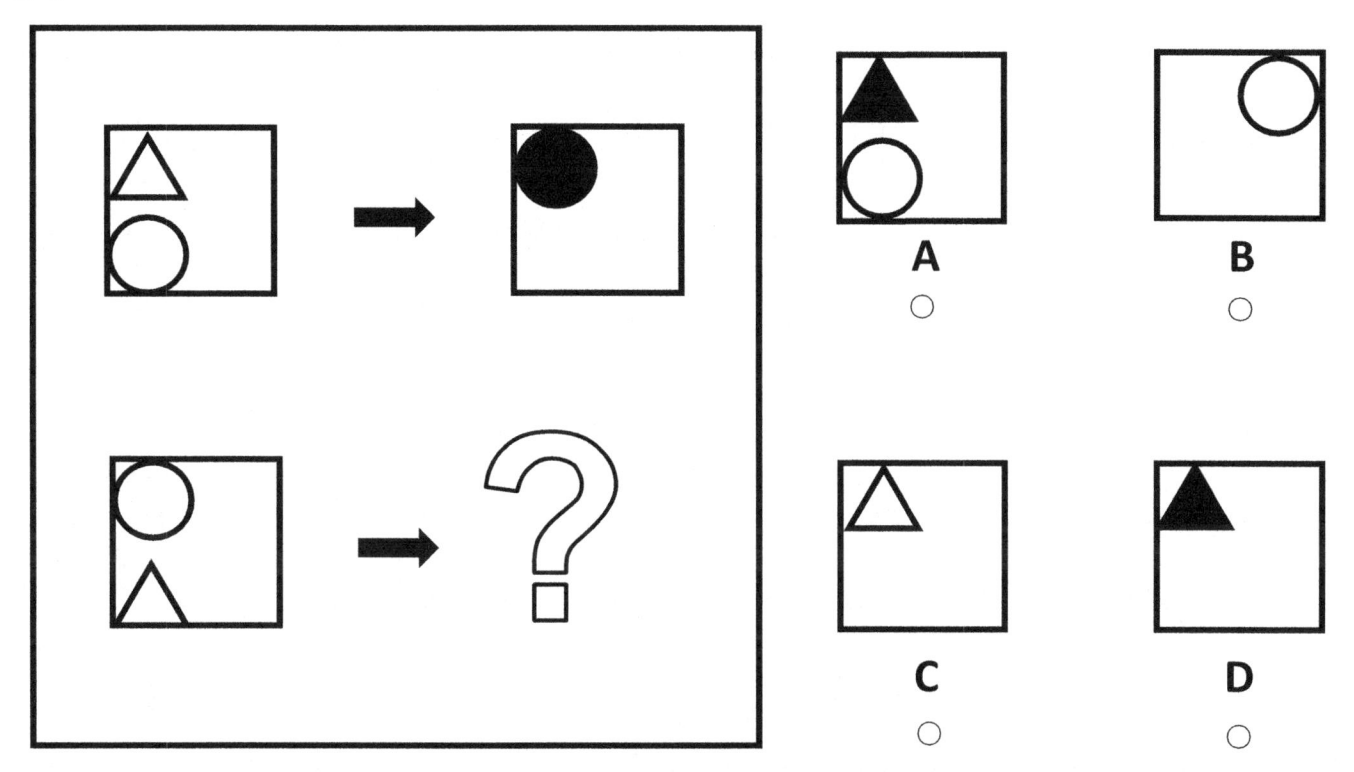

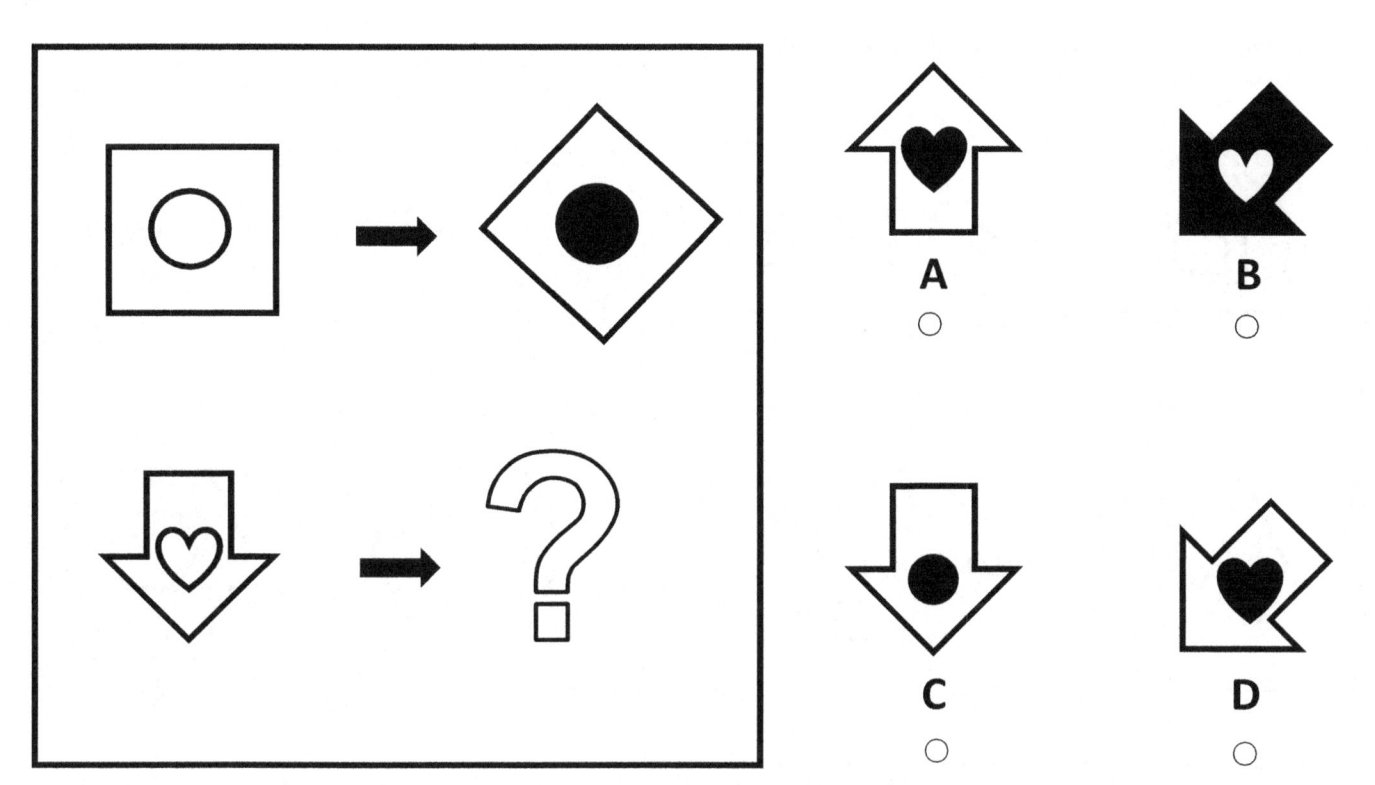

7.

8.

187

PRACTICE TEST GRADE 2

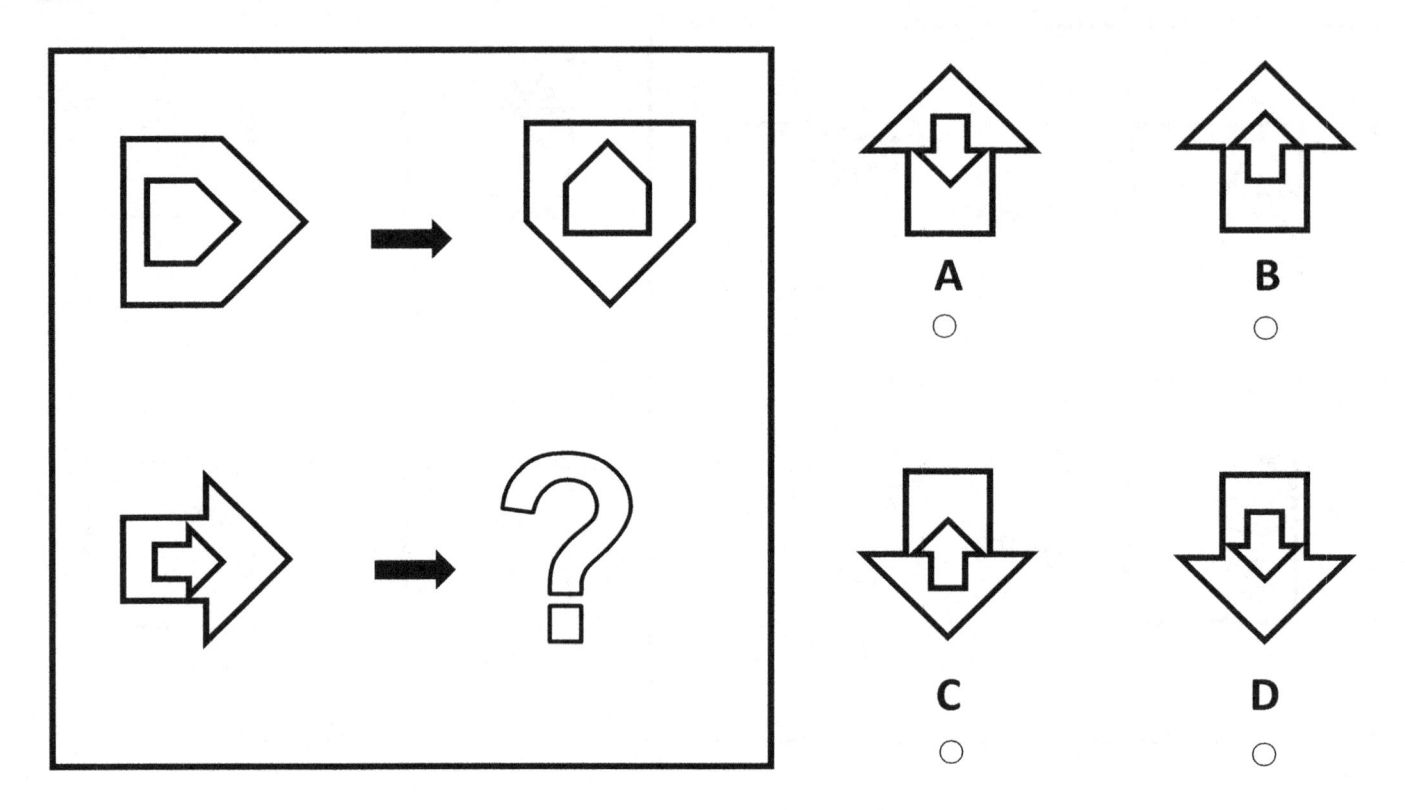

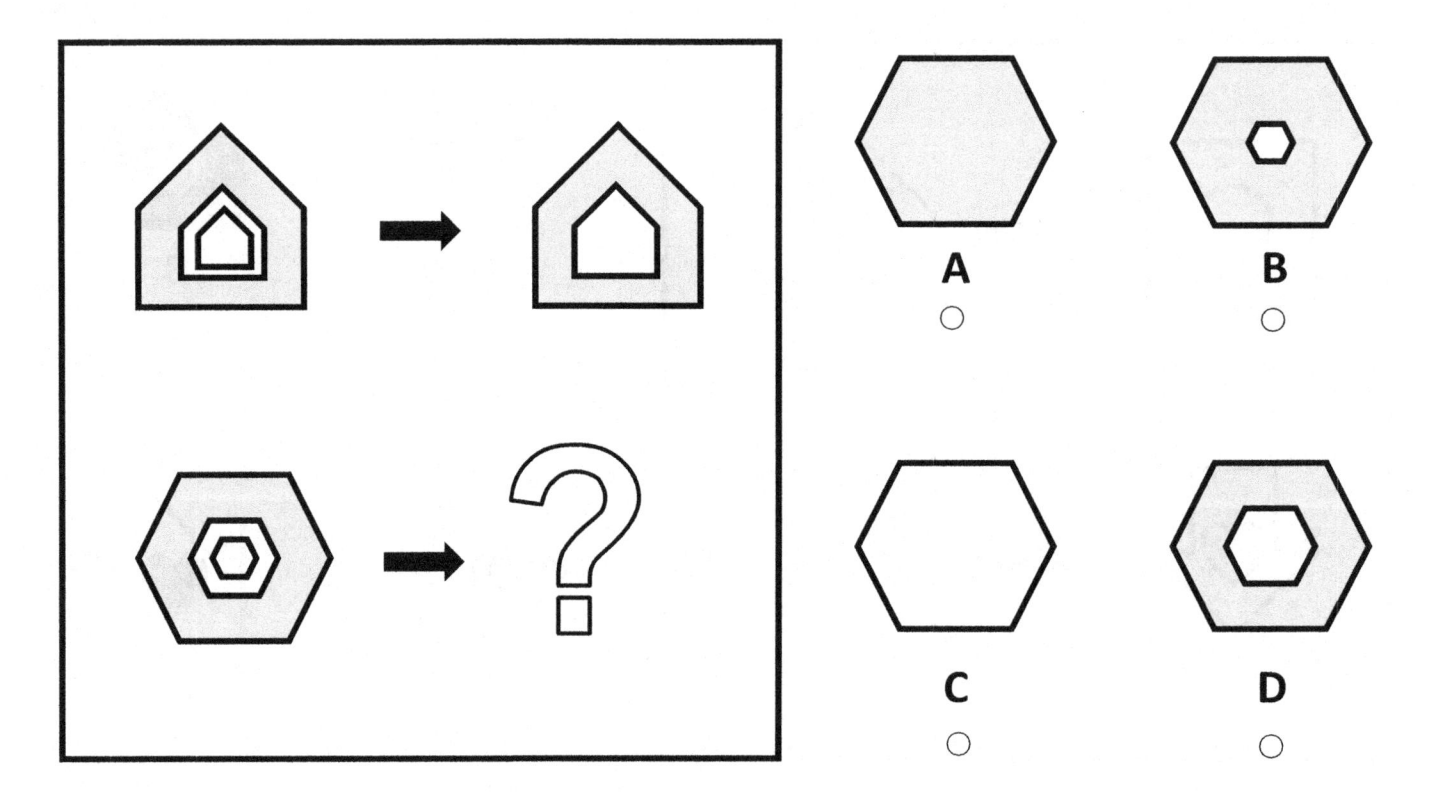

9.

10.

188

PRACTICE TEST GRADE 2

11.

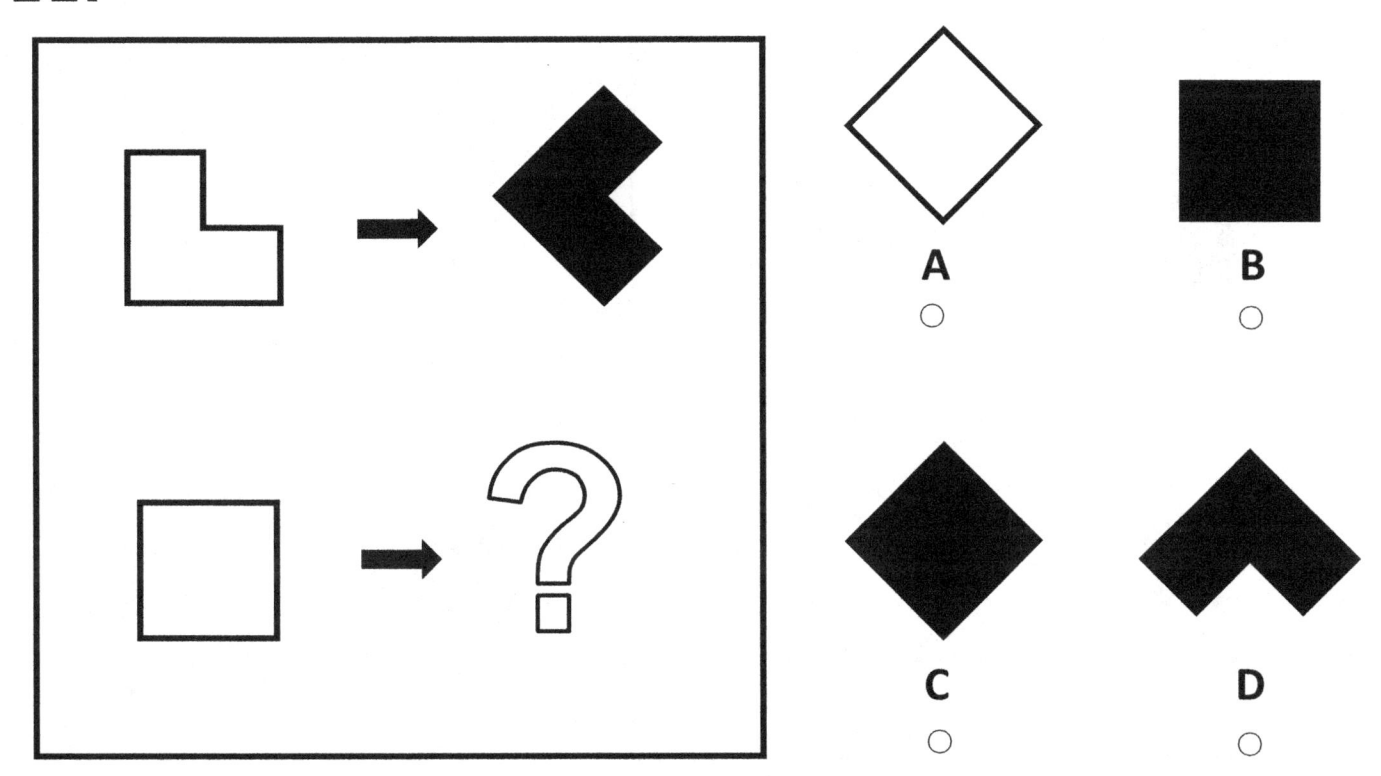

12.

189

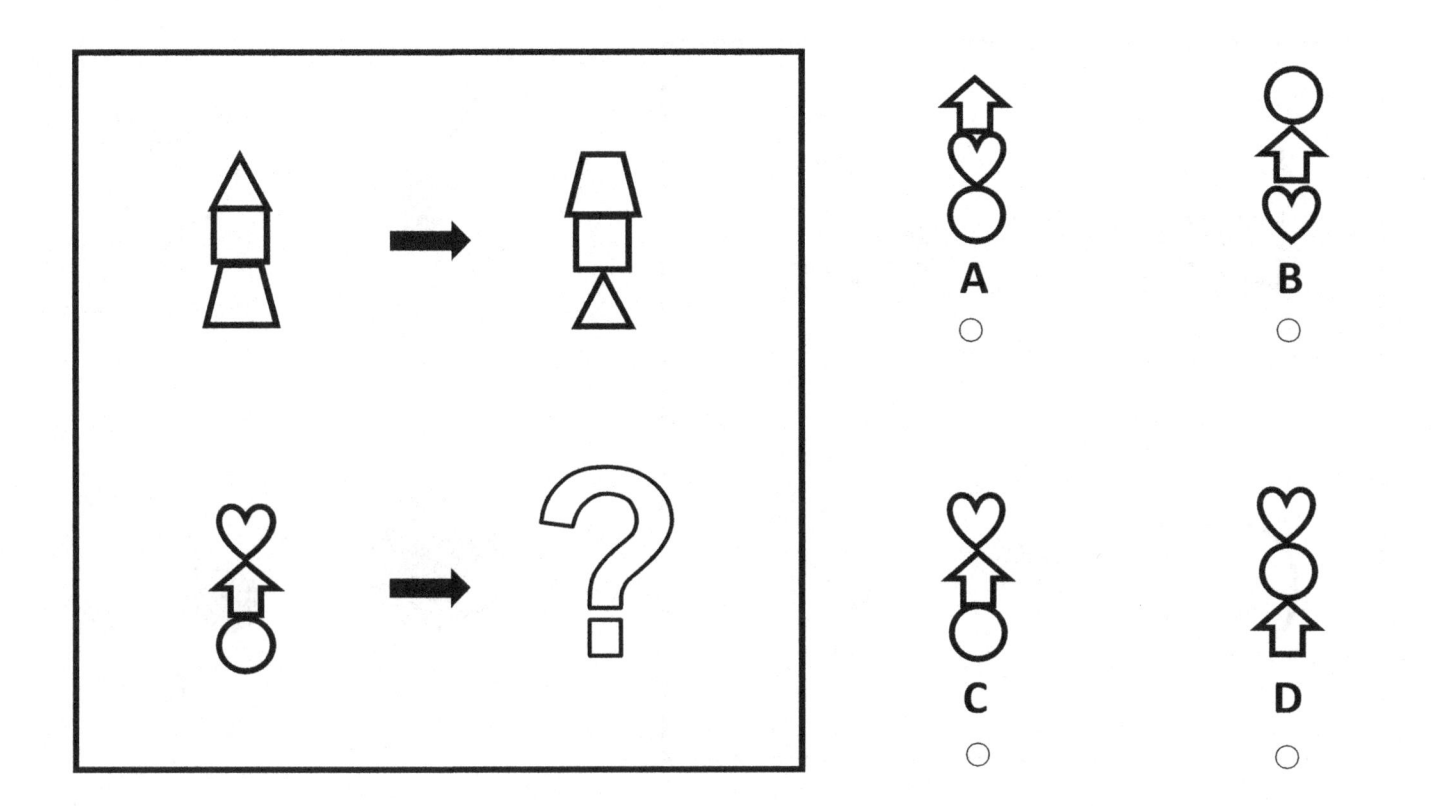

PRACTICE TEST GRADE 2

13.

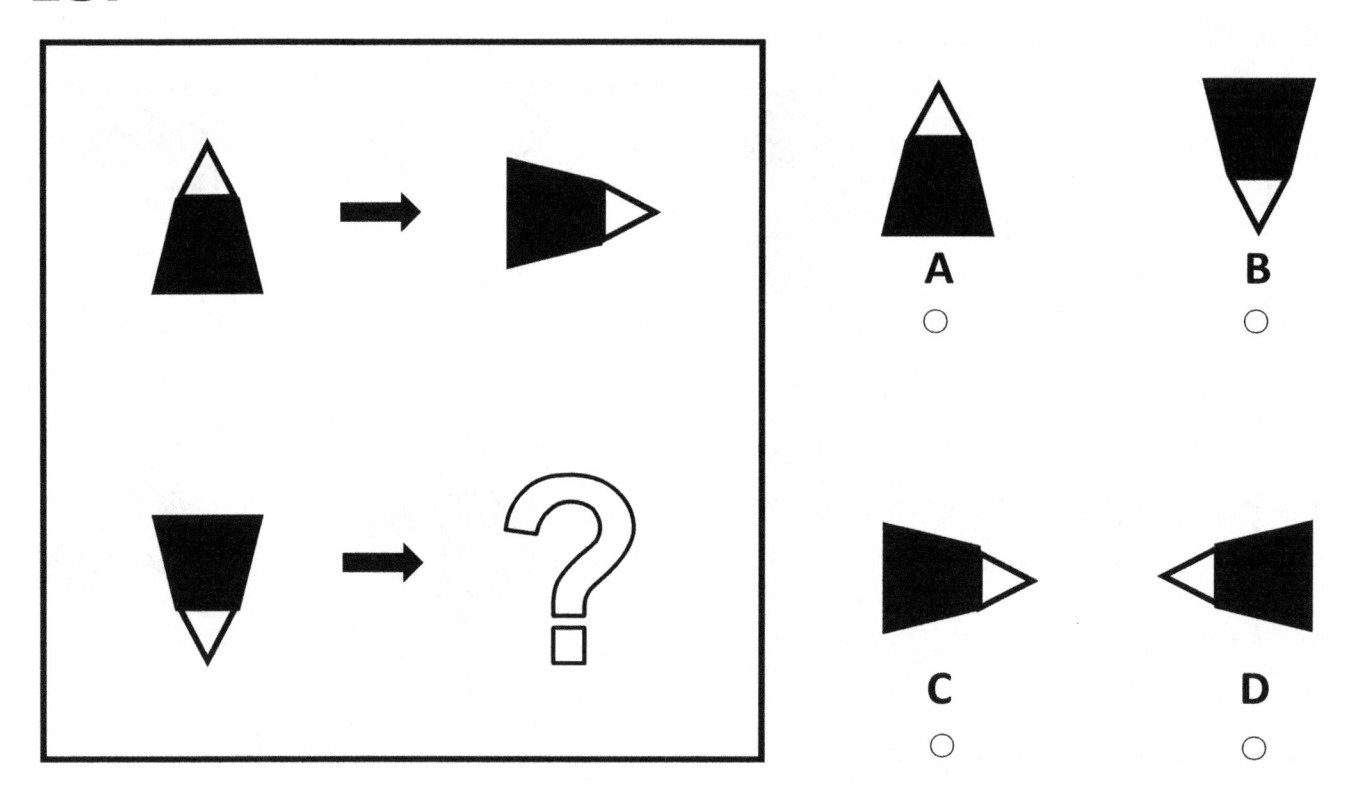

A
B
C
D

14.

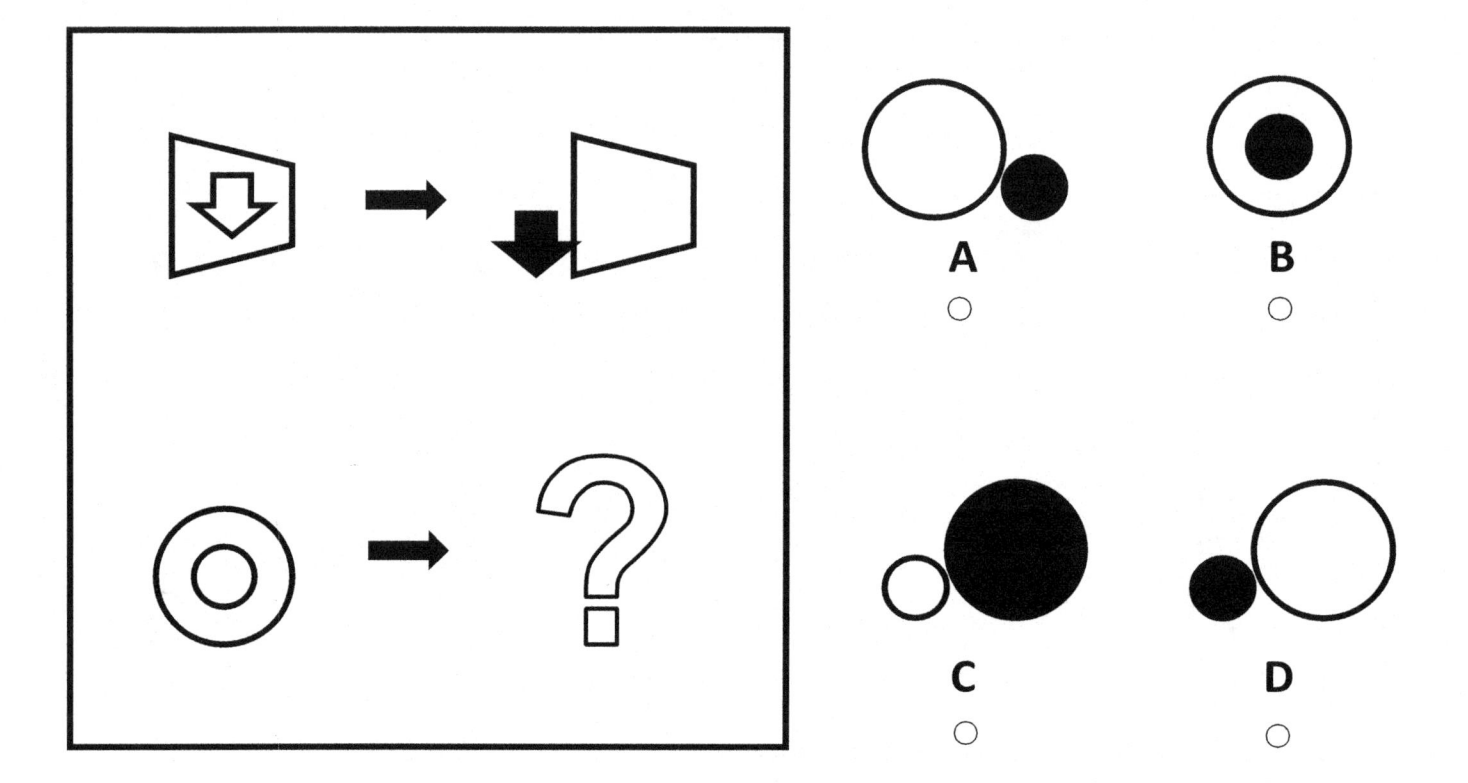

A
B
C
D

190

PRACTICE TEST GRADE 2

15.

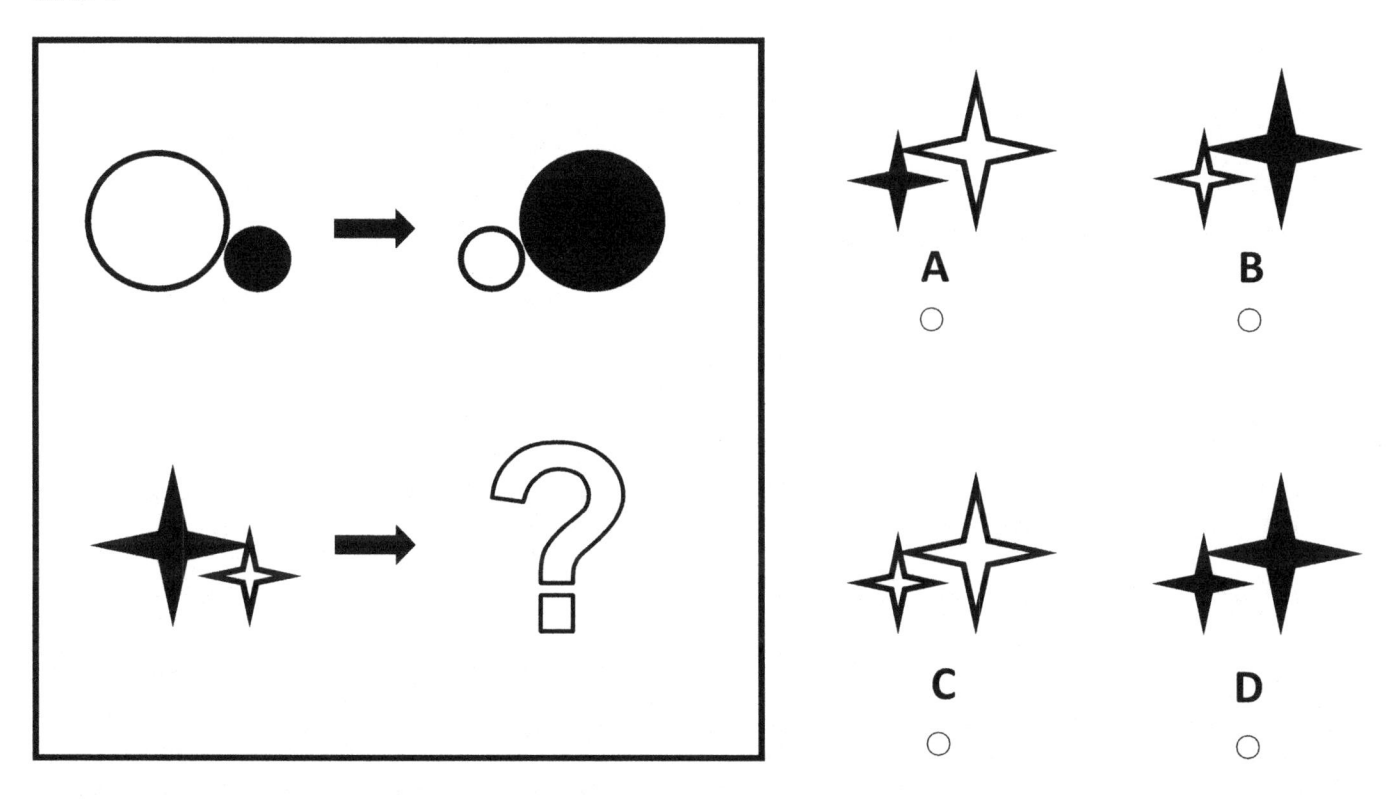

A
B
C
D

16.

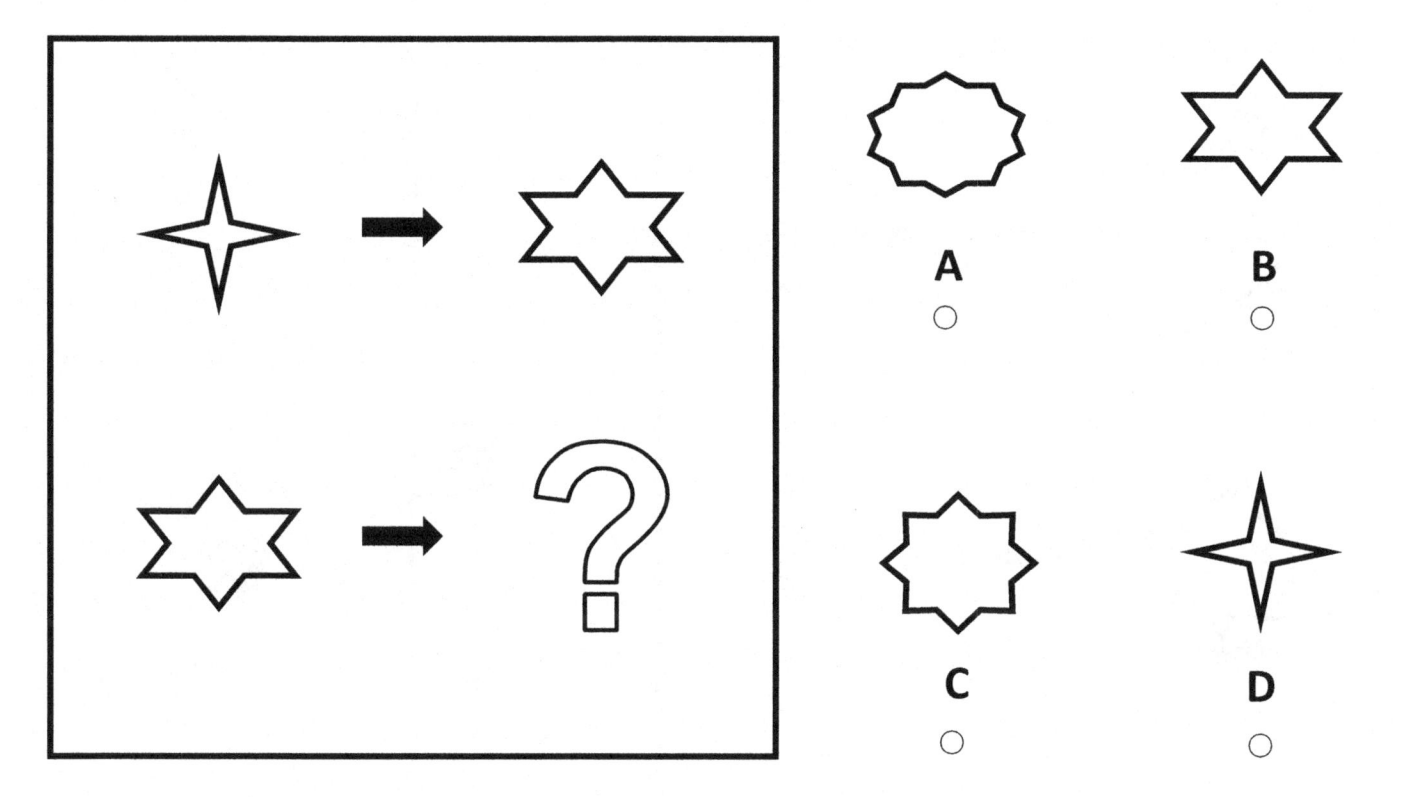

A
B
C
D

191

PRACTICE TEST GRADE 2

17.

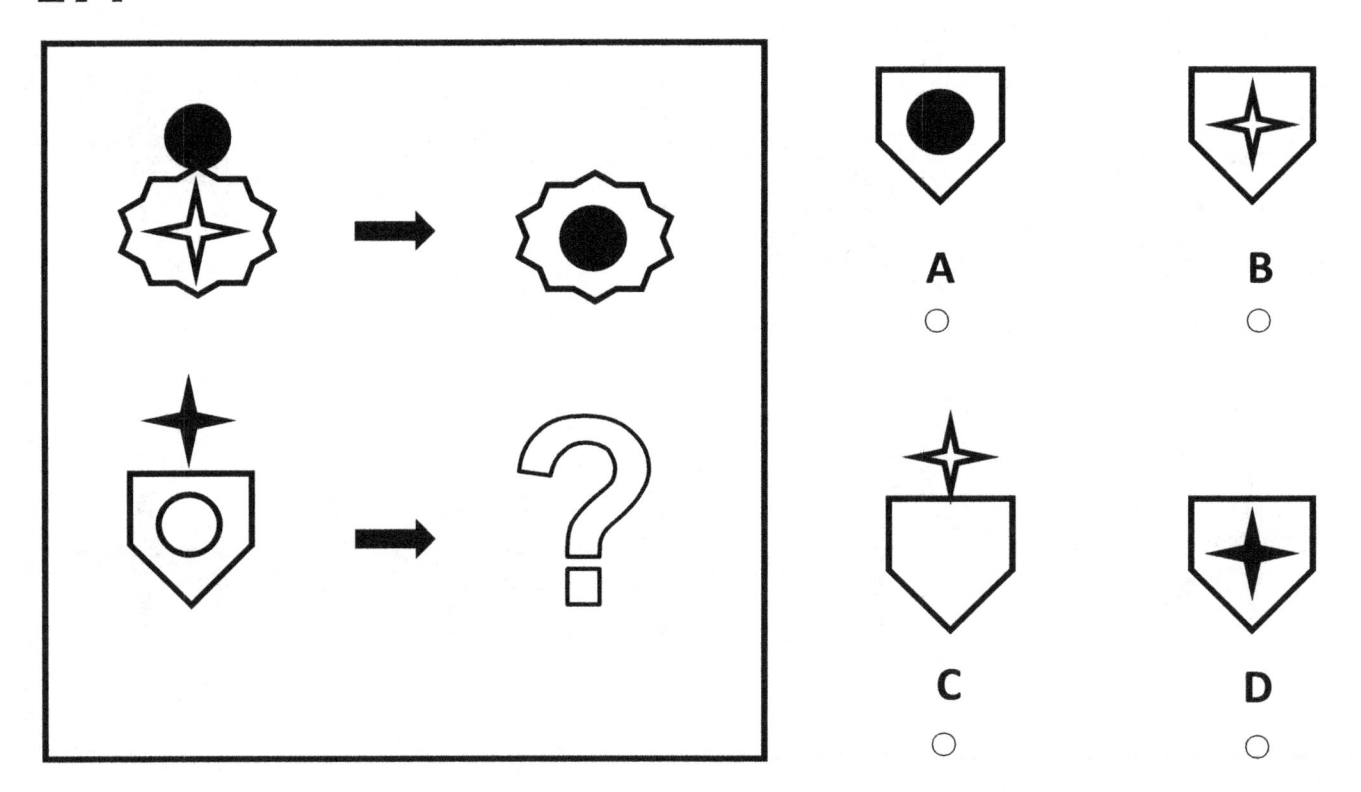

A B C D

18.

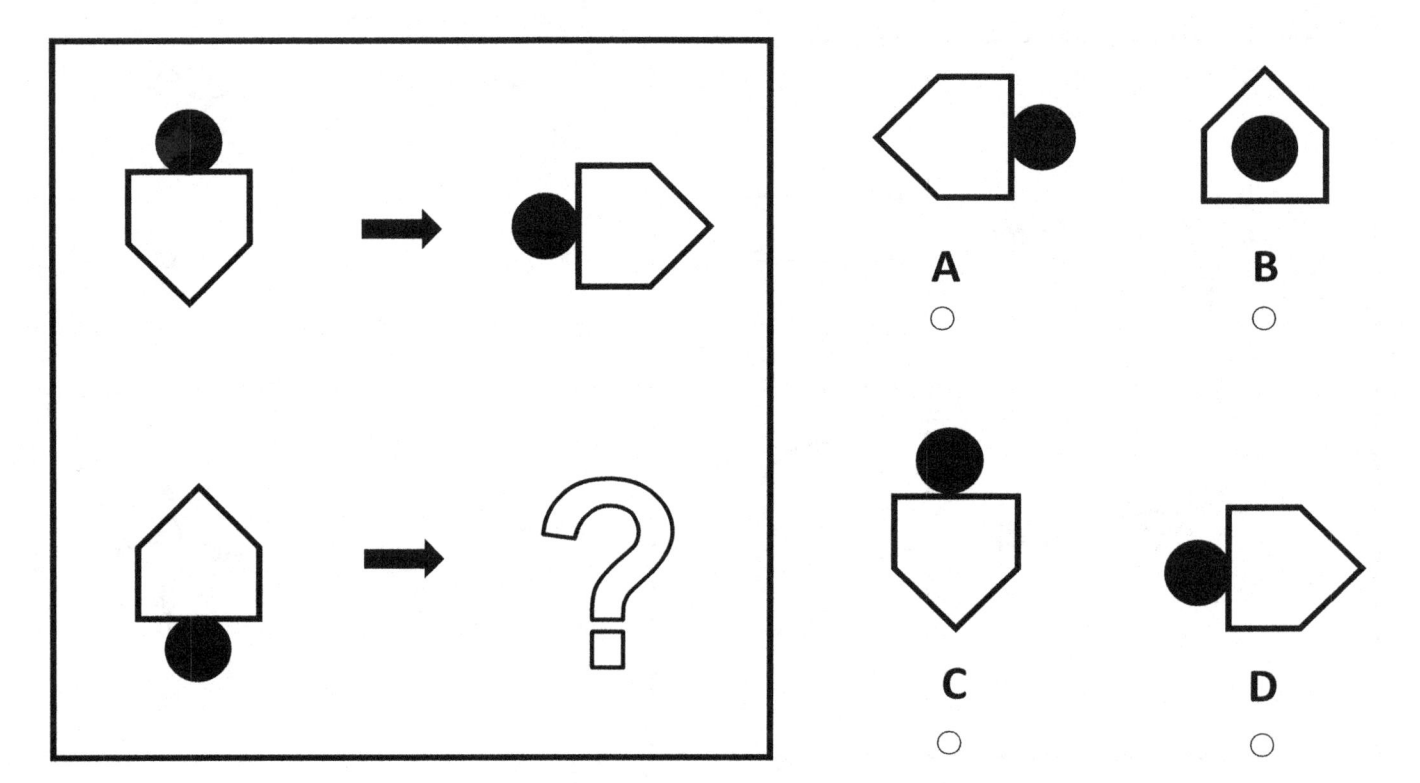

A B C D

192

PRACTICE TEST GRADE 2

Figure Classification

Students are provided with three shapes and they have to select the answer choice that should be the fourth figure in the set, based on the similarity with the other three figures. The intention is to test the student's ability to recognize similar patterns and to make a rational choice.

Example

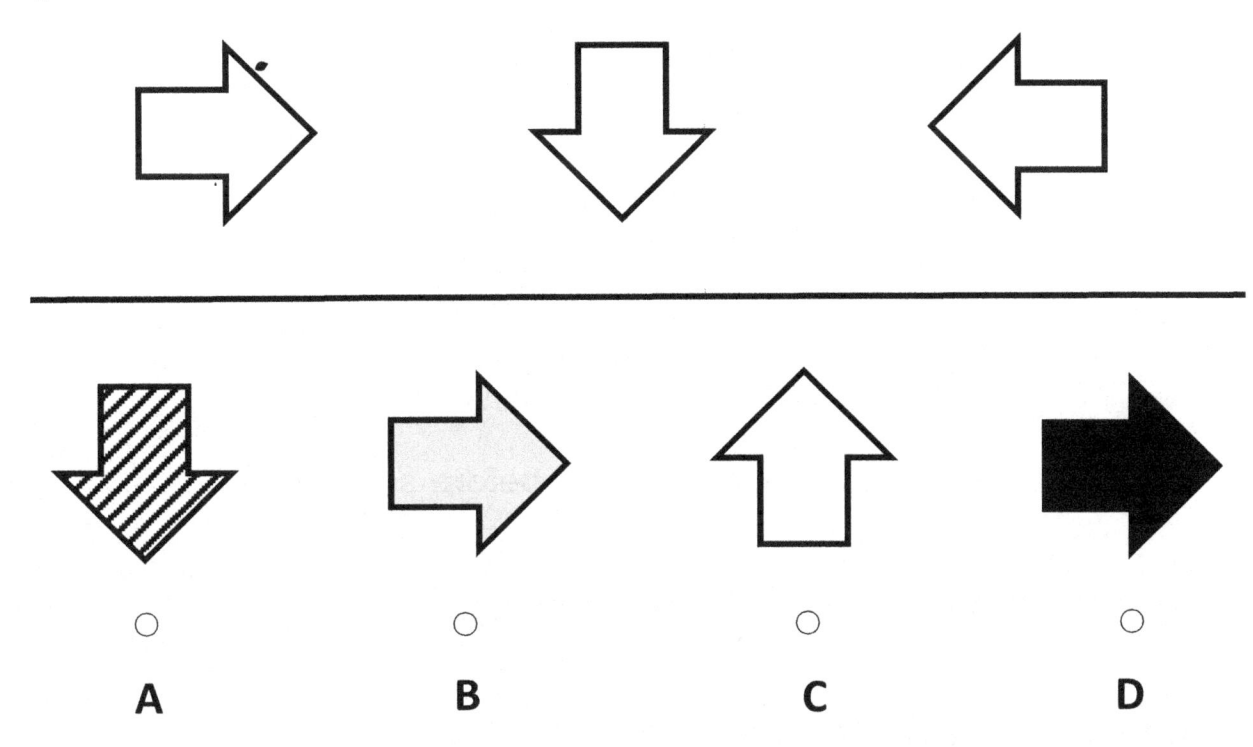

Look at the three pictures on the top. What do these three figures have in common?
You can see three white arrows in the same size.
Now, look at the shapes in the row of the answer choices. Which image matches best the three shapes in the top row?

The image of the answer choice must be a white arrow. The right answer is "C".

PRACTICE TEST GRADE 2

Tips for Figure Classification

- Be sure to review all answer choices before selecting one.

- Try to use logic and sequential reasoning.

- Carefully consider the elements of each figure:

6. color
7. form
8. number of sides
9. orientation
10.   number of elements inside each figure

- Try to exclude the obviously wrong options to reduce the answer choices.

PRACTICE TEST GRADE 2

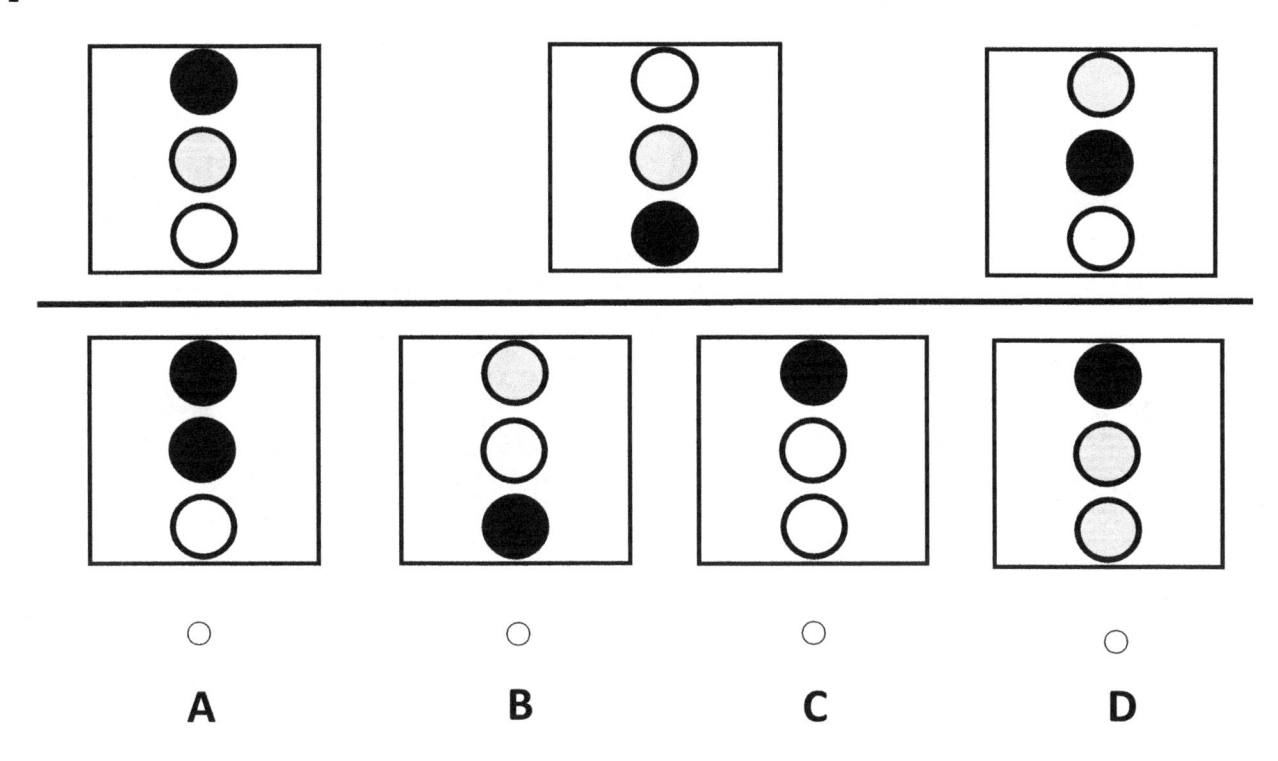

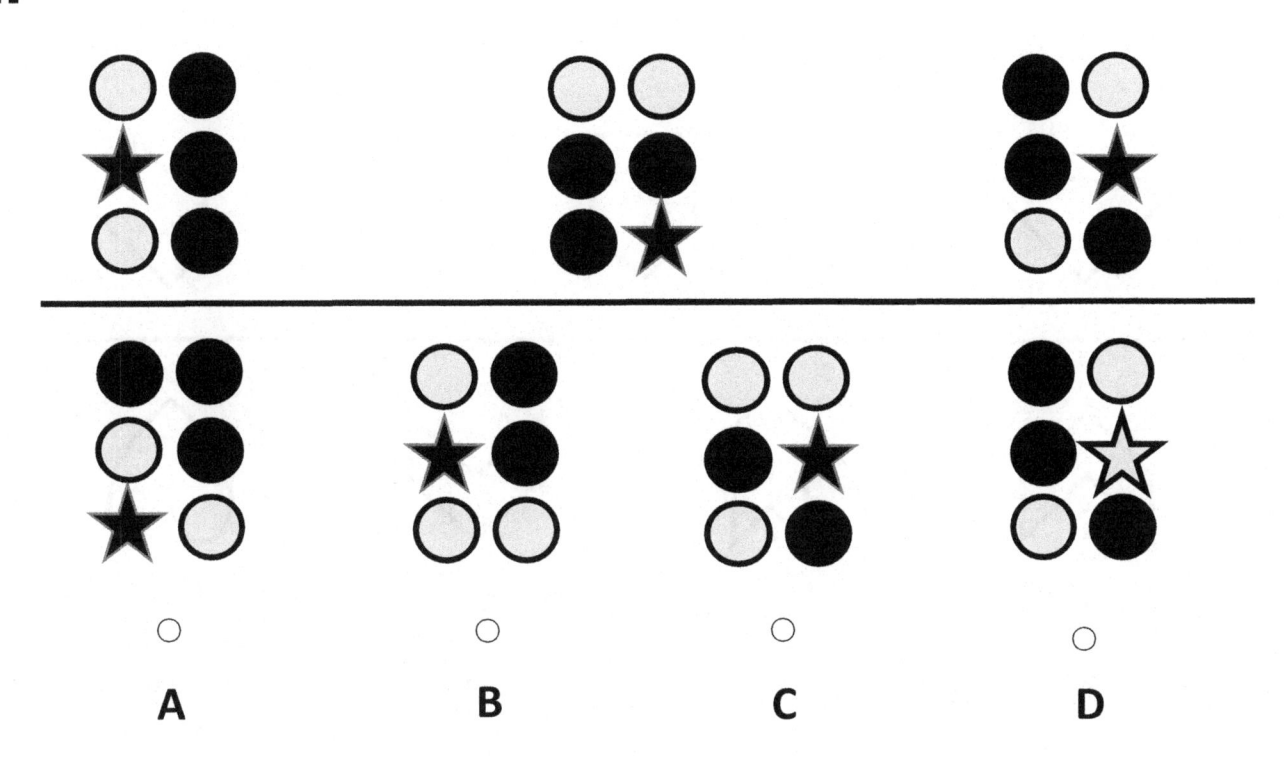

1.

2.

195

PRACTICE TEST GRADE 2

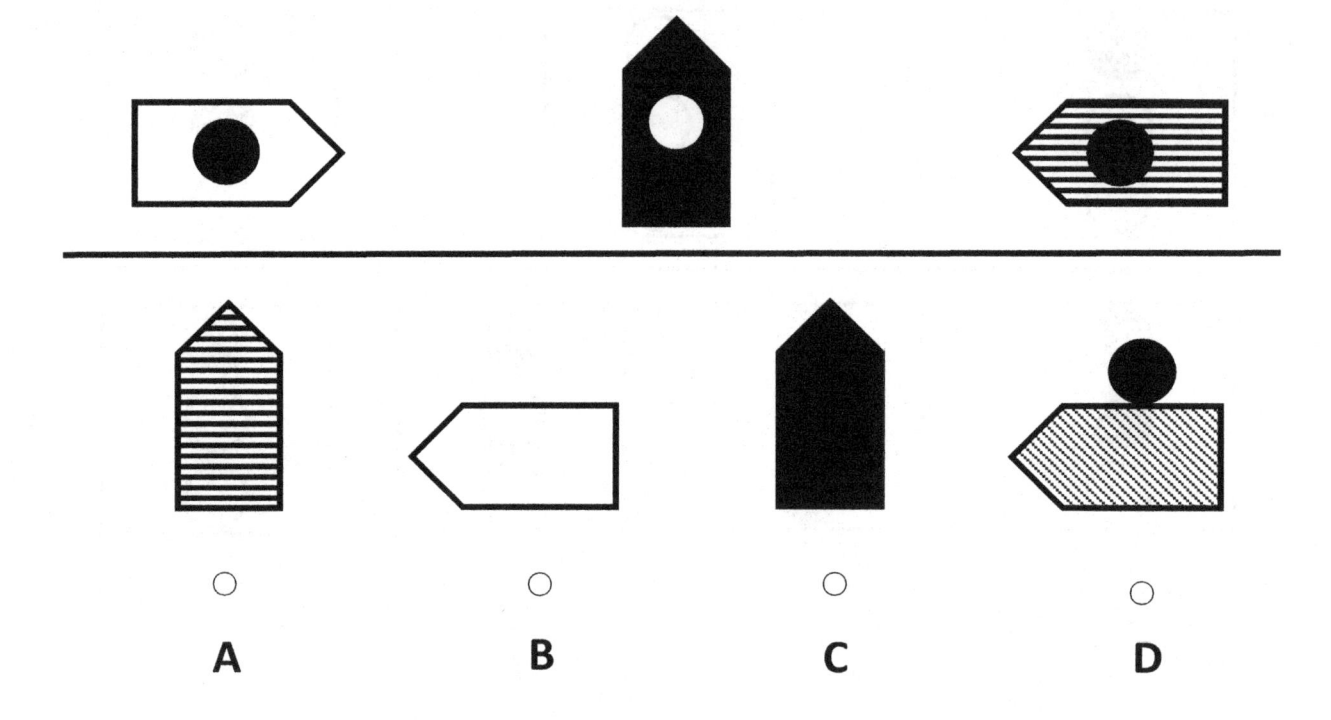

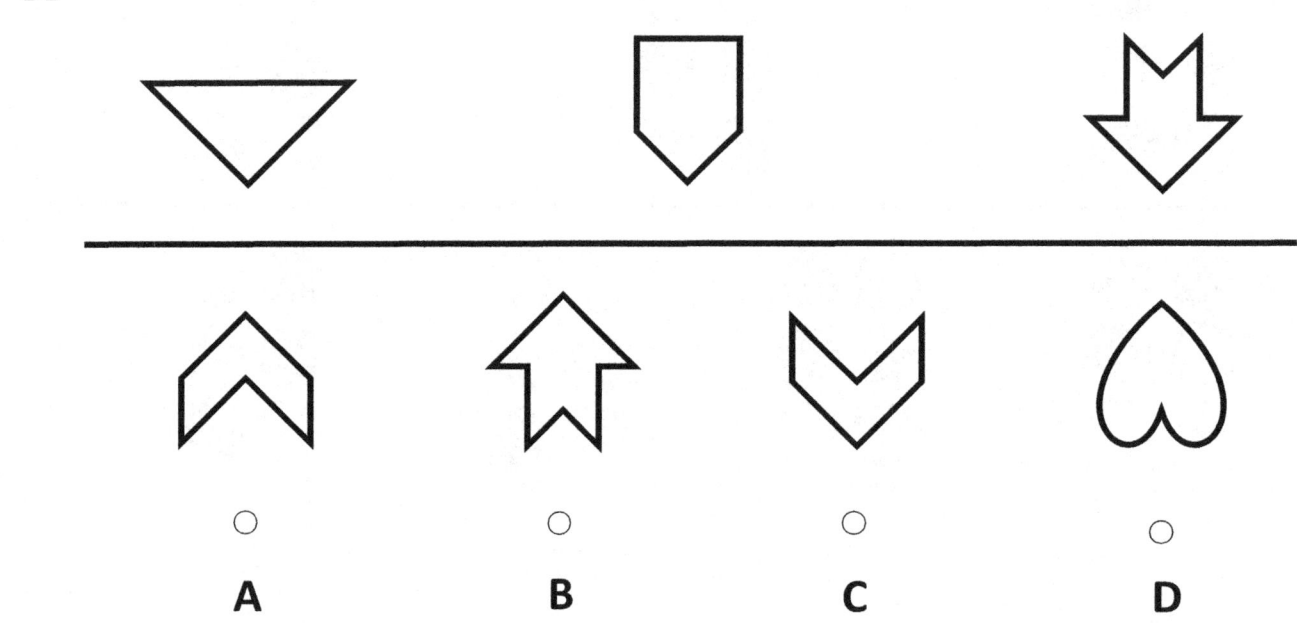

3.

4.

196

PRACTICE TEST GRADE 2

5.

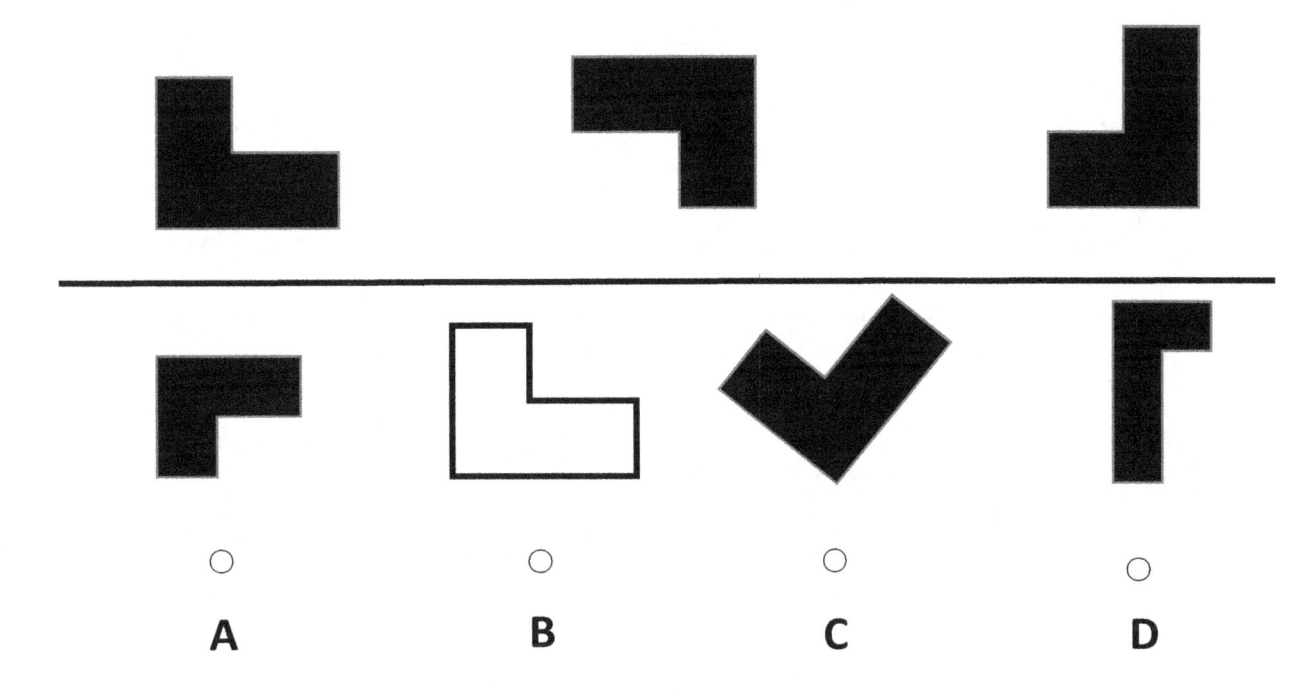

○ A   ○ B   ○ C   ○ D

6.

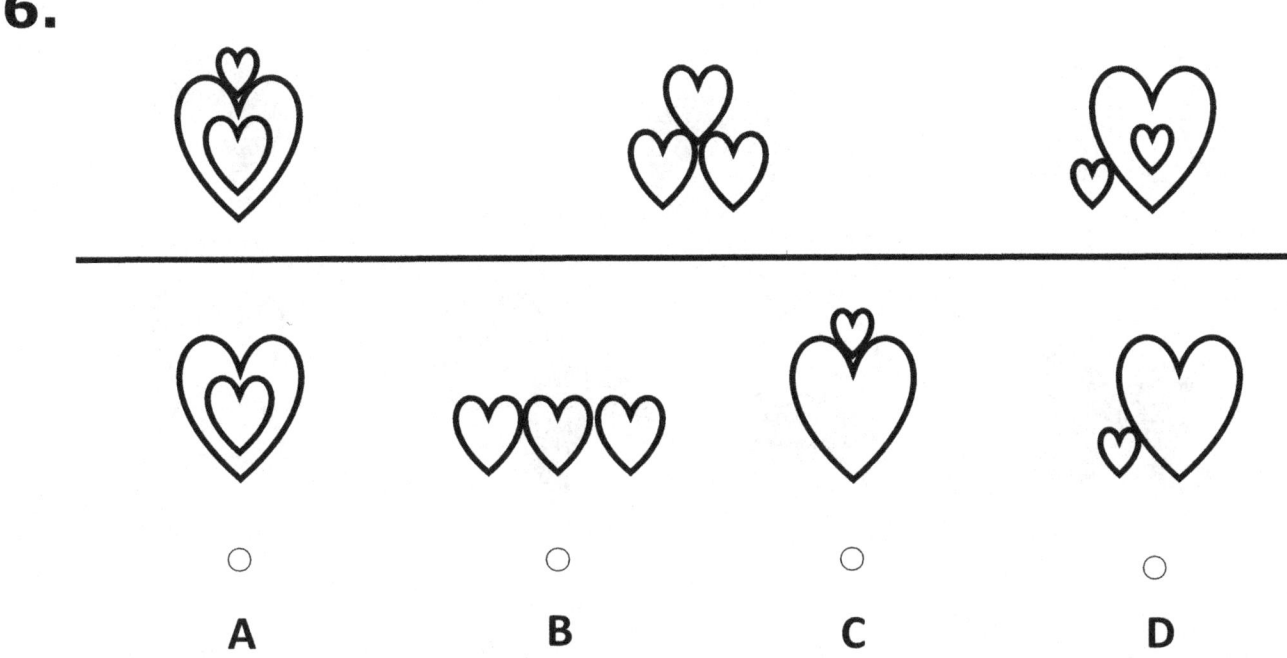

○ A   ○ B   ○ C   ○ D

197

PRACTICE TEST GRADE 2

7.

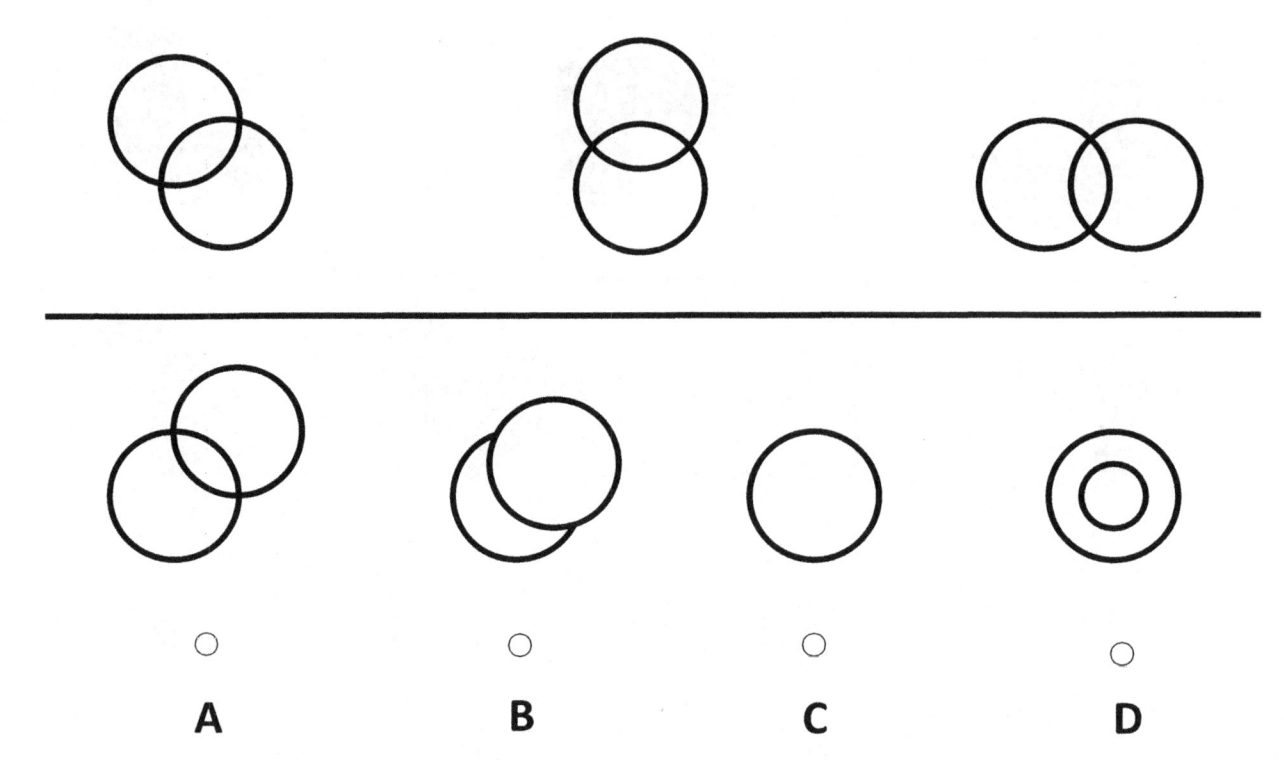

○ A   ○ B   ○ C   ○ D

8.

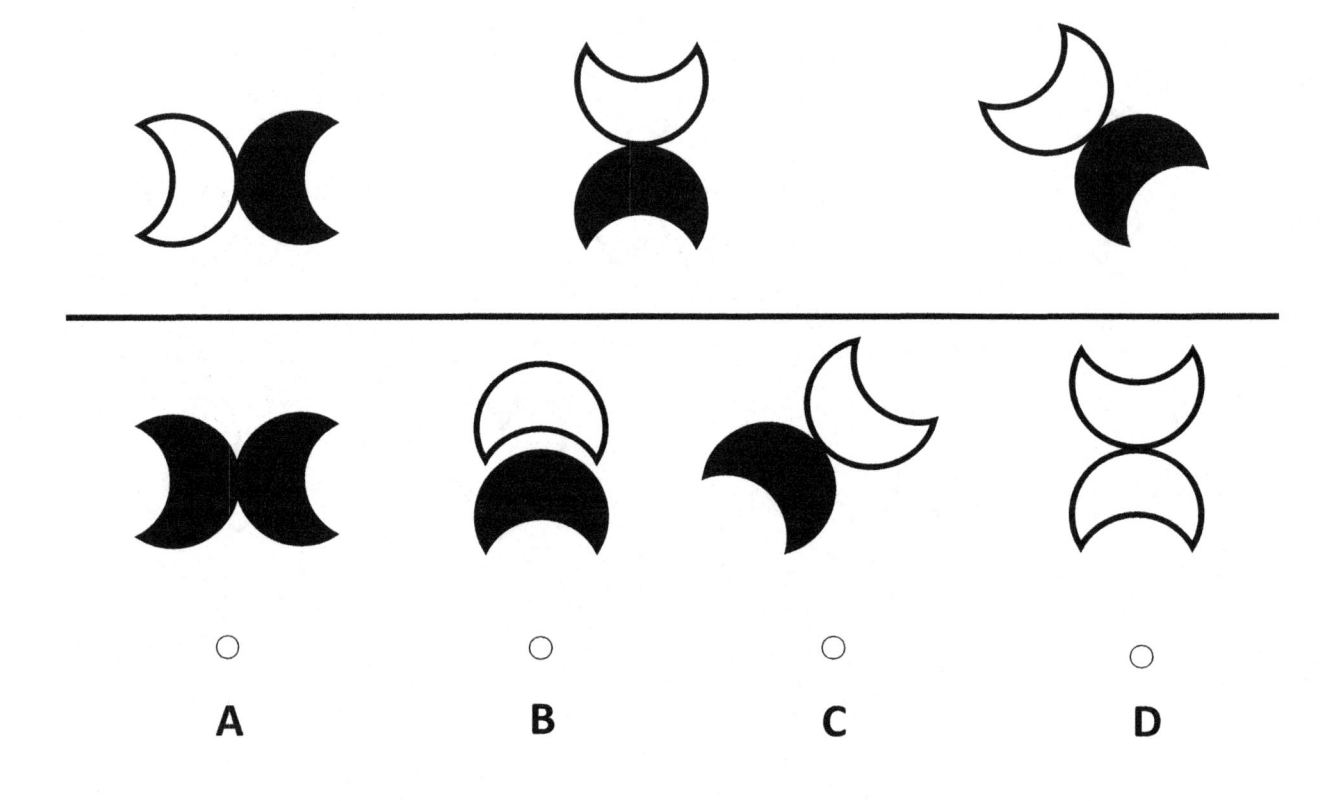

○ A   ○ B   ○ C   ○ D

198

PRACTICE TEST GRADE 2

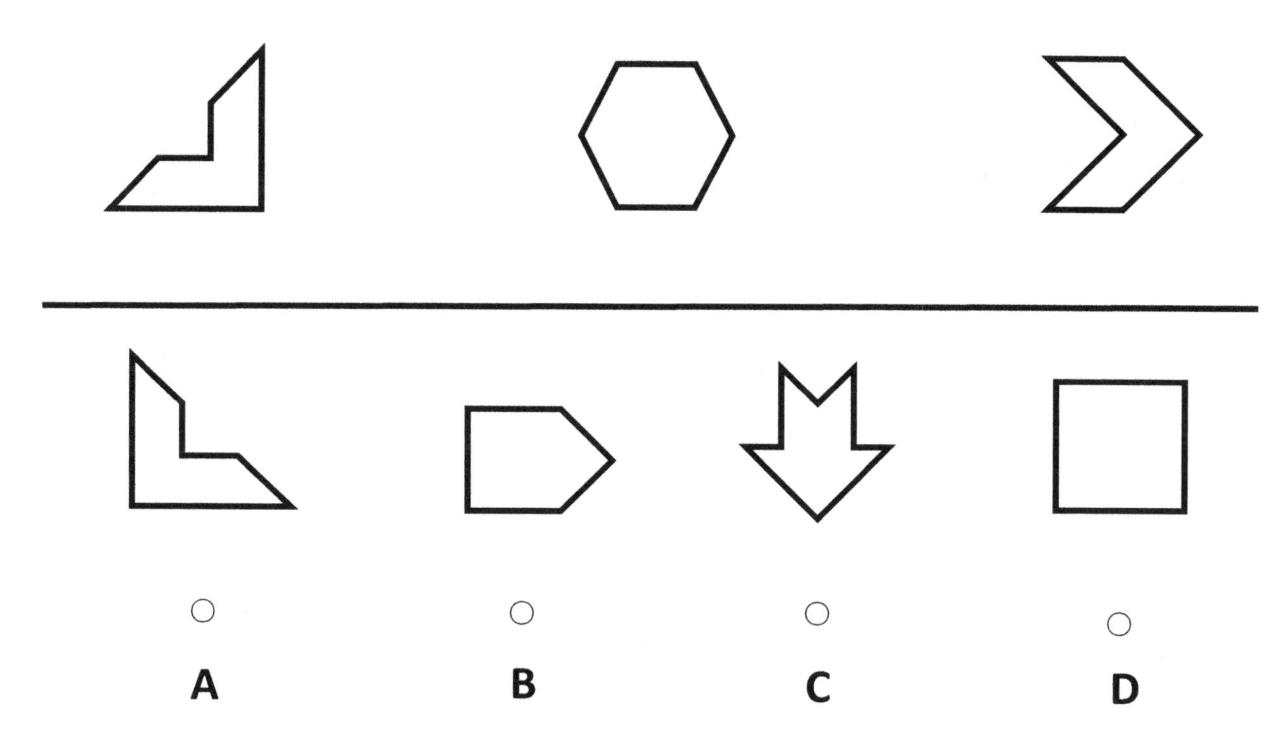

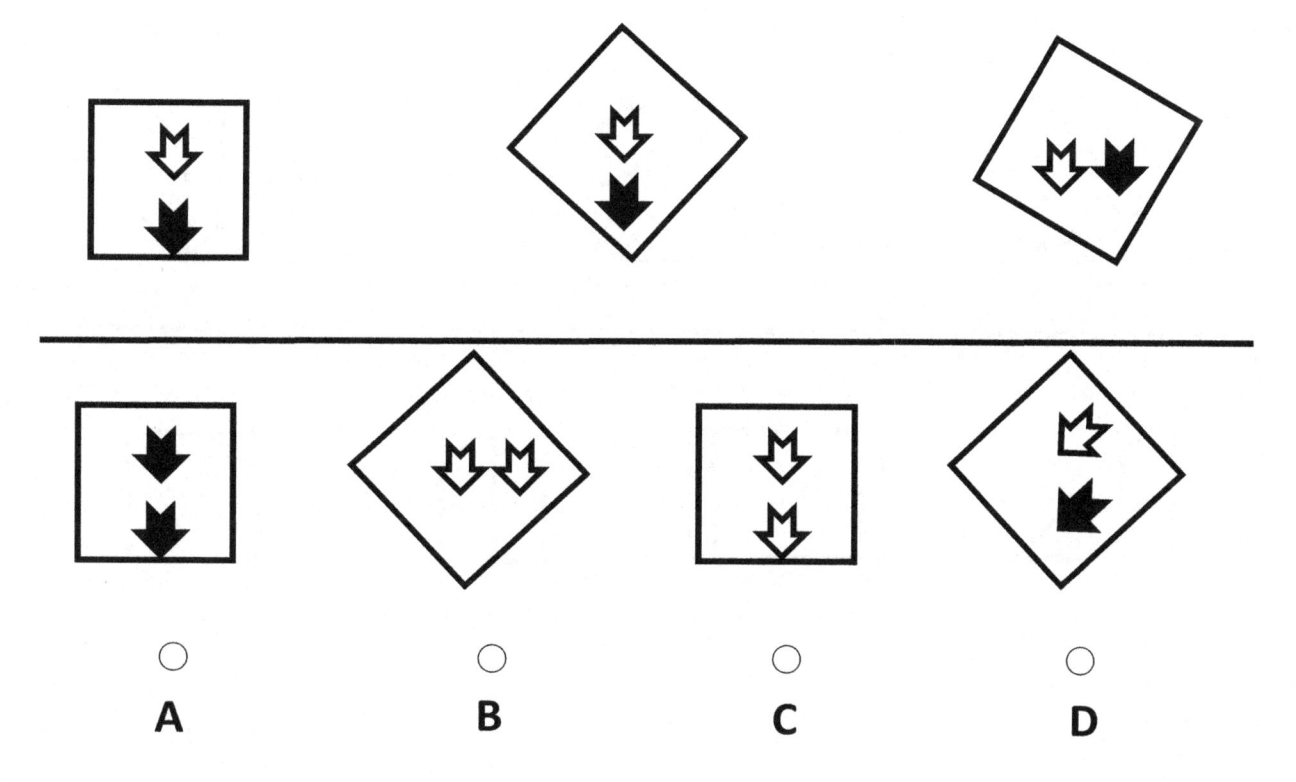

9.

10.

199

PRACTICE TEST GRADE 2

11.

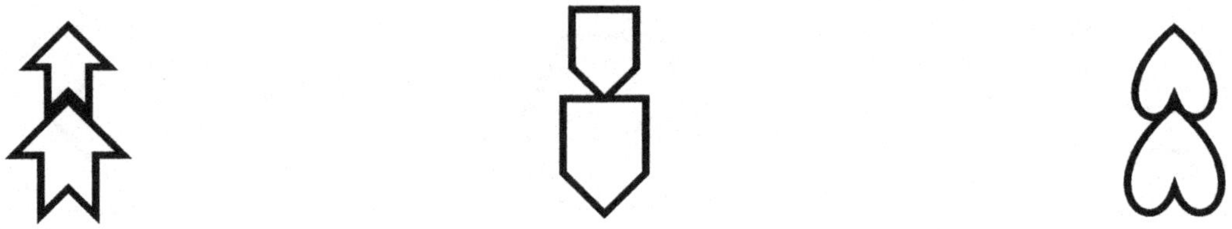

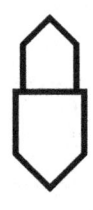

○ A   ○ B   ○ C   ○ D

12.

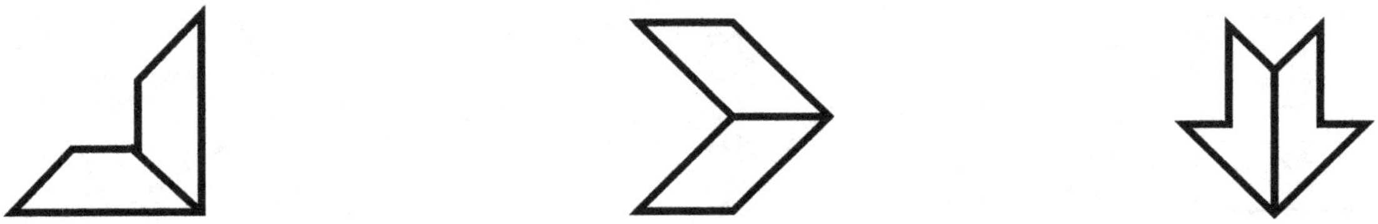

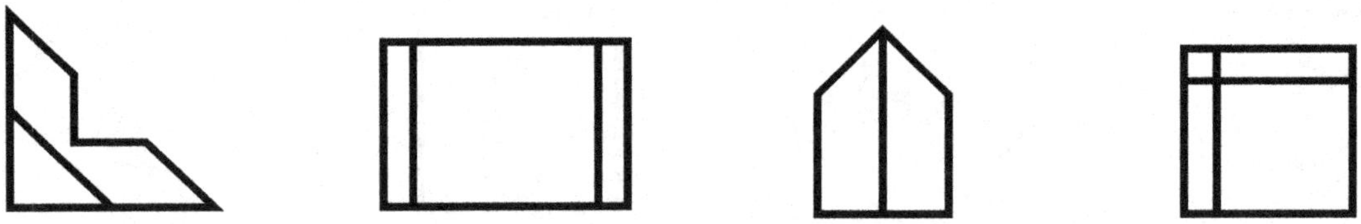

○ A   ○ B   ○ C   ○ D

200

PRACTICE TEST GRADE 2

13.

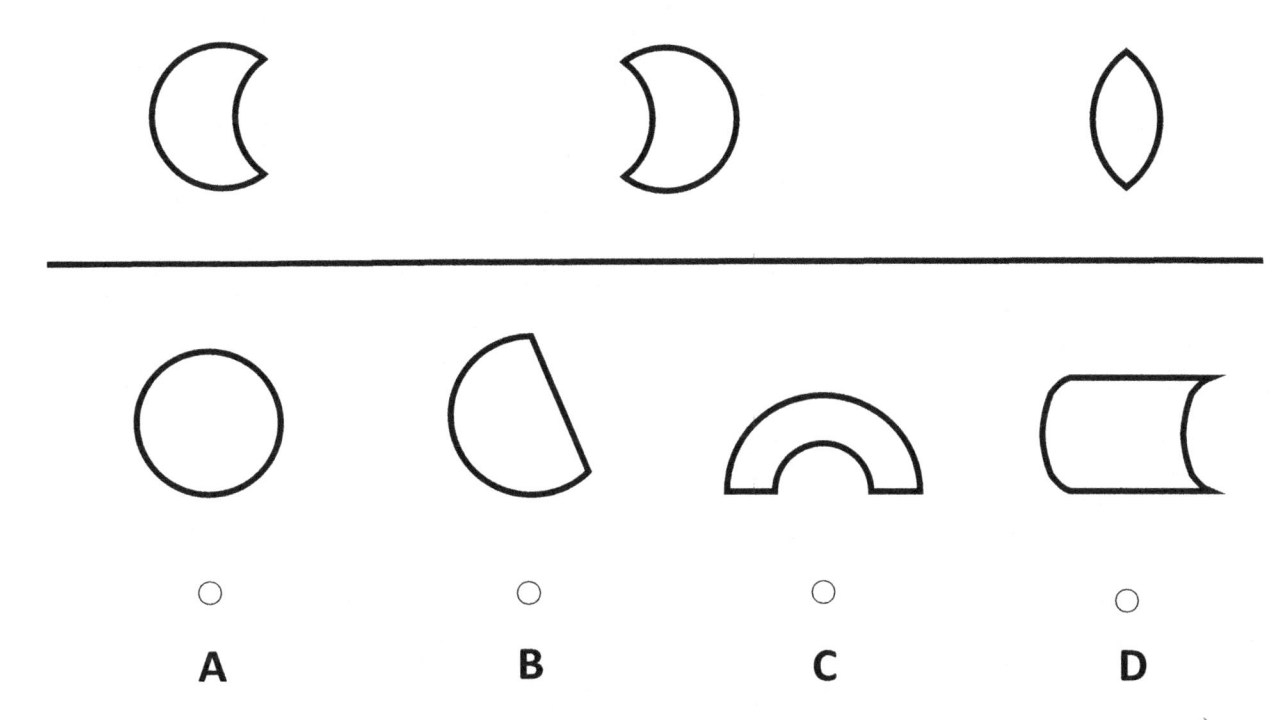

14.

201

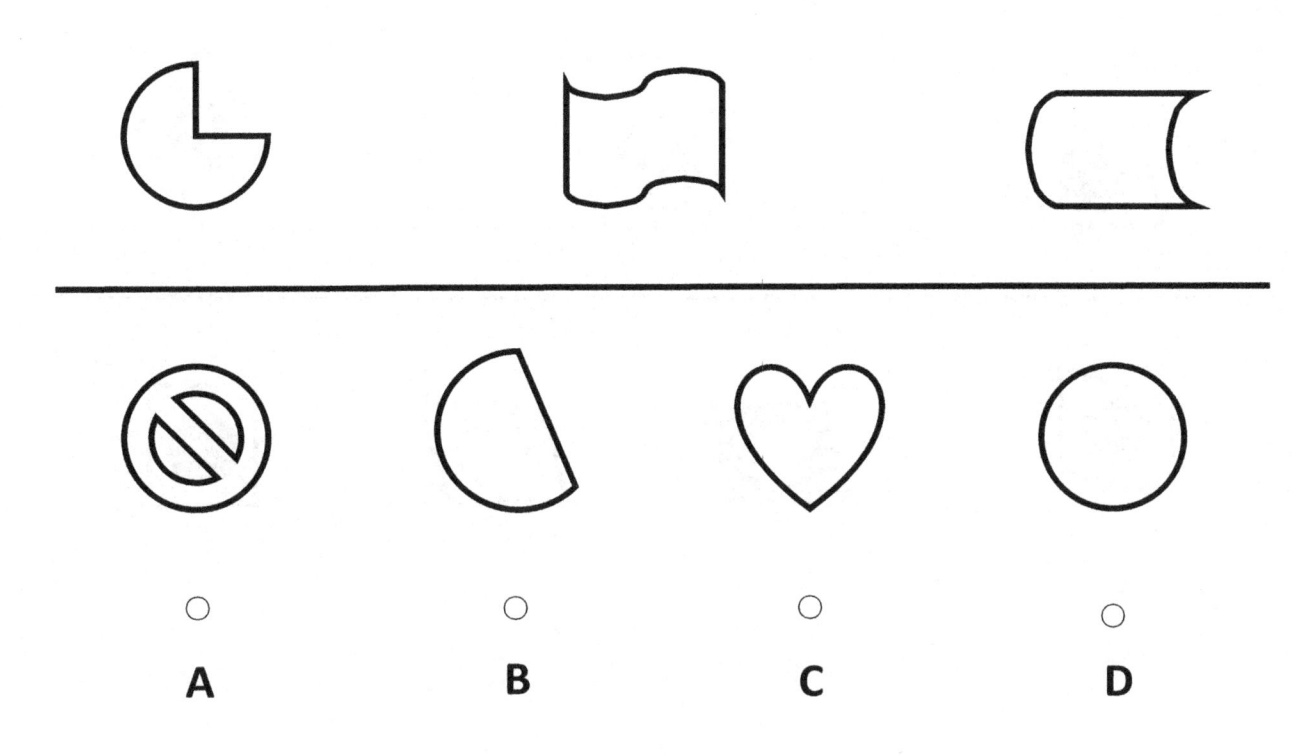

PRACTICE TEST GRADE 2

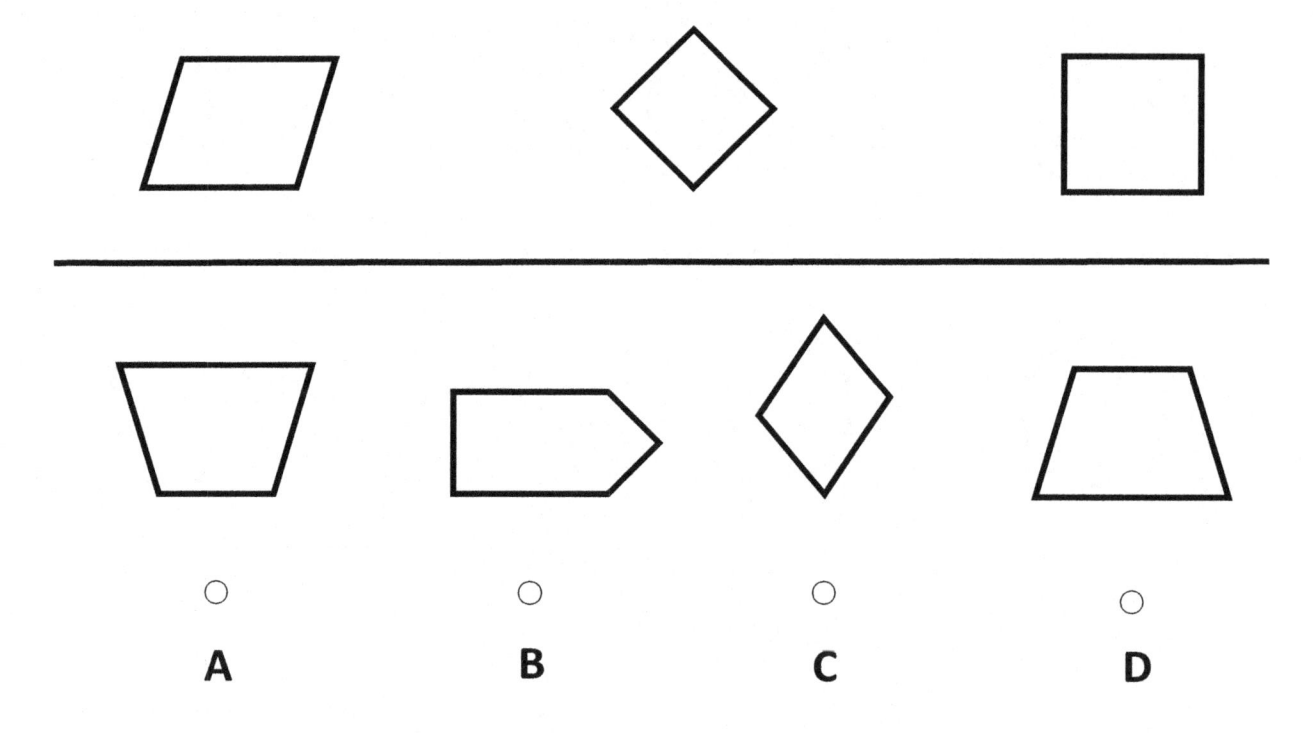

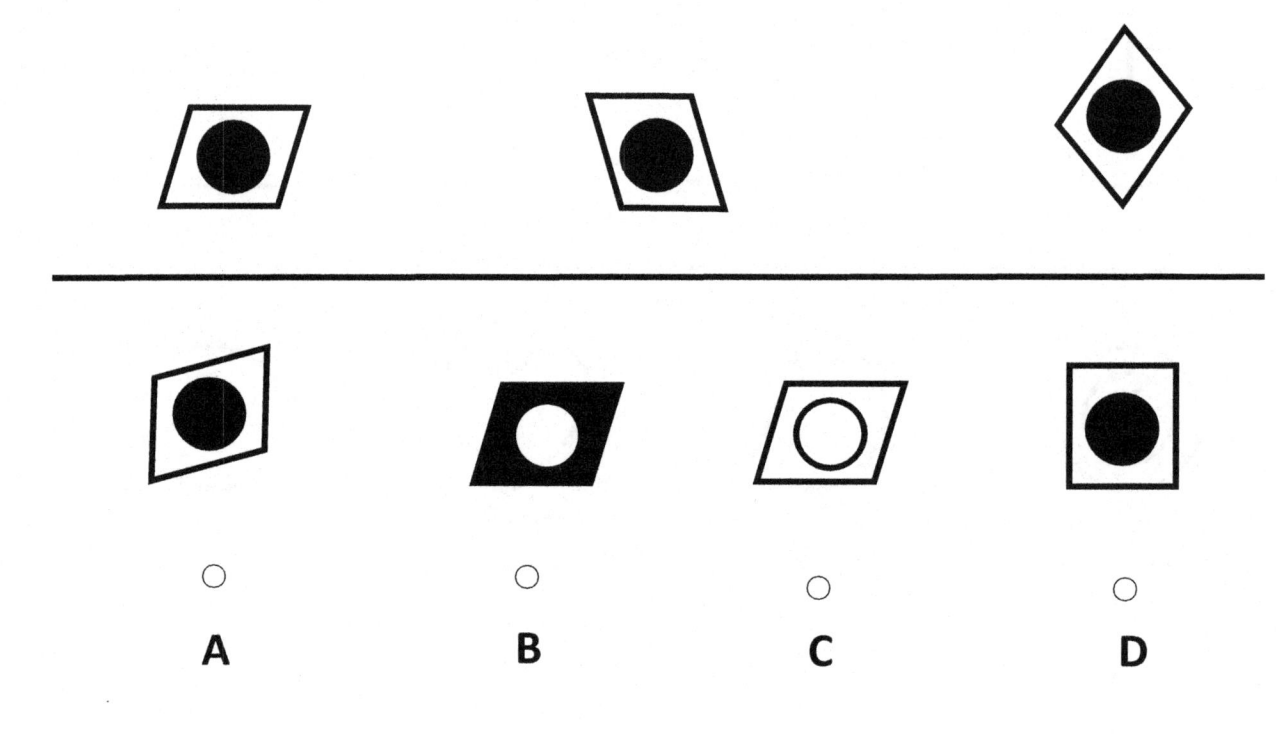

15.

16.

202

PRACTICE TEST GRADE 2

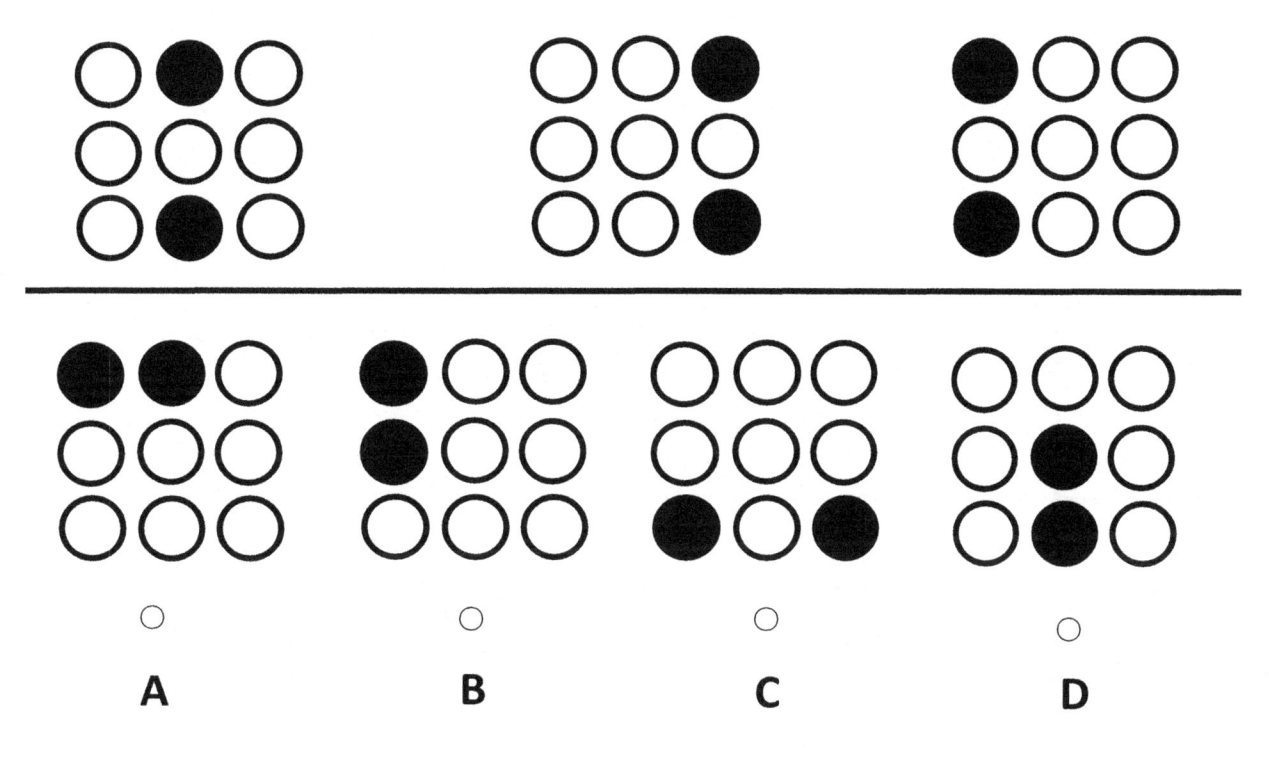

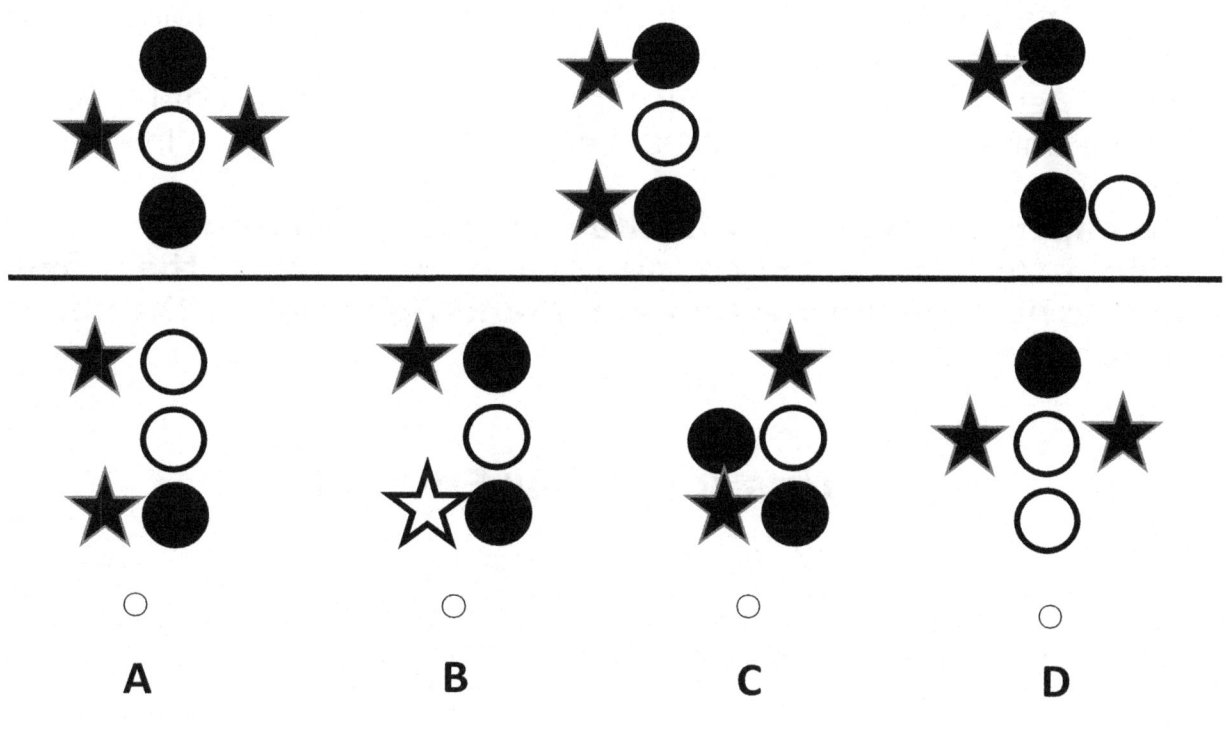

17.

18.

203

PRACTICE TEST GRADE 2

Paper Folding

Children need to determine the appearance of a perforated and folded sheet of paper, once opened.

Example

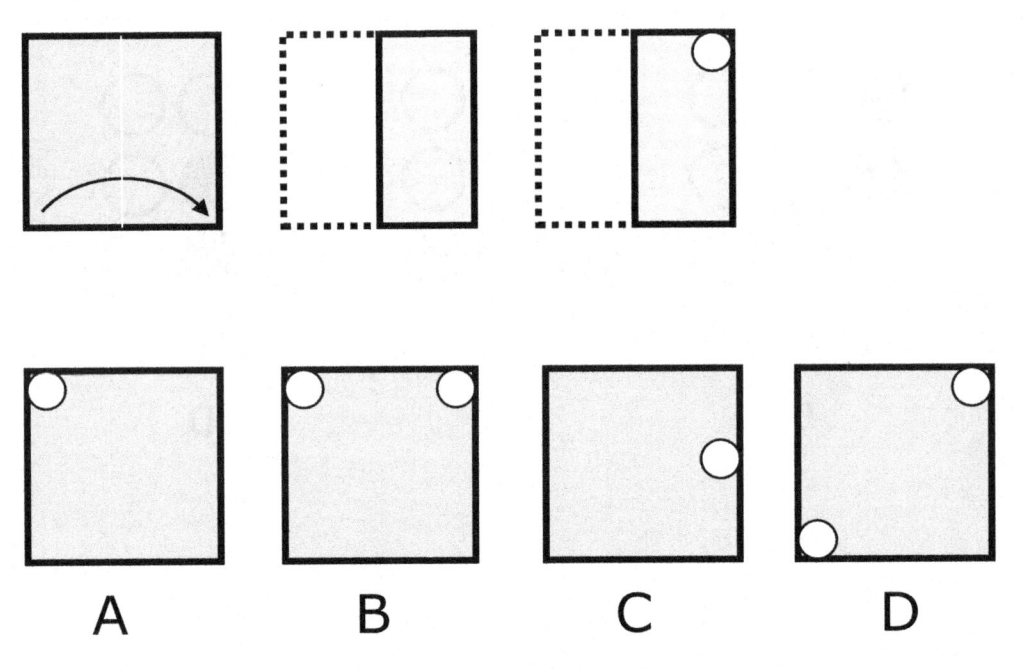

A   B   C   D

The figures at the top represent a square piece of paper being folded, and the last of these figures has one hole on it.

One of the lower three figures shows where the perforation will be when the paper is fully unfolded. You have to understand which of these images is the right one.

First, the paper was folded horizontally, from left to right.
Then, one hole was punched out. Therefore, when the paper is unfolded the hole will mirror on the left and right side of the sheet.
The right answer is "B".

Tips for Paper Folding

The best way to get ready for these challenging questions is to practice. The patterns that show up on the test can confuse students, so the demonstration of folding and unfolding real paper can be very helpful.

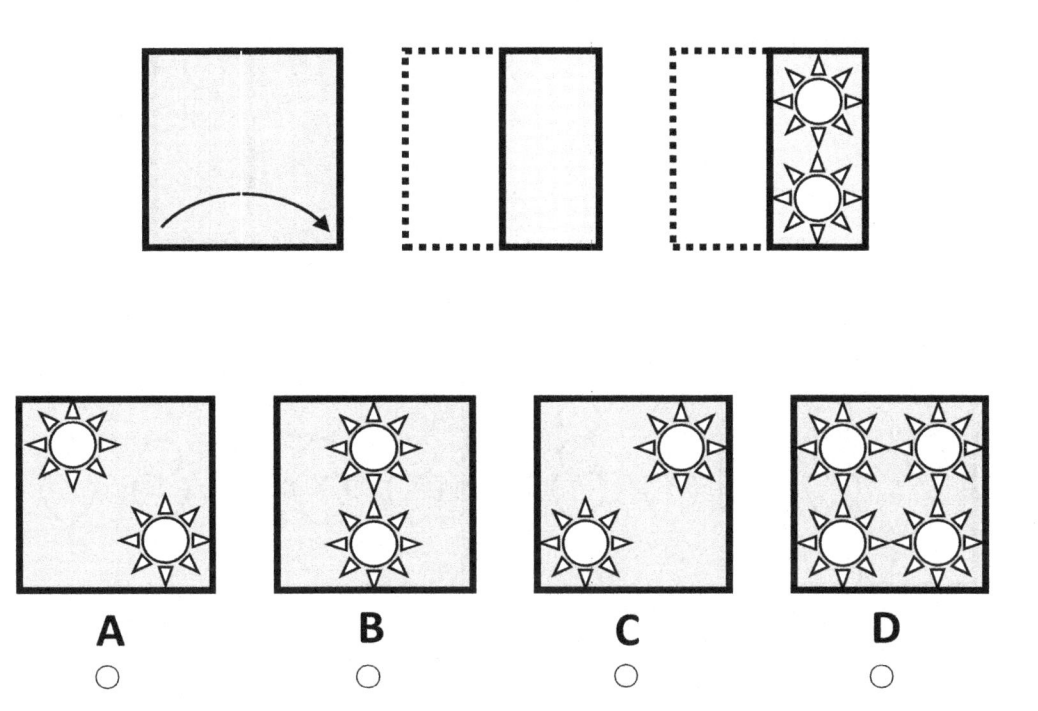

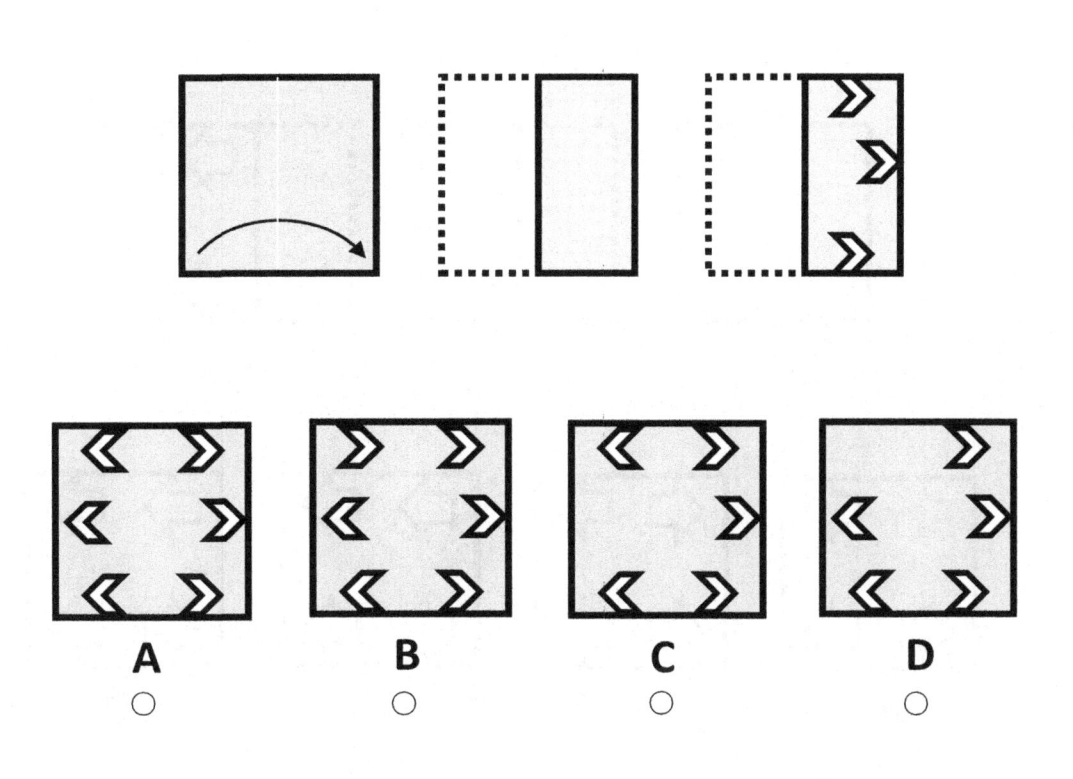

PRACTICE TEST GRADE 2

1.

2.

205

PRACTICE TEST GRADE 2

3.

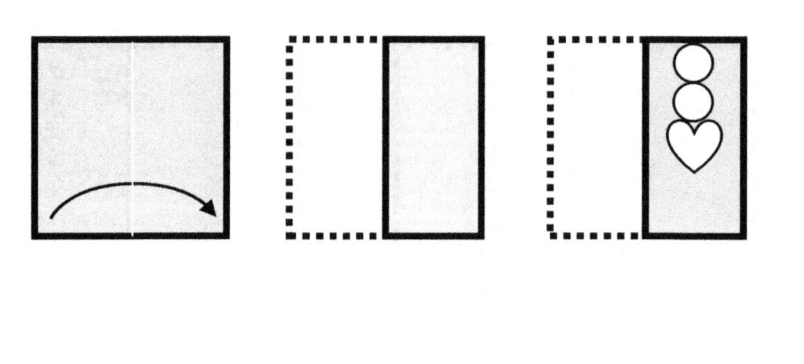

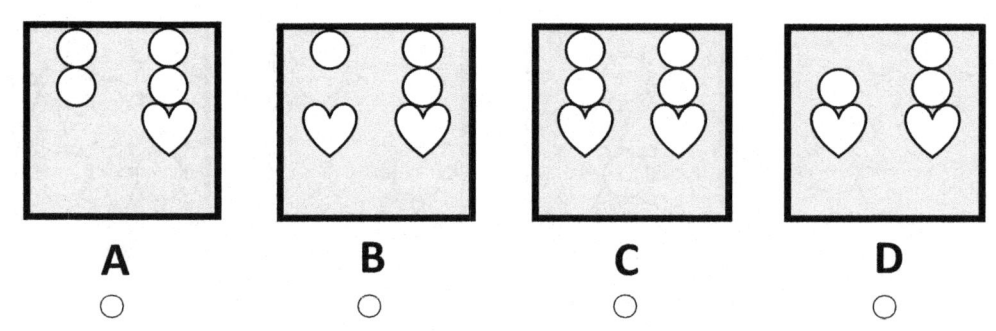

A   B   C   D

4.

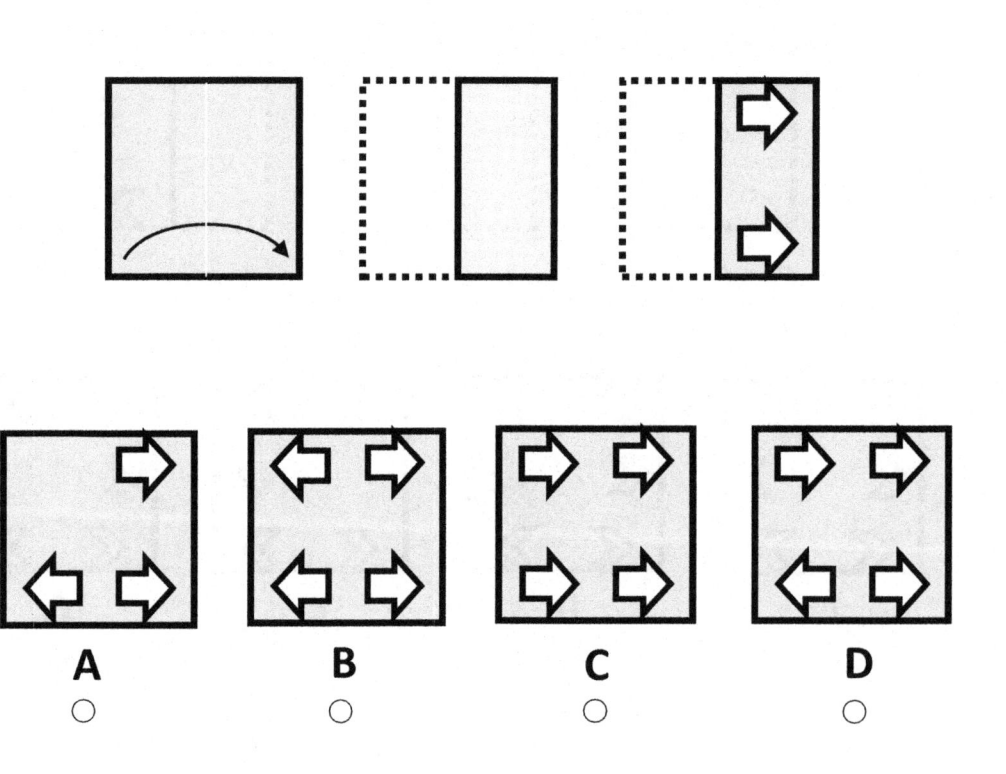

A   B   C   D

206

PRACTICE TEST GRADE 2

5.

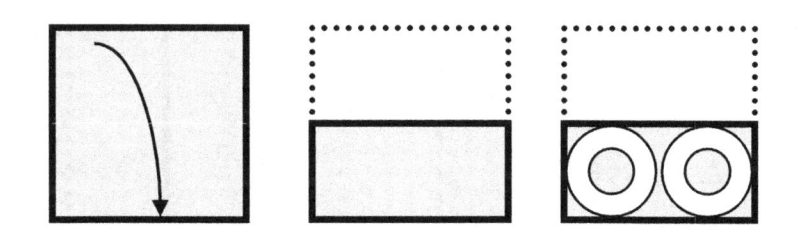

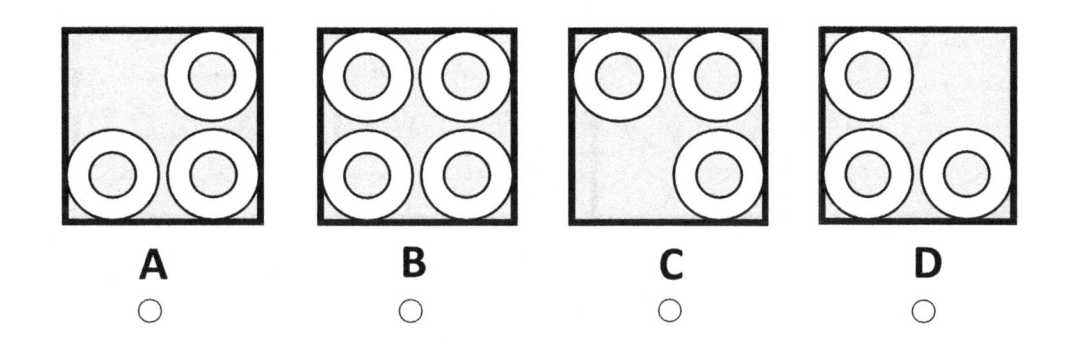

A B C D

6.

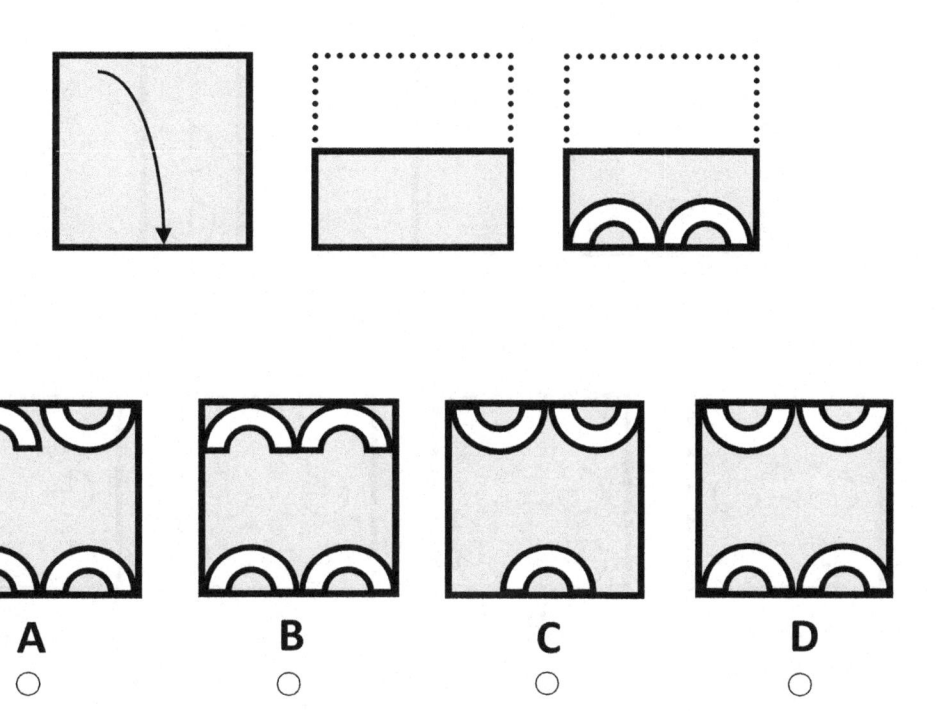

A B C D

207

PRACTICE TEST GRADE 2

7.

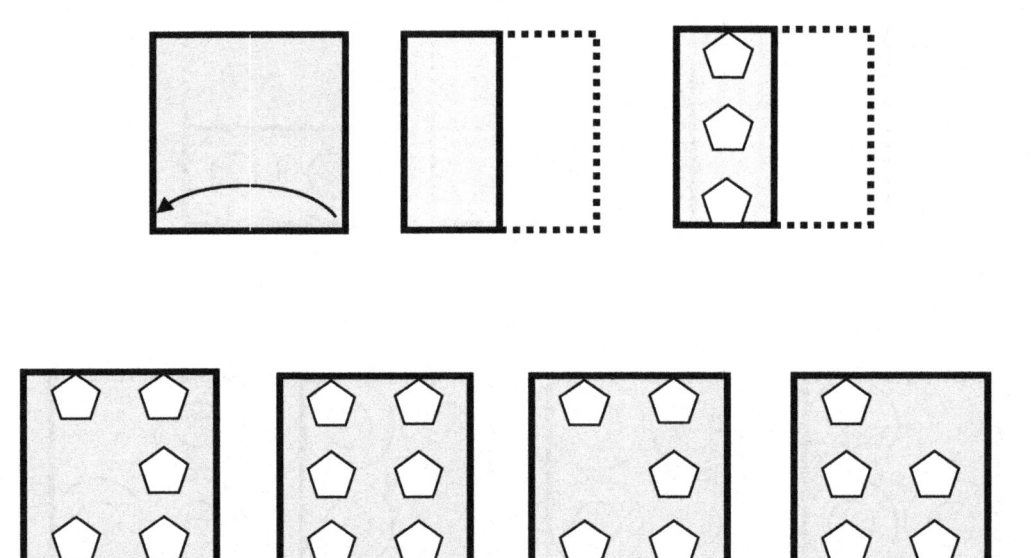

A B C D

8.

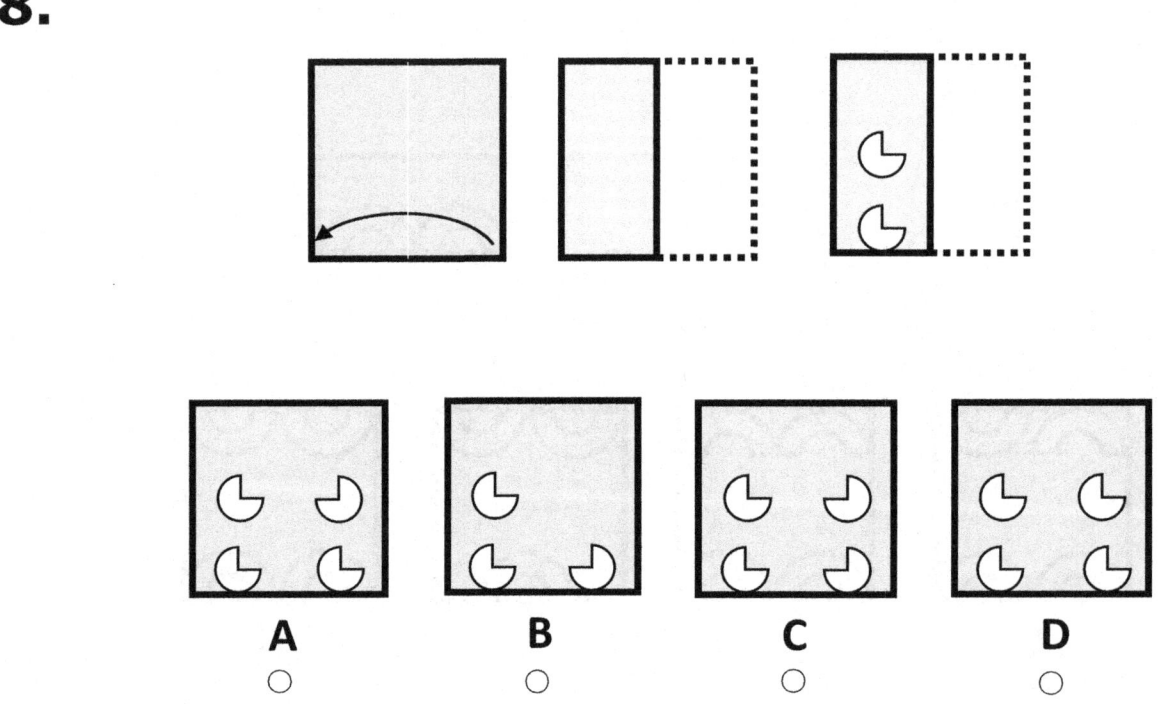

A B C D

208

PRACTICE TEST GRADE 2

9.

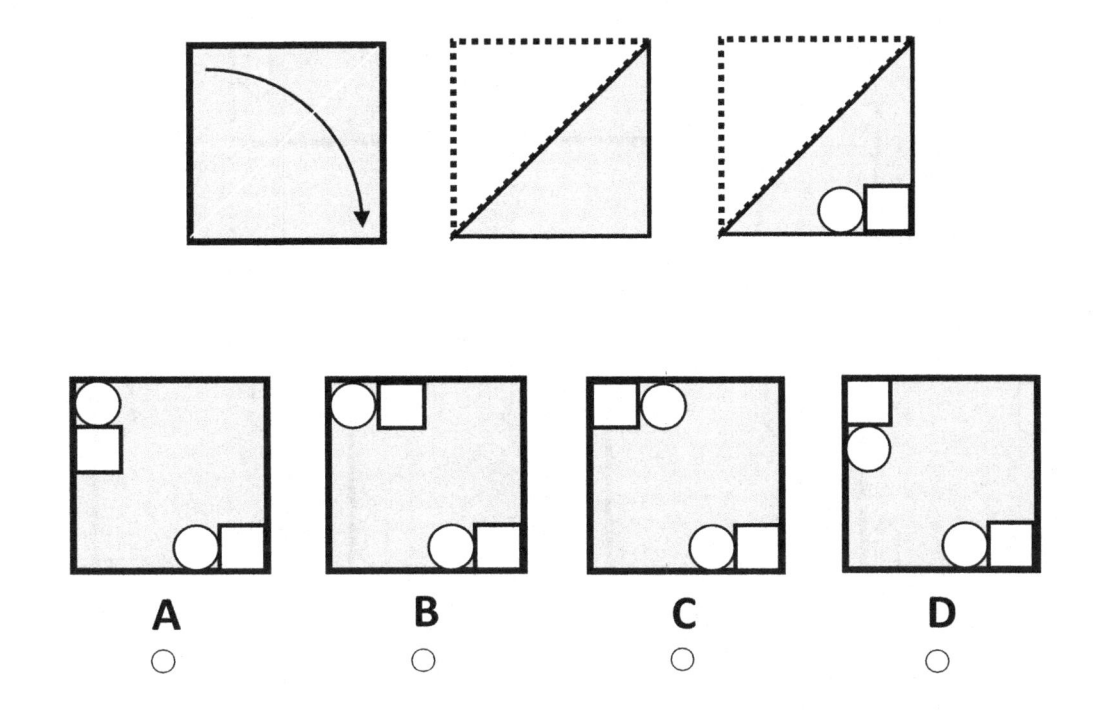

A **B** **C** **D**

10.

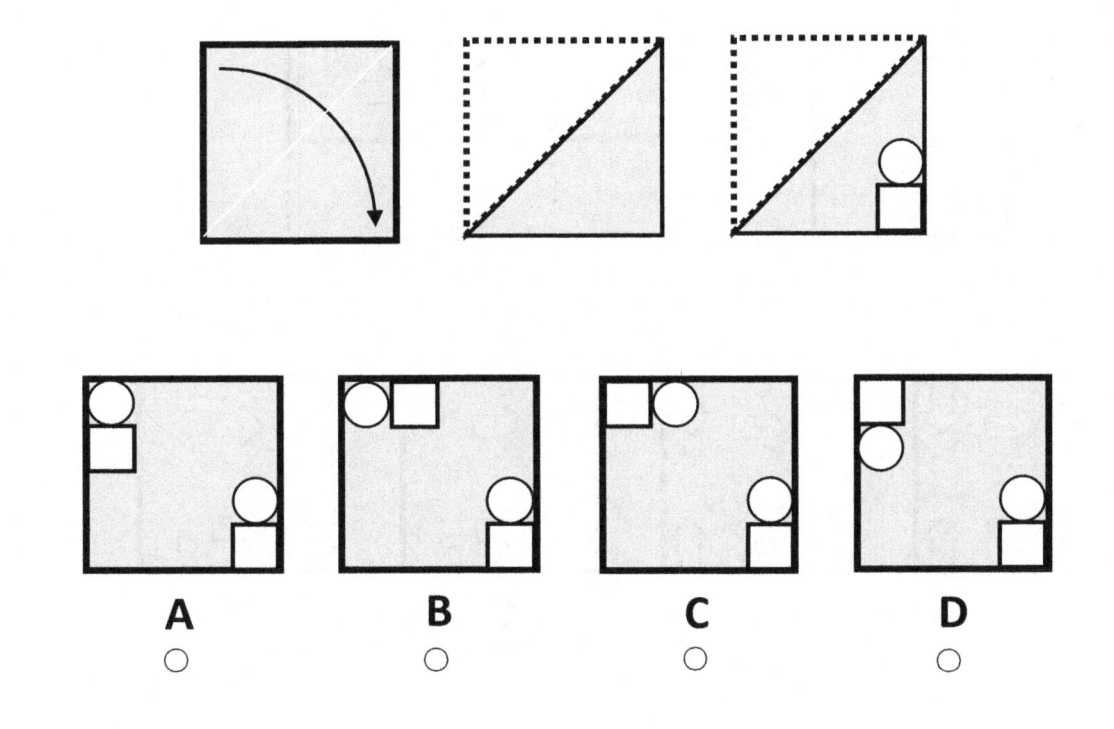

A **B** **C** **D**

209

PRACTICE TEST GRADE 2

11.

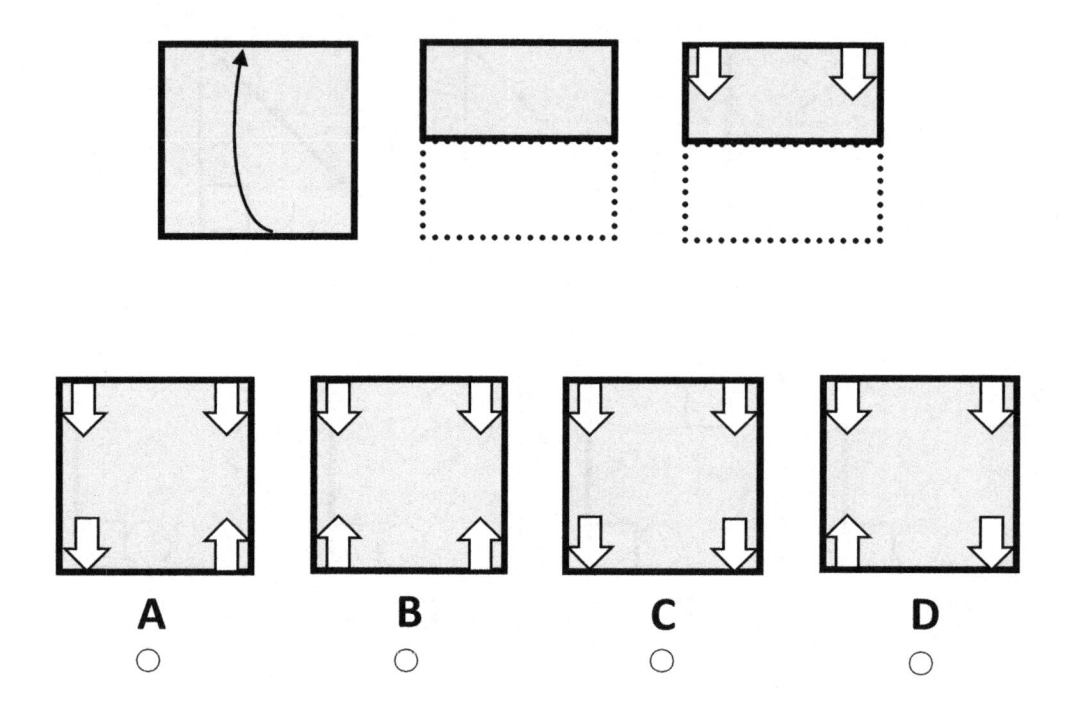

A **B** **C** **D**

12.

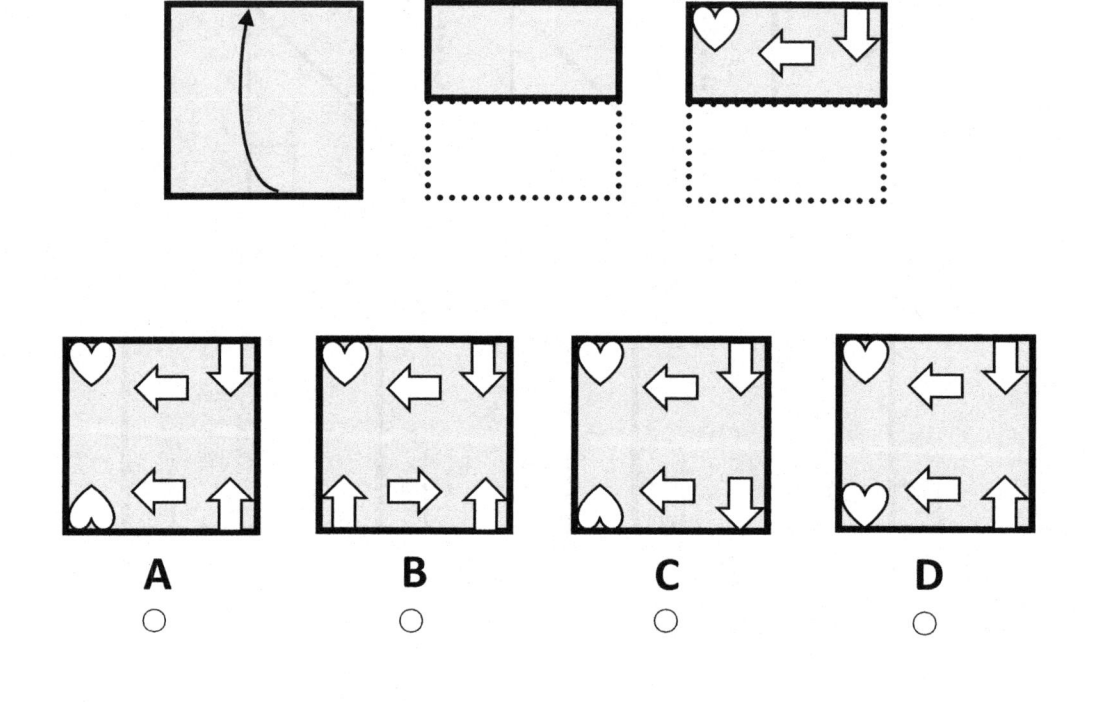

A **B** **C** **D**

PRACTICE TEST GRADE 2

13.

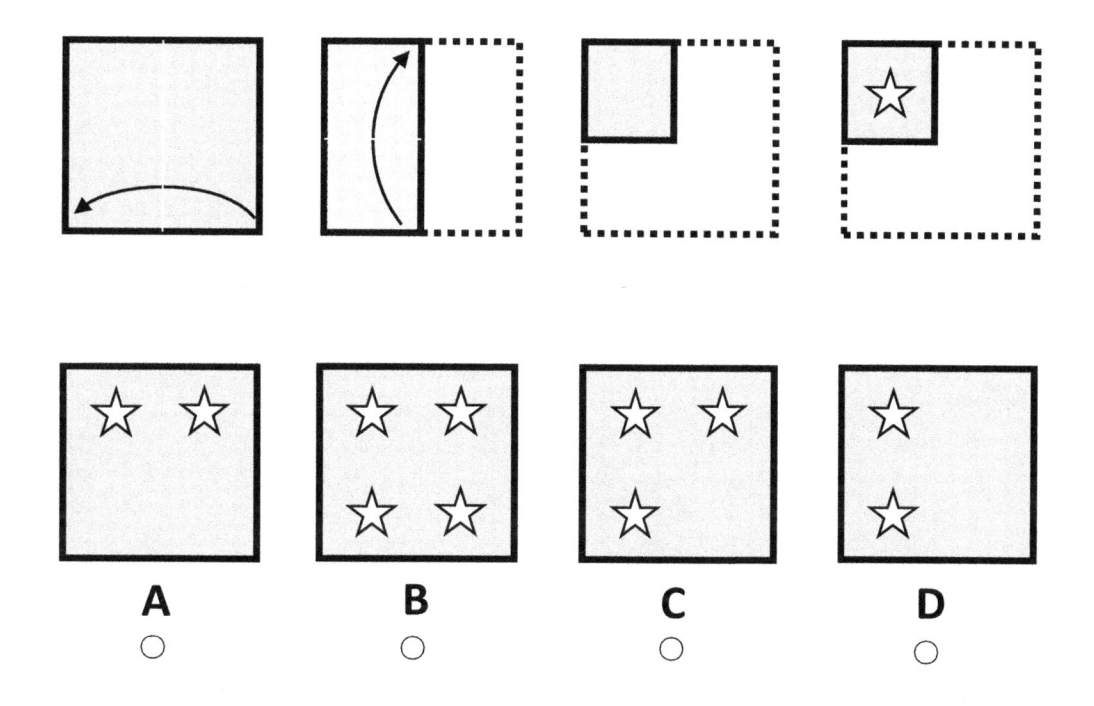

A   B   C   D

14.

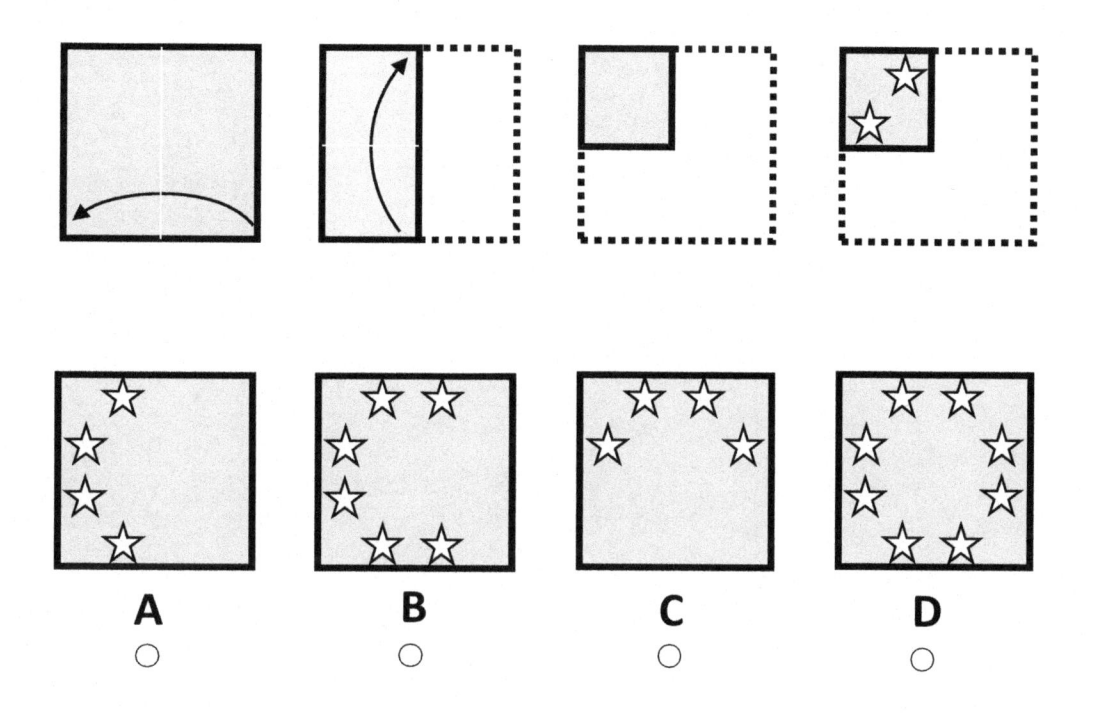

A   B   C   D

211

PRACTICE TEST GRADE 2

PRACTICE TEST QUANTITATIVE BATTERY

This section introduces abstract reasoning and problem-solving skills to learners and is one of the most challenging sections in the test.

Number Puzzle

Students are required to solve basic mathematical equations. An equation says that two things are equal. It will have an equals sign "=" like this:

$$4 + 2 = 10 - 4$$

The equation says that what is on the left (4 + 2) is equal to what is on the right (10 − 4).

Example 1

$$? - 15 = 4$$

A 10   B 19   C 1   D 7   E 16

- The right side of the equal sign is 4. Which answer should be given in place of the question mark, so that the left side of the equal is also 4?

$$19 - 15 = 4; 4 = 4$$
The right answer is "B".

Tips for Number Puzzle

- Deeply understand the meaning of "equal", as the purpose is to provide the missing information that will make the two parts of the equation the same.

- Train yourself to solve simple basic equations.

- Practice with numbers and problem solving.

PRACTICE TEST GRADE 2

1.

$$7 = 2 + ?$$

8	5	6	1
○	○	○	○
A	B	C	D

2.

$$6 = 8 - ?$$

8	2	6	1
○	○	○	○
A	B	C	D

3.

$$3 = 10 - 4 - ?$$

1	2	3	4
○	○	○	○
A	B	C	D

4.

$$12 = 8 + 2 + ?$$

4	4	2	1
○	○	○	○
A	B	C	D

5.

$$10 = 8 + 3 - ?$$

1	3	6	2
○	○	○	○
A	B	C	D

6.

$$12 = 5 - 3 + ?$$

11	10	6	4
○	○	○	○
A	B	C	D

7.

$$5 = 3 + 9 - ?$$

8	9	4	7
○	○	○	○
A	B	C	D

8.

$$12 = 10 - 5 + ?$$

8	7	1	9
○	○	○	○
A	B	C	D

9.

$$9 = 3 + 8 - ?$$

1	4	2	3
○	○	○	○
A	B	C	D

PRACTICE TEST GRADE 2

10.

$$20 = 11 + 2 + \;?$$

5	3	7	9
○	○	○	○
A	B	C	D

11.

$$9 = 11 - 10 + \;?$$

8	2	3	5
○	○	○	○
A	B	C	D

12.

$$2 = 9 + 5 - \;?$$

13	12	10	9
○	○	○	○
A	B	C	D

PRACTICE TEST GRADE 2

13.

$$18 = 7 + 2 + \;?$$

10	14	15	9
○	○	○	○
A	B	C	D

14.

$$1 = 15 + 5 - \;?$$

10	17	19	8
○	○	○	○
A	B	C	D

PRACTICE TEST GRADE 2

Number Analogies

Children will be provided with 2x2 basic matrices. Each box of the matrices contains a certain number of objects. In the lower row, the child must identify the same relationship as in the upper row and select the answer option that best fits the box with the question mark.

Example

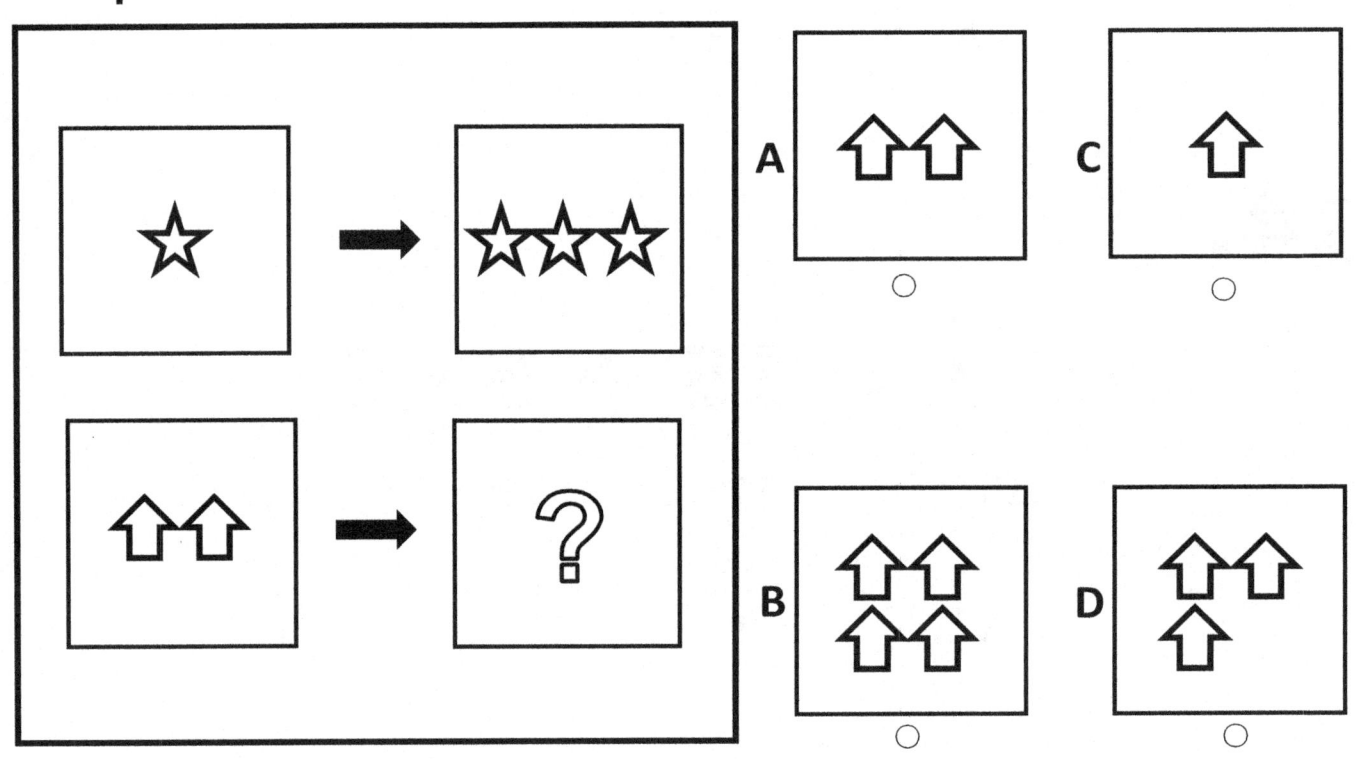

- First, identify the relationship between the objects in the upper squares.

  What is the relationship between "1 stars" and "3 stars"?

  3 is greater than 1 by 2 (1 + 2 = 3).

- Now, look at the objects in the lower squares. In the left box we have 2 arrows.
- Which of the possible choices follows the previous rule?

  In the right box, we should have 2 more arrows. Therefore, the correct answer is B (2+2=4).

Tips for Number Analogies

- Step 1: Acquire all the information from the two given pairs (relationships, sums, subtractions, etc.).

- Step 2: Apply the same rules, relations, formulas that you correctly identified in step 1.

- Step 3: Double-check that the rule has been properly applied.

- Train yourself to solve simple additions and subtractions.

- Work with real objects to understand the concepts.

- Start with simple numerical analogies and gradually increase the level of complexity.

PRACTICE TEST GRADE 2

1.

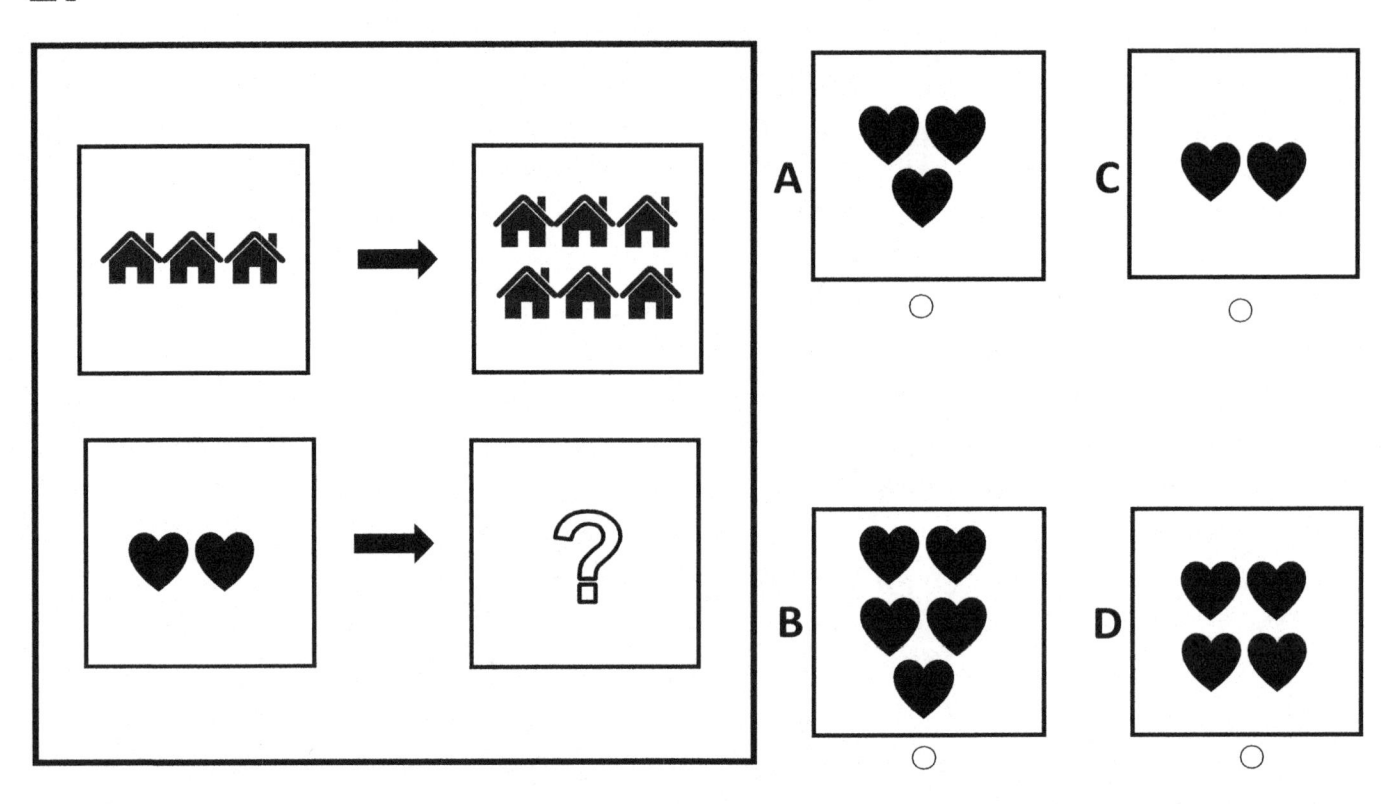

2.

222

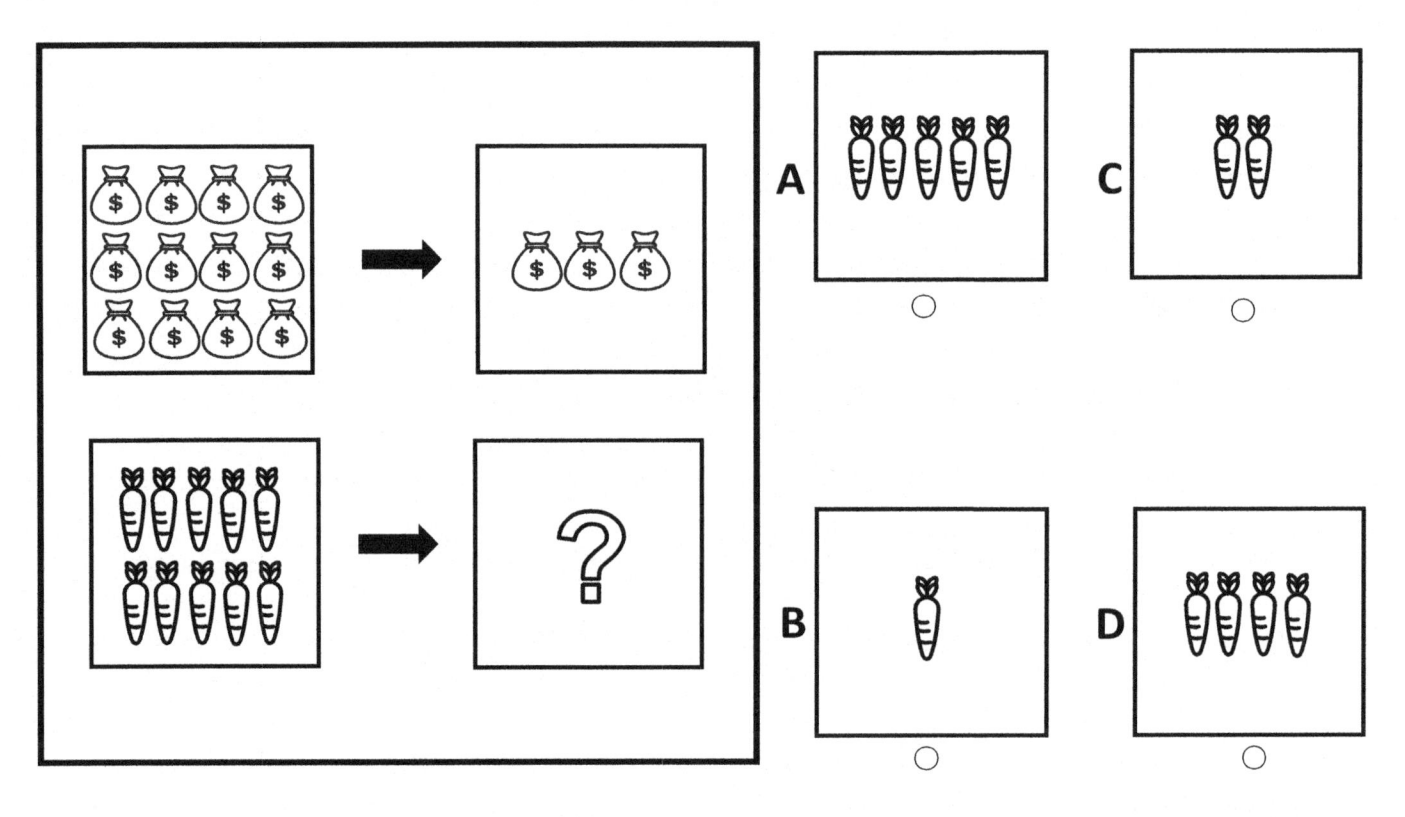

PRACTICE TEST GRADE 2

3.

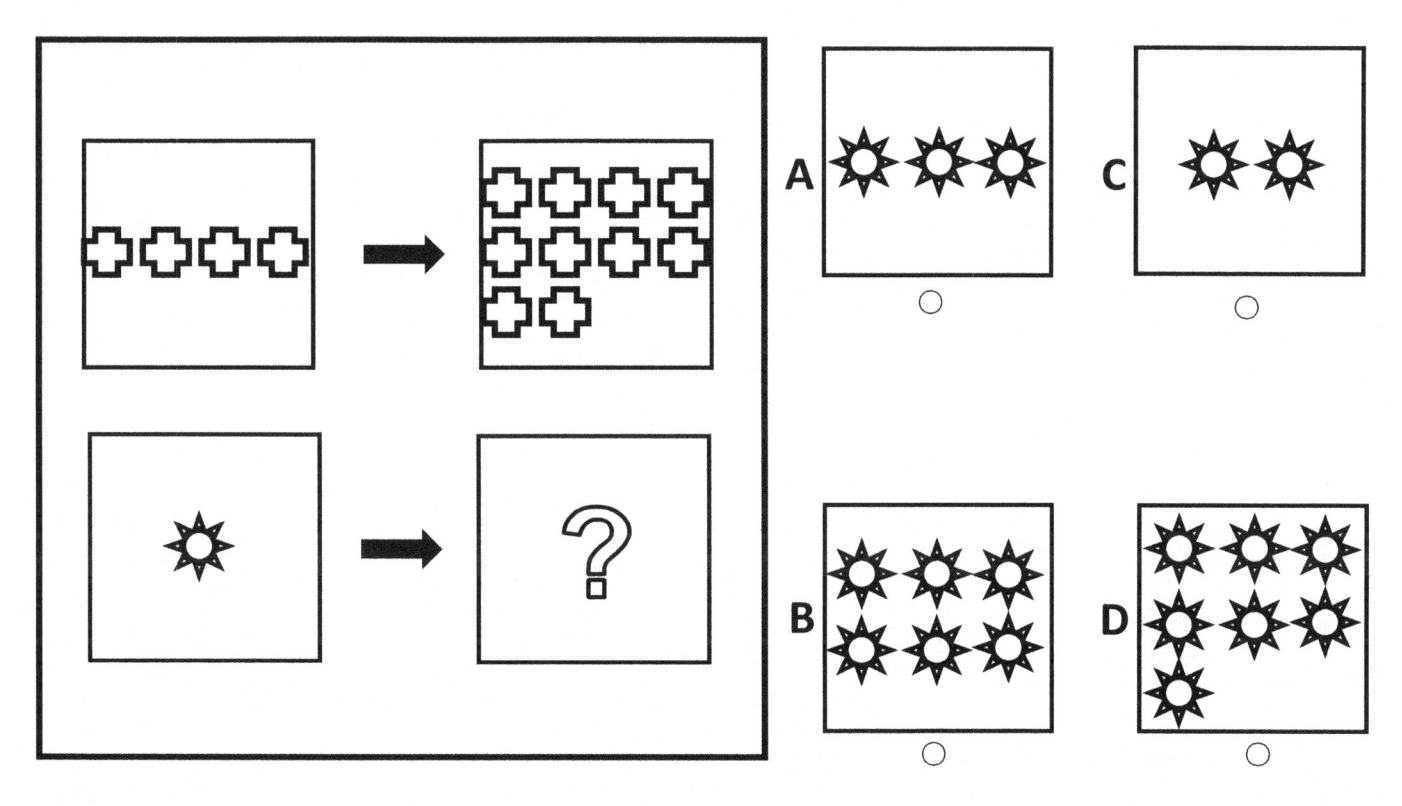

4.

223

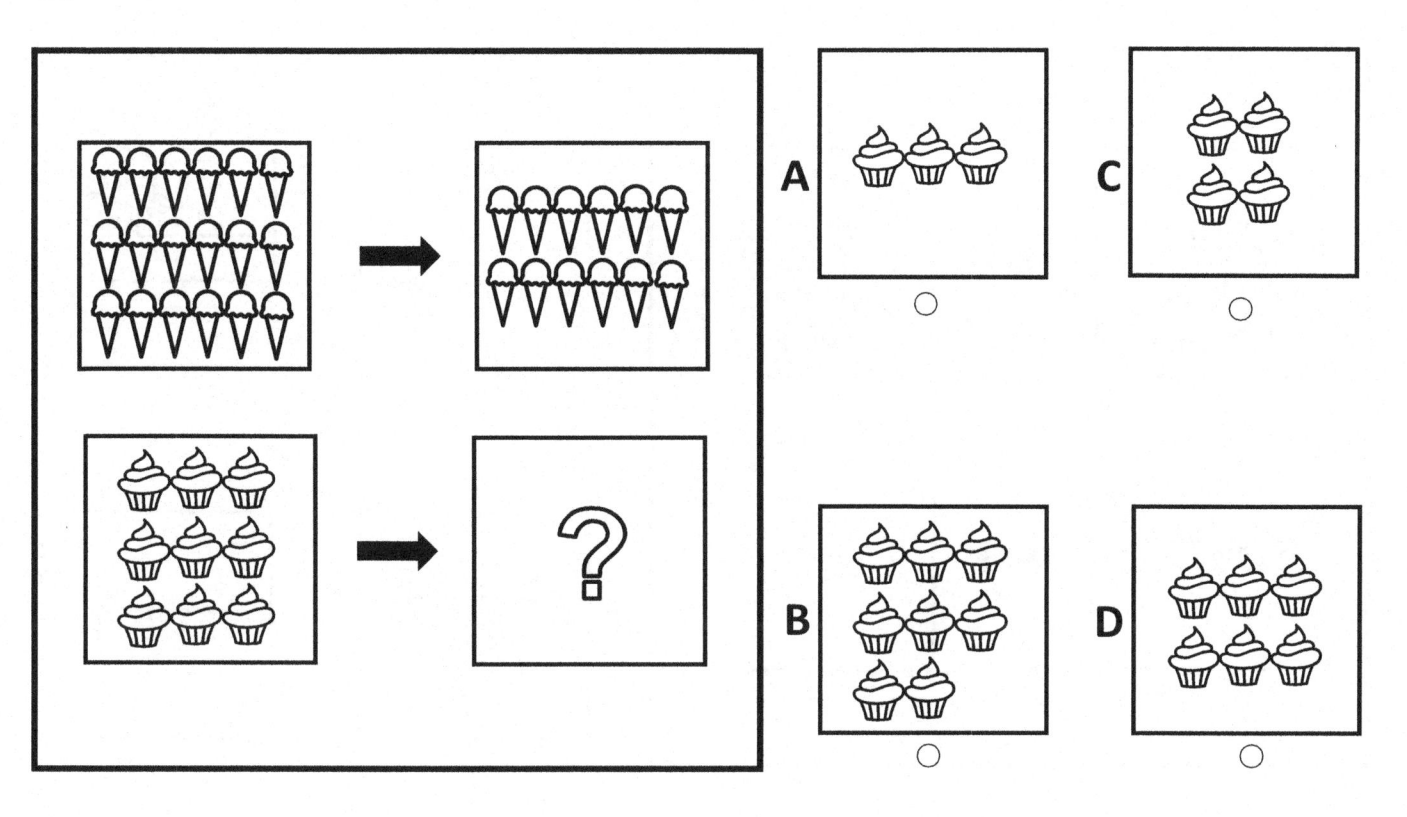

PRACTICE TEST GRADE 2

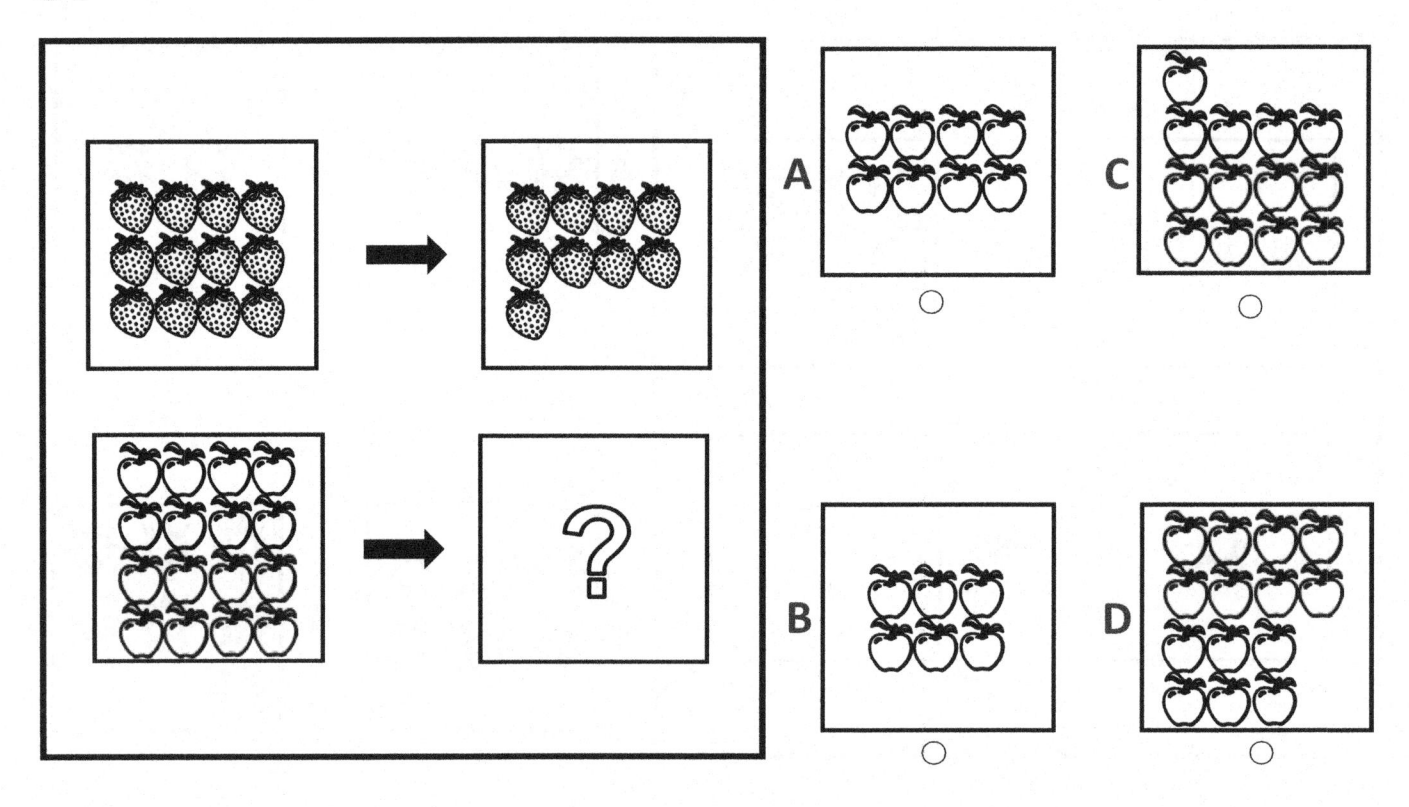

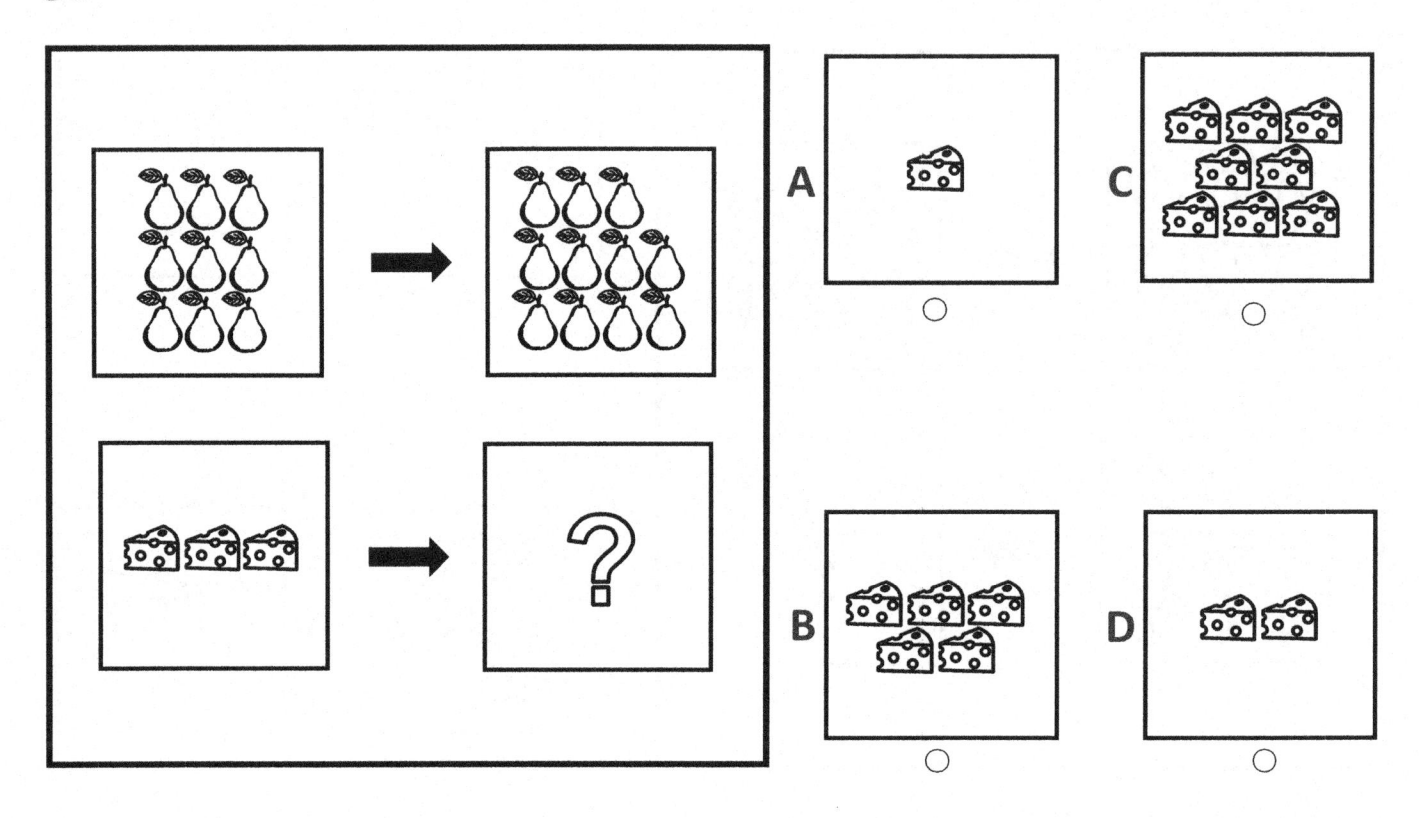

5.

6.

224

PRACTICE TEST GRADE 2

7.

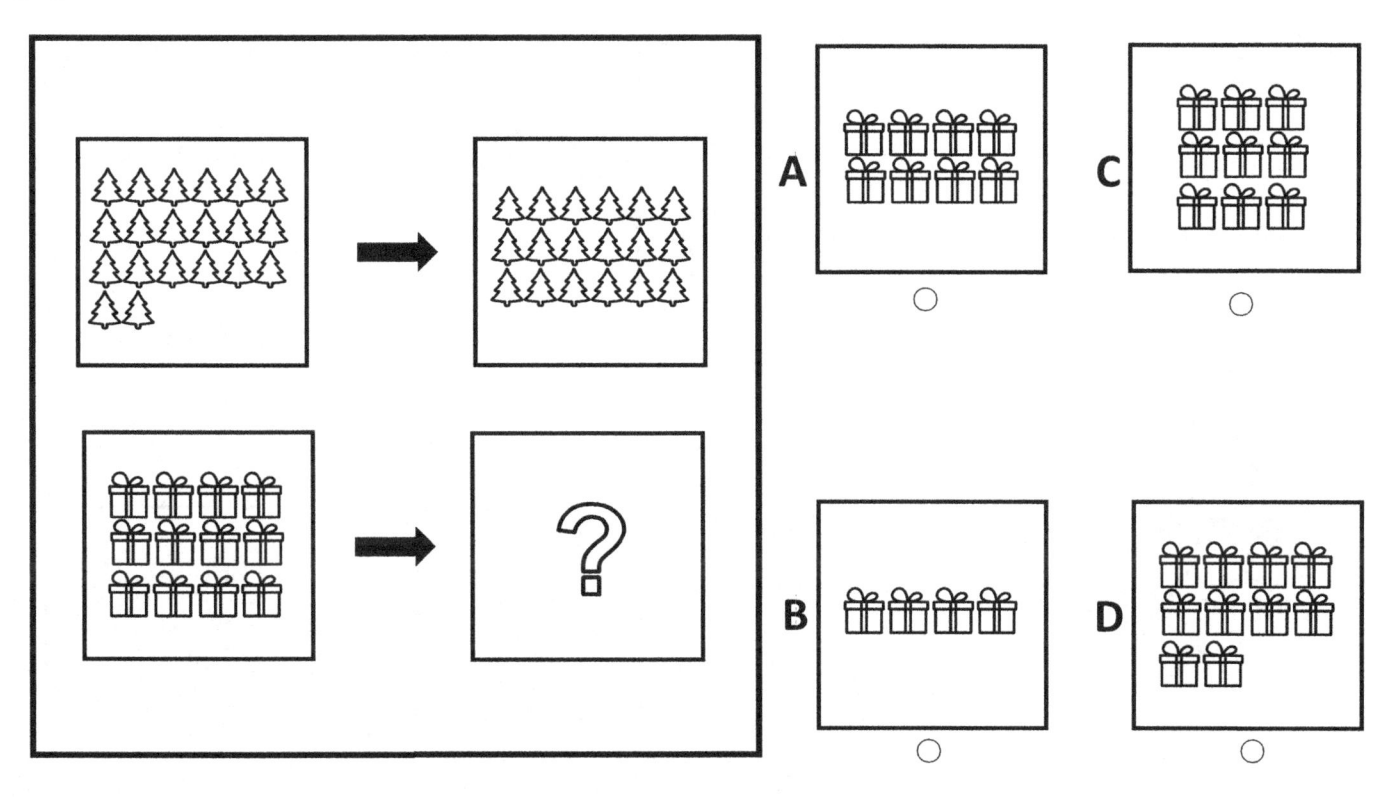

8.

225

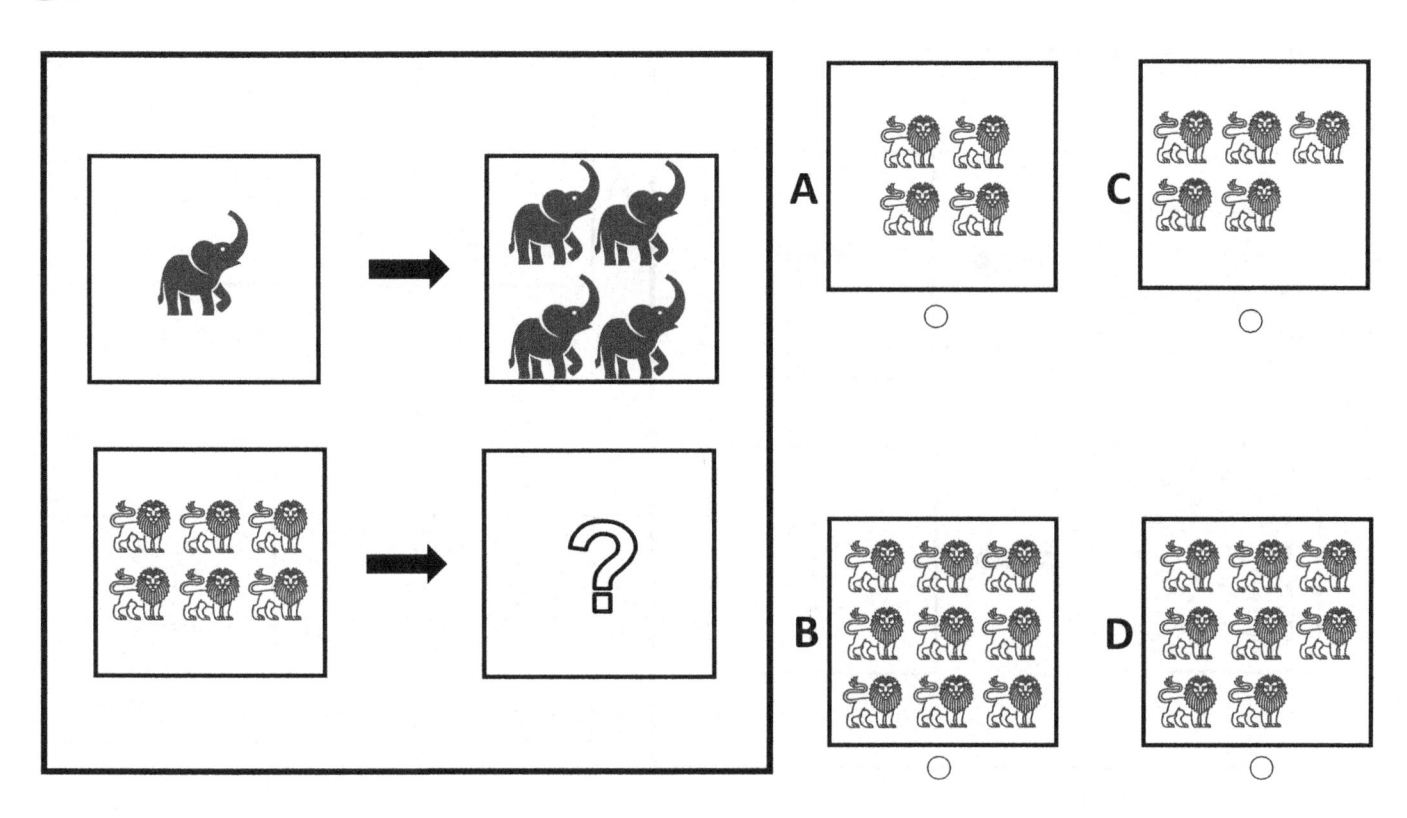

PRACTICE TEST GRADE 2

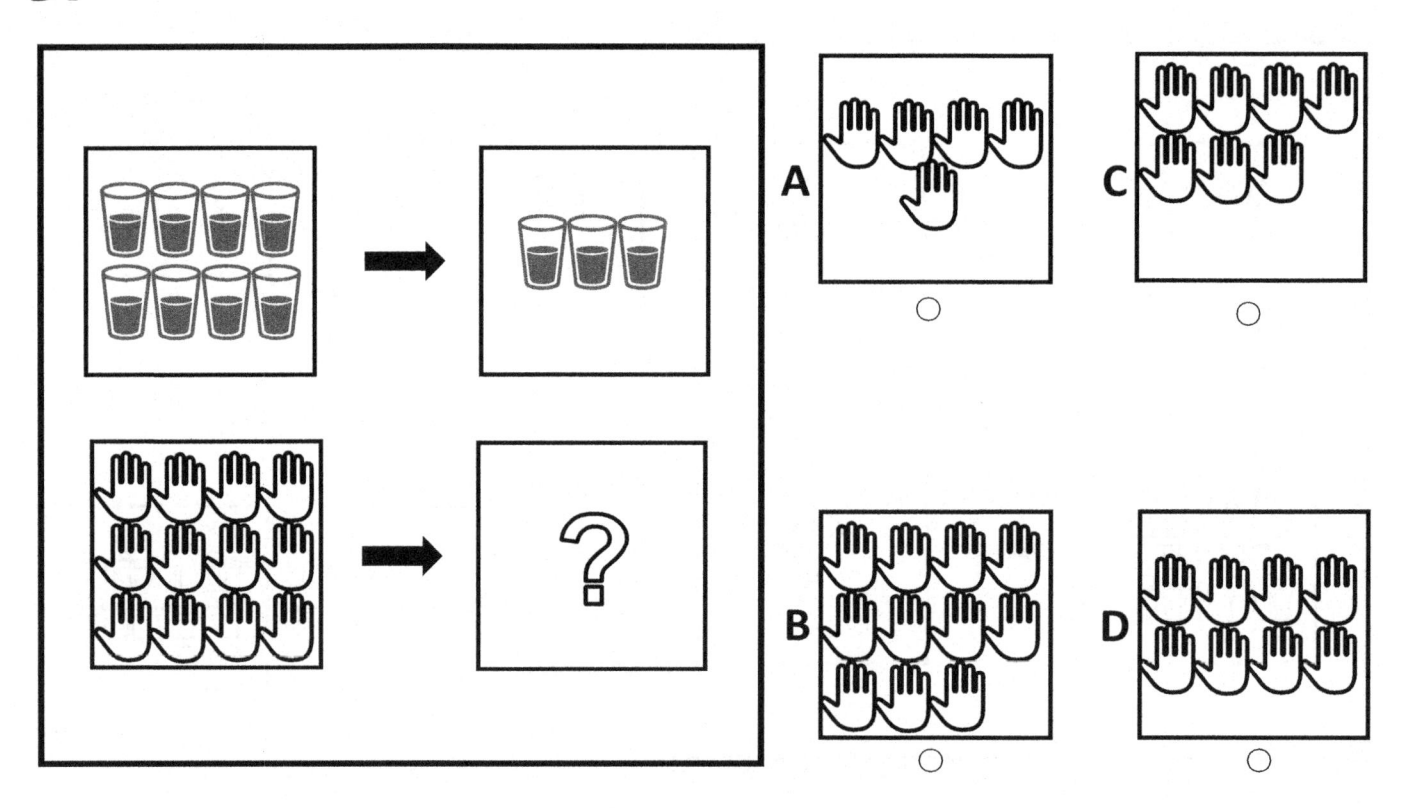

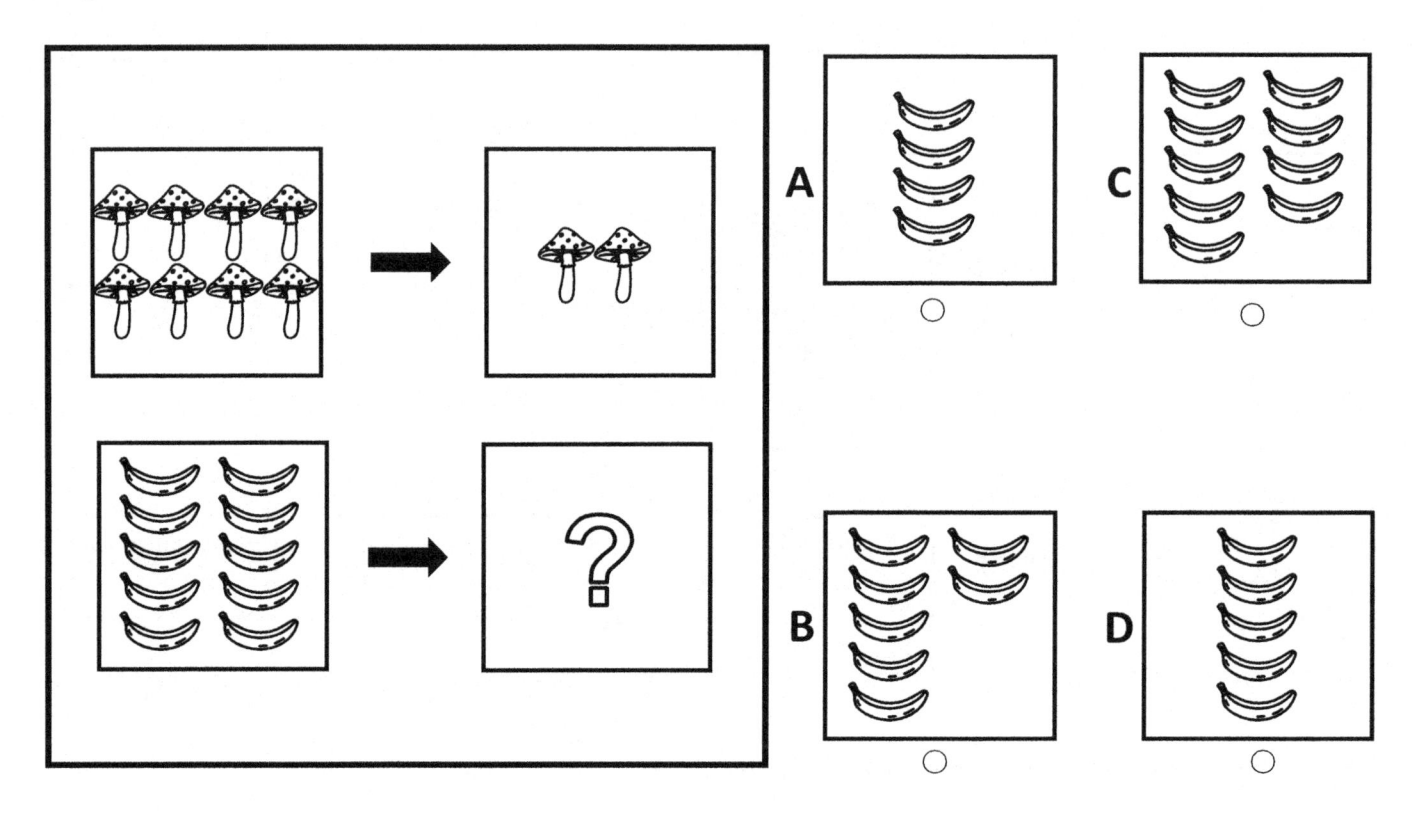

9.

10.

226

PRACTICE TEST GRADE 2

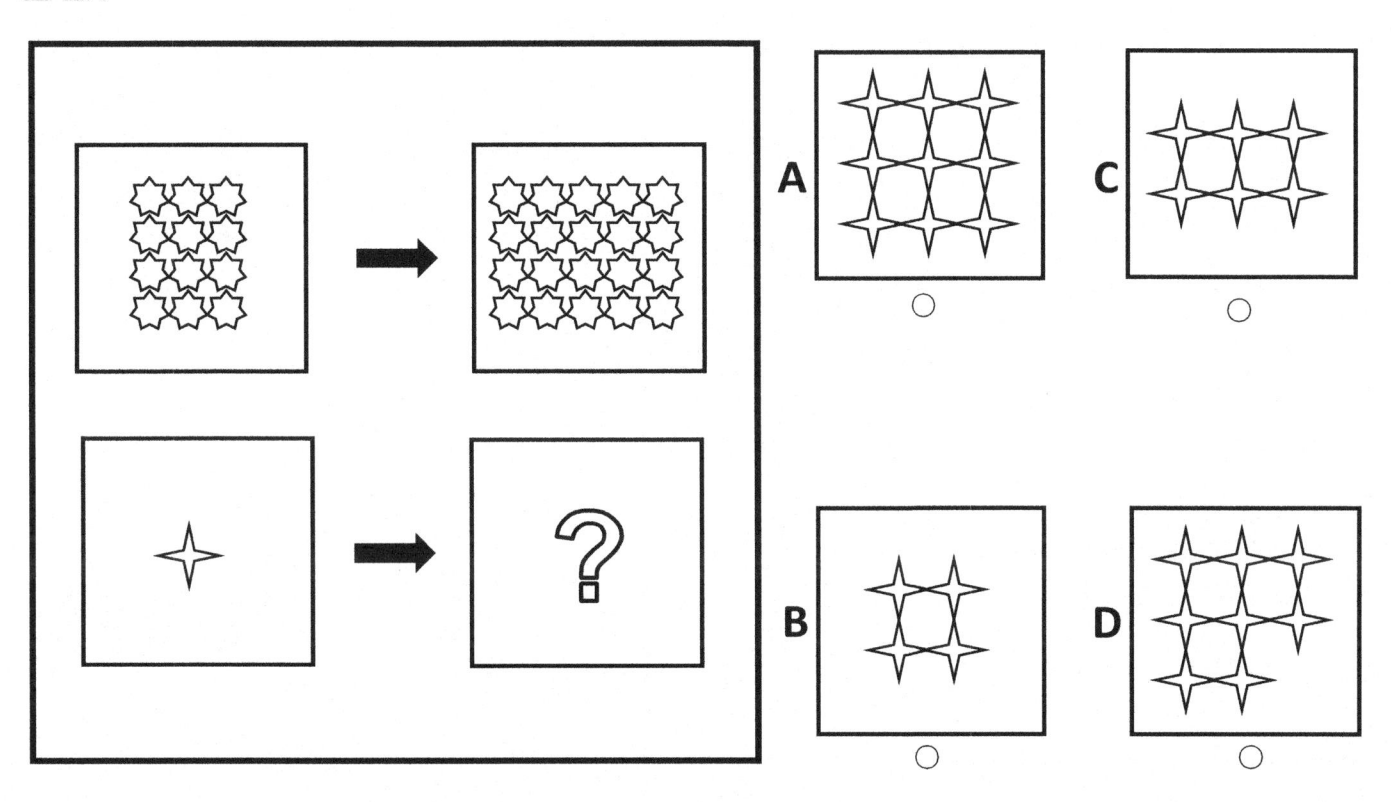

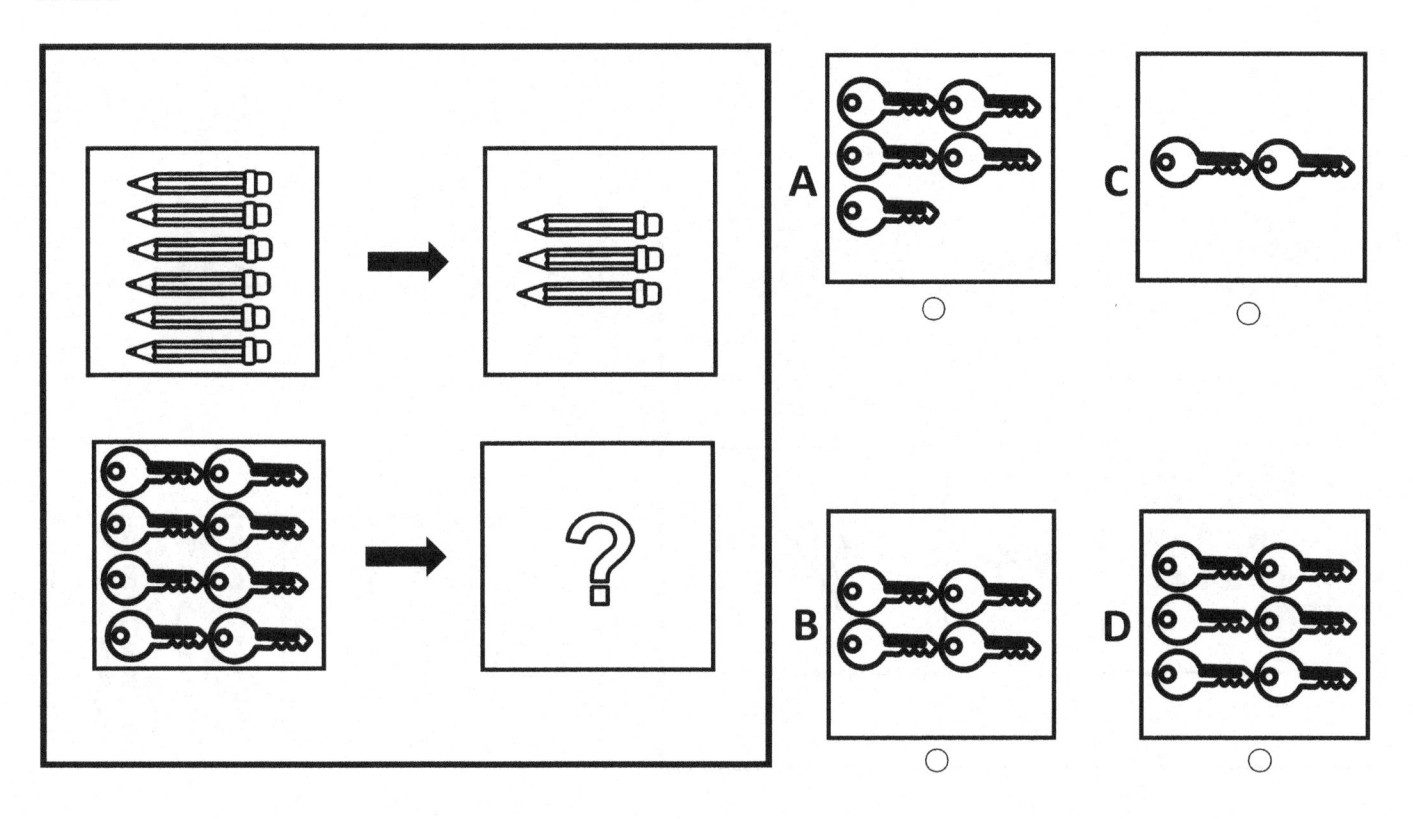

11.

12.

227

PRACTICE TEST GRADE 2

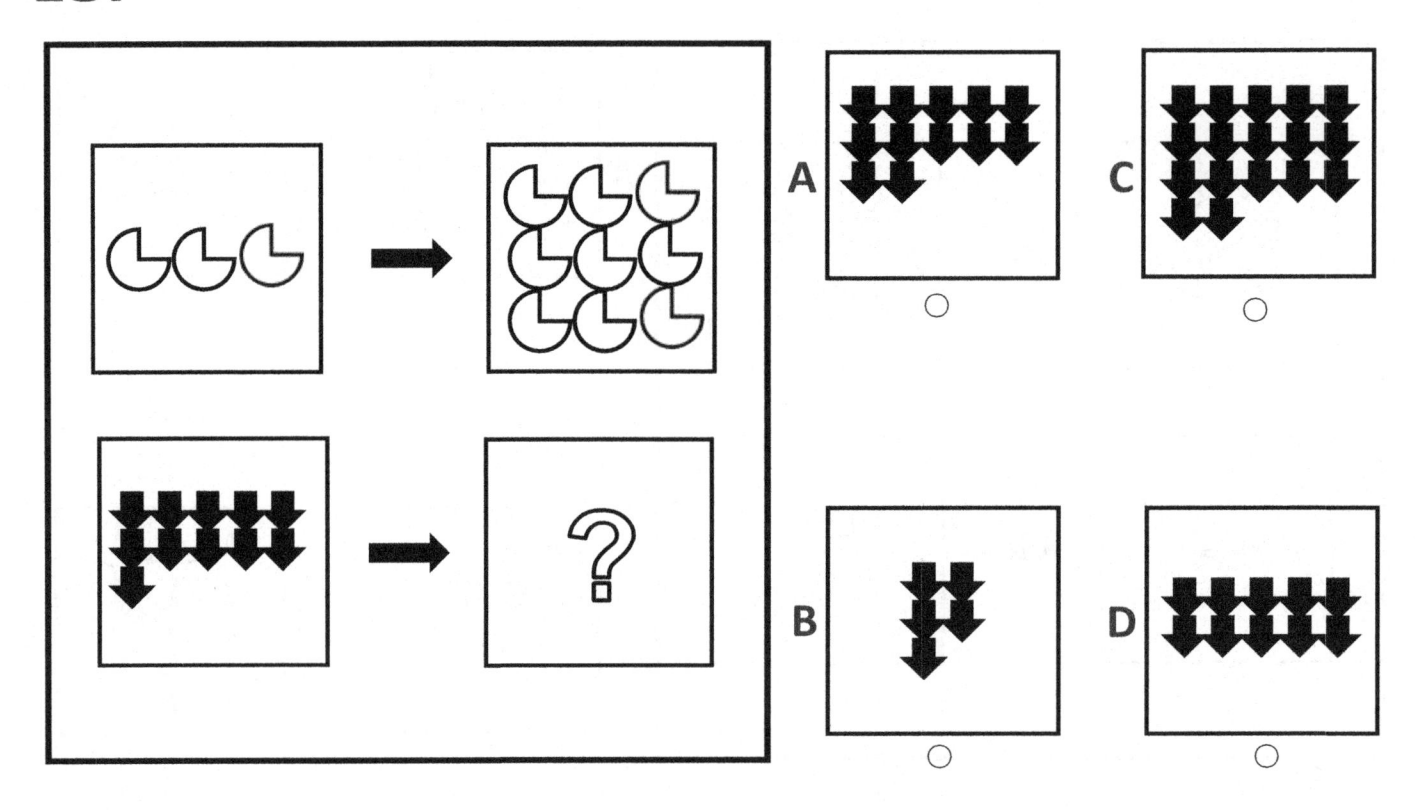

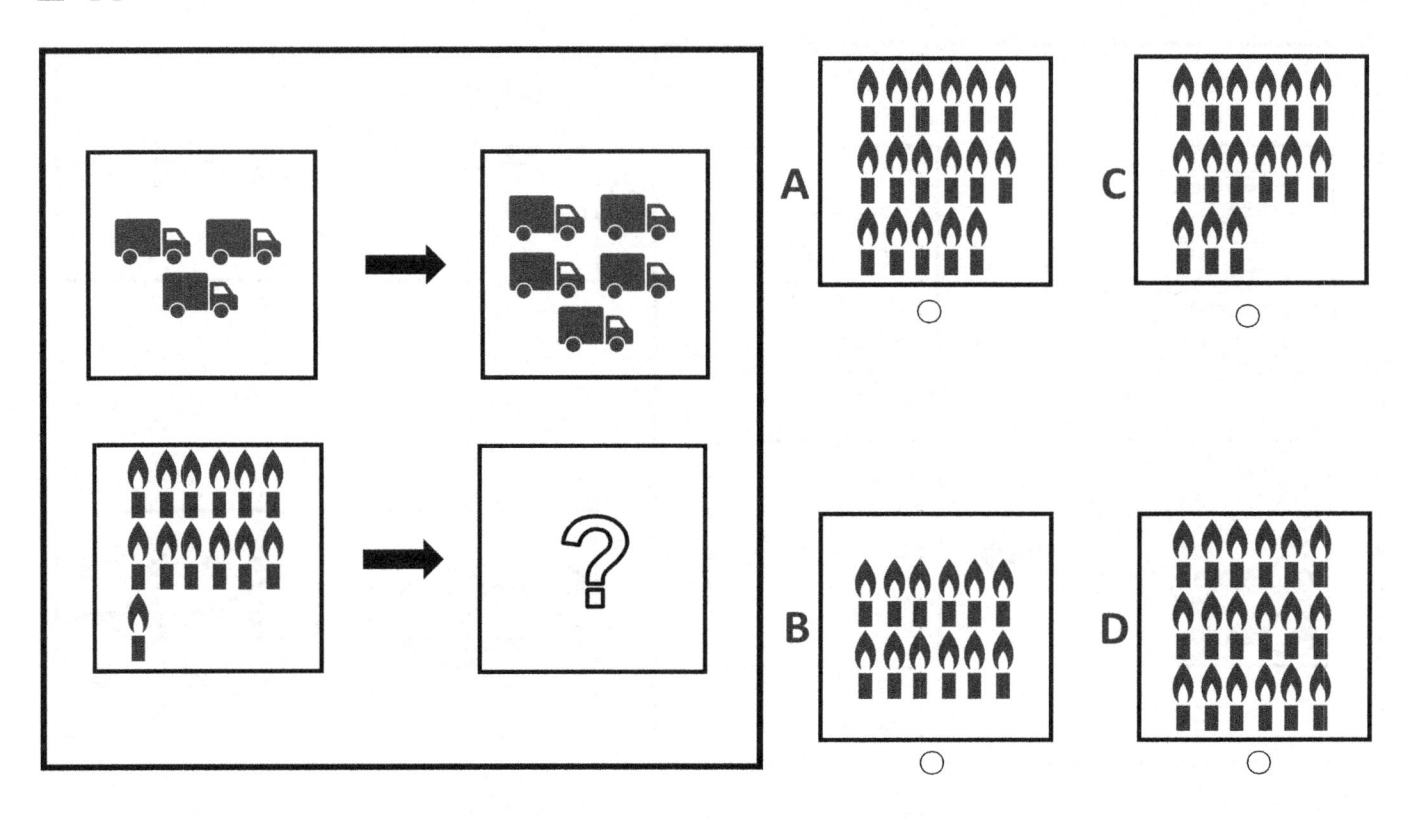

13.

14.

228

PRACTICE TEST GRADE 2

15.

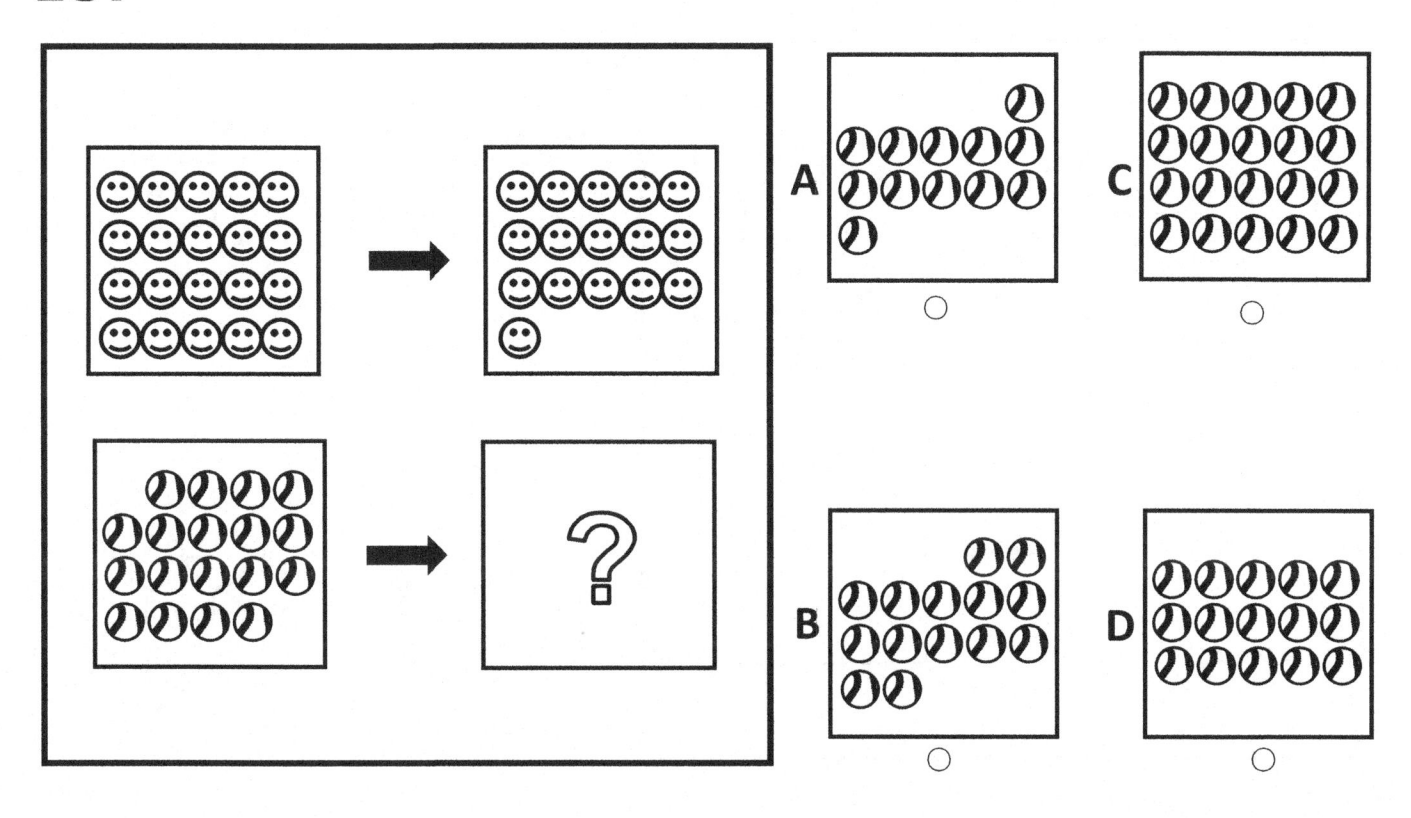

16.

229

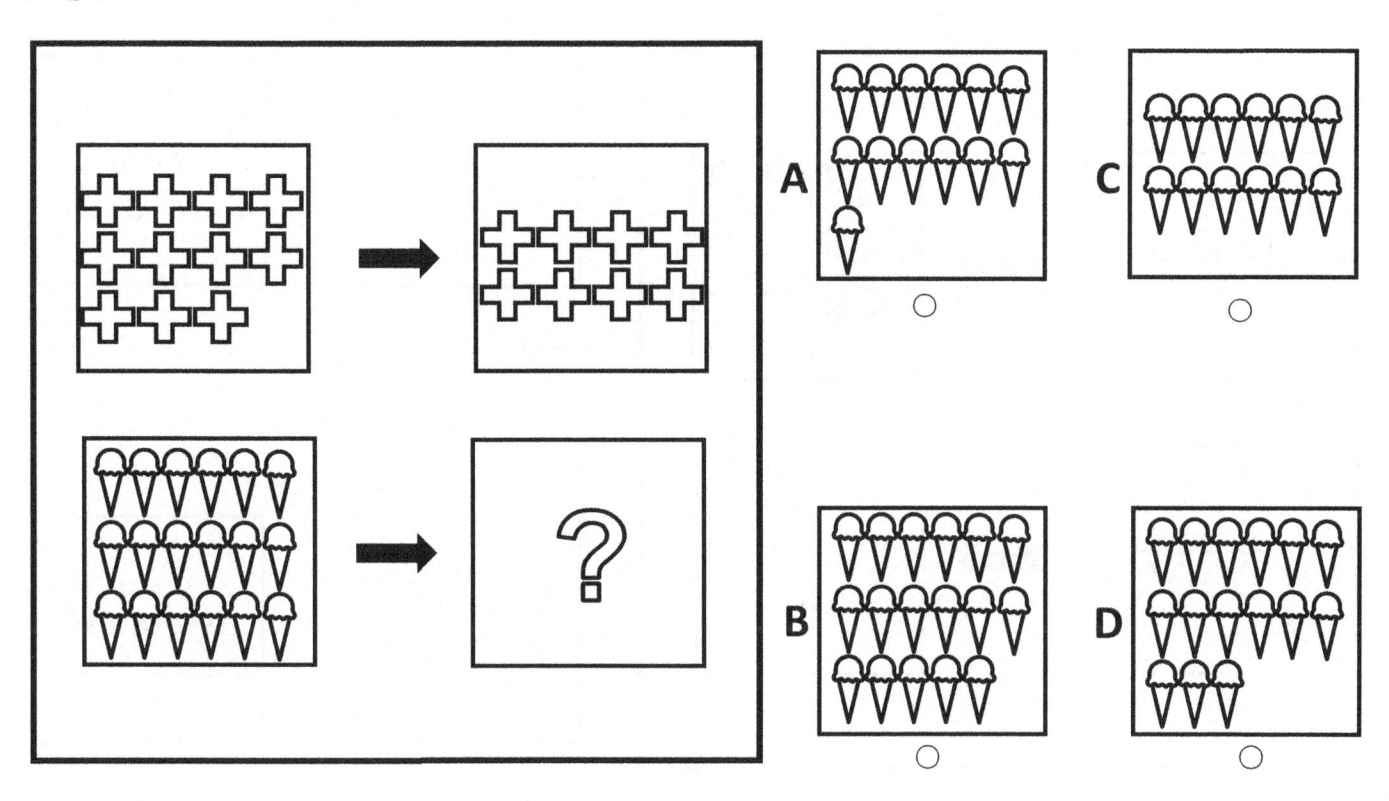

PRACTICE TEST GRADE 2

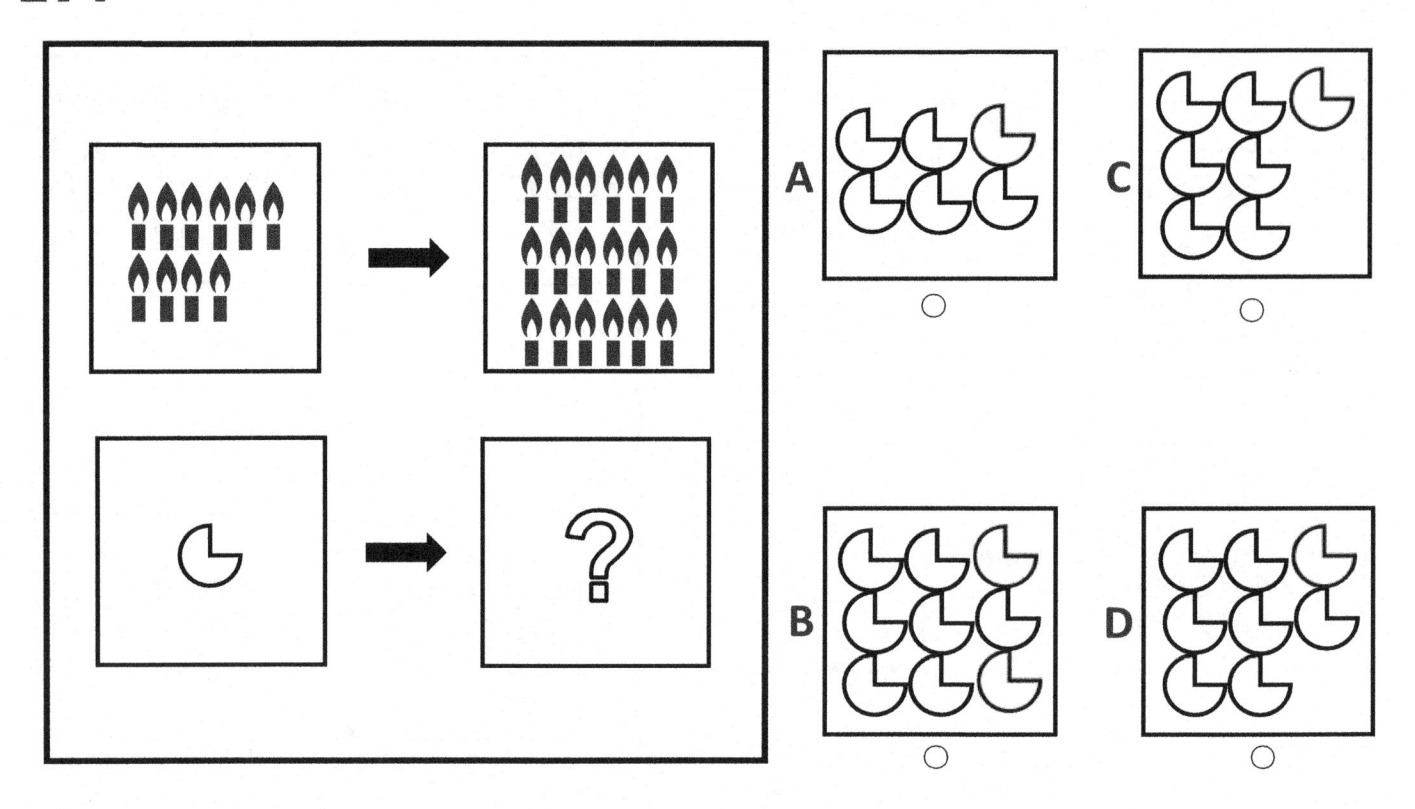

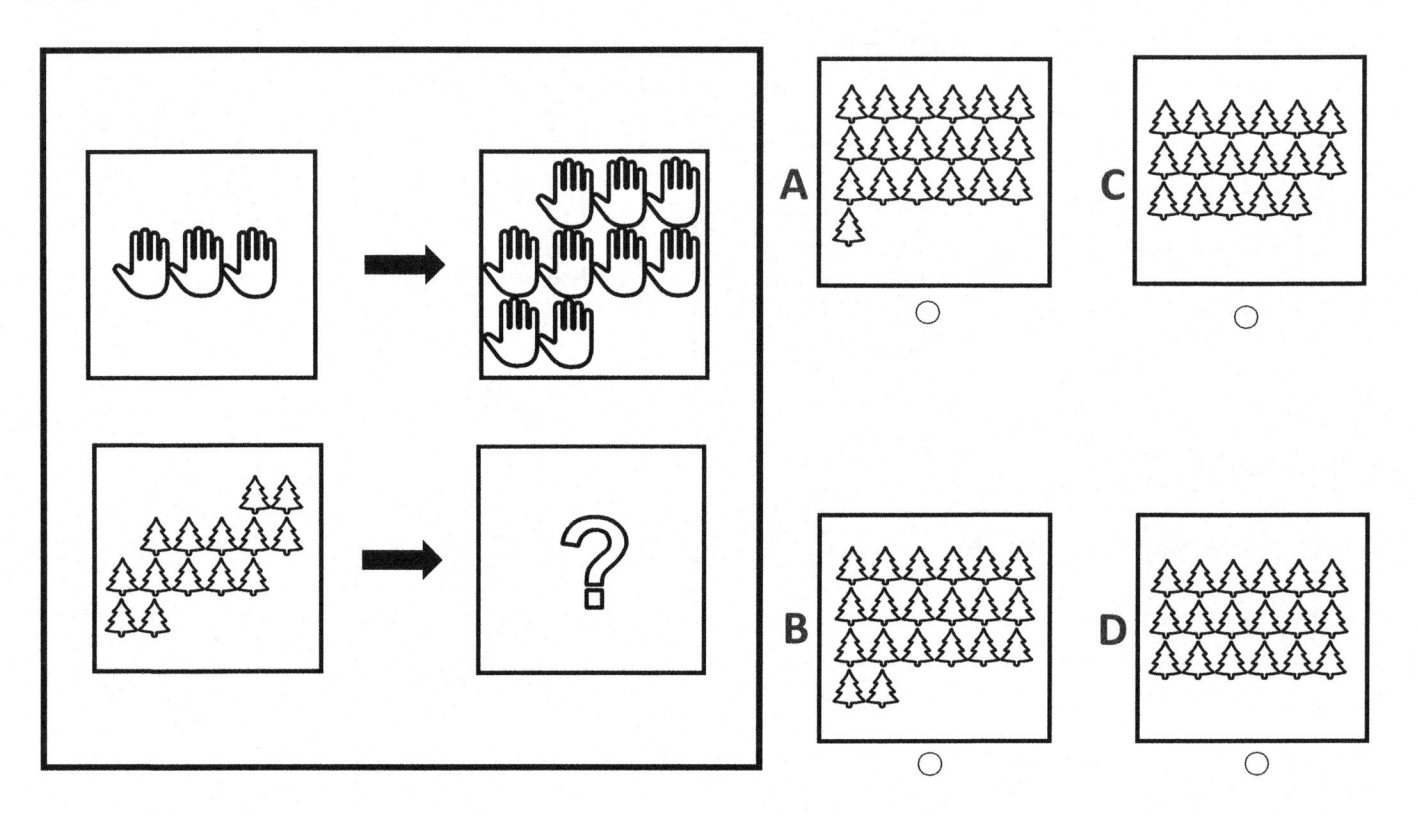

17.

18.

230

PRACTICE TEST GRADE 2

Number Series

Children are required to determine which string of beads is needed to complete a sequence that follows a specific pattern by observing an abacus.

Example 1

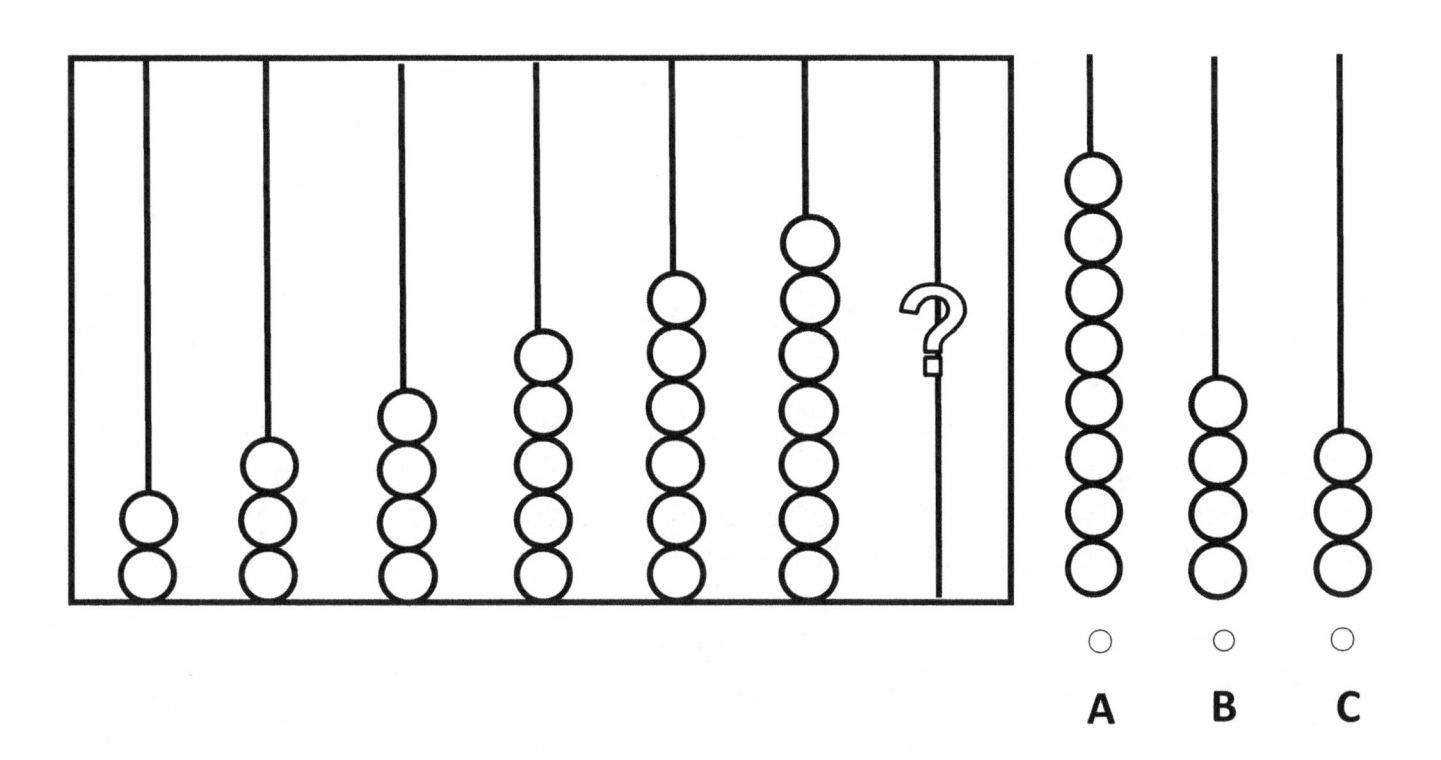

- The sequence is: 2   3   4   5   6   7   ?
- It's easy to realize that each number in the sequence increases by 1. 2+1=3; 3+1=4; 4+1=5; 5+1=6; 6+1=7; etc.
- Apply the same rule to the number 7.

7 + 1 = 8 The right answer is "A"

PRACTICE TEST GRADE 2

Example 2

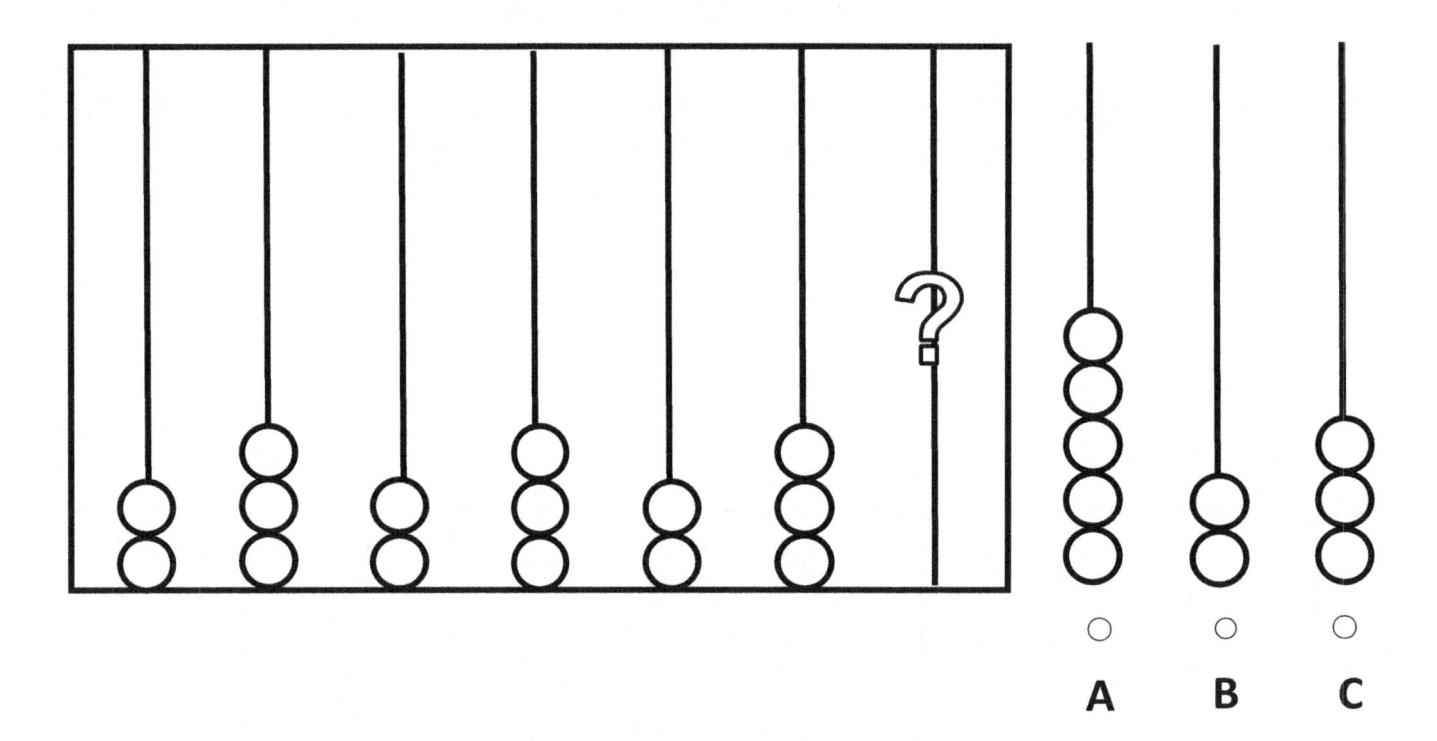

- The sequence is: 2 3 2 3 2 3 ?
- It's easy to realize that each number in the sequence increases by 1 and then decreases by 1.
- 2+1=3; 3-1=2; 2+1=3; 3-1=2; 2+1=3 etc...
- Apply the same rule to the number 3.

3-1=2 The right answer is "B"

Tips for Number Series

To answer these questions, children will need to be able to identify the patterns in a sequence of numbers and provide the missing item. Therefore, it is necessary to perform as many exercises as possible, moving from the easiest to the hardest.

In the beginning, to make the logic of the sequences easier, it is useful to work with real objects.

PRACTICE TEST GRADE 2

1.

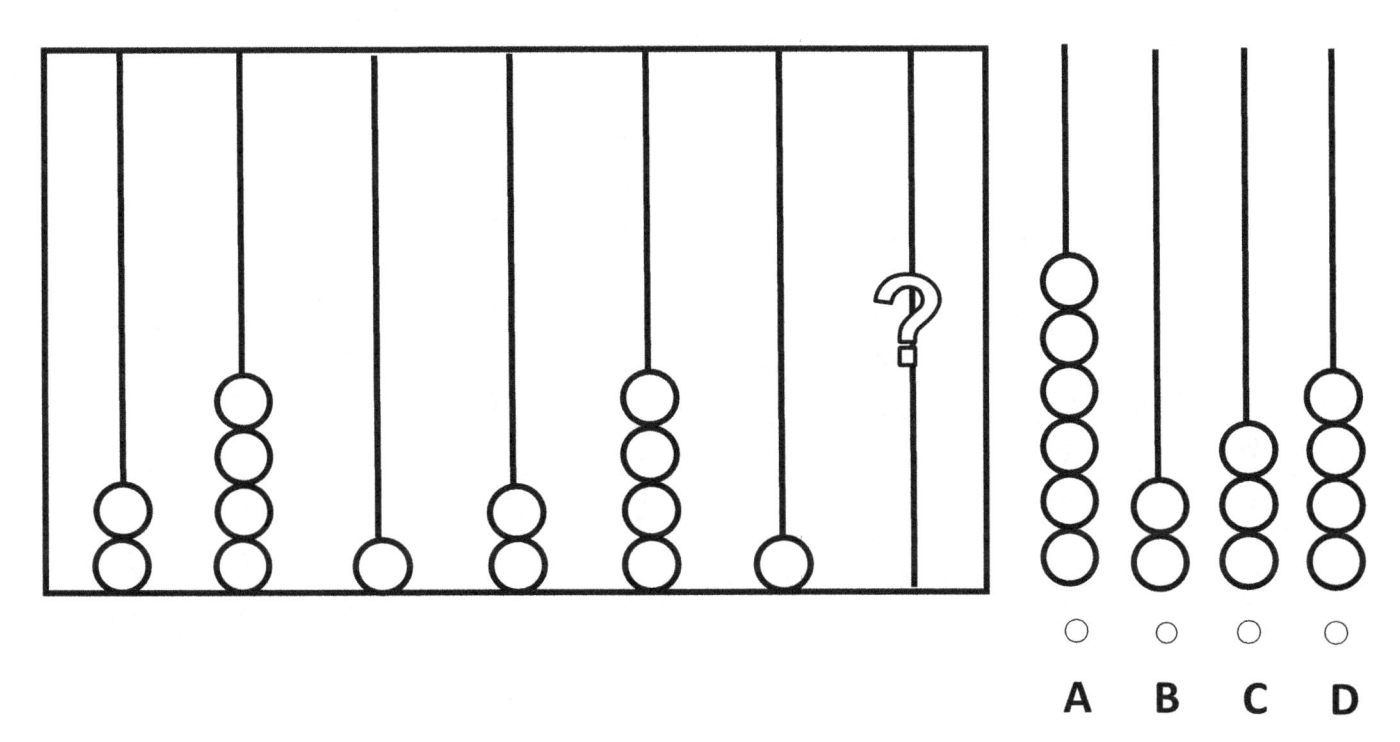

2.

233

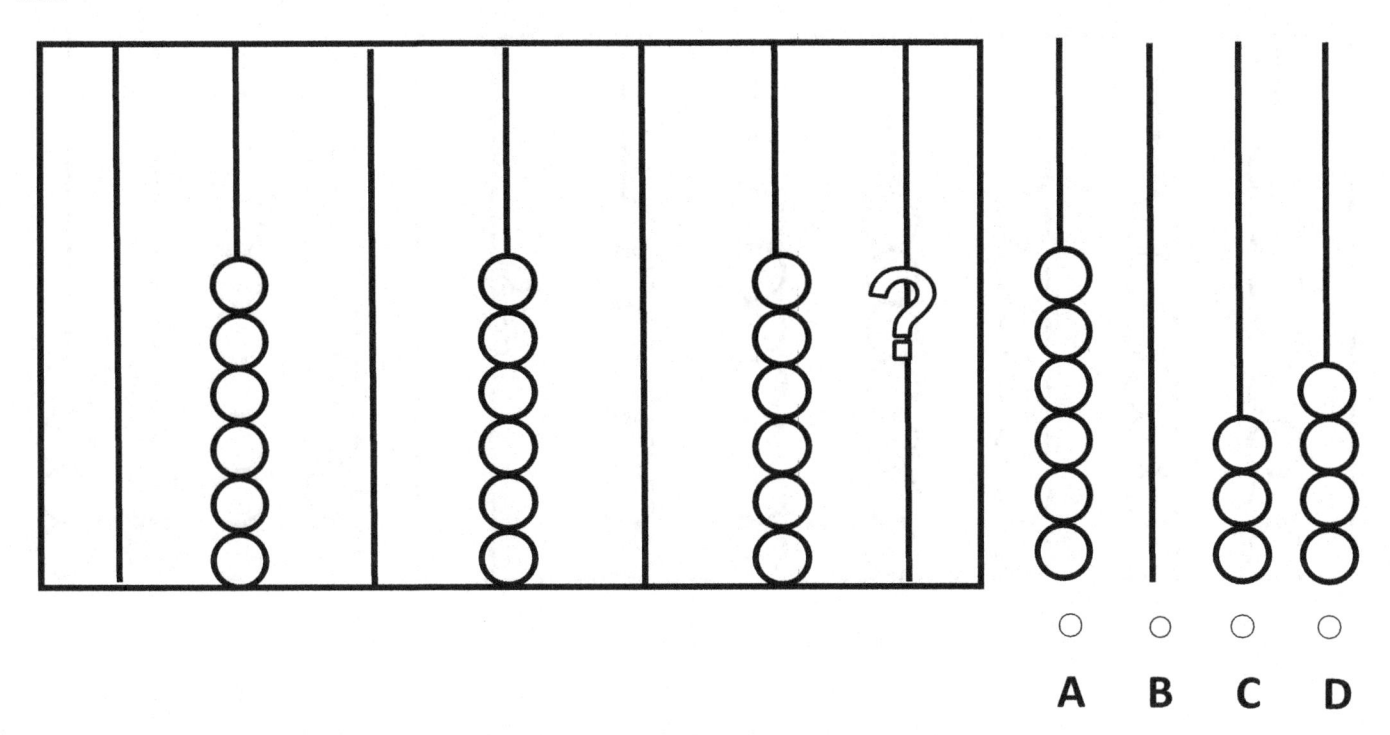

PRACTICE TEST GRADE 2

3.

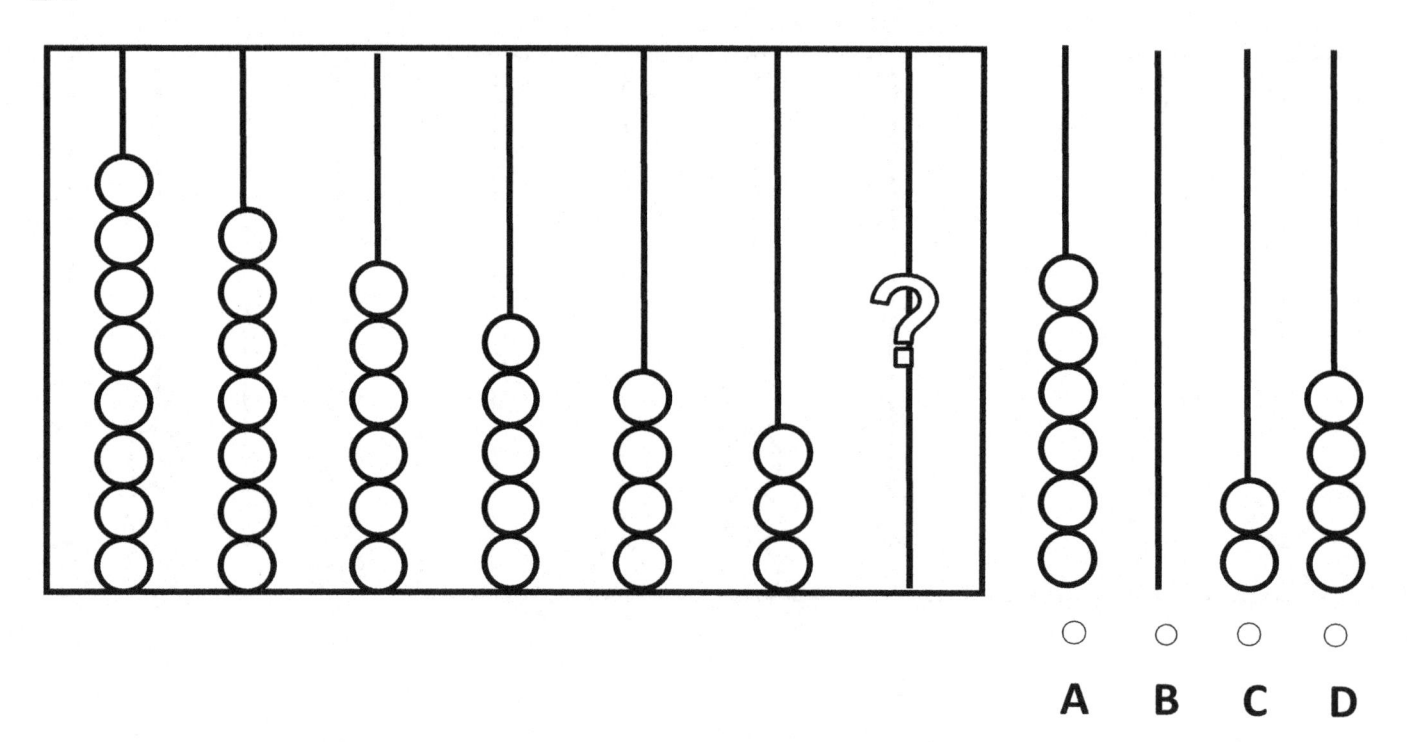

○ ○ ○ ○
A B C D

4.

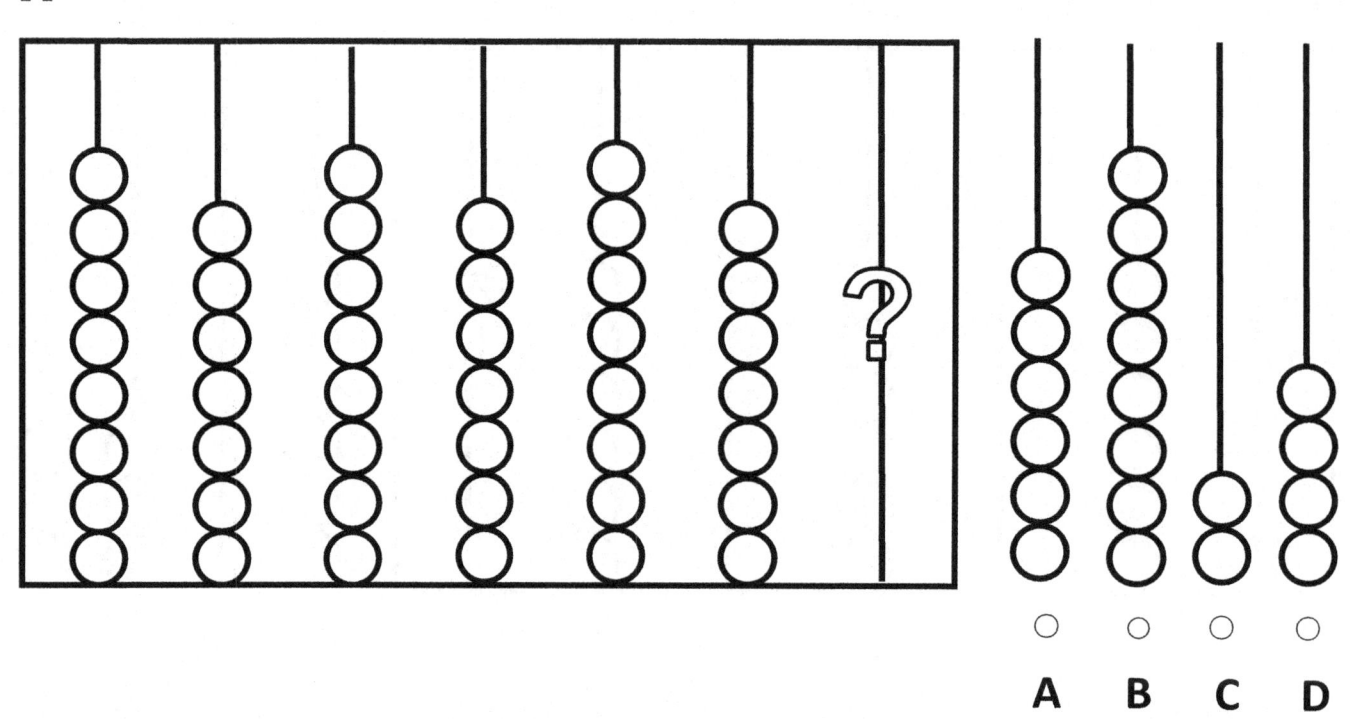

○ ○ ○ ○
A B C D

234

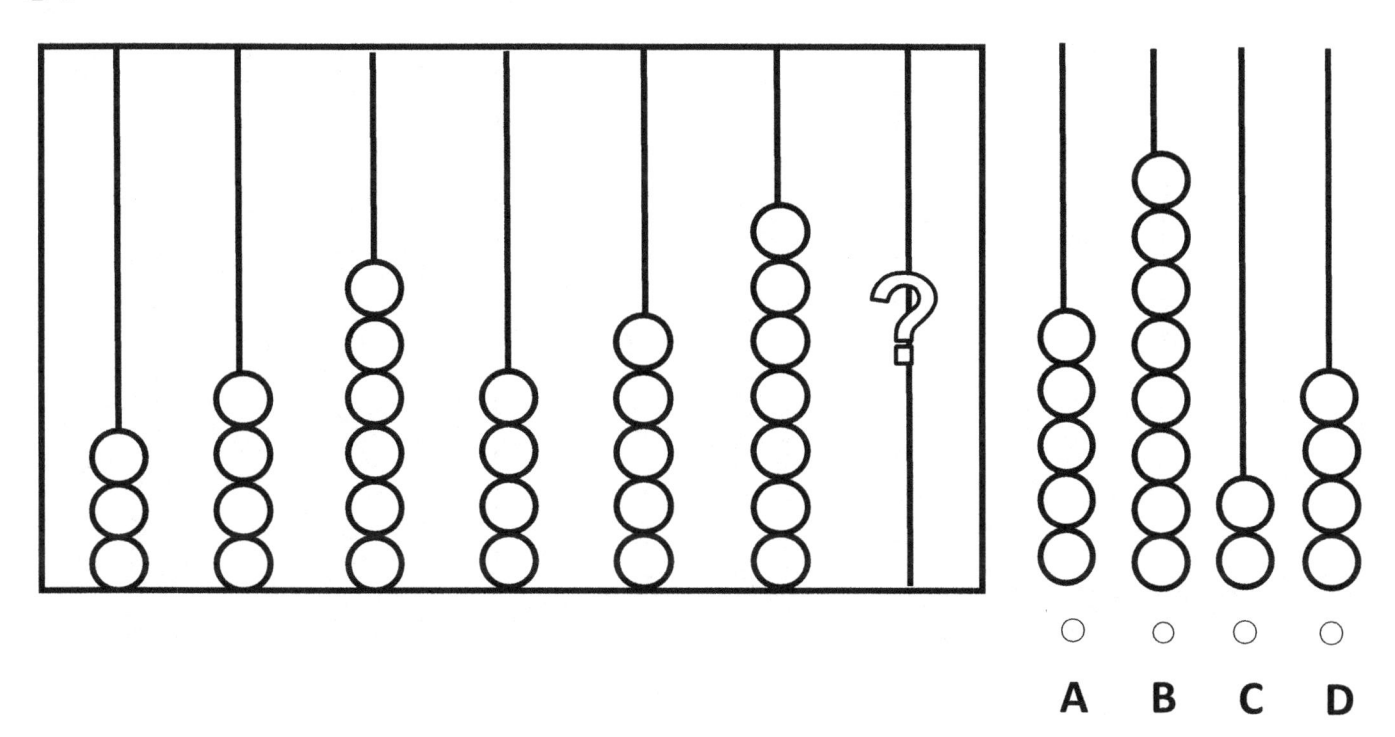

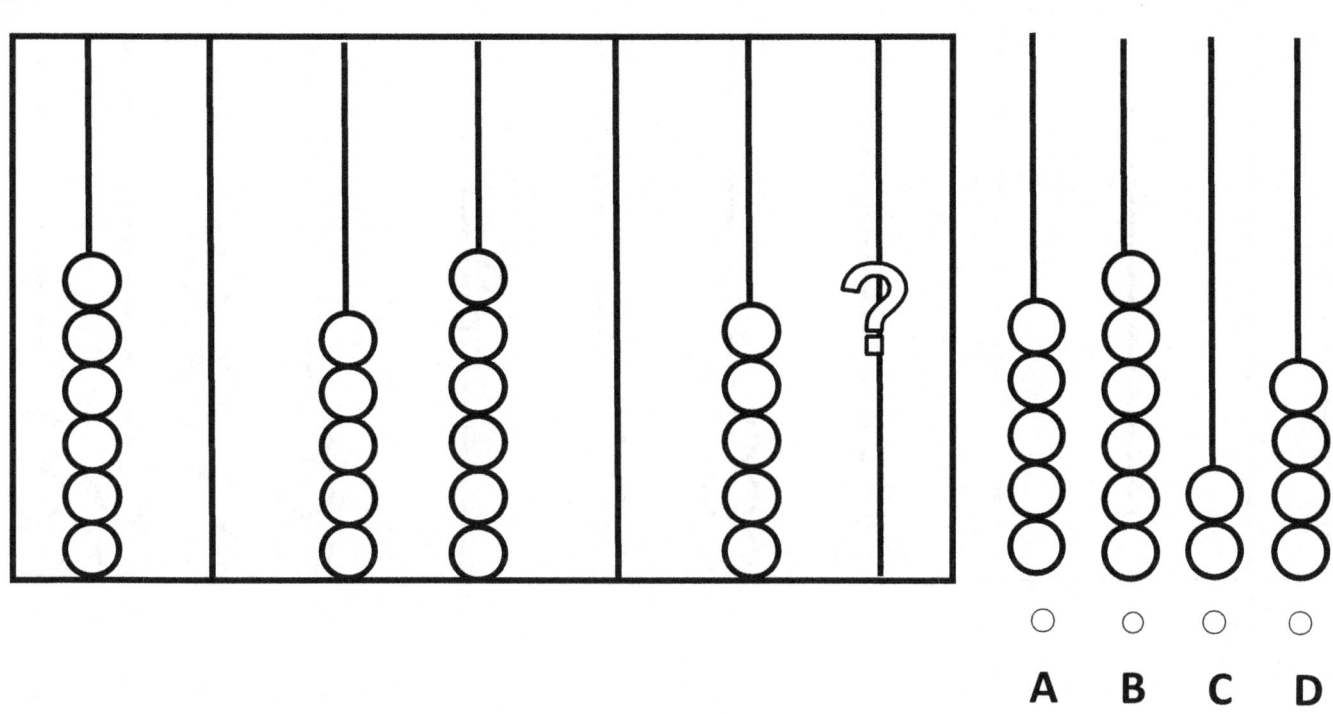

PRACTICE TEST GRADE 2

5.

6.

235

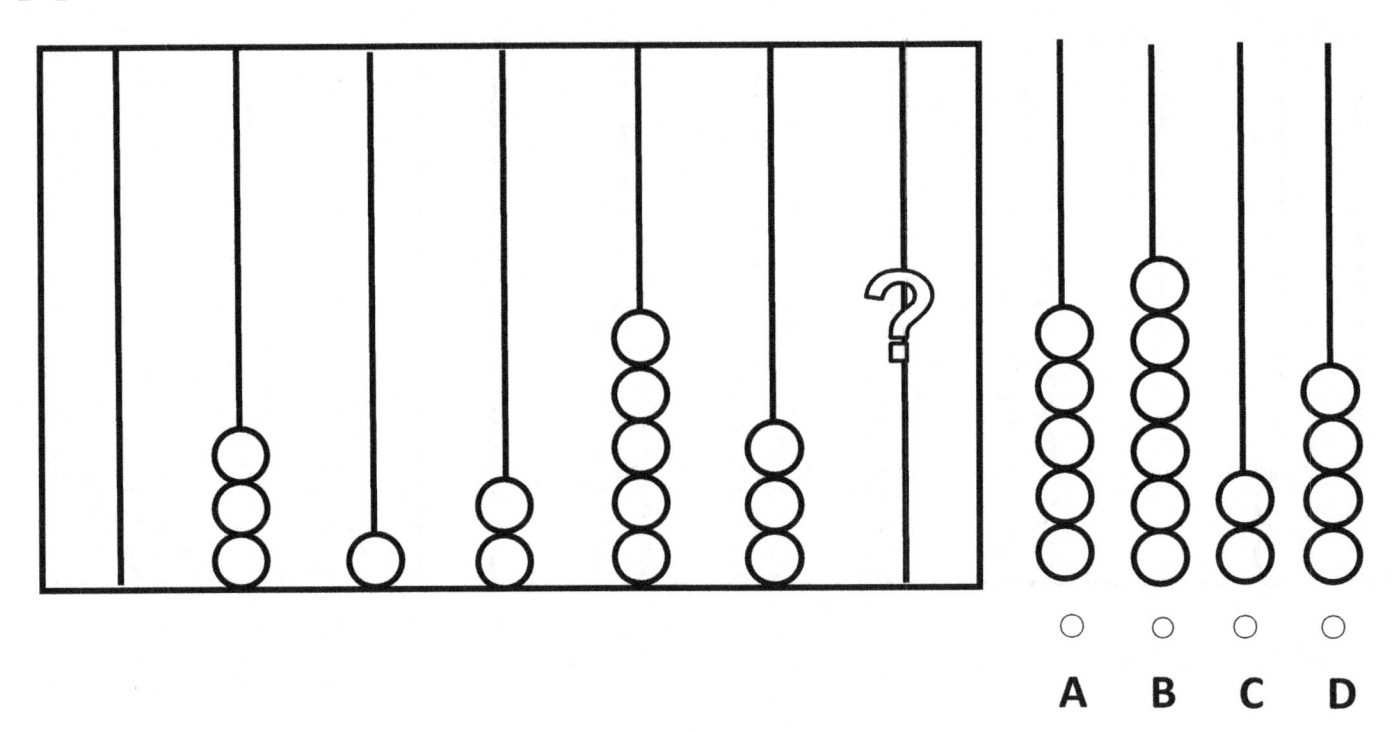

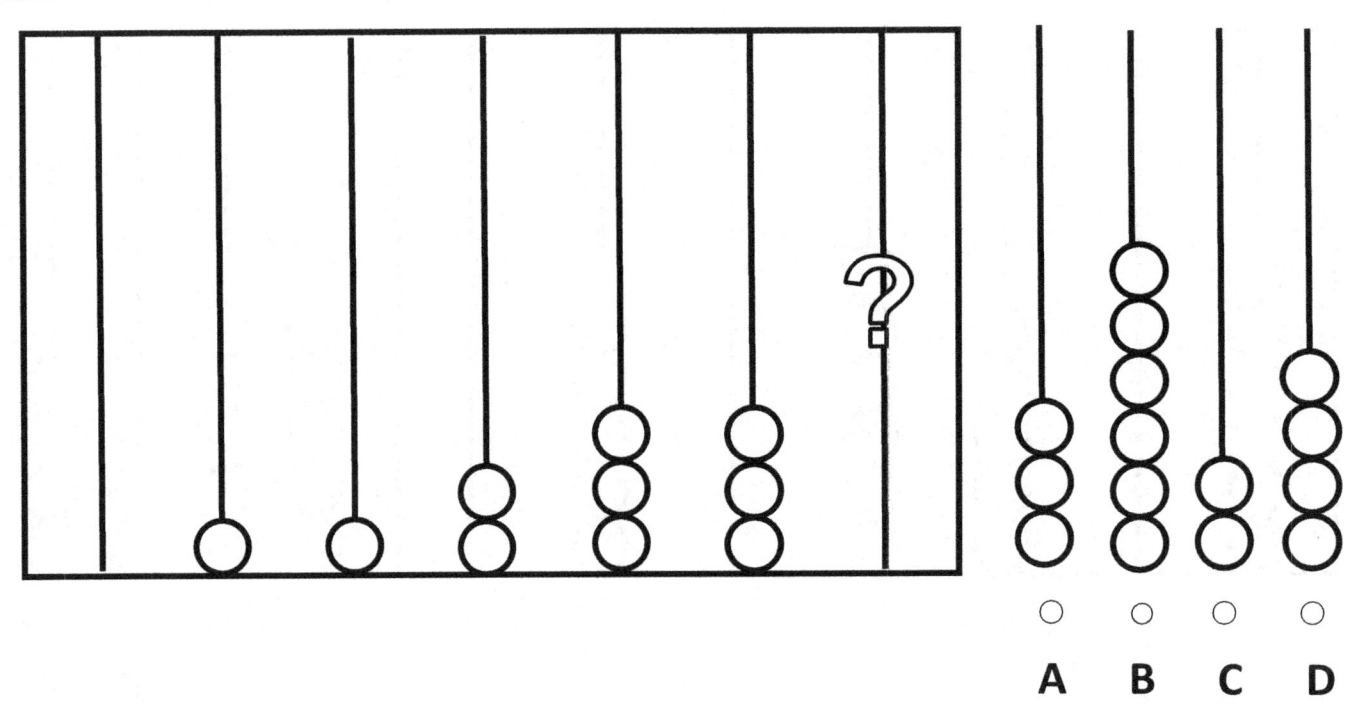

PRACTICE TEST GRADE 2

7.

8.

236

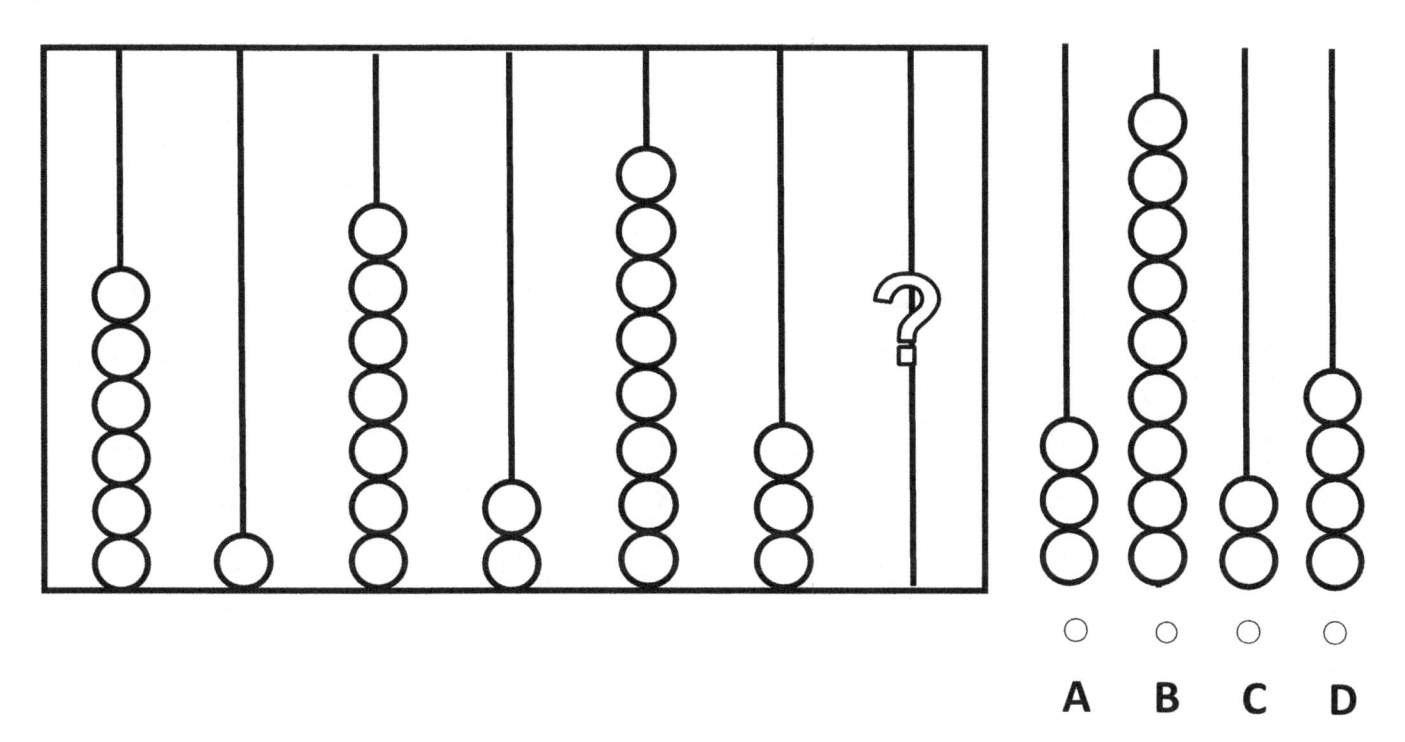

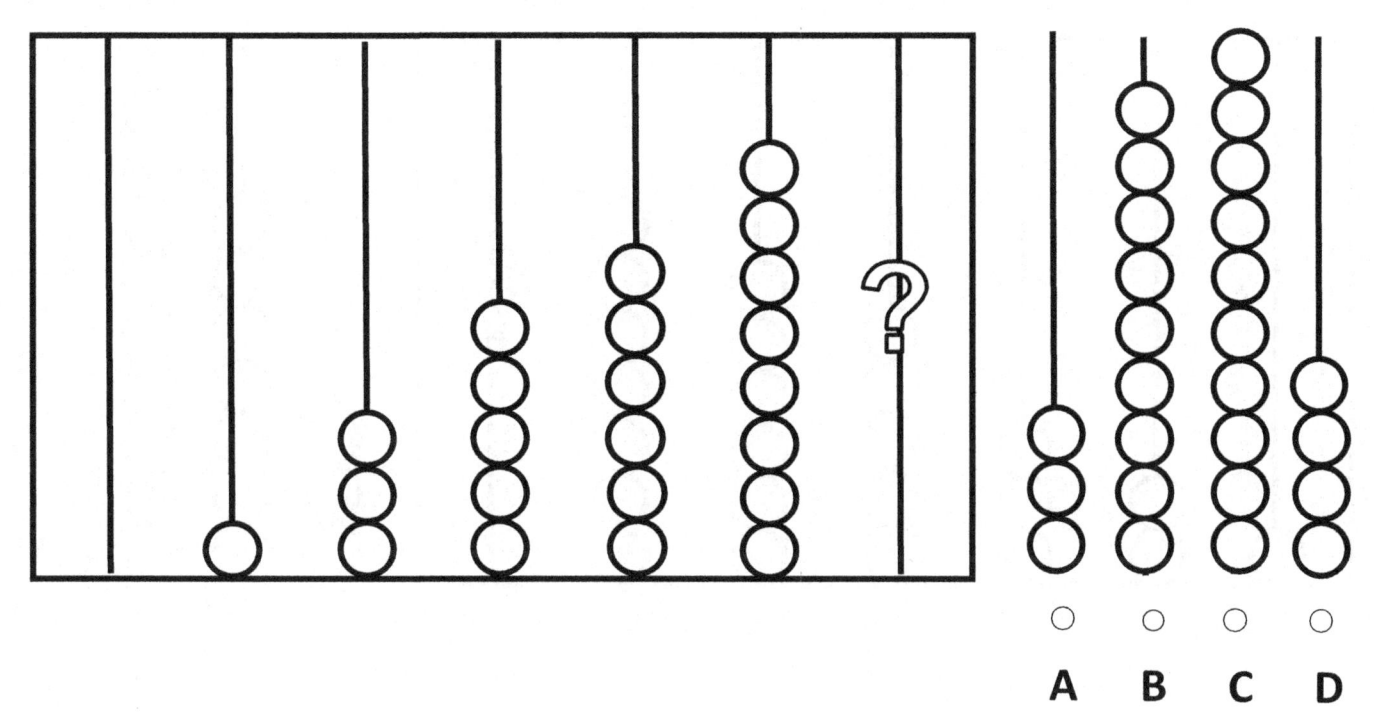

PRACTICE TEST GRADE 2

9.

10.

237

PRACTICE TEST GRADE 2

11.

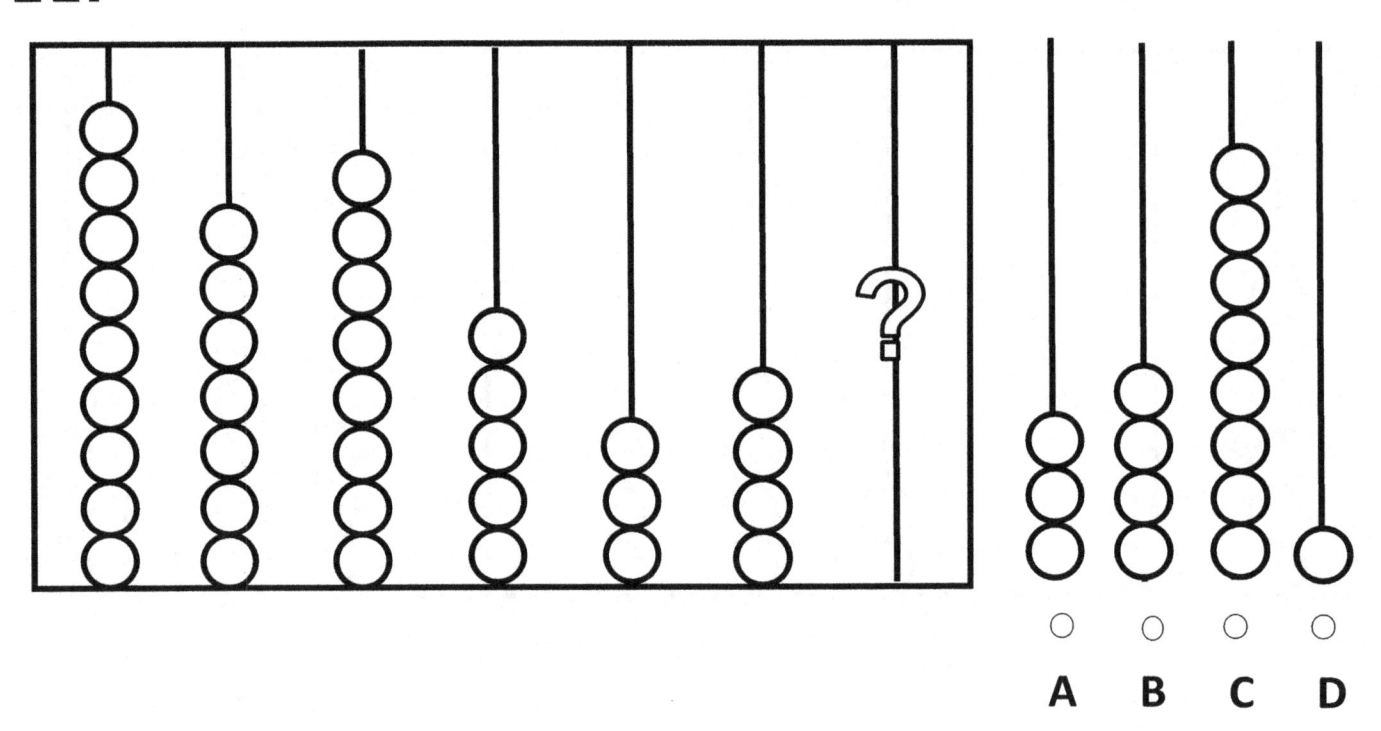

12.

238

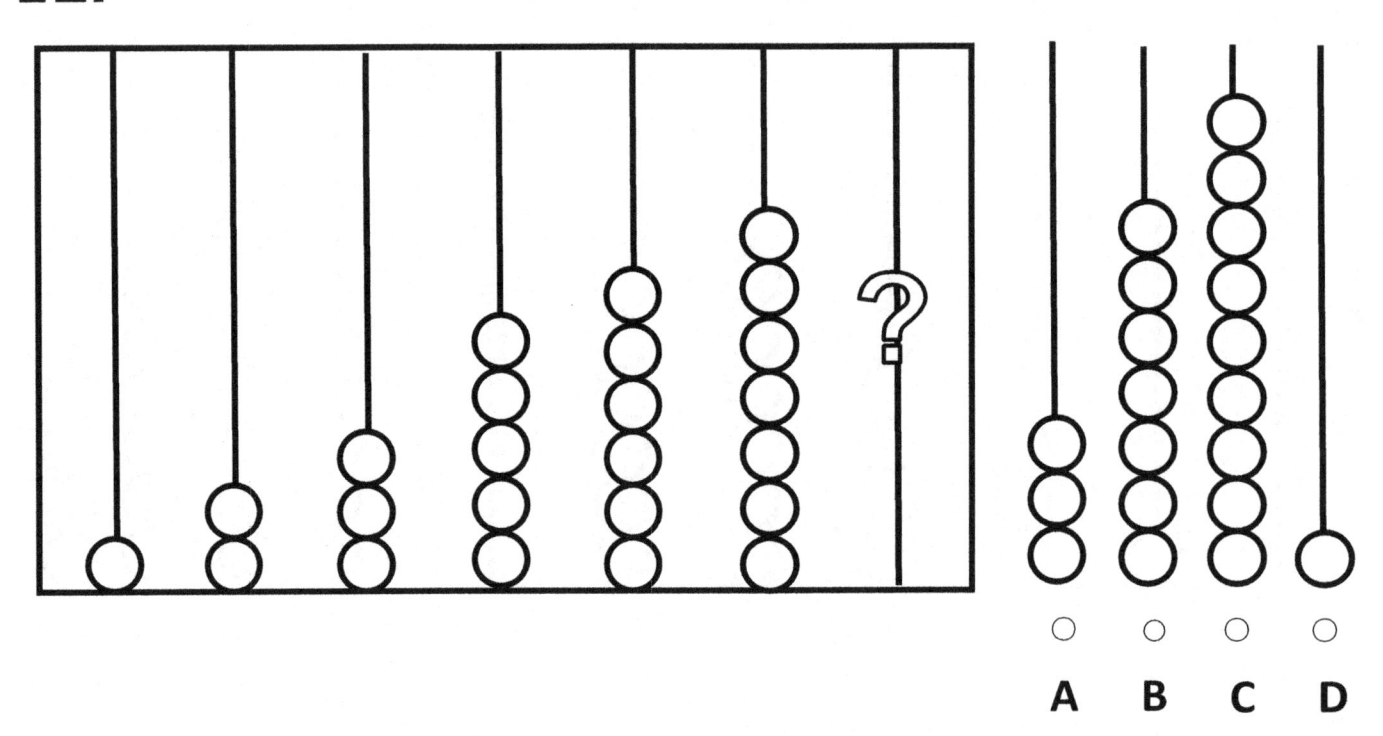

PRACTICE TEST GRADE 2

13.

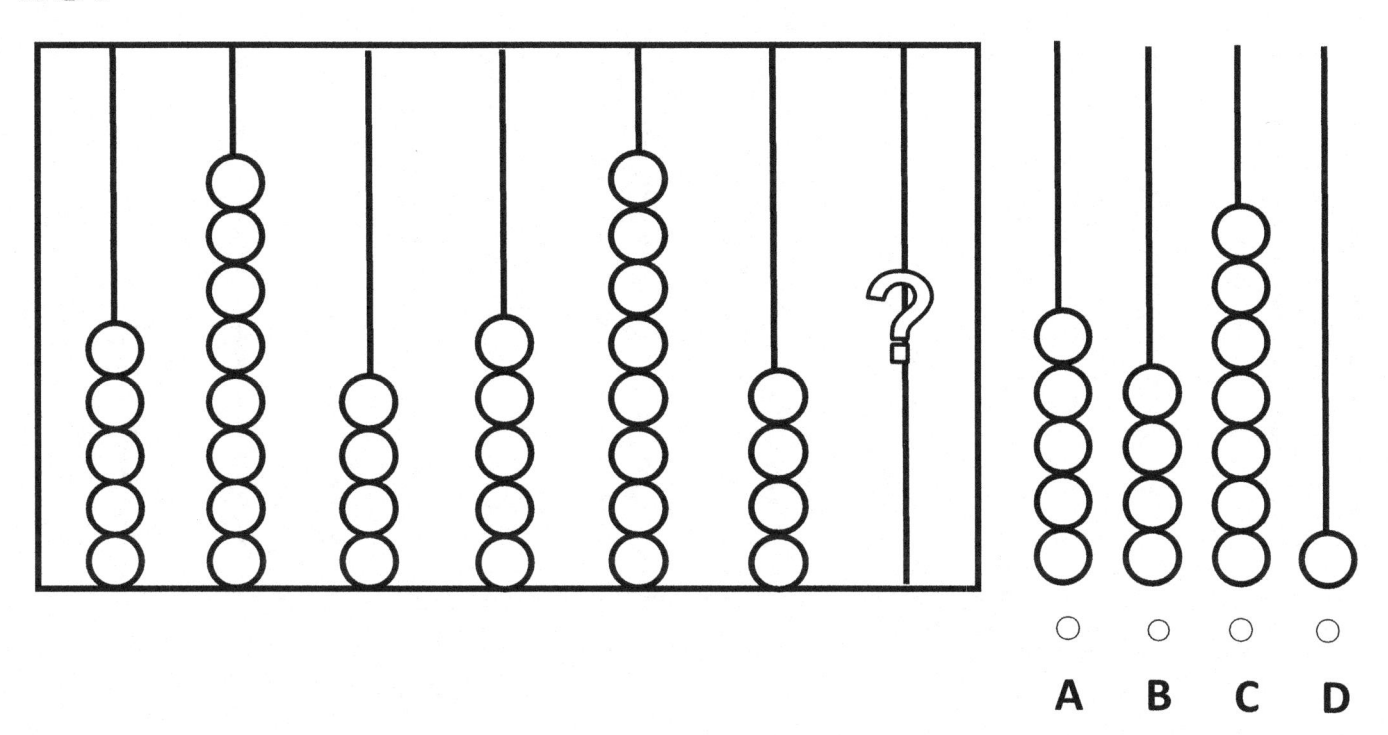

14.

239

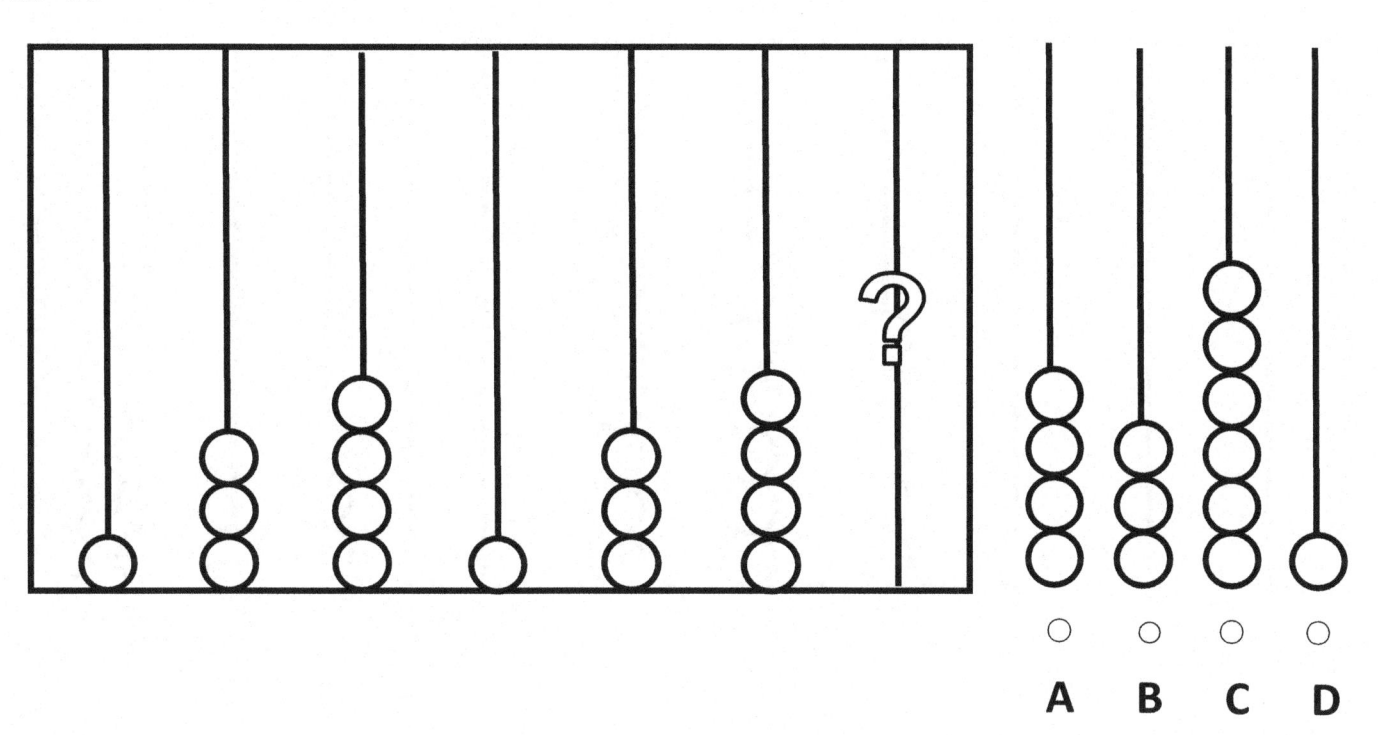

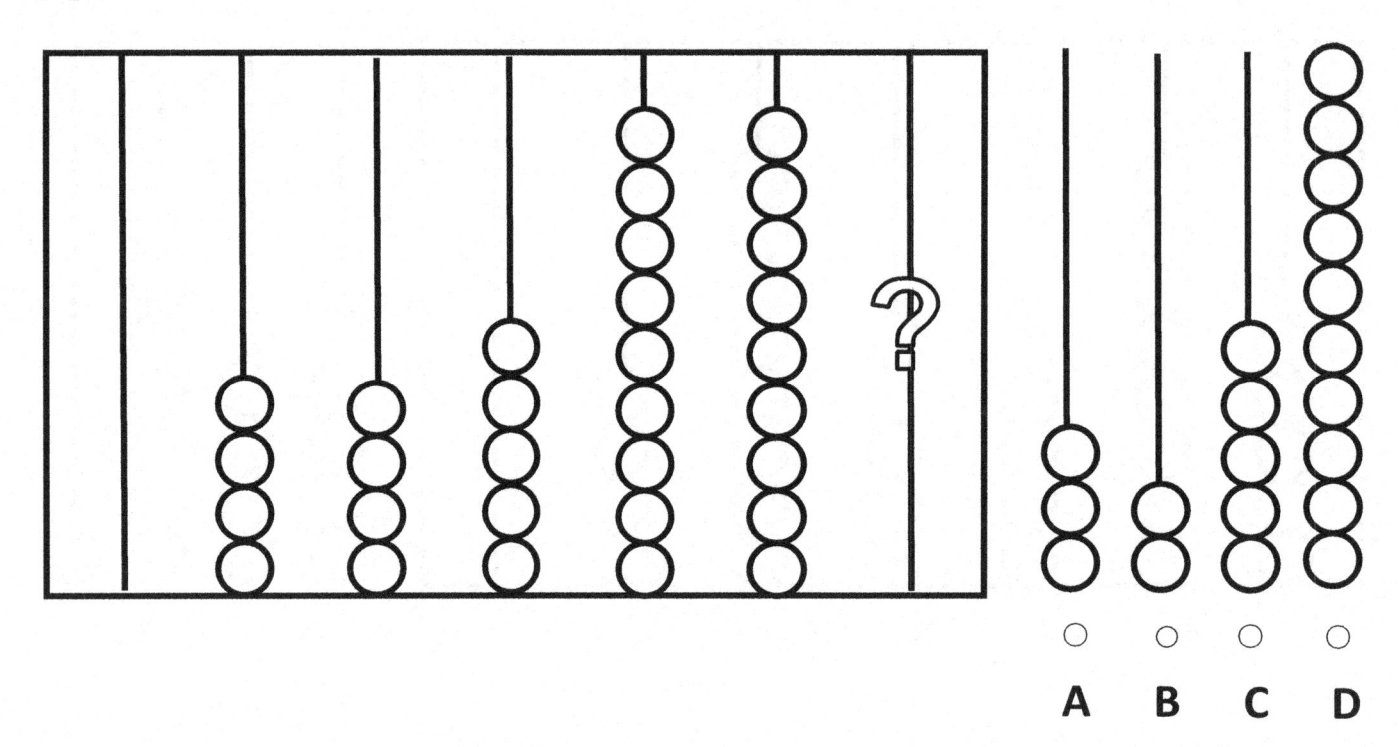

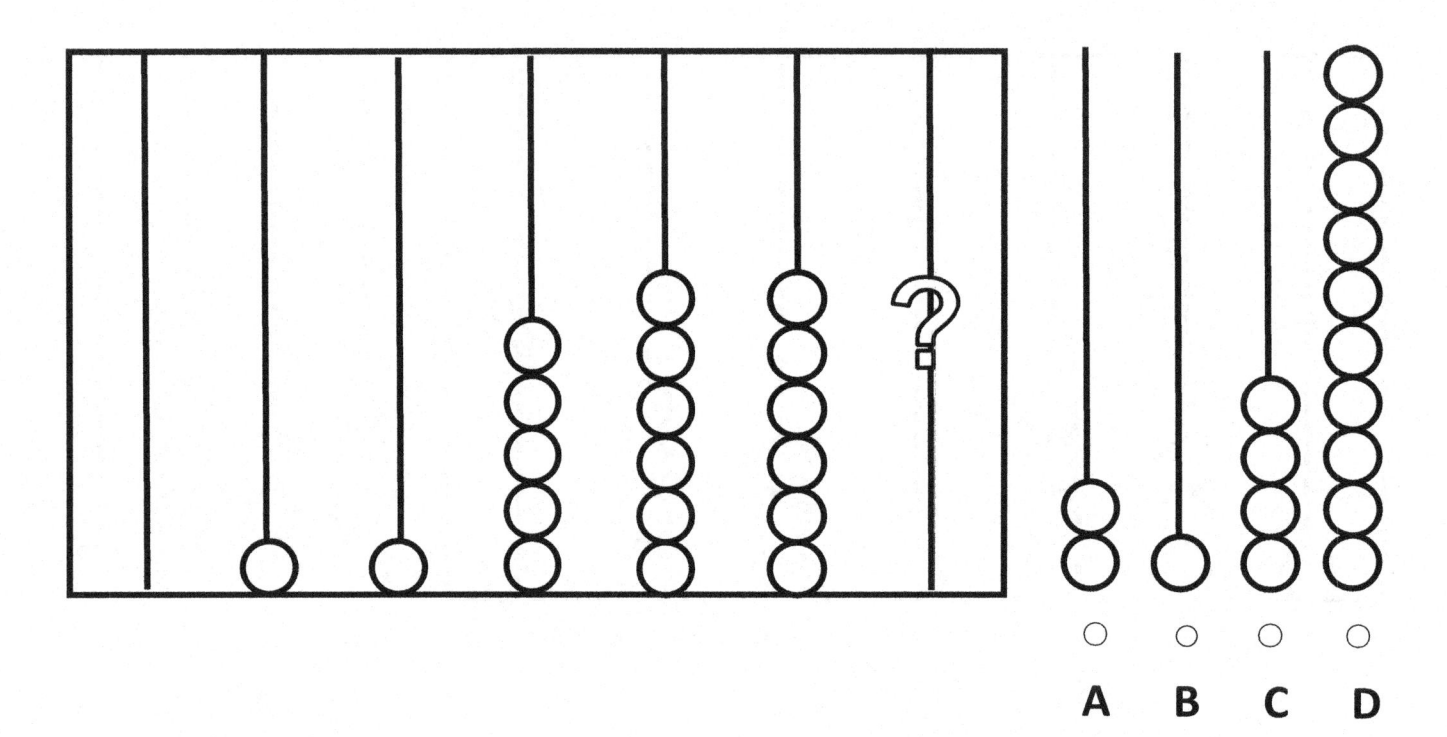

PRACTICE TEST GRADE 2

15.

16.

240

PRACTICE TEST GRADE 2

17.

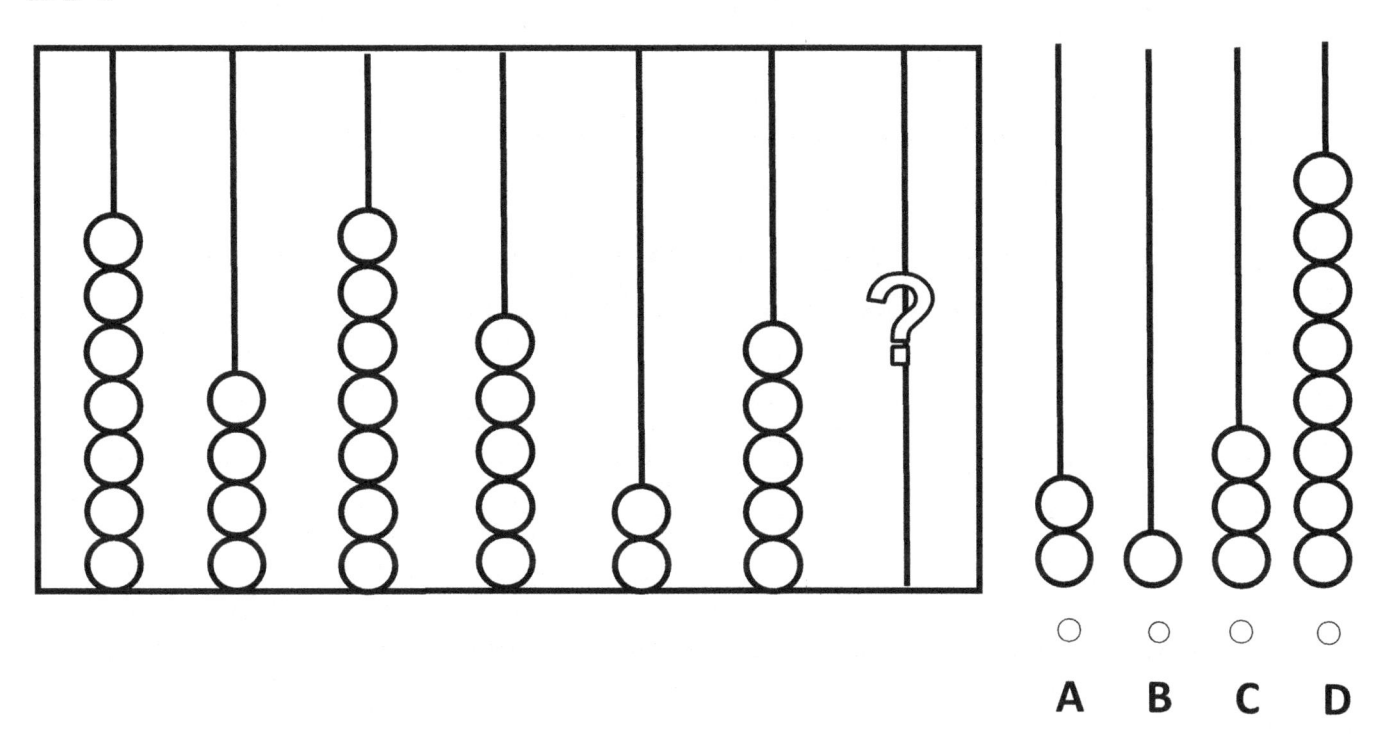

18.

241

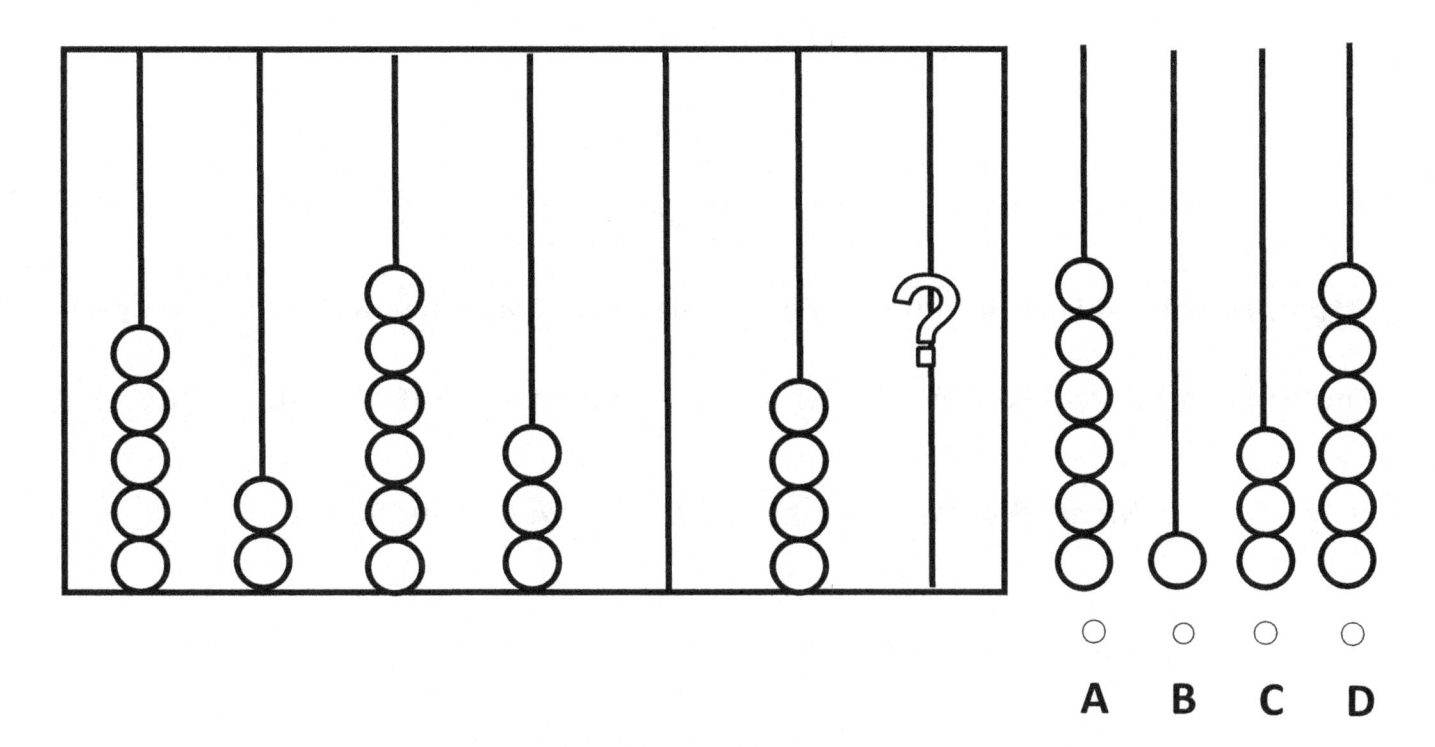

ANSWER KEY GRADE 2

HOW TO DOWNLOAD 54 BONUS QUESTIONS

Thank you for reading this book, we hope you really enjoyed it and found it very helpful.

PLEASE LEAVE US A REVIEW ON THE WEBSITE WHERE YOU PURCHASED THIS BOOK!

By leaving a review, you give us the opportunity to improve our work.

A GIFT FOR YOU!
FREE ONLINE ACCESS TO 54 BONUS PRACTICE QUESTIONS.

Follow this link:

⬇

https://www.skilledchildren.com/free-download-cogat-grade-2-test-prep.php
You will find a PDF to download: please insert this PASSWORD: 080131

Nicole Howard and the SkilledChildren.com Team

www.skilledchildren.com

THANK YOU PAGE GRADE 2

ANSWER KEY FOR GRADE 2

THANK YOU PAGE GRADE 2

Picture Analogies Practice Test
p.140

1.
Answer: option D
Explanation: Surfboards are used at the beach; skis are used in the mountains.

2.
Answer: option B
Explanation: Windows are found in houses; portholes are found in ships.

3.
Answer: option D
Explanation: Stars go on top of the Christmas trees; candles go on top of the birthday cakes.

4.
Answer: option B
Explanation: Eyebrows are located above the eyes; mustaches are located above the mouth.

5.
Answer: option B
Explanation: Fries are cooked in the fryer; chicken is cooked in the oven.

6.
Answer: option B
Explanation: The tablecloth is placed on the table; the blanket is placed on the bed.

7.
Answer: option B
Explanation: The iron is used to smooth out shirts; the hair straightener is used to straighten hair.

THANK YOU PAGE GRADE 2

8.
Answer: option C
Explanation: To wash dishes you use the dishwasher; to wash shirts you use the washing machine.

9.
Answer: option A
Explanation: The diving mask is worn on the face; fins are worn on the feet.

10.
Answer: option A
Explanation: The polisher is used to clean the floor. The vacuum cleaner is used for the carpet.

11.
Answer: option C
Explanation: Kneepads protect the knees; helmets protect the head.

12.
Answer: option A
Explanation: The teacher works in the school; the doctor works in the hospital.

13.
Answer: option A
Explanation: Arms are for canoeing; legs are for biking.

14.
Answer: option B
Explanation: The padded jacket is used when it snows; the swimsuit is used when it's sunny.

15.
Answer: option A
Explanation: The lawnmower is used to cut grass; the razor is used to trim beards.

THANK YOU PAGE GRADE 2

16.
Answer: option B
Explanation: The skeleton belongs to man; the bone belongs to fish.

17.
Answer: option C
Explanation: The ruler is for drawing lines; the compass is for drawing circles.

18.
Answer: option D
Explanation: The wrench is for turning bolts; the screwdriver is for turning screws.

Picture Classification Practice Test
p.151

1.
Answer: option A
Explanation: Hens, penguins, ostriches, and turkeys are non-flying birds.

2.
Answer: option C
Explanation: The colander, microwave, blender, toaster are items that are used in the kitchen.

3.
Answer: option B
Explanation: The chess horse, playing cards, puzzles, dominoes are board games.

4.
Answer: option A
Explanation: The iron, washing machine, iron board and basket with dirty laundry are items that are found in the laundry room.

5.
Answer: option C
Explanation: Hummingbirds, eagles, parrots and owls are flying birds.

6.
Answer: option B
Explanation: The lawnmower, rake, watering can and wheelbarrow are gardening items.

7.
Answer: option B
Explanation: The school, the museum, the hospital, and the house are all buildings for humans.

8.
Answer: option C
Explanation: Rhinos, elephants, lions and gazelles are all animals living in the African savannah.

9.
Answer: option D
Explanation: Dolphins, dogs, tigers, and whales are all mammals.

10.
Answer: option D
Explanation: Fridges, safes, backpacks and bookcases are made to store items.

11.
Answer: option B
Explanation: The microwave, deep fryer, electric oven and frying pan are for cooking food.

12.
Answer: option C
Explanation: The birdcage, fish bowl, birdhouse and doghouse are structures made for animals.

13.
Answer: option A
Explanation: The boat, life buoy, canoe and balloon can float in the water.

14.
Answer: option A
Explanation: Apatosaurus, triceratops, t-rexes, and stegosaurs were dinosaurs.

15.
Answer: option A
Explanation: Snow, rain, wind, and tornadoes are weather phenomena.

16.
Answer: option B
Explanation: Santa Claus, the Witch, the Wizard and the Mermaid are fantastic characters.

17.
Answer: option C
Explanation: Cheese, milk, ham, and eggs are foods of animal origin.

18.
Answer: option D
Explanation: The dragon, the unicorn, the three-headed monster and the frog prince are characters from fairy tales.

Sentence Completion Practice Test
p.163

1.
Answer: option A
Explanation: Penguin is classified as bird.

2.
Answer: option D
Explanation: The swimsuit doesn't protect against the cold.

3.
Answer: option C
Explanation: The oven will not be found in the garden.

4.
Answer: option B
Explanation: Bats are mammals.

5.
Answer: option D
Explanation: John will use the ball in the D box.

6.
Answer: option C
Explanation: Spiders aren't insects. The group is called the Arachnida.

7.
Answer: option D
Explanation: The head contains the brain.

8.
Answer: option A
Explanation: Trucks have wheels.

9.
Answer: option A
Explanation: You need a telescope.

10.
Answer: option C
Explanation: You can use a battery-powered flashlight.

11.
Answer: option B
Explanation: Ham does not contain sugar.

12.
Answer: option D
Explanation: Eggplants don't grow on trees.

13.
Answer: option B
Explanation: Planet Earth never stands still.

14.
Answer: option D
Explanation: A compass is generally not found in the laundry room.

15.
Answer: option C
Explanation: Horses don't eat meat.

16.
Answer: option B
Explanation: The TV remote control works with batteries.

17.
Answer: option D
Explanation: Seals don't lay eggs.

18.
Answer: option B
Explanation: A seamstress doesn't use a saw.

Figure Matrices Practice Test
p.184

1.
Answer: option B
Explanation: The white figure rotates by 180 degrees and turns black.

2.
Answer: option D
Explanation: Both figures rotate by 180 degrees and the inside shape turns white.

3.
Answer: option C
Explanation: The larger figure gets smaller and stands next to the others.

4.
Answer: option C
Explanation: The two inside figures are placed to the left of the larger figure.

5.
Answer: option B
Explanation: The two figures are placed side by side horizontally and become white.

6.
Answer: option A
Explanation: The lower figure rotates by 180 degrees, turns white, and moves on top of the other.

THANK YOU PAGE GRADE 2

7.
Answer: option D
Explanation: The upper figure disappears. The lower figure takes the place of the other one and turns black.

8.
Answer: option D
Explanation: The larger figure rotates by 45 degrees clockwise. The inside shape turns black.

9.
Answer: option C
Explanation: The larger figure rotates by 90 degrees clockwise. The inner figure rotates by 90 degrees counterclockwise.

10.
Answer: option D
Explanation: The internal figure is removed.

11.
Answer: option C
Explanation: The figure rotates by 45 degrees clockwise and turns black.

12.
Answer: option B
Explanation: The higher figure takes the place of the lower one and vice versa.

13.
Answer: option D
Explanation: The 2 figures rotate by 90 degrees clockwise.

14.
Answer: option D
Explanation: The smaller figure moves to the left of the larger one and turns black.

THANK YOU PAGE GRADE 2

15.
Answer: option A
Explanation: The two figures switch places and colors.

16.
Answer: option C
Explanation: The right stars have 2 more points than the one on the left.

17.
Answer: option D
Explanation: The inside shape is removed. The upper shape moves inside the larger figure.

18.
Answer: option A
Explanation: Figures rotate 90 degrees counterclockwise.

Figure Classification Practice Test
p.195

1.
Answer: option B
Explanation: 3 circles, one black, one gray and one white, in different positions.

2.
Answer: option A
Explanation: Combos of 2 gray circles, 3 black circles and a black star.

3.
Answer: option D
Explanation: Combos of a 5-sided figure and a circle.

4.
Answer: option C
Explanation: Figures pointing down.

5.
Answer: option C
Explanation: Same black rotated figure.

6.
Answer: option B
Explanation: Combos of three hearts.

THANK YOU PAGE GRADE 2

7.
Answer: option A
Explanation: 2 intersecting circles.

8.
Answer: option C
Explanation: 2 identical figures, one white and one black, pointing in opposite directions.

9.
Answer: option A
Explanation: Six-sided shapes.

10.
Answer: option D
Explanation: Combos of a white square, a black arrow and a white arrow.

11.
Answer: option A
Explanation: Two shapes pointing in the same direction.

12.
Answer: option C
Explanation: Figures divided into 2 equal parts.

13.
Answer: option A
Explanation: Figures consisting only of curved lines.

14.
Answer: option A
Explanation: 2 straight lines in each figure.

THANK YOU PAGE GRADE 2

15.
Answer: option C
Explanation: Parallelograms.

16.
Answer: option A
Explanation: Same rotated figures and same colors.

17.
Answer: option C
Explanation: 7 white circles and 2 black circles. The 2 black circles are always separated by a white circle.

18.
Answer: option C
Explanation: Combos of 2 black circles, 1 white circle and 2 black stars.

Paper Folding Practice Test
p.205

1.
Answer: option D

2.
Answer: option A

3.
Answer: option C

4.
Answer: option B

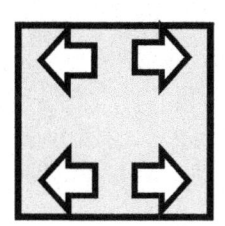

THANK YOU PAGE GRADE 2

5.
Answer: option B

6.
Answer: option D

7
Answer: option B

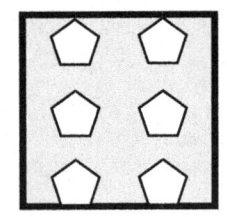

8.
Answer: option C

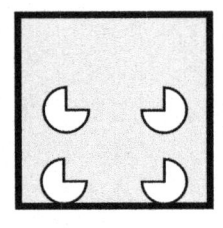

9.
Answer: option D

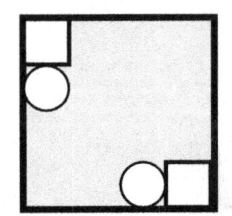

THANK YOU PAGE GRADE 2

10.
Answer: option C

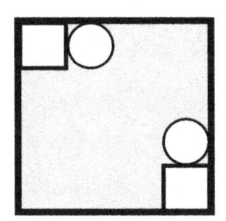

11.
Answer: option B

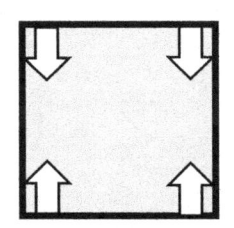

12.
Answer: option A

13.
Answer: option B

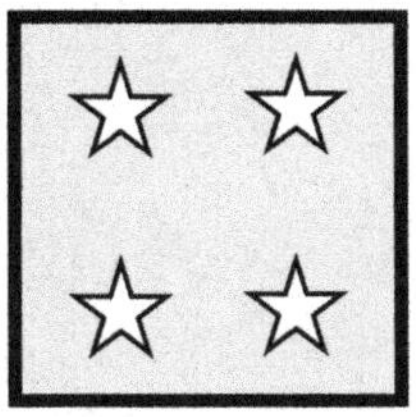

THANK YOU PAGE GRADE 2

14.
Answer: option D

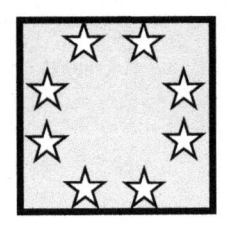

Number Puzzle Practice Test
p.215

1.
Answer: option B
Explanation: 7=2+5

2.
Answer: option B
Explanation: 6=8-2

3.
Answer: option C
Explanation: 3=10-4-3

4.
Answer: option C
Explanation: 12=8+2+2

5.
Answer: option A
Explanation: 10=8+3-1

6.
Answer: option B
Explanation: 12=5-3+10

7.
Answer: option D
Explanation: 5=3+9-7

THANK YOU PAGE GRADE 2

8.
Answer: option B
Explanation: 12=10-5+7

9.
Answer: option C
Explanation: 9=3+8-2

10.
Answer: option C
Explanation: 20=11+2+7

11.
Answer: option A
Explanation: 9=11-10+8

12.
Answer: option B
Explanation: 2=9+5-12

13.
Answer: option D
Explanation: 18=7+2+9

14.
Answer: option C
Explanation: 1=15+5-19

Number Analogies Practice Test
p.222

1.
Answer: option B
Explanation: 3 more.

2.
Answer: option B
Explanation: 9 less.

3.
Answer: option D
Explanation: 6 more.

4.
Answer: option A
Explanation: 6 less.

5.
Answer: option C
Explanation: 3 less.

6.
Answer: option B
Explanation: 2 more.

7.
Answer: option D
Explanation: 2 less.

THANK YOU PAGE GRADE 2

8.
Answer: option B
Explanation: 3 more.

9.
Answer: option C
Explanation: 5 less.

10.
Answer: option A
Explanation: 6 less.

11.
Answer: option A
Explanation: 8 more.

12.
Answer: option A
Explanation: 3 less.

13.
Answer: option B
Explanation: 6 less.

14.
Answer: option C
Explanation: 2 more.

15.
Answer: option B
Explanation: 4 less.

16.
Answer: option D
Explanation: 3 less.

17.
Answer: option B
Explanation: 8 more.

18.
Answer: option B
Explanation: 6 more.

Number Series Practice Test

p.233

1.
Answer: option B
Explanation: +2 -3, +1, +2, -3, +1, etc.

2.
Answer: option B
Explanation: +6, -6, +6, -6, +6, -6, etc.

3.
Answer: option C
Explanation: -1,-1,-1,-1,-1,-1, etc.

4.
Answer: option B
Explanation: -1, +1, -1, +1, -1, +1, etc.

5.
Answer: option A
Explanation: +1, +2, -2, +1, +2, -2, etc.

6.
Answer: option B
Explanation: -6, +5, +1, -6, +5, +1, etc.

7.
Answer: option D
Explanation: +3, -2, +1, +3, -2, +1, etc.

THANK YOU PAGE GRADE 2

8.
Answer: option D
Explanation: +1, +0, +1, +1, +0, +1, etc.

9.
Answer: option B
Explanation: -5, +6, -5, +6, -5, +6, etc.

10.
Answer: option C
Explanation: +1, +2, +2, +1, +2, +2, etc.

11.
Answer: option D
Explanation: -2, +1, -3, -2, +1, -3, etc.

12.
Answer: option C
Explanation: +1, +1, +2, +1, +1, +2, etc.

13.
Answer: option A
Explanation: +3, -4, +1, +3, -4, +1, etc.

14.
Answer: option D
Explanation: +2, +1, -3, +2, +1, -3 etc.

15.
Answer: option D
Explanation: +4, +0, +1, +4, +0, +1 etc.

THANK YOU PAGE GRADE 2

16.
Answer: option D
Explanation: +1, +0, +4, +1, +0, +4 etc.

17.
Answer: option C
Explanation: -3, +3, -2, -3, +3, -2 etc.

18.
Answer: option B
Explanation: -3, +4, -3, -3, +4, -3 etc.

Made in the USA
Las Vegas, NV
30 January 2023